CHINESE THEORIES OF LITERARY CREATION

CHINESE THEORIES OF LITERARY CREATION

A Historical and Critical Introduction

ZONG-QI CAI

A PRISM MONOGRAPH

Supplement to *Prism: Theory and Modern Chinese Literature*, Volume 20
Zong-qi Cai, Series Editor

© 2023 Lingnan University
ISBN: 978-1-4780-2699-0
Cataloging-in-Publication information is available at the Library of Congress.
Printed and bound by CPI Group (UK) Ltd, Croydon, CR0 4YY

Contents

Acknowledgments

I owe a debt of gratitude to Lingnan University for funding a postdoctoral position with a duty to assist with my research. During her tenure as a postdoctoral fellow, Dr. Zhang Chen fulfilled this duty in a most diligent and professional manner, producing rough translations of various narrative sections of this book. The degree to which I have benefited from these translations varies from chapter to chapter, and they surely helped speed up the manuscript completion. My heartfelt thanks go to Cara Ryan for meticulously editing all chapters and to Leon Chai for sharing his insights into various issues of Western literary theory. I also wish to thank Patricia J. Watson for her meticulous copy-editing of the entire manuscript, Charles Brower of Duke University Press for overseeing the editorial process in a most helpful and professional manner, and Matthew Ching Hang Cheng for helping with the back matter, as well as two anonymous readers for their insightful comments and suggestions.

Finally, a personal note of profound thanks to my wife, Changfen Zheng, for her kind tolerance of my countless evenings, weekends, and extended leaves devoted to this and other projects instead of her and the family.

PRISM: THEORY AND MODERN CHINESE LITERATURE • 20 (ANNUAL SUPPL.) • DECEMBER 2023
DOI 10.1215/25783491-11246701 • © 2023 LINGNAN UNIVERSITY

Introduction: Highlights of Chinese Theories of Literary Creation

This book is the first installment of a four-part project, with roughly concurrent publication in Chinese and English: the first three of my Chinese monographs will appear with Shanghai guji chubanshe in the first half of 2025, soon after the publication of this first English monograph. It will take somewhat more time to bring out the remaining monographs in the English series. As works treating Chinese theories of literature, literary creation, interpretation, and aesthetic judgment, respectively, they're all subtitled *A Historical and Critical Introduction* to emphasize their broad chronological coverage and their original and analytical nature. Each book presents much material never presented in either Chinese- or English-language scholarship. On both the macro level (each book's conceptual framework) and the micro level (my topic selection and commentary), I believe my work is decidedly new. At the same time, I mean to make my critical inquiry accessible to as broad a readership as possible.

Gaping Lacunae

To begin, let us survey what has been done on Chinese literary theory to date. In English-language scholarship, very little has been written on China's literary theory in general, and even less on literary creation. Lin Shuen-fu's and Ronald Egan's chapters in my edited book *A Chinese Literary Mind: Culture, Creativity, and Rhetoric in "Wenxin diaolong"* (2001) are perhaps the only publications devoted to this topic. In contrast to the plethora of books on Chinese poetry, fiction, and drama, publications on Chinese literary theory are exceedingly scarce. The only comprehensive treatment in English, James J. Y. Liu's *Chinese Theories of Literature* (1979), is now nearly half a century old. Stephen Owen's *Readings in Chinese Literary Thought* (1992) stands as the lone source book on the subject. Such neglect of Chinese literary theory naturally constitutes a serious impediment to the study of Chinese literary genres. Without knowing what traditional Chinese critics wrote about various aspects of literature, one cannot understand

PRISM: THEORY AND MODERN CHINESE LITERATURE • 20 (ANNUAL SUPPL.) • DECEMBER 2023
DOI 10.1215/25783491-11080835 • © 2023 LINGNAN UNIVERSITY

how broad aesthetic ideals have guided creative endeavors and led to continual transformation of literary genres over millennia. To neglect Chinese literary theory is, so to speak, to ignore the forest for the trees.

The late 1970s to early 1980s saw a brief but important flourishing of Chinese scholarship on the creative process. The in-depth, fruitful research of four leading scholars produced three influential monographs, beginning in 1979 with Wang Yuanhua's 王元化 (1920–2008) *The Theory of Literary Creation in Liu Xie's Literary Mind and the Carving of Dragons* 劉勰文心雕龍創作論. This comprehensive study organizes Liu Xie's (ca. 465–ca. 520) theory of literary creation around eight topics: (1) the relationship between subjectivity and objects, (2) artistic imagination, (3) the writer's creative style, (4) affective metaphor and imagery, (5) emotion and intent, (6) the progressive relationship of *si* 思–*yi* 意–*yan* 言 (thought-conception-words), (7) compositional structure, and (8) the immediacy of creation. In exploring these eight core topics, Wang draws extensively from pre-Qin and Han philosophical texts as well as Lu Ji's 陸機 (261–303) "*Fu* Exposition on Literature" (Wenfu 文賦). In 1982, Mou Shijin 牟世金 (1928–1989) and Lu Kanru 陸侃如 (1903–1978) published their book on the same subject, titled *Liu Xie on Literary Creation* 劉勰論創作. One year later, Zhang Shaokang 張少康 published *Chinese Theory of Literary Creation through the Ages* 中國歷代文學創作論. Zhang's work broadens the scope of investigation beyond Liu Xie's magnum opus, *Literary Mind and the Carving of Dragons* 文心雕龍 (hereafter *Literary Mind*), as it traces the historical evolution of key terms and concepts on creative conception, poetic imagery, compositional methods, and style. After this book, no substantial book-length study has been published on premodern Chinese theories of literary creation.

With this brief review, we can clearly see gaping lacunae waiting to be filled in both English- and Chinese-language scholarship—in the former representing something of a total blank rather than mere gaps. In the latter, the biggest lacuna is the absence of any comprehensive studies of the post–Six Dynasties writings on literary creation, an absence made all the more glaring by an almost excessive attention on Lu Ji's and Liu Xie's theoretical expositions. In my view, the overemphasis on the Six Dynasties period and neglect of later periods have much to do with overly rigid subscription of the modern notions of theory. Rigorously structured and comprehensively argued, Lu Ji's and Liu Xie's works perfectly measure up to what we currently call *theory*. It's no wonder they have become modern scholars' favorites. Mou Shijin and Lu Kanru and Wang Yuanhua all make Liu Xie's *Literary Mind* the exclusive subject of their investigation. Although Zhang Shaokang extends his typological study of terms and concepts beyond the Six Dynasties, he clearly does not consider post–Six Dynasties texts on a par with Lu Ji's and Liu Xie's works. Apparently, modern scholars still do not fully accept and appreciate the post–Six Dynasties mode of critical discourse. Beginning with the Tang, critics adopted informal writings—including letters, prefaces or post-scripts, poetry manuals, and poetry talks—as the primary means of expressing their thoughts about literature. Instead of presenting abstract, well-rounded expositions, they took delight in sharing their flashes of critical insight on specific issues. If measured by our modern notions of theory, this mode of critical discourse is decidedly unsystematic, but it nonetheless prevails for nearly one and a half millennia, from the Tang through the end of the Qing. In my view, gross neglect of these voluminous post–Six Dynasties discussions on literary creation belies a regrettable prejudice and presumption that such works represent a decline in intellectual rigor resulting from the jettisoning of systematic thought. This false assumption, explicit or otherwise, inevitably leads to an even more sweeping false belief: that China does not have an unbroken, continuous tradition of theorizing literary creation.

Aims and Approaches

In publishing this book, I aim not just to add the first monograph entry in the list of English publications on the subject but to do what has not been done before: to rediscover theoretical value in the voluminous post–Six Dynasties discussions on literary creation and thereby establish a complete trajectory of Chinese thinking about literary creation from antiquity through the Qing. For this purpose, I have availed myself of two critical approaches: analytical and analytical-reconstructive.

A straightforward analytical approach is applied to the three Six Dynasties comprehensive theories developed by Lu Ji, Liu Xie, and Zong Bing 宗炳 (375–443). An analytical-reconstructive approach processes the huge body of subsequent scattered discussions on literary creation. This approach aims to piece together isolated comments made by multiple authors over different times into a "theoretic collage."

The undertaking of this analytical-reconstructive work has been exceptionally time-consuming, as well as intellectually daunting. It has taken me about two decades, starting in 2003, to read through an enormous number of primary texts, including all the major collections of poetry talks (*shihua* 詩話) from the Song through the Qing, and to write commentaries on several hundred selected passages, many of which I have come to see as undiscovered gems of Chinese literary thought. In digesting this huge body of material, I have learned to grasp the multivalence of key terms and statements accrued over centuries and exercise careful contextualization to determine what concepts they convey in a particular text. By sorting out the interconnections among these concepts, I have mapped out the complex routes taken by traditional critics to probe different aspects and phases of literary creation.

Persistent practice of this inductive close reading has yielded three important discoveries. First, many post–Six Dynasties critics continued to think about literary creation within the *yi→xiang→yan* 意→象→言 (conception-image-word) paradigm of their predecessors Lu Ji and Liu Xie, albeit with significant modifications in some cases. Second, though his critical comments were only randomly collected, Tang critic Wang Changling 王昌齡 (ca. 698–ca. 756) seems to be the only major post–Six Dynasties critic who explored all phases of literary creation as Lu Ji and Liu Xie had done. Third, Yuan and Ming-Qing critics tend to share interest in particular phases of literary creation based on their precise historical period or membership in a particular school. These discoveries, derived from close reading of primary texts, provided the solid foundation from which I reconstructed eleven Yuan and Ming-Qing theories of literary creation. These reconstructed theories display affinities with the three Six Dynasties theories in that they, too, focus on various critical issues lying at the heart of the *yi→xiang→yan* paradigm. Together, three Six Dynasties theories, three Tang-Song theories, and eleven Yuan and Ming-Qing theories represent a coherent, continuous tradition of thinking about literary creation.

An Overview of Major Findings

This book consists of nine chapters, threading through all of China's historical periods, followed by a tenth chapter in conclusion.

Chapter 1 presents the philosophical foundations laid by pre-Qin and Han-Wei thinkers for the subsequent rise of literary creation. In particular, it compares and differentiates Confucian, Daoist, and syncretic expositions on six key terms: *yi* 意 (conception), *xiang* 象 (image), *yan* 言 (word), *xin* 心 (heart/mind), *xing* 形 (bodily form), and *shen* 神 (spirit). In early pre-Qin times, Daoists conceptualized the first three as a prototriad marking a descent from the metaphysical, through the semimetaphysical, to the physical. For their part, Confucians dismissed *yi* as speculative thought and ignored the term *xiang* while dwelling on the relationship between *yan* (words) with verifiable realities (*shi* 實). Beginning in the late Warring States period, *yi*, *xiang*, and *yan* began to be used together, first as an essentialist triad, as in *Commentary on the Appended Phrases* (Xici zhuan 繫辭傳), and later as a deconstructive triad, as in the writings of Wang Bi 王弼 (226–249). The emergence of the *yi→xiang→yan* 意→象→言 (conception→image→word) triad proves a boon for the subsequent rise of literary creation theory, as it provides a useful paradigm for conceptualizing the entire creative process.

The other three terms examined in this chapter, *xin* 心 (heart/mind), *xing* 形 (bodily form), and *shen* 神 (spirit), are equally indispensable for developing a literary creation theory, as their rich reservoir of accrued meanings enables critics to explore dynamic workings of the heart/mind, body, and spirit at different phases of literary creation.

Chapter 2 is an in-depth study of China's only two comprehensive, self-consciously constructed theories of literary creation developed respectively by Lu Ji's *"Fu* Exposition on Literature" and by Liu Xie in his chapters "Nourishing

Lifebreath" (Yangqi 養氣), "Sensuous Appearances of Things" (Wuse 物色), and "Spirit-Thinking" (Shensi 神思), all from his *Literary Mind*. Conceptualizing literary creation within the *yi→xiang→yan* paradigm, Lu and Liu carefully examine all five major phases of literary creation: (1) the writer's cultivation of optimal physical and mental conditions, (2) emotional response to external stimuli, (3) a two-way flight of imagination, (4) the envisaging (of the work-to-be), and (5) the compositional process transforming the vision into an actual work of language.

The first phase is barely noted by Lu but is the sole topic of discussion in Liu's "Nourishing Lifebreath." The second phase attracts serious attention from both: while Lu dwells on this second phase at the beginning of his essay, Liu gives it a fuller treatment in his "Sensuous Appearances of Things." The third and fourth phases are the real focus of attention for both Lu and Ji. This flight of imagination is called "mind-roaming" by Lu and "spirit-thinking" by Liu. And though both Lu and Liu are inspired by Zhuangzi's 莊子 (369–298 BCE) idea of transcendent roaming, neither strives for a no-return transcendence and eternal union with Dao. Instead, they emphasize that their mind-roaming or spirit-thinking is a two-way journey: after transcending time and space in a spiritual flight beyond the world's boundaries, the mind returns to activate intense interactions among emotions, phenomena, and language, culminating in the formation of what Liu calls the "conception-image" (*yixiang* 意象). The fifth, most technical phase proves the hardest to crack for both Lu and Liu. Both know that using concrete words to fully capture the virtual conception-image is as challenging a task as blindfolded Butcher Ding, fabled character in the *Zhuangzi*, somehow effortlessly cutting an ox. To accomplish such a feat, Lu and Liu believe, a master must ceaselessly learn and internalize compositional rules until he can transcend them all and produce great works spontaneously. For this reason, Lu devotes the greater part of his essay to expounding compositional and rhetorical principles while praising inspiration as the ultimate factor for the birth of a great work. In describing this final phase of literary creation, Liu takes the same dual approach. On one hand, he devotes many chapters to discussing all kinds of compositional issues, ranging from structure to rhetorical devices and meter. On the other, he alludes to Zhuangzi's fabled artisans like Carpenter Bian to emphasize the need to transcend all rules. What Lu and Liu fail to do is find a key term that encompasses both the sublime exercise of the mind and the mundane ordering of words at the final phase of literary creation. This gives later critics like Wang Changling an opportunity to make breakthroughs by incorporating compositional issues as an integral part of their theories of literary creation. Seen in broad historical perspective, Lu's and Liu's well-structured theories provide a good baseline for evaluating post–Six Dynasties theories of literary creation. Many of these later theories strike us as elucidations, extrapolations, emendations, or expansions of parts of Lu's and Liu's theories within the broad *yi→xiang→yan* paradigm.

Chapter 3 turns to examine the burgeoning impact of Buddhist thought on the theory of artistic creation by revisiting Zong Bing's famed essay "Preface to the Painting of Landscape" 畫山水序 (hereafter "Preface"). Zong Bing is most likely the first to transcend the limits of native Daoist and Xuanxue privileging of insubstantial *xiang* 象 (image) and to consciously adopt Buddhist concepts to probe transcendental significance in actual objects, visual images, and visual perception itself. This broad intellectual reorientation is clearly affirmed by a subsequent debate between Zhou Yong 周顒 (fl. 493?) and Zhang Rong 張融 (444–497) on the similarities and differences between Daoism and Buddhism. Whereas Zhang Rong cites Zhuangzi's remark "Dao abides in what meets the eye" to illustrate the likeness of Daoism and Buddhism, Zhou Yong counters with his philosophical proposition "A Piercing Glance Elevates the Mind" (*Muji gaoqing* 目擊高情), claiming the unique power of visualization makes Buddhism different from and superior to Daoism. This forgotten Zhou-Zhang debate provides an important perspective from which to look anew at Zong Bing's "Preface" and recognize its pivotal significance in introducing the Buddhist notions of *xiang* (image) and *shen* (spirit) into art criticism. By interpreting Zong's key terms and statements—long misconstrued as Daoist and/or Confucian—in light of Buddhist writings by Zong's teacher Huiyuan 慧遠 (334–416), as well as his own treatise "Elucidating Buddhism" (Ming fo lun 明佛論), I have ascertained that Zong's essay articulates a coherent and systematic Buddhist view of art and literature. In historical perspective, Zong's "Preface" opens up a new horizon for the Tang poet-critic Wang Changling to formulate his famous poetic theory of "three inscapes," discussed in detail in chapter 4.

Chapters 4 and 5 turn to the Tang and Song, seeking to reconstruct two distinct theories of literary creation. Chapter 4 addresses the *yi*-focused theory of Wang Changling. Unlike Lu Ji and Liu Xie, Wang did not adopt the form of a formal treatise or seek to build a comprehensive, rigorously argued theory. Instead he offered a large body of scattered comments on various aspects of literary creation, as collected in "On the Roles of *Yi* in Refined Writing" (Lun wenyi 論文意), a section in *The Literary Mirror and the Secret Repository of Literature* (Bunkyō Hifuron 文鏡秘府論) compiled by the famous Japanese monk Kūkai 空海 (774–835). However, if these fragmentary comments are re-arranged along the axis of the creative process, there emerges a coherent, comprehensive theory with critical acumen. Not only did Wang reconceptualize the key term *yi* in Buddhist terms, he also creatively applied the Buddhist concept *jing* 境 (inscape) to expand Lu Ji's and Liu Xie's *yi→xiang→yan* into a *yi→jing→xiang→yan* paradigm. With this four-phase paradigm, Wang reconceptualized the creative process, adding highly original and incisive comments on each of the four phases, as well as their interrelationships.

The theory discussed in chapter 5 is almost diametrically opposed to Wang's in that it emphasizes spontaneity and dismisses the notion of *yi* with its subjective intention, specifically "to act deliberately." This theory is reconstructed not, as with Wang, from a single person's writings but with writings by a host of critics united by their shared advocacy of spontaneity. Upholding the spontaneous nature of literary creation, Chen Zi'ang 陳子昂 (ca. 659–ca. 700) and Bai Juyi 白居易 (772–846) emphasized the stirring of emotions. In the same vein, ancient-style masters Han Yu 韓愈 (768–824) and Su Shi 蘇軾 (1037–1101) set store by the overflow of *qi* or vital breath, and Yan Yu 嚴羽 (?–ca. 1245) and other Buddhist-minded critics championed Chan-style enlightenment as a way of writing great poetry.

Chapters 6–9 comb through voluminous discussions on literary creation from the Ming-Qing period and reconstruct three distinct types of literary creation theory: *canwu* 參悟 (meditation-enlightenment)-centered theories, *yi*-centered theories, and *qing* 情-centered theories. Chapter 6 examines the *canwu*-centered theories of literary creation developed during the Yuan, Ming, and Qing dynasties. These theories are reconstructed from a large body of comments on the transcendent mental activity at the initial phase of literary creation. Compared with Lu Ji's thoughts on mind-roaming, Liu Xie's on spirit-thinking, or Wang Changling's on "activating *yi*," these later comments are often more detailed and insightful. In sorting them out, I found a convenient classificatory scheme in the two-character compound *canwu* 參悟, meaning "to meditate and achieve enlightenment." The two characters making up this compound can each be used independently, in which case *can* 參 functions as a transitive verb, meaning "to meditate on something," while *wu* 悟 functions primarily as a noun meaning "enlightenment." Yan Yu has apparently split the compound *canwu* in such a way. While speaking of *miaowu* 妙悟 (wondrous enlightenment) for poetry writing, he dwells on the importance of *can* or meditating and immersing oneself in the greatest of Tang poems as a means of achieving "wondrous enlightenment" in poetic art.

To go beyond Yan Yu, I would further propose to broaden *canwu*'s scope of reference to include non-Buddhist expositions of transcendent mental activity. Thinking along this line, I have discovered that Yuan and Ming-Qing critics conceived four distinct types of transcendent mental activity, induced respectively by meditating nature's formless process of change, physical landscapes, written texts, and human emotions. In describing these transcendent mental activities, Yuan and Ming-Qing critics keenly perceived four distinct modi operandi: dynamic mind-roaming, tranquil union with the ultimate reality, spiritual communion with the authorial consciousness in texts, and empathetic intuition. The first three modes manifest influences from Zhuangzi's philosophy, Buddhism, and Tang-Song Confucian hermeneutics, respectively. As for the last mode, it seems to originate from the late Qing scholar Kuang Zhouyi's 況周頤 (1895–1926) own writing and life experiences. A concurrent rise of four different modes of meditation-enlightenment is a phenomenon not seen in any other historical period.

Chapter 7 discusses the *yi*-centered theory. It begins by mapping out five different meanings of *yi* employed in earlier theories of literary creation and then proceeds to discuss *yi*'s new meaning among Ming-Qing critics. Unlike Lu Ji, Liu Xie, and Wang Changling, Ming-Qing critics showed little interest in probing the entire creative process, focusing their attention instead on one particular creative phase or activity. Compared to those of their predecessors, their understanding of many critical issues strikes us as more incisive and profound. For example, if Wang Changling had only obliquely touched on the suprasensory dimension in "activating *yi*" and "bringing forth *yi*" at the final creative phase, Yuan critic Yu Ji 虞集 (1272–1348), and the Ming critic Wang Tingxiang 王廷相 (1474–1544) thoroughly elucidated this suprasensory exercise of the mind during compositional execution. This is no small achievement. Lu Ji and Liu Xie had tried but failed to connect the writer's imaginative *yi* with his act of casting words. Wang Changling was the first to assume that imaginative *yi* threads through the final compositional phase, but he did not develop this assumption into a full-fledged theory of deploying *yi*. Picking up where Wang left off, Ming-Qing critics achieved a major theoretical breakthrough when they demonstrated how the imaginative concept (*yi*) propels composition on all levels, from generating the momentum (*shi* 勢) of writing to finding a proper structure, selecting key images, and finally deploying words and phrases. Seen in a broader perspective, this breakthrough also has a profound impact on the development of so-called composition studies (*wenzhang xue* 文章學), injecting creative psychology into what is otherwise mere technical study of compositional forms and rules.

Chapters 8 and 9 examine the *qing*-centered theory of literary creation. China's poetic tradition has a long history of valuing *qing* (emotions), evidenced in the prominence of the dicta "Poetry expresses the heart's intent" (*Shi yan zhi* 詩言志) and "Poetry coarises with emotions" (*Shi yuan qing* 詩緣情)—similar words, but if we a look at these two statements' provenance and historical reception, we realize they signal very different views of emotion. "Poetry expresses the heart's intent" is almost as old as poetry itself: it was allegedly said by the legendary Emperor Shun on a totemic dance, according to the *Book of Documents* 尚書 (Shang shu). During the Han, however, this statement was appropriated by the author of the "Great Preface to the *Book of Poetry*" (*Shi da xu* 詩大序) to articulate an instrumental view of poetry, one that sanctifies emotions as positive and potentially transformative response to sociopolitical realities. This understanding of emotion has been embraced ever since by all Confucian-minded scholars. The other statement, "Poetry coarises with emotion," made by Lu Ji when praising belletristic poetry, has been taken to express a bellestristic view of poetry as an artistic patterning of emotions.

Although emotion or *qing* had long been valued for a variety of reasons, not until the mid-Ming did it begin to emerge as the primary factor in the creative process. Ming critics may even be roughly divided into two camps:, the Archaists (Fugu pai 復古派) and the Anti-Archaists (Fan fugu pai 反復古派), which held divergent and even diametrically opposing views on artistic, social, and moral issues. Despite their different positions, they agreed on the importance of emotions, and there were no direct debates between them on this topic. In theorizing literary creation, however, the two camps held opposing views of emotion in ways later echoed in the West by William Wordsworth (1770–1850) and T. S. Eliot (1888–1965). The Anti-Archaists valued emotion as unmediated response to life and advocated a spontaneous, powerful expression of it as a way to assert one's individuality (Wordsworth would say something very similar). The Archaists, in contrast, approached emotion in a way that might be said to anticipate Eliot: divorcing emotion from the writer's life experience and contemporary sociopolitical events and seeking to refine it through sophisticated linguistic patterning and fusing it with natural images (Eliot's "objective correlatives").

From the late Ming through the mid-Qing, the line between the Anti-Archaist and Archaist stance on emotion became increasingly blurred. Huang Zongxi 黃宗羲 (1610–1695), Shen Deqian 沈德潛 (1673–1769), and various leading figures in the Changzhou school of *ci* poetry tended to blend the nonbelletristic with the belletristic, the ethical-sociopolitical with the aesthetic, often to the point of complete fusion. For instance, when discussing the interplay of emotion and natural images, Zhou Ji 周濟 (1781–1839) did not indulge in either moral allegorizing or pure aesthetic inquiry. Instead, he strove for an ideal fusion of moral consciousness with aesthetic experience. In the late Qing, however, we see a radical revival of the Anti-Archaist stance on emotion. While reform-minded thinkers Gong Zizhen 龔自珍 (1792–1841) and Liang Qichao 梁啟超 (1873–1929) turned to emotion as a driving force for sociopolitical change, the revolutionary Lu Xun 魯迅 (1881–1936) lauded Byron's "demonic" emotion as the means of destroying the old society to build a new one. Apparently, he considered literary creation and the creation of a new world parts of the same project.

In Comparative Perspective

Having described major Chinese theories of literary creation, in chapter 10 I conclude by reflecting on their distinctive features through comparison with their Western counterparts. To facilitate this comparison, I find another use of the *yi→xiang→yan* paradigm. Rooted in early Chinese philosophical thought, this paradigm serves well as a critical reference point in chapters 1–9. Each of the examined theories may be situated and distinguished in terms of its full embrace, expansion on, or partial adoption of the *yi→xiang→yan* paradigm, even though the radical branches of the *canwu*-centered and *qing*-centered theories apparently jettison this paradigm. The *yi→xiang→yan* paradigm also facilitates comparative reflections as it sets forth the three levels on which we can fruitfully compare

Chinese and Western theories of literary creation: *yi* or suprasensory conception at a metaphysical level, *xiang* or envisagement at the mediating level, and *yan* or deployment of words at the practical level of composition.

On the metaphysical level of *yi*, both Chinese and Western critics believe that suprasensory mental activity approximates an intuition of the ultimate reality, but there are fundamental differences in their notions of what ultimate reality is. In the West, it usually refers to the absolute spirit essence, while Chinese take it to be the eternal Dao of cosmic transformations or the Buddha nature that transcends the subject-object divide. Chinese and Western critics envision different routes to achieving union with the ultimate reality and producing great poetry. Under the abiding influence of Neoplatonism, Western critics commonly believe that, through vestiges of the highest spirit subsisting in the mind, and through communion with the same spirit abiding in nature, the writer can produce the finest poetry. Wordsworth's philosophical poem *The Prelude* and Samuel Taylor Coleridge's "primary imagination" both describe this mode of tranquil spiritual communion. Meanwhile, critics under the sway of German metaphysics tend to emphasize the proactive use of a priori knowledge in the mind for creative imagination, as shown in Coleridge's notion of "secondary imagination." By contrast, Chinese critics who are devout believers of Buddhism would guide the writer to enlightenment through tranquil contemplation of the landscape. And those who hold the Daoist worldview stress that the writer should suspend sight and hearing to activate a dynamic interplay of emotions, images, and words until they fuse into a perfect "conception-image" (*yixiang*), which is the virtual form of the work-to-be.

On the mediating level of *xiang* (image or envisagement), there are many points of similarity between Chinese and Western thought. Both Chinese and Western literary critics regard envisagement as an important medium to render transcendental experience into words. For Western critics, the core issue is usually transcendental imagination, for which the Latin root, *imāginātiō*, can also mean illusory image or "fancy." For Chinese critics, too, the internalized "virtual image" is a topic for great investment of attention. For example, the *Commentary on the Attached Phrases* (Xici zhuan 繫辭傳) says, "The sage created *xiang* to fully set forth the *yi* (the intuition of the ultimate reality)" 聖人立象以盡意.[1] The *xiang* here refers not to external objects but to the virtual image in the sage's mind. Daoists and thinkers of Abstruse Learning (Xuanxue 玄學) set great store by this virtual image.

All in all, the differences between Western and Chinese discussions of envisagement far outweigh their similarities. There are two reasons for this. First, the ultimate reality to which the envisagement opens is of a fundamentally different nature in China and the West. In the latter, it means spiritual essence, while in the former, it is usually the highest principle of objective transformations of the universe. Even though the Buddhist notion of the ultimate reality appears to have some subjective characteristics, Buddhist enlightenment is not a realization of the ontological spirit but, rather, a leap beyond the subjective-objective divide. The second factor fundamentally setting the Chinese concept of *xiang* apart from Western notions is their drastically different understandings of the relationship between mental image, visual perception, and the phenomenal world. In the tradition of Western metaphysics, visual perception is the preferred instrument by which ontological spirit injects itself into the phenomenal world, rather than the medium by which human beings perceive objective reality. Precisely because of this, from Plato onward, most Western literary critics would emphasize (to the point of extreme exaggeration) the faculty of vision when discussing artistic imagination. Contrary to this tendency of valorizing visual perception, indigenous Chinese thinkers have always regarded visual and acoustic perceptions as impediments to apprehend the highest cosmic principle, Dao. The ultimate cosmic reality, if manifested, would be the elusive "Grand Image" of which Laozi (ca. 600–501 BCE) speaks, or something that eludes the sight of even Lizhu 離珠 (Zhuangzi's symbolic character of superhuman vision). Precisely because of this, Lu Ji emphasizes that at the start of the creative process the author must "withdraw his sight and retract his hearing" and let his spiritual essence roam to the fringes of the world.[2] In Liu Xie's "Spirit-Thinking" chapter, the writer's spirit roams with phenomena without involving visual perception. Ultimately, the writer fuses feelings, phenomena, and words into a mental image of the work-to-be (conception-image)—a virtual image of the external world that eludes physical perception. From this we see how Lu and Liu both believe that the primary objective of transcendent mind-roaming or spirit-thinking is to form the elusive mental image. Having fused together emotions, external phenomena, and words, this mental image is ample preparation for composition. Of course, this does not mean that Lu and Liu have completely overlooked the importance of visual and acoustic perceptions, only that their function is limited to inciting emotions and expressive intent. It is not until the advent of Buddhism in China that Zong Bing, Wang Changling, and other Buddhist-minded critics began to recognize and appreciate the potential of spiritual enlightenment through visual engagement with landscape.

On the practical level of *yan*, there are fewer areas for comparison between the Chinese and Western theories of literary creation. Western critics usually reject any relationship between transcendental imagination and language, believing that the use of language is a quotidian technical matter. Although literary language received some attention from the neoclassic critics of the eighteenth century, subsequent Romantic-era literary critics contended with one another to develop unique theories of literary creation focused almost exclusively on transcendental imagination. Thus, deployment of language was excluded from their discussions of creativity, or was even viewed as an impediment to artistic creation.

Chinese critics, on the contrary, investigate the entire creative process from the initial transcendent mental activity to literary composition. The establishment of *yi*-centered discourse in the Ming-Qing period is immensely significant because it successfully infuses transcendent spirit-thinking, along with the interaction between emotions, scenery, and objects it incites, into every step of the compositional phase. The deployment of language thus becomes a rhythmic movement driven by the thrust of creative conception. The *yi*-centered theory should be of special value to Western critics, as it might inspire them to reflect on how to expand the scope of inquiry to include the entire creative process, from transcendental imagination to the final act of writing.

///////////////////////////////////////

Notes

1. *Zhou yi zhengyi*, in *SSJZ*, 1:70. All translations are the authors' own unless otherwise noted.
2. *WFJS*, 36.

Chapter 1

The Philosophical Foundations

In studying literary creation, Chinese critics follow an approach markedly different from that of Western critics, who tend to dwell on abstract theoretical questions regarding its origin and ontotheological implications.[1] Chinese critics, in contrast, focus on the actual creative process itself. What interests Chinese critics most is how an author reaches *yi* 意, an intense, preexpressive state of mind, and then translates that mental state into *yan* 言, a refined pattern of words or simply a literary text. Both *yi* and *yan* are very important terms in early philosophical discourse, denoting from very early on the signified and the sign, respectively, in linguistic and cognitive processes and over time acquiring a rich polysemy. This polysemy, in turn, provides a treasure trove of concepts necessary for distinguishing complex mental and linguistic activities at different stages of literary creation. The term *yi* 意 captures a broad array of preexpressive mental experiences, ranging from clear ideas to artistic envisagement that defies conceptualization. Meanwhile *yan* 言 encompasses all formal aspects of a work: its structure, texture, rhetoric, phrasing, and so forth. In the Warring States text *Commentary on the Attached Phrases* (Xici zhuan 繫辭傳), the *yi-yan* dyad eventually evolved into a broad cosmic-epistemological paradigm that would be adopted by Lu Ji 陸機 (261–303) and Liu Xie 劉勰 (ca. 465–532?) in their comprehensive theories of literary creation. Their work established a baseline against which we can evaluate and distinguish later theories of literary creation.

Another important difference between Western and Chinese approaches to exploring literary creation is the West's exclusion of the body from the creative process versus the Chinese emphasis on it. What enables the Chinese to think of mind and body integrally are the two spirit-form paradigms developed by Han-Wei thinkers on ideas found in *Zhuangzi* 莊子 and *Guanzi* 管子 compilations. In tracing the rise of these paradigms, I closely examine many related concepts and expositions from which later critics consistently draw to formulate original views on the productive interplay between mind and body in the creative process.

PRISM: THEORY AND MODERN CHINESE LITERATURE • 20 (ANNUAL SUPPL.) • DECEMBER 2023
DOI 10.1215/25783491-11080845 • © 2023 LINGNAN UNIVERSITY

Pre-Qin Concepts of *Yi* 意 (Conception), *Xiang* 象 (Image), and *Yan* 言 (Language)

The rise of the *yi→xiang→yan* paradigm for the creative process was long and gradual, beginning with the clash between Confucian essentialist and Daoist nonessentialist views on language and realities. The *yi-yan* dyad, a protoform of the *yi→xiang→yan* paradigm, evolved into the later triadic paradigm thanks to the Daoist introduction of *xiang* 象. The pairing of *yi-yan* is a completely natural occurrence due to their etymological bond. In *Explanations of Simple and Compound Characters* (Shuowen jiezi 說文解字), Xu Shen 許慎 (30–124) provides this gloss for *yi*:

§1

means *zhi*. It is constituted of the parts *xin* (heart) and *yin* (sound). By observing words one can get to know *yi*.

志也。从心音。察言而知意.[2]

Xu points out *yi*'s inherent relation to *yan* (word) as revealed in its character formation— 音 (sound) + 心 (heart). Because *yi* is the "sound in the heart," Xu maintains that "it can be known through an examination of words [*yan*]." In addition, he describes *yi* as synonymous with *zhi*, a word that literally means the movement of the heart and, by extension, intent and volitional or moral preference. Elaborating on Xu's gloss, Duan Yucai 段玉裁 (1735–1815) writes,

§2

Zhi means cognizance (*shi*). It is what is recognized by the mind. The word *yi* may be glossed as "to fathom" and "to record." . . . "To record" is like what we nowadays say "to remember."

志即識。心所識也。意之訓為測度，為記 . . . . . . 記者，如今人云記憶是也.[3]

Duan deemphasizes the moral implication of *zhi* and redefines it solely in cognitive terms. According to Duan, *yi*, as a noun, denotes mental cognizance or awareness and, as a verb, refers to the mental act of fathoming or conjuring up something absent and restoring it in memory.

Given the inherent etymological connection between *yi* and *yan*, it comes as no surprise that the two terms appear together very early on and that their mutual relationship became a subject of intense debate on various levels among early Chinese thinkers. Broadly speaking, these thinkers fall into three camps. The first comprises thinkers who believe that "*Yan* can fully express *yi*" 言可盡意 and boasts an eminent line of Confucian thinkers, beginning with Confucius (551–478 BCE) himself, followed by Xunzi 荀子 (ca. 313–238 BCE), Dong Zhongshu 董仲舒 (179–104? BCE), Ouyang Jian 歐陽建 (?–300), and others. The second camp consists of thinkers who hold the opposite view, that "*Yan* does not fully express *yi*" 言不盡意. Among its luminaries are Laozi 老子 (ca. 600–501 BCE) and Zhuangzi 莊子 (ca. 369–286 BCE), the two greatest Daoist philosophers, and Wang Bi 王弼 (226–249), the preeminent master of the Abstruse Learning (Xuanxue 玄學). The relatively smaller third camp is made up of syncretic thinkers, like the author of *Commentary on the Attached Phrases*, who seek to reconcile the opposing views of the first two groups.

Confucian Essentialist Views of Language (*Yan*)

The thinkers of the first camp share a common belief in the inseparability of names (*ming* 名) with external actualities (*shi* 實), on the one hand, and internal thought (*yi* 意), on the other. Any gaps that exist between names and their referents, they believe, can be closed through a rectification of names so they become unmediated representation, even embodiment of external actualities or internal thought.

In the *Analects*, we discern this essentialist view of language (*yan*) as Confucius discusses names (*ming* 名) and phrases (*ci* 辭). When a disciple asks what his first task would be if he were governing a country, Confucius replies:

§3

It would certainly be to correct names. . . . If names are incorrect, what is said does not accord with what is meant; and if what is said does not accord with what is meant, what is to be done cannot be effected. If what is to be done cannot be done, then rites and music will not flourish. If rites and music do not flourish, then mutilations and lesser punishments will go astray. And if mutilations and lesser punishments go astray, the people have nowhere to put hand or foot. Therefore the gentleman uses only such names as are proper for speech, and only speaks of what would be proper to carry into effect. The Gentleman, in what he says, leaves nothing to mere chance.[4]

必也正名乎。 ……名不正。則言不順。言不順。則事不成。事不成。則禮樂不興。禮樂不興。則刑罰不中。刑罰不中。則民無所措手足。故君子、名之必可言也。言之必可行也。君子於其言。無所苟而已 矣。(*LYYD*, 25/13/3)

Here Confucius identifies the rectification of names as the paramount task of his government. To him, names constitute the basis of human speech and action. The correct use of names will ensure unimpeded, effective use of speech, and the right speech will in turn guarantee proper employment of rituals and the laws. This passage clearly reveals Confucius's belief in an inherent, inseparable bond between language (*yan, ming*) and ethico-sociopolitical realities. Only because he sees names as bound up with these realities does he believe a rectification of names all but guarantees success in his sociopolitical endeavors.

Confucius also believes in an inherent bond of *yan* with what lies in the human mind, or *yi*:

§4

The master said, phrases are to get [things] across—no more to it.

子曰。辭達而已矣。(*LYYD*, 33/15/41)

In this statement, "phrases" may be seen as synonymous with *yan*, and what they "get across" or convey (*da* 達) is in all likelihood one's idea, intent, will—all of which can be subsumed by *yi*. Judging by the tone of this statement, Confucius apparently believes that *ci* or *yan* can fully express *yi* and that it is fairly straightforward to accomplish that. Although Confucius does not use the word *yi* as a noun, he does use it and its variant *yi* 億 as a verb (to fathom, to speculate), altogether three times in the *Analects*. And each time he dismisses speculative thinking (*yi*) as unworthy of a gentleman.[5] This seems a logical stance for Confucius to take. Since he refrains from probing the supernatural, he naturally finds little use for any speculative flight of thought ungrounded in external realities.

The task of explaining the ground for seeing names as endowed with ethico-sociopolitical realities is left to Xunzi. He accomplishes this in his lengthy essay "Rectification of Names" (Zhengming 正名). He begins by showing the paramount importance of the correct use of names, introducing two opposite kinds of historical evidence to prove his point. The first is the peace and prosperity of the early Zhou stemming from its rulers' correct employment of names; the other is the collapse of ethico-sociopolitical order due to the "rise of flamboyant phrases undermining correct names" (*qici yi luan zhengming* 奇辭以亂正名). Next, he proceeds to the more difficult task of proving the inherent bond between names and realities:

§5

Names have no correctness of their own. The correctness is given by convention. When the convention is established and the custom formed, they are called correct names. If they are contrary to convention, they are called incorrect names. Names have no corresponding actualities by themselves. The actualities ascribed to them are given by convention. When the convention is established and the custom is formed, they are called names of such-and-such actualities. But some names are felicitous in themselves. When a name is direct, easy to understand, and self-consistent, it is called a felicitous name.[6]

名無固宜，約之以命。約定俗成謂之宜，異於約則謂之不宜。名無固實，約之以命實，約定俗成謂之實名。名有固善，徑易而不拂，謂之善名。(*XZJJ*, 2:22.420)

Xunzi first concedes that names have no actualities of and in themselves and then asserts that correct, felicitous names can nonetheless become identical with actualities by virtue of convention. He calls this wedding of names with actualities "the establishment of names" (*chengming* 成名) and considers it the key to the success of the late kings (rulers of the early Zhou). He contends that a ruler "cannot afford not to examine the late kings' establishment of names" 後王之成名，不可不察也 (*XZJJ*, 2:22.420)

§6

When names are heard, actualities are made known. This is the function of names. When names accumulate and display a pattern, we have the embellishment of names. A man who has utilized both the function and embellishment of names is called the one who knows names. Name is that which is used to differentiate actualities. Phrase is that which combines differentiating names to elucidate one meaning. Argumentative discourse is that which does not merely differentiate actualities but also makes known the Dao of alternating movement and inaction.[7]

名聞而實喻，名之用也。累而成文，名之麗也。用、麗俱得，謂之知名。名也者，所以期累實也。辭也者，兼異實之名以論一意也。辨說也者，不異實名以喻動靜之道也。(*XZJJ*, 2:22.422–23)

Xunzi depicts the "interface" of language with actualities on three levels. On the first level, names are employed to the effect that they become practically wedded to external actualities. On the second, the accumulation of names produces a refined phrase or statement, which illuminates an internal reality—one particular meaning or thought (*yiyi* 一意). This pairing of *ci* with *yi* provides a good answer to what Confucius thinks *ci* is supposed to get across (§4). On the third level, argumentative discourse (*bianshuo* 辨說), made up of phrases and sentences, reveals/shows the Dao of alternating movement and inaction. To reiterate his quasi-essentialist view of *yan*, Xunzi retraces this chain of links between *yan* and actualities from top down:

§7

What lies in the heart accords with the Dao; argumentative discourse accords with what lies in the heart; and phrases accord with argumentative discourse.

心合於道，說合於心，辭合於說。(*XZJJ*, 2:22.423)

He 合, the key word of this passage, is very hard to translate. It seems to suggest a degree of integration somewhere between "being matched" and "being fused." In Xunzi's view, appropriate language and actualities are closer to each other than just "matching" but are not yet fused into one. It seems no English word or phrase exactly captures this degree of integration: "accord with" is an imperfect choice.

If Xunzi reveals a tendency among Confucian thinkers to close the gaps between language and realities, we find a culmination of this trend in the unabashed reification of *yan* by Dong Zhongshu. In his "An In-Depth Examination of Names and Appellations" (Shen cha ming hao 深察名號), a chapter of his *Luxuriant Gems of the Spring and Autumn Annals* (Chunqiu fan lu 春秋繁露), Dong writes:

§8

The correctness of names and appellations is derived from heaven and earth. Heaven and earth are the great meaning of names and appellations. The ancient sages howled and followed [*xiao*] heaven and earth, and this is called *hao* or appellation. They called out [*ming*] and issued an order, and this is called *ming* or name. The utterance of names means calling out and issuing an order. The utterance of appellations means howling and following. Therefore, howling and following heaven and earth is called "appellation"; and calling out and issuing an order is called "name." Name and appellation are different in pronunciation but have the same basic sense. They both make sounds to convey heaven's will. Heaven does not speak, but lets man express his will; heaven does not act, but lets man act under it. So names are that by which the sages expressed heaven's will, and they must be subjected to a thorough examination.

名號之正，取之天地，天地為名號之大義也。 古之聖人，而效天地謂之號，鳴而施命謂之名。 名之為言，鳴與命也，號之為言，謞而效也。謞而效天地者為號，鳴而命者為名。 名號異聲而同本，皆鳴號而達天意者也。 天不言，使人發其意；弗為,使人行其中。 名則聖人所發天意，不可不深觀也。受命之君，天意之所予也。[8]

Dong unequivocally seeks to reify the words *ming* (name) and *hao* (appellation), making them the embodiment of *yi* or, rather, *tianyi* 天意 (heaven's will). To this end, he employs a fairly complicated scheme of phonological gloss (*yinxun* 音訓). First, he locates an onomatopoetic homonym for *ming* 名 (name): *ming* 鳴 (to call out, to crow); and an onomatopoetic near-homonym for *hao* 號 (appellation): *xiao* 謞 (to howl). Then, by glossing each pair as interchangeable in meaning, Dong traces the origins of "name" and "appellation" to the ancient sages' howling and calling. As howling and calling are sounds of nature, he contends that names and appellations derived from those sounds are not empty man-made signs but the natural utterances of heaven. To make this point absolutely clear, Dong stresses that "heaven does not speak, but lets man express his will." In other words, names and appellations are nothing but the expression of the divine will through the mouths of sages. Having completed this radical reification of name and appellation, Dong proceeds to reify a set of key Confucian names and appellations and thereby divinize the Confucian sociopolitical hierarchy.

Thanks to the concerted efforts of Xunzi, Dong Zhongshu, and other Confucian thinkers to endow actualities and even divinity in language (*yan*), the entire Confucian ethico-sociopolitical system was eventually codified under *ming* (name) itself and became known as *mingjiao* 名教 (the teaching of names). Thus, upholding the endowed actualities of name or language (*yan*) practically means defending the Confucian ethico-sociopolitical system. So, when *mingjiao* came under intense attack during the Wei-Jin period, Ouyang Jian rose to defend the sacredness of *yan* in his famous essay "A Discourse on *Yan* Fully Expressing *Yi*" (Yan jin yi lun 言盡 意論).

Ouyang's essay takes the form of a brief dialogue between two fictitious characters, the Gentleman of Stale Consensus (Lei tong junzi 雷同君子) and Mr. Maverick (Wei zong xiansheng 違眾先生). In the first half of the essay, the Gentleman of Stale Consensus asks why Mr. Maverick refuses to accept the "*yan* does not fully express *yi*" theory, even though it is all the rage in their time and has been consistently invoked by prominent figures like Jiang Ji 蔣濟 (?–249), Zhong Hui 鍾會 (225–264), and Fu Gu 傅嘏 (Three Kingdoms period). To this question, Mr. Maverick, Ouyang's mouthpiece, gives a brief and clear answer:

§9
Mister (Maverick) replies: Heaven does not speak and yet the four seasons progress; the sages do not speak and yet their insightful knowledge survives. Without depending on names, physical shapes manifest roundness and squareness; without being referred to by names, the sensuous world displays black and white. Nonetheless, to objects, names are that which does not bestow; to the principles of things, words (*yan*) are that which performs no action.

先生曰。夫天不言。而四時行焉。聖人不言。而鑒識存焉。形不待名。而方 圓已著。色不俟稱。而黑白以彰。然則名之於物無施者也。言之於理無為者也。

Yet in both ancient and present times efforts are made to rectify names, and the sages did not dispense with language—what are the reasons for this? Principles of things are comprehended in the mind, but they cannot be fully conveyed without language. Things do exist out there, but they cannot be differentiated without language. If there is no language to facilitate the mind's movement, the mind has no way to engage [the principles of things]. If there are no names to differentiate things, we cannot make judgment and knowledge apparent. When judgment and knowledge are apparent, names and categories are differentiated; when words and names match things, our emotions and intent move smoothly.

而古今務於正名。聖賢不能去言。其故何也。誠以理得於心。非言不暢。物
定於彼。非言不辯。言不暢志。則無以相接。名不辯物。則鑒識不顯。鑒識顯而
名品殊。言稱接而情志暢。

Let us investigate the cause and find out why it is so. It is not that things have the names in and of themselves or that the principles must be called what they are called by internal necessity. If we want to distinguish the actualities of things, we must give them distinctive names. If we want to facilitate the inner tendencies, we must establish a clear reference for them. Names evolve as they follow [the changes of] things; words change as a result of [the changes of] the principles. The case is like this: when a sound is made an echo follows, or when a physical shape exists, a shadow attaches itself to it. Thus we cannot distinguish them as two. If they are not two, there is nothing that words cannot fully express. Therefore, I contend that words fully express [yi].

原其所以。本其所由。非物有自然之名。理有必定之稱也。欲辯其實。則殊
其名。欲宣其志。則立其稱。名逐物而遷。言因理而變。此猶聲發響應。形存影
附。不得相與為二。苟其不二。則無不盡。吾故以為盡矣。[9]

To repudiate the "*yan* does not fully express *yi*" theory, Ouyang does not avail himself of Dong Zhongshu's reifying argument probably because it was already badly discredited. Instead, he goes further back to Xunzi and rehashes his rational analysis of names and actualities. In the long passage cited above, he recapitulates the essential points made by Xunzi 荀子 (ca. 313–238 BCE) in his "Rectification of Names" (§§5–7). Like Xunzi, he first acknowledges the absence of actualities in names themselves, but he goes on to stress that without names we can neither differentiate realities nor comprehend the principles of things. Again, like Xunzi, he confidently speaks of the binding of names with realities as he compares their mutual bond to that of sound and echo, shape and shadow. In a way, he elevates words to an even higher status than Xunzi did. In describing names as "that which does not bestow" and words as "that which performs no action," he is in fact transferring to names and words the customary Daoist praise of the Dao. In traditional Daoist works, both the Dao and ancient sages are lauded for benefiting the world without bestowing or contriving action. Ouyang's borrowing of this prominent Daoist parlance aptly betrays the syncretic tendency characteristic of his time.

Daoist Antiessentialist Views of Language (*Yan*)

Since the Confucian hierarchal ethico-sociopolitical system rests in large measure on the reification of *yan*, it is only natural that the Daoists, their archrivals, spare no effort to dereify *yan* by stressing the gaps that separate it from external realities (ranging from the Dao to concrete things) and from internal *yi*. This clear anti-Confucian agenda, however, is generally kept in the background in most Daoist expositions on the insubstantiality of *yan*. It seems they prefer to explore the relation of *yan* to the Dao and *yi* on a lofty philosophical plane.

§10

The way that can be spoken of	道可道，
Is not the constant way;	非常道；
The name that can be named	名可名，
Is not the constant name.	非常名。[10]

This famed opening statement of the *Laozi* 老子 (*Dao de jing* 道德經) spells out the best-known Daoist perspective on *yan*: an emphasis on the inability of names to embody realities, especially the Dao. The paradoxical fact that Laozi goes on to use names to depict the Dao reveals the concomitant Daoist perspective on *yan*—a recognition of its indispensable value to suggest what lies beyond itself. An elucidation of these two Daoist perspectives is given in the *Zhuangzi*:

§11

Before we can speak of coarse or fine, however, there must be some form. If a thing has no form, the numbers cannot express its dimensions, and if it cannot be encompassed, then numbers cannot express its size. We can use words to talk about the coarseness of things and we can use our minds to visualize the fineness of things. But what words cannot describe, and the mind cannot succeed in visualizing—this has nothing to do with coarseness and fineness.[11]

夫精粗者，期於有形者也；無形者，數之所不能分也；不可圍者，數之所不能窮也。可以言論者，物之粗也；可以意致者，物之精也；言之所不能論，意之所不能察致者，不期精粗焉。(*ZZJS*, 3:17.572)

This passage tells us that *yan* can reveal only crude appearances, while *yi* reaches the refined essence of things. It also identifies something, hidden beyond the reach of even *yi*, that transcends the distinction of the crude and refined. The use of *yi* as a pointer to something hidden can be traced to its etymology. The name Jisun Yiru, a person mentioned several times in the *Spring and Autumn Annals*, has been consistently written as 季孫意如 in the *Zuo Commetaries* (Zuozhuan 左傳) and the *Guliang Commentaries* (Goling zhuan 穀梁傳), but as 季孫隱如 in the *Gongyang Commentaries* (Gongyang zhuan 公羊傳).[12] This would indicate that *yi* and *yin* 隱 (hiddenness) were interchangeable at the time those three commentaries were written. In any event, Zhuangzi does foreground the sense of hiddenness in his use of the word *yi*. According to him, *yi* not only reveals things' refined essence, hidden from the senses as well as language, but also points to what lies further hidden beyond the refined essence. This notion of a three-stage progression from the obvious to the hidden to the most hidden is reiterated in the following passage:

§12

Men of the world who value the Way all turn to books. But books are nothing more than words. Words have value; what is of value in words is what lies in the mind (*yi*). What lies in the mind has something it is pursuing, but the thing that it is pursuing cannot not be put into words and handed down. The world values words and hands down books but, though the world values them, I do not think them worth valuing. What the world takes to be value is not real value.[13]

世之所貴道者書也。書不過語，語有貴也。語之所貴者意也，意有所隨。意之所隨者，不可以言傳也，而世因貴言傳書。世雖貴之，我猶不足貴也，為其貴非其貴也。(*ZZJS*, 2:13.488)

What does Zhuangzi mean when he says "what lies in the mind has something it is pursuing" 意所隨 (*yi suo sui*)? While he does not explicitly tell us, we easily infer that it is the ultimate reality of the Dao. Thus the three-stage progression denotes an epistemological process from tangible *yan* through inward cognizance (*yi*) to the supersensible Dao. Having deconstructed Confucian essentialist views of *yan*, it is out of the question for Zhuangzi to see *yan*, *yi*, and the Dao as contiguously linkable or "mergeable." He must conceive of this epistemological process as a series of leaps from separated, unbridgeable categories of existence.

§13

The fish trap exists because of the fish; once you've gotten the fish, you can forget the trap. The rabbit snare exists because of the rabbit; once you've gotten the rabbit, you can forget the snare. Words exist because of meaning; once you've gotten the meaning, you can forget the words. Where can I find a man who has forgotten words so I can have a word with him?[14]

荃者所以在魚，得魚而忘荃；蹄者所以在兔，得兔而忘蹄；言者所以在意，得意而忘言。吾安得夫忘言之人而與之言哉! (*ZZJS*, 4:26.944)

The famous metaphors of the fish trap and rabbit snare are obviously meant to underscore the role of *yan* as a springboard for reaching higher realities while reaffirming the insubstantiality and deficiency of *yan*. Although these metaphors somewhat alleviate the tension between the two Daoist perspectives on *yan*, true relief of this tension occurs only later in *Commentary on the Attached Phrases*.

Two Competing *Yi→Xiang→Yan* Paradigms: Protocosmological vs. Ontoepistemological

Arguably the most important of the so-called Ten Wings (Shi yi 十翼 or *Ten Commentaries on the Book of Changes*), *Commentary on the Attached Phrases* is traditionally attributed to Confucius. Most modern scholars, however, have dismissed this attribution as legend and consider it an anonymous work composed during the Warring States period. Some have even questioned its status as a canonical Confucian text on account of its embrace of many prominently Daoist ideas. One may not want to go so far as to call it a Daoist text, but its syncretic blending of Confucian and Daoist ideas must be recognized.[15] Its blending of Confucian and Daoist views on the *yan-yi* relationship is particularly noteworthy in its two consecutive quotations of Confucius:

§14

The Master said, "Writing does not exhaust words, and words do not exhaust what lies in the mind [*yi*]. If it is so, does this mean that what lies in the mind of the sages cannot be discerned?"

子曰。書不盡言。言不盡意。然則聖人之意。其不可見乎。[16]

This first quotation begins with a prominently Daoistic statement: "Writing does not exhaust words, and words do not exhaust ideas." Despite its attribution to Confucius, this statement runs diametrically opposed to what Confucius says about the *ci*'s complete expressive power in the *Analects* (see §4) and, in fact, unequivocally reaffirms the first Daoist perspective (§10). The ensuing question, "If it is so, does this mean that the inward conception of the sages cannot be discerned?" points to the second Daoist perspective—an acknowledgment of *yan* as a useful but expendable tool like Zhuangzi's fish trap for conveying *yi* (see §13).

§15

The Master said, "The sages established images in order to express what lies in their mind exhaustively. They established the hexagrams in order to treat exhaustively the true innate tendency of things and their countertendencies to spuriousness. They attached phrases to the hexagrams in order to exhaust what they had to say. They let change occur and achieve free flow in order to exhaust the potential of the benefit involved. They made a drum of it, made a dance of it, and so exhausted the potential of its numinous power."

子曰。聖人立象以盡意。設卦以盡情偽。繫辭焉以盡其言，，。變而通之以盡利。鼓之舞之以盡神。[17]

This second quotation, however, sets us back firmly on the path of Confucian thinking.

While the first quotation twice uses the phrase *bu jin* 不盡 (does not fully [do something]), this quotation contains a series of five neatly paralleled statements, each containing an auxiliary clause of purpose led by the phrase *yi jin* 以盡 (in order to fully [do something]). The five auxiliary clauses set forth what the sages sought to accomplish to the fullest in constructing and employing the trigrams and hexagrams:

1. to fully express their cognizance of the cosmic secrets (*jinyi* 盡意) by "imaging" the workings of the universe (*lixiang* 立象);
2. to fully reveal true innate tendencies of things and their countertendecies (*jin qing wei* 盡情偽) by devising trigrams and hexagrams based on that image (*shegua* 設卦);
3. to fully express what can be said of the trigrams and hexagrams by appending phrases to them (*xici* 繫辭);
4. to fully yield the benefits of the *Changes* (*jinli* 盡利) by allowing changes to occur and flow smoothly; and
5. to fully exploit the numinous power (*jinshen* 盡神) by making full use of the *Changes*.

This series of five *yi jin* phrases undoubtedly underscores a Confucian belief in the magical power of language or graphic signs to make manifest all realities, including the cosmic ultimate.

Of the five statements, the first is the most important, as it entails an ingenious appropriation of the Daoist views on *xiang* (image) and *yi* (idea). While harping on the deficiency of *yan* as speech or writing, both Laozi and Zhuangzi valorize *xiang* (the formless, shadowy image) as an unmediated manifestation of the Dao. In the *Dao de jing*, Laozi identifies this suprasensory image with the Dao itself:

§16

As a thing the way is	道之為物，
Shadowy, indistinct.	惟恍惟惚。
Indistinct and shadowy,	惚兮恍兮。
Yet within it is an image;	其中有象，
Shadowy and indistinct,	恍兮惚兮。
Yet within it is a substance.[18]	其中有物。

To differentiate this shadowy and indistinct image of the Dao from ordinary visual images, he calls it the "Great Image":

§17

The great note is rarefied in sound,	大音希聲，
The great image has no shape.	大象無形。
The way conceals itself in being nameless.	道隱無名，
It is the way alone that excels in bestowing and in accomplishing.	夫唯道善貸且成。[19]

While Laozi distinguishes ordinary visual images from the suprasensory image of the Dao, Zhuangzi tells of two corresponding human faculties required for their respective perception:

§18

The Yellow Emperor went wandering north of the Red Water, ascended the slopes of Kun-lun, and gazed south. When he got home, he discovered he had lost his Dark Pearl. He sent Knowledge to look for it, but Knowledge couldn't find it. He sent Keen-Eyed [Li Zhu] to look for it, but Keen-Eyed couldn't find it. He sent Wrangling Debate to look for it, but Wrangling Debate couldn't find it. At last he tried employing Image Shadowy, and Image Shadowy found it. The Yellow Emperor said, "How odd!—in the end it was Image Shadowy who was able to find it."[20]

黃帝遊乎赤水之北，登乎崑崙之丘而南望，還歸，遺其玄珠。使知索之而不得，使離朱索之而不得，使喫詬索之而不得也。乃使象罔，象罔得之。黃帝曰："異哉，象罔乃可以得之乎?" (ZZJS, 2:12.414)

This fable tells of four ways of knowing: conceptual thought (Knowledge 知), verbal argument (Wrangling Debate 喫詬), visual perception (Keen-Eyed 離朱), and intuitive envisagement (Image Shadowy 象罔). It explains that the Dao (Dark Pearl 玄珠) is accessible only to Image Shadowy. Two of these four ways, Keen-Eyed and Image Shadowy, may seem similar but are fundamentally different. According to Zhuangzi, intuitive envisagement is far more powerful and penetrative than visual perception. If the latter merely brings forth outer appearances of things, it reveals the Dao (Dark Pearl) through its shadowy, indistinct image. In creating the allegorical figure Image Shadowy, Zhuangzi introduces a new perspective on *xiang*. If the Laozi sees the suprasensory *xiang* as a form of primordial, undifferentiated existence, Zhuangzi examines it in its verbal sense: as an act of intuitive "imaging" or envisagement. Later, following this new direction of Zhuangzi, Han Fei 韓非 (ca. 280–ca. 233 BCE) describes how Laozi's sages, by virtue of intuitive envisagement, perceive the Dao:

§19

People can rarely see a living elephant. When they get the bones of a dead elephant, they use them as a visual hint and conjure up how it looked when alive. Therefore, what those people conjure up (*yixiang*) is called image (*xiang*). Now even though the Dao can not be heard or seen, the sage dwells upon things accomplished by the Dao to envisage its shape. Therefore, [Laozi] says "the shape without shape, the image without image."

人希見生象也，而得死象之骨，案其圖以想其生也，故諸人之所以意想者 皆謂之象也 。今道雖不可得聞見，聖人執其見功以處見其形，故曰：「無狀之狀，無物之象。」[21]

In explaining Laozi's notion of "shape without shape and image without image," Han Fei stresses the dynamic role of *yixiang* 臆想 (or *yi* 臆), an act of conjuring up or imagining something absent. While Confucius dismisses such mental activity as speculative and untrustworthy,[22] Laozi, Zhuangzi, and other Daoists obviously rely on it to leap beyond the boundaries of time and space toward the metaphysical Dao. According to Han Fei's explanation, this act begins with the stimuli of the actual world (the bones of a dead elephant) and ends with a mental image of some actual existence (the living elephant). Just as common people conjure up absent physical things, Han Fei explains, the sages can envisage the metaphysical Dao as "shape without shape and image without image" or simply the "Great Image."

This brings us back to the similar act of intuitive envisagement depicted in the statement, "The sages established images in order to express their ideas exhaustively." There is little doubt that the ideas (*yi*) referred to here are not abstract concepts but the sages' intuitive cognizance of the Dao. Their "establishing" of "images" is in many ways comparable to Image Shadowy's capture of the Dark Pearl (the Dao).

Reconciling Opposite Theories on the *Yan-Yi* Relationship: *Commentary on the Attached Phrases*

If Laozi's "Great Image" and Zhuangzi's "Image Shadowy" originally have no connection whatsoever with *yan* (language), the author of *Commentary on the Attached Phrases* seeks to establish this connection. Through parallel phrasing, he links *xiang* (the sages' intuitive envisagement) first with written signs (trigrams and hexagrams) and then with actual written words (attached phrases). Thanks to this linkage, the author endows *yan* with the same divine power Laozi and Zhuangzi did *xiang*. Indeed, he extols the trigrams and hexagrams as capable of "exhausting the inner tendencies and countertendencies" of things. Elsewhere in

Commentary on the Attached Phrases he attempts an even more explicit reification of *yan*.

§20a

To plumb the mysteries of the world to the utmost is dependent on the hexagrams; to drum people into action all over the world is dependent on the phrases.

極天下之賾者。存乎卦。鼓天下之動者。存乎辭。[23]

§20b

As a book, the *Changes* is something which is broad and great, complete in every way. There is the Dao of heaven in it, the Dao of Man in it, and the Dao of Earth in it. It brings these three powers together and doubles them. This is a reason for there being six lines. What these six lines embody is nothing other than the Dao of the three powers.

易之為書也。廣大悉備。有天道焉。有人道焉。有地道焉。兼三才而兩之。故六。六者非他也。三才之道也。[24]

Since this reification of *yan* is entirely premised on its intrinsic link with *xiang*, it speaks to the author's feat in blending the Daoist notions of the suprasensory *xiang* with the Confucian belief in the magic power of graphic signs and language.

Reconceptualizing the *Yi→Xiang→Yan* Triad as an Ontoepistemological Paradigm: Wang Bi

If there is only an implicit, unpronounced *yi→xiang→yan* paradigm in *Commentary on the Attached Phrases*, we observe a reformulation of it as a grand ontoepistemological paradigm in the writings of Wang Bi. In the "Clarifying Image" (Ming xiang 明象) section of his *General Remarks on the Book of Changes* (Zhou yi lüe li 周易略例), Wang gives a clear exposition of the triad as an ontoepistemological paradigm:

§21

Images are the means to express ideas. Words are the means to explain the images. To yield up completely, there is nothing better than images, and to yield the meaning of the images, there is nothing better than words. The words are generated by the images, thus one can ponder the words and so observe what the images are. The images are generated by ideas, thus one can ponder the images and so observe the ideas there. The ideas are yielded up completely by images, and the images are made explicit by the words.

夫象者，出意者也。言者，明象者也。盡意莫若象，盡象莫若言。言生於象，故可尋言以觀象；象生於意，故可尋象以觀意。意以象盡，象以言著。[25]

Judging by the repeated use of the word *jin* (exhaust, exhaustively), this opening paragraph is most likely inspired by the depiction of the making of the *Book of Changes* in the *Commentary on the Attached Phrases* (§14). However, if we compare this passage with §14, we notice two important differences. In §14, *yi*, *xiang*, and *yan* pertain to a series of actions by the sages—the intuition of the Dao, the envisagement of the Dao, the devising of trigrams and hexagrams, and the attachment of verbal phrases. But with Wang Bi, the three terms have become broad philosophical categories, indicating three main stages of an ontological transformation from nonbeing to being. Second, if the author of *Commentary on the Attached Phrases* merely implies a causal link in the sages' actions, Wang Bi describes the triad in explicit terms of one producing another. If produced by *xiang*, it must follow that *yan* partakes in the divine power of both *xiang* and *yi* and thus possesses ontological essence in and of itself. This essentialist conclusion, however, is subverted by what Wang says in the very next paragraph:

§22

Thus, since the words are the means to explain ideas, once one gets the ideas, he forgets the images. Similarly, "the rabbit snare exists for the sake of the rabbit; once one gets the rabbit, he forgets the snare. And the fish trap exists for the sake of fish; once one gets the fish, he forgets the trap." If this is so, then the words are snares for the images, and the images are the traps for the ideas. Therefore, someone who stays fixed on the words will not get the images, and someone who stays fixed on the images will not get the ideas.

故言者所以明象，得象而忘言；象者，所以存意，得意而忘象。猶蹄者所以在兔，得兔而忘蹄；筌者所以在魚，得魚而忘筌也。然則，言者，象之蹄也；象者，意之筌也。是故，存言者，非得象也；存象者，非得意者也。[26]

If the preceding paragraph reiterates the essentialist view of the *Commentary on the Attached Phrases*, this paragraph presents a distinctly deconstructive view. Indeed, Wang goes all out to demonstrate the unbridgeable gaps between the three terms. To begin with, he recasts Zhuangzi's metaphors of the fish trap and the rabbit snare (§13) by adding *xiang* between *yan* and *yi*. As *yan* is merely the fish trap or the rabbit snare for *xiang*, so is *xiang* for *yi*. Consequently, *yan* cannot be one and the same as *xiang*. The same goes for *xiang*'s relationship with *yi*. To go one step further in this deconstructive exercise, Wang Bi contends that only by forgetting or disposing of *yan* and *xiang* successively can one hope to become cognizant of *yi*, the ultimate reality.

Why does Wang Bi present two mutually contradictory views in the same breath? We may point to his eclectic turn of mind as a simple answer. In my opinion, his eclecticism springs from practical needs of different kinds. As he is elaborating on the meaning of the *Book of Changes*, the essentialist view of the *Commentary on the Attached Phrases* is simply too influential for him to ignore. Hence he feels compelled to reiterate that view (see §22). Of course, his need to invoke the *Commentary on the Attached Phrases* does not necessarily preclude the possibility of a genuine if qualified embrace of that essentialist view. By the same token, Wang Bi's dramatic switch to a deconstructive argument may stem from his desire to undermine a rigid obsession with concrete images among Han *Yijing* exegetes, especially those of the Images and Numbers school (Xiangshu pai 象數派). Of Wang's essentialist and deconstructive strains of thought, it is definitely the latter that has wielded the greatest influence in his and later times. In fact, the weaker, essentialist angle, inherited from the *Commentary on the Attached Phrases*, is rarely acknowledged in either traditional or modern studies of his philosophical thought. In the development of literary creation theory, however, it is this forgotten tradition of essentialist thinking that wields significant, productive influence. This is particularly true of its impact on the development of Lu Ji's and Liu Xie's theories of literary creation (see chap. 2).

Two Views on the Transcendental Mind: Zhuangzi and the *Guanzi*

In addition to the *yi→xiang→yan* paradigm facilitating the study of the entire creative process, early philosophical discourse also offers literary critics two alternate spirit-form paradigms to explore the dynamic interplay between the literary mind and the body, and between mental and linguistic activities at different stages of literary creation. These two spirit-form paradigms evolved from Zhuangzi's and *Guangzi* compilers' divergent views on *xin* 心 (mind) and *xing* 形 (bodily form, external form).

In the extant texts of the Spring and Autumn period, *xin* (mind) is not a topic of serious philosophical inquiry. Confucius's *Analects*, for instance, has *xin* as an internalization of ethics and morals, with minor philosophical implications. But in philosophical texts produced during the mid-Warring States period, including the *Mencius* 孟子, the *Zhuangzi* 莊子, and the *Guanzi* 管子, *xin* (the mind) rises to prominence as one of the most discussed topics. In discussing *xin*, these texts almost uniformly focus on the ancient sages in their respective traditions: the Confucian sages in the *Mencius*; the "Perfected Man" 至人," "True Man 真人," and "Divine Man 神人" in the *Zhuangzi*; and the unnamed Daoist sages in the *Guanzi*.

In exploring the sage mind, Warring States thinkers conceptualized its transcendent omnipotence and omniscience in terms of the mind's union with the cosmic Dao. To describe how this union is possible, they variously emphasize the endowment of *qi* 氣 or cosmic life force and the ability to transcend the senses to roam with the suprasensible Dao. The *Guanzi* (core text of the Jixia 稷下 school of Daoism) stresses the full endowment of the cosmic lifebreath (*qi*) as the reason for the sage mind's omnipotent power. This is made very clear in the following passage:

§23

When the mind-lifebreath takes form, it is more luminous than the sun and the moon and displays keener perception than the father and mother [observing their children]. Rewards are not enough to guide people to be good, and punishments are not enough to deter transgressions. When the lifebreath-intent is attained the whole world submits; when the mind-intent is secured, the whole world listens. The lifebreath accumulates to a miraculous degree, it contains ten thousand things within itself. Can one accumulate [lifebreath]? Can one conform to oneness? Can one know good fortunes and misfortunes without casting divining stems? Can one know when things end and achieve completion? Can one seek and know all within oneself without seeking others' help? Thinking and thinking, again thinking and thinking, but one still cannot think through. Ghosts and spirits help one to think through. No, it is not due to the power of ghosts and spirits; it is all because of the perfecting of essence-lifebreath.

心氣之形，明於日月，察於父母。賞不足以勸善，刑不足以懲過。氣意得而天下服，心意定而天下聽。搏氣如神，萬物備存。能搏乎？能一乎？能無卜筮而知吉凶乎？能止乎?能已乎？能勿求諸人而得之己乎？思之思之，又重思之。思之而不通，鬼神將通之。非鬼神之力也，精氣之極也。(*GZJZ*, 943)

In my view, the very uncommon English compound "life-breath," derived from the more familiar phrase "breath of life," is a fitting translation of the Chinese term *qi* as it captures the term's essence: a dynamic flow that imparts and sustains life. Here, *life-breath* is dehyphenated for a more succinct rendering of four *qi*-compounds: mind-lifebreath (*xinqi* 心氣), lifebreath-intent (*qiyi* 氣意), mind-intent (*xinyi* 心意), and essence-lifebreath (精氣). While the first three of these are very uncommon and may even be coinages of the *Guangzi*, they reveal the author's unique understanding of lifebreath as the supreme cosmic force transcending the divide between subject and object, mind and body. Indeed, this lifebreath is construed elsewhere in the *Guangzi* as one and the same as the Dao. Little wonder, then, that accumulation of "essence-lifebreath" endows the sage with (1) absolute ethico-sociopolitical authority ("all under heaven submits . . . all under heaven listens"), (2) omnipotence ("it contains ten thousand things all within itself"), and (3) omniscience ("know good fortunes and misfortunes without casting divining stems . . . know all within oneself without seeking other's help").

The Zhuangzi school of Daoism also regards *qi* or lifebreath as a conduit to union with the Dao, as shown in Zhuangzi's famous remarks on mental fasting:

§24

Lifebreath is what remains unoccupied and waits for [external] things. Only in the unoccupied does *Dao* come to roost. This state of being unoccupied is the fasting of the mind.

回曰：“敢問心齋。”仲尼曰：“若一志，無聽之以耳而聽之以心；無聽之以心而聽之以氣。耳止於聽，心止於符。氣也者，虛而待物者也。唯道集虛。虛者，心齋也。”(*ZZJS*, 1:147).

Here Zhuangzi lists an ascending scale of knowing, with aural reception at the bottom, the mind's understanding in the middle, and the lifebreath's union with the Dao at the top. Unlike the compilers of *Guangzi*, however, Zhuangzi does not build his Daoist metaphysics through an in-depth investigation of the *qi* in both physical-physiological and metaphysical realms. Instead, he tends to focus on the metaphysical implications of lifebreath: "Let your mind roam in the bland, let your lifebreath converge on the boundless, let things follow their natural course and allow no partiality, and then the whole world will be well-governed" 汝遊心於淡，合氣於漠，順物自然而無容私焉，而天下治矣 (*ZZJS*, 1:294).

Here the pairing of the compound "mind-roaming" with "convergence of lifebreath with the boundless" shows Zhuangzi's full acknowledgment of lifebreath's metaphysical efficacy. However, compared to the *Guangzi* compilers, Zhuangzi talks a lot more about mind-roaming than about accumulation of lifebreath. This divergence of interest inevitably leads to their opposing views on the mind-body relationship.

The roaming of the mind presupposes a view of the body as a bondage from which the mind must free itself in order to freely roam in the universe, so it is only natural that Zhuangzi would often speak disparagingly of the body as a hindrance to be rid of. This belief is encapsulated by his famous dictum "leave behind physical form and abandon wisdom" (*lixing quzhi* 離形去知). In "The Seal of Virtue Complete" (Dechongfu 德充符) chapter, Zhuangzi lavishes praise on many imaginary deformed characters whose minds, in spite or, rather, because of their bodily deformities, freely roam between heaven and earth. Such anecdotes underscore the extent to which Zhuangzi privileges spirit at expense of body.

Contrary to Zhuangzi's view, compilers of the *Guanzi* believe in a deep inter-dependence between a sage's mind and his body. This symbiotic notion of mind and body is most clearly articulated here:

§25

As one's mind reaches its fullest internally, so does one's body externally, becoming invulnerable to disasters from heaven as well as human harm. Such a person is what we call a sage. If one can maintain uprightness and quietude and has calm complexion, sharp hearing, keen eyesight, firm sinews and strong bones, he can uphold the round heaven and walk across the square earth.

心全於中，形全於外。不逢天菑，不遇人害，謂之聖人。人能正靜，皮膚裕寬，耳目聰明，筋信而骨強，乃能戴大圜而履大方。(*GZJZ*, 938)

Here, *Guangzi* compilers conceptualize the mind's fullest realization not like Zhuangzi's disembodied spirit roaming the universe but through a transforma-tion that simultaneously includes the body. "Body-bound" though it is, this out-come is just as miraculous—with the sage upholding the round heaven and walk-ing across the square earth—as Zhuangzi's roaming mind.

This "metaphysical" description of the sage body reveals *Guangzi* compilers' penchant for overturning traditional conceptual hierarchies (mind vs. body, meta-physical vs. physical) by arguing a two-way movement between bipolar terms. They trace the cosmic lifebreath, for instance, both as it descends into the sage's mind and body and as it flows from the sage back out into the universe:

§26

The essence exists and grows inside, and the outer enjoys peace and flourishes. What is harbored inside becomes the source of a spring—expansive and peaceful, and a deep receptacle of lifebreath. This receptacle does not dry up and therefore the whole body is firm and strong. With this inexhaustible spring and his nine outlets wide open, the sage traverses heaven and earth and blesses the four seas.

精存自生，其外安榮。內藏以為泉原，浩然和平，以為氣淵。淵之不涸，四體乃固，泉之不竭，九竅遂通，乃能窮天地，被四海。(*GZJZ*, 938)

The use of the word *haoran* 浩然 to describe the expansive flow of cosmic life-breath immediately makes us think of the famous passage by Mencius (372–289 BCE) on "the flood-like overflow of lifebreath" (*haoran zhi qi* 浩然之氣):

§27

"May I ask what your strong points are?"
"I have an insight into words. I am good at cultivating my 'flood-like *qi*.'"

"May I ask what this 'flood-like *qi*' is?

"It is difficult to explain. There is *qi* which is, in the highest degree, vast and unyielding. Nourish it with integrity and place no obstacle in its path and it will fill the space between Heaven and Earth. It is the *qi* which unites rightness and the Way. Deprive it of these and it will collapse. It is born of accumulated rightness and cannot be appropriated by anyone through a sporadic show of rightness."[27]

"敢問夫子惡乎長？"曰："我知言，我善養吾浩然之氣。""敢問何謂浩然之氣？"曰："難言也。其為氣也，至大至剛，以直養而無害，則塞於天地之間。其為氣也，配義與道；無是，餒也。是集義所生者，非義襲而取之也。"[28]

This passage advances a similar proposition of dynamic movement of lifebreath overflowing from a human being to affect the whole world. As we cannot accurately and conclusively date the *Mencius* and the *Guangzi*, we cannot say whether Mencius appropriated this idea from the *Guangzi* compilers or the other way around. But if I were to venture a guess, I would most likely vote for the former scenario and then suggest that Mencius added some distinctly Confucian elements to the *Guangzi* proposition. First, he changes the subject from the ancient sage to himself, a sage wannabe. Second, he blends a Confucian moral ideal into cosmic lifebreath. Finally, discussing deployment of words and the cultivation of this cosmic-moral lifebreath in such proximity, Mencius implies a connection between them.

Two Alternate Spirit-Form Paradigms in the Han: Hierarchical vs. Equalistic

Expositions on the mind continue to figure prominently in Han-Wei philosophical discourse, displaying both continuity with and divergence from earlier Warring States texts. Han-Wei thinkers alternately inherited the opposing stances on mind and body taken by Zhuangzi and the *Guanzi* compilers and, consequently, developed two corresponding conceptual paradigms. One is the Zhuangzian hierarchical spirit-form paradigm, established by Liu An 劉安 (179–122 BCE), main compiler of the *Huananzi* 淮南子, characterized by a consistent privileging of spirit over form and at times a celebration of spirit from form. The other is the *Guanzi*an interdependent spirit-form paradigm fashioned by Huang-Lao Daoists.

Against the backdrop of this general continuity, however, we find significant divergences from earlier philosophical discourse clearly reflected in the naming and application of the two paradigms. Han-Wei thinkers' increasing use of the term *shen* (spirit) in place of *xin* is one such refraction of the momentous changes occurring in philosophical discourse. Where mid–Warring States discussions of *xin* are concerned with ancient sages—their main goal to illustrate exemplars of ideal rulers to the various feudal lords—Han debates on *shen* carried greater urgency in practical politics as they preached Daoist "inner sagehood" to Han emperors and offered strategies for preserving *shen* or spirit. Along with this shift in terminology, Han thinkers went well beyond imagining the minds of ancient sages to develop two alternate spirit-form paradigms as they applied these paradigms to the sociopolitical issues of their time.

Liu An's hierarchical spirit-form paradigm is not particularly original, largely representing a codification of Zhuangzi's ideas, somewhat randomly and figuratively expressed, in expository form, as shown in this exposition on the spirit-form relationship:

§28

If one takes spirit as the master and lets form follow, it will be auspicious. On the contrary, if one puts form in charge and lets spirit follow, it will be harmful.

故以神爲主者，形從而利；以形爲制者，神從而害。(*HNHLJJ*, 41)

Obviously borrowing Zhuangzi's celebration of mind liberated from the body and freely roaming the universe, the innovation comes in the shift in discourse mode and the intended reader. Where Zhuangzi's stories of "perfected" and "true" men (as well as deformed figures) addressed politics-weary individuals yearning for personal freedom, Liu An proposes Zhuangzi's view as a guiding principle for a new audience: emperors and their ministers seeking optimal governance. His sociopolitical adaptation of Zhuangzi's formulation is clearly seen in his move to correlate spirit-form with the traditional hierarchy of distinguished heaven over the humble earth:

§29

The refined spirit is received from heaven and the physical form is granted by earth. . . . The mind is the master of form and spirit is the master of mind.

夫精神者，所受於天也；而形體者，所稟於地也 . . . . . . 故心者，形之
主者。(*HNHLJJ*, 219, 226)

Given the primacy of spirit through its inherent bond with heaven, Liu recommends to interested rulers a new route to achieve inner sagehood: transcendental roaming in the great harmony of spirit:

§30

So the sage pursued inner cultivation in the Daoist vein and did not seek outer embellishments of benevolence and righteousness. Impervious to the influx from ears and eyes, they roamed in the great harmony of spirit. Consequently, they fathomed the three springs below and probed the nine heavens above, traversed the six directions, and coursed through ten thousand things. This is the roaming of the sages.

是故聖人內修道術，而不外飾仁義，不知耳目之宣，而游于精神之和。若然者，下揆三泉，上尋九天，橫廓六合，揲貫萬物，此聖人之游也。(*HNHLJJ*, 60–61)

This adaptation of Zhuangzi's "mind-roaming" as a means of "achieving sagehood within and thereby demonstrating powerful kingship" (*neisheng waiwang* 內聖外王) reflects the eclectic spirit of the times. Influenced by this prevalent eclecticism, Han Confucian thinkers, too, appropriated Daoist notions of mind-roaming or spirit-roaming for their own purposes. For instance, Yang Xiong 揚雄 (53–18 BCE) harnesses it as a transcendent thrust to commune with the ancient sage:

§31

"May I ask what 'spirit' is?"

"It is the mind."

"Could you explain it?"

"When imperceptibly reaching heaven, spirit is heaven. When imperceptibly reaching earth, spirit is earth. Heaven and earth are unfathomable, but through its imperceptible movement, spirit can fathom them let alone the human world or its affairs and principles."

"May I beg to ask if the sages are capable of such an imperceptible movement of the mind?"

"In the past, Confucius's mind imperceptibly moved toward King Wen and reached it. Yan Yuan's mind moved toward Confucius but could not quite reach it. Spirit exists in such an imperceptible form." . . . Possessing such spirit and reaching the ultimate, the sages made possible the smooth operations of the world, bestowed enormous benefits on it, brought heaven and humans seamlessly together into great harmony.

或問 "神"。曰："心。" "請問之。" 曰："潛天而天，潛地而地。天地，神明而不測者也。心之潛也，猶將測之，況於人乎？況於事倫乎？" "敢問潛心于聖。" 曰："昔乎，仲尼潛心於文王矣，達之。顏淵亦潛心於仲尼矣，未達一間耳。神在所潛而已矣。" . . . . . . 聖人存神索至，成天下之大順，致天下之大利，和同天人之際，使之無間也. (*FYYS*, 137–41)

Thanks to his deft adaptation of Daoist spirit-roaming, Yang Xiong conceives a new way to intuitively commune with ancient sages and cosmic process to bring the greatest benefits for the human world. His description of this transcendental exercise of the mind is much clearer and more detailed than those in earlier

Confucian texts and may be seen as a distant source for Ming-Qing concepts of intuitive communion with ancient literary masters.

To sum up my discussion of Liu An's hierarchical spirit-form paradigm, I might say that it works well as a guide for Han rulers to strive for spiritual transcendence or so-called inner sagehood. However, grounded in the "otherworldly" *Zhuangzi*, this seems less applicable than the competing, "equalizing" spirit-form paradigm grounded in the more earthbound *Guangzi*. Characterized by a drastically broadened view of both spirit and form, the latter seems to undergird the whole-person approach taken by Huang-Lao Daoists to nurture ideal empire rulers. Spirit now denotes not just a transcendental flight of the mind as in the *Zhuangzi* but actually encompasses the entire ambit of consciousness, including thoughts, emotions, and mental equilibrium. Likewise, the human form of a ruler is broadly reconceptualized as a microcosm of the entire polity or even world. Given this, the primary duty of a ruler is the cultivation of life, that is, to achieve the optimal state of both mind and body, as well as a perfect balance between them. During the Han, this new thinking of spirit and form was so extensively applied in medical, physiological, and sociopolitical discourse that it became a ubiquitous practical framework for evaluating nearly all earthly phenomena. It is worth looking at some examples of how this spirit-form conception buttressed a variety of evaluations across the period.

Turning first to the early Han grand historian Sima Tan's 司馬談 (ca. 169–110 BCE) comparative evaluation of Confucian and Daoist thought in his short essay "The Essentials of Six Philosophical Schools." In the *History of the Former Han* (Han shu 漢書) version, we read:

§32
That by which people obtain life is spirit, and that which embodies life is form. If spirit is overused, it will be exhausted. If the form is overworked, it deteriorates. When form and spirit become separate, one dies. The dead cannot be brought back to life, and what is separated cannot be put back together. Therefore, the sages attached great importance to this [spirit and form]. Judging by this, we know that spirit is the basis of life and form is the vehicle of life. Not having first steadied his spirit and form, a ruler still claims, "I have the wherewithal to rule the world." What is the ground for making this claim?

凡人所生者神也，所託者形也。神大用則竭，形大勞則敝，形神離則死。死者不可復生，離者不可復合，故聖人重之。由是觀之，神者生之本，形者生之具。不先定其神形，而曰"我有以治天下"，何由哉?[29]

This passage gives one of the clearest expositions on the spirit-form paradigm predicated on inseparability and interdependence of the two. What is most noteworthy about Sima Tan's essay, however, is not its lucidity but its truly original application of this spirit-form parity to assess Confucian and Daoist schools. According to Sima Tan, the Confucian school compares unfavorably with the Daoist school because its overly proactive sociopolitical agendas and endeavors are bound to exhaust both spirit and form/body of the ruler, threatening his very life in the worst of circumstances. For this reason, he (unsubtly) mocks Confucians for claiming to "have the wherewithal to rule the world" while being oblivious to the harm done to the ruler's spirit and form. Sima Tan declares that "the Confucians talk broadly but lack the essentials; they toil but achieve little. Therefore, it is difficult to follow in all of their endeavors" 儒者博而寡要，勞而少功，是以其事難盡從. In contrast, he maintains that "the Daoists let people focus their spirit, accord with the formless in their movement, and provide adequate sustenance for the myriad things" 道家使人精神專一，動合無形，瞻足萬物. Sima Tan's argument might sound odd if we know little about Han thought, but it makes perfect sense once we know the widely held Han belief in the emperor's spirit and form as the microcosm of the world. Sima Tan believes the Daoist nonaction approach leads to optimal conditions for the ruler's spirit and form and therefore ensures peace and prosperity in the world.

By the middle of the Former Han, the equalistic spirit-form paradigm became so dominant and persuasive that even Dong Zhongshu, preeminent Confucian thinker of his time, made conspicuous use of it when expounding on what he calls "primordial spirit" (*yuanshen* 元神), the foundational concept of his cosmological-political doctrine.

§33

For the one who is lord of people, it is imperative to value spirit. Spirit is what no one can see or gets to hear. It comes close to us, and yet its form cannot be seen and its sound cannot be heard. . . . What cannot be seen or heard is called "obscure and shadowy." By being dark, one can illuminate, and by being shadowy, one can display brilliance. The one who can be obscure and shadowy is a divine man. The lord values staying in obscurity and, in so doing, makes his standing luminous; he positions himself in the shadows but tends toward the yang or brightness. . . . Therefore ministers take the yang position but belong to the yin, and their lord takes the yin position but belong to the yang. The way of the yin lies in physical form and therefore exhibits their nature. The way of the yang is traceless and therefore values spirit.

為人君者，其要貴神。神者，不可得而視也，不可得而聽也，是故親而不見其形，聽而不聞其聲。......不見不聞，是謂冥昏。能冥則明，能昏則彰。能冥能昏，是謂神人。君貴居冥而明其位，處陰而向陽。......故人臣居陽而為陰，人君居陰而為陽。陰道尚形而露情，陽道無端而貴神。(*CQFLYZ*, 171–72)

Here we can observe Dong's simultaneous appropriation of both spirit-form paradigms. First he defines the all-important lord-minister relationship in terms of Liu An's spirit-form hierarchy: borrowing Liu's transcendental spirit-roaming as imperative for the lord, Dong simply identifies the lord with the cosmic spirit itself, calling him "primordial spirit." However, when he comes to explain the lord-ministers relationship, he avails himself of the equalizing spirit-form paradigm to stress their mutual interdependence. By further correlating this interdependence with that of the cosmic yin-yang, he hits two birds with one stone. First, the notion of distinguished yang and humble yin helps reaffirm his hierarchical definition of the lord-minister relationship. Second, the yin-yang dialectical interaction leads him very conveniently to describe or, rather, prescribe the proper conduct for lord and ministers alike.

Because the schematic implications emerging from this correlation is rather complicated, I want to spell it out further. As the first step, Dong identifies the lord with "spirit" and his ministers with "form." Next he reaffirms the lord/spirit as the privileged yang and the ministers/form with the underprivileged yin. Dong's third step is to demonstrate the dialectical modus operandi of both yin and yang: yang achieves its dominant potential through passivity; yin reveals its submissive status through activity or proactivity. Translated into political terms, this convoluted reasoning simply means that, as the lord is the primordial spirit without a form, he should withdraw himself from all activities before the public eye. But ironically, or dialectically, it is by following this passive course of nonaction that he consummates his role as the spirit/lord. Conversely, ministers belong to the submissive yin and must, by virtue of its dialectical logic, take the prominent role of political action and thereby reaffirm their subordinate status.

In the Eastern Han, we observe applications of the equalistic spirit-form paradigm to practical sociopolitical issues not directly related to empire rulership. A good example is this new exposition on the spirit-form by prominent Eastern Han thinker Wang Chong 王充 (27–ca. 97):

§34

What gives birth to humans are yin and yang lifebreath. Yin lifebreath produces bones and flesh, while yang lifebreath produces spirit. Humans are born with both yin and yang lifebreath intact, so their bones and flesh are firm, and their essence-spirit is abundant. Essence-lifebreath produces wisdom, while bones and flesh produce strength. While essence-spirit [enables] speech, the physical body firmly guards [vitality]. Intricately intertwined, bones and flesh and spirit depend on and sustain each other to the effect that both can be observed and do not perish. If the life-breath, reaching major yang, becomes overabundant and entertains no yin, it cannot take shape as physical form and appear merely as images. Without bones and flesh, the essence-lifebreath appears like a flash before our eyes and dies out instantly.

夫人所以生者，陰、陽氣也。陰氣主爲骨肉，陽氣主爲精神。人之生也，陰陽氣具，故骨肉堅，精氣盛。精氣爲知，骨肉爲強。故精神言談，形體固守。骨肉精神，合錯相持，故能常見而不滅亡也。太陽之氣，盛而無陰，故徒能爲象，不能爲形。無骨肉，有精氣，故一見恍惚，輒復滅亡也。[30]

Here Wang Chong is probing an issue—that of afterlife or its impossibility—at once more philosophical and more practical than those addressed by Sima Tan and Dong Zhongshu. It is more philosophical because Wang deals head on with the ultimate existential question that inevitably arises from a persistent emphasis on the interdependence of spirit and form: would spirit, if so dependent on form, continue to exist after the dissolution of the form? By giving the logical answer of no, Wang Chong aims to solve once and for all an issue plaguing Eastern Han society: the entrenched and widespread customs of lavish burial. By arguing against afterlife on the ground of absolute spirit-form interdependence, Wang Chong strives to undermine the very rationale for lavish burials: the filial duty of providing sustenance for the departed.

The dominance of this spirit-form paradigm, along with its earlier mind-form in the *Guanzi*, profoundly shapes the intellectual landscape for nascent thinking about art and literature during the Han-Wei transition. This early thinking is characterized by an overriding emphasis on the form or human body in the creation of art. For instance, Zhao Yi 趙壹 (fl. 168–189) regards fine calligraphy as born of natural combination of a fine mind and a dexterous hand:

§35
Men have different compositions of lifebreath and blood, and their sinews and bones differ as well. Their minds can be simple and sophisticated, and their hands dexterous or clumsy. Whether writing looks beautiful or ugly has much to do with the mind and the hand—how can it be arbitrarily pursued? Just as people have beautiful or ugly appearances, how they become like others by imitating? In the past, the beautiful? Xi Shi felt heart pain and frowned, and stupid people imitated her look, only to make themselves look all the more horrid. The Lady of the Zhao was good at dancing and walked with enchanting grace. Those who imitated her ended up losing balance and crawling.

凡人各殊氣血，異筋骨。心有疏密，手有巧拙。書之好醜，在心與手，可強爲哉？若人顏有美惡，豈可學以相若耶？昔西施心疹，捧胸而矉，衆愚效之，秖增其醜；趙女善舞，行步媚蠱。學者弗獲，失節匍匐。 (*FSYL*, 2)

Cao Pi 曹丕 (187–226), Emperor Wen of the Wei, puts even more emphasis on the bodily form when making the first Chinese statement on refined literature:

§36
Literature is primarily constituted of lifebreath. One's lifebreath is by nature clear or turgid and therefore cannot be arbitrarily altered. Take music as example, although there are uniform measures and set rhythms, people draw breath variously and therefore give skillful or clumpy performances accordingly. Even if one's father and elder brothers possess [the art of performance], they cannot pass it to their sons or younger brothers.

文以氣爲主。氣之清濁有體，不可力強而致。譬諸音樂，曲度雖均，節奏同檢，至於引氣不齊，巧拙有素，雖在父兄，不能以移子弟。(*ZGLDWLX*, 1:158–59)

This statement has often been compared (and even equated) by many Chinese scholars with Georges Buffon's pithy "the style is the man." Surely, the comparison makes a valid point that both Cao Pi and Buffon deterministically link author and text, but it misses the essential difference between the two statements. In speaking of "the man," Buffon is thinking of the author's subjectivity rather his physiological constitution. But the reverse is true of Cao Pi's statement, which amounts to a physiological definition of literature, a definition probably unimaginable in the Western critical tradition.

I hope the broad survey in this chapter sheds light on the philosophical foundations for the development of literary creation theories examined in later chapters. In discussing these theories in chapters 2–9, I will repeatedly refer to the passages discussed above and show how Chinese literary critics consistently conceptualized the creative process within the *yi→xiang→yan* paradigm, how they tried to understand the transcendental spirit-thinking within the hierarchical spirit-form paradigm, and how they availed themselves of the two alternate spirit-form paradigms to probe the dynamic interplay between mind and body, inspiration and conscious endeavors, creative conception and compositional execution. By tracing these theories to their philosophical sources, we can better understand why and how traditional Chinese critics did what they did under given historical and cultural circumstances. The findings of my historicized and "culturalized" studies of these theories, in turn, provide solid ground for broad cross-cultural reflections in chapter 10.

////////////////////////////////

Notes
1   A notable exception is Wordsworth's detailed description of the creative process in his "Preface to *Lyrical Ballads*" (1800). I have compared his description with Liu Xie's in my

Configurations of Comparative Poetics, chapter 6. For a comprehensive study on Western theories of creative imagination, see Engell, *Creative Imagination*.

2   Xu. *Shuowen jiezi*, 10.502.

3   Ibid.

4   Waley, *Analects of Confucius*, 171–72. To be more faithful to the original, I have replaced "language" (Waley's choice) with "names" as the English translation of the term *ming*.

5   See *LYYD*, 16/9/4, 21/11/18, 29/14/31.

6   Chan, *Source Book in Chinese Philosophy*, 126.

7   My translation is based on the textual notes collected in *XZJJ*.

8   *CQFLYZ*, 10.285.

9   Collected in Ouyan, *Yi wen lei ju*, 1:19.348.

10 Wang Bi, *Laozi Daodejing zhu*, in *Wang Bi ji jiaoshi*, 1:1; translation from Lau, *Lao Tsu*, 57.

11 Watson, *Complete Works of Chuang Tzu*, 178.

12 See Gao, *Gu zi tong jia hui dian*, 374.

13 Watson, *Complete Works of Chuang Tzu*, 152, with modifications.

14 Ibid., 302.

15 For a summary of the debate on the character of the *Commentary on the Attached Phrases* from the Song to the late 1950s, see Peterson, "Making Connections." For an account of the most recent work on the *Commentary on the Attached Phrases*, see Chen G., *Yi zhuan yu Daojia sixiang*, 232–76. Chen seeks to establish the Daoist character of this commentary through textual collations. Comparing the commentary's standard text with the extant oldest silk text unearthed in the Mawangdui Tomb in the 1970s, Chen notes the absence in the latter of several passages expounding Confucian ideas and regards those passages as latter-day interpolations into a text of Daoist origins. To demonstrate the commentary's Daoist origins, Chen also traces its key philosophical concepts to a broad array of Daoist texts and presents the results of his textual collations in a convenient chart (225–31).

16 *Zhou yi zhengyi*, in *SSJZ*, 1:70; translation from Lynn, *Classics of Changes*, 67.

17 *Zhou yi zhengyi*, in *SSJZ*, 1:70; translation from Lynn, *Classics of Changes*, 67, with modifications.

18 Wang Bi, *Laozi Daodejing zhu*, chap. 21, in *Wang Bi ji jiaoshi*, 1:52; translation from Lau, *Lao Tsu*, 78.

19 Wang Bi, *Laozi Daodejing zhu*, chap. 41, in *Wang Bi ji jiaoshi*, 1:112; translation from Lau, *Lao Tsu*, 102.

20 Watson, *Complete Works of Chuang Tzu*, 302, with slight modification.

21 Wang X., *Hanfeizi*, 20.148.

22 See *CQFLYZ*, 10.285.

23 *Zhou yi zhengyi*, in *SSJZ*, 1:71; translation from Lynn, *Classics of Changes*, 68.

24 *Zhou yi zhengyi*, in *SSJZ*, 1:78; translation from Lynn, *Classics of Changes*, 92.

25 Lou Yulie, *Wang Bi ji jiaoshi*, 2:609; translation from Lynn, *Classics of Changes*, 31.

26 Lou Yulie, *Wang Bi ji jiaoshi*, 2:609; translation from Lynn, *Classics of Changes*, 31.

27 Lau, *Mencius*, 1:57; with modifications.

28 Yang, *Mengzi yizhu*, 61–62.

29 Ban, *Han shu*, 2713–14.

30 Huang H., *Lunheng jiaoshi*, 3:946.

Two Six Dynasties Theories of Literary Creation
Lu Ji and Liu Xie

The Six Dynasties period (222–589) is seen by many Chinese scholars as an era of "literary self-consciousness" (*wenxue zijue* 文學自覺) a phrase coined by Lu Xun 魯迅 (1881–1936) to describe the ambitious pursuit of glory by literary masters of the Jian'an reign of the Han (196–220) and their Wei-Jin followers. In my view, the indisputable evidence of this literary self-consciousness is not literature itself but the theorizing of it by Six Dynasties literati devoted to exalting the significance of this nascent belletristic literature and elevating its authors' status. At the pinnacle of these critical writings are China's first and only comprehensive theories of literary creation, in Lu Ji's 陸機 (261–303) *Fu Exposition on Literature* (hereafter *Exposition*) and Liu Xie's 劉勰 (ca. 465–532?) magnum opus, *Literary Mind and the Carving of Dragons* 文心雕龍 (hereafter *Literary Mind*).[1]

Written shortly before his death in 303, Lu Ji's *Exposition* occupies a pivotal position in the historical development of Chinese literary theory. Looking backward, it forms a good complement to Cao Pi's 曹丕 (187–226) essay "On Literature" (Lunwen 論文) written roughly eighty years earlier, around 218. There seems a perfect division of labor between the authors. Cao Pi did what befitted a crown prince patron of literature: declaring belletristic literature "a great enterprise in governing the state and a pursuit that gives one an immortal name" 經國之大業，不朽之盛事.[2] By so doing, he installed a new elite class he called "men of letters" (*wenren* 文人), lavishing praise on the most accomplished of those closest to him, namely the so-called Seven Masters of the Jian'an (Jianan qizi 建安七子). By contrast, Lu Ji did what befitted a prominent man of letters: describing and elucidating the miraculous process of literary creation to justify Cao Pi's claims for men of letters like himself.

Fast forward a couple hundred years and Lu Ji's essay finds itself nicely complemented by Liu Xie's chapters on literary creation in his *Literary Mind*. Here we note a perfect partnership between an original thinker and a great synthesizer. While Lu brought forth original ideas about the workings of the literary

PRISM: THEORY AND MODERN CHINESE LITERATURE • 20 (ANNUAL SUPPL.) • DECEMBER 2023
DOI 10.1215/25783491-11080855 • © 2023 LINGNAN UNIVERSITY

mind, Liu absorbed, expanded, and integrated these ideas as a coherent whole along four stages of the creative process: mental and psychological preparedness, emotional response to the outer world, the transcendent flight of the creative mind that culminates in the formation of "conception-image," and finally the translation of that conception-image into a work of language. Given this, it seems most productive to arrange and compare Lu's and Liu's thoughts along these four stages and thereby distinguish their comprehensive theories of literary creation.

Conceptualizing Literary Creation within the *Yi*→*Xiang*→*Yan* Paradigm

Before exploring Lu's and Liu's discussion of the four creative stages, let's consider how they adapted the *yi→xiang→yan* paradigm to theorize literary creation. The adoption of this paradigm is obviously a conscious decision, as both Lu and Liu explicitly identify literary creation as a process of transforming *yi* (inward conception) into *yan* (words) and give a poetic description of *xiang* (envisagement), the intermediary of this transformation. Thus, Lu Ji prefaces his *Exposition* with a personal reflection on the *yi-yan* relationship:

§37

Whenever I observe compositions by men of talent, I feel I have a way of grasping the strenuous efforts of their minds. Though there are many divergences in the ways they articulate their words and deploy phrases, we can still grasp and talk about the value and beauty, merits and demerits of their works. Whenever I myself write a literary piece, I keenly envision their state of mind. I, too, constantly fear about conceptions (*yi*) not matching actual things and writing not matching conceptions. To understand all this is not difficult, but to be able to write well is. Here I write *A Fu Exposition on Literature* to pass on the splendid craft of past writers and to illuminate the reasons for success and failure in writing, hoping that someday it will be known for exhausting all the subtleties of writing.[3]

余每观才士之所作，窃有以得其用心。余每觀才士之所作，竊有以得其用心。夫放言遣辞，良多变矣，妍蚩好恶，可得而言。夫放言遣辭，良多變矣。妍蚩好恶,可得而言。 每自属文，尤见其情，恒患意不称物，文不逮意，盖非知之难，能之难也。每自屬文，尤見其情，恆患意不稱物，文不逮意。蓋非知之難，能之難也。 故作文赋，以述先士之盛藻，因论作文之利害所由，佗日殆可谓曲尽其妙。故作《文賦》，以述先士之盛藻，因論作文之利害所由，佗日殆可謂曲盡其妙。至於操斧伐柯，虽取则不远，若夫随手之变，良难以辞逮，盖所能言者，具於此云。(*WFJS*, 1)

This preface introduces a new concept of literary creation not seen in earlier writings: literary work as an externalization of *yi* (creative conception), not the traditional *zhi* (heart's intent). "Shi yan zhi" 詩言志 (Poetry expresses the heart's intent), common in pre-Qin and Han texts, reveals the often strategic importance of *zhi*. Given the contexts for its appearance, *zhi* usually denotes a volitional intent or attitude toward certain sociopolitical events or conditions. Expression of *zhi* often becomes a sociopolitical act, performed on public occasions, praising or criticizing the state of governance or delivering a diplomatic message.

At their etymological roots, *yi* and *zhi* are cognates denoting "the movement of the heart" and often merged into a compound (*zhiyi* 志意).[4] Despite this cognate bond, *yi*, when used alone, carries no ethico-sociopolitical meaning or even connotations. Thus, by substituting this neutral *yi* for the sociopolitically loaded *zhi*, Lu Ji effectively gets rid of all the sociopolitical baggage and rethinks the creative process in terms of a self-conscious, private act of pure artistic creation. This de-sociopoliticization of the creative process is not the only benefit of substituting the *yi-yan* paradigm for the old *zhi-yan* paradigm. As discussed in chapter 1 (see §§20–22), *yi* has accrued much transcendent significance in the Daoist and Abstruse Learning (Xuanxue 玄學) cosmological-epistemology discourse and readily lends itself to Lu Ji and Liu Xie for exploring the subtlest use of the literary mind.

Lu Ji's statement that "I, too, constantly worry about conceptions [*yi*] not matching actual things and writing not matching conceptions" has been traced by many to Zhuangzi's 莊子 (ca. 369–286 BCE) remarks about *yi* and *yan* (see §§11–13). In my opinion, Lu Ji's statement expresses a belief diametrically opposed to Zhuangzi's. Zhuangzi's remarks are "antiessentialist" in that they stress unbridgeable gaps between *wu* 物 (things) and *yi* and between *yi* and *yan*. By contrast, Lu Ji's fear of not being able to close these gaps belies an opposite belief in the possibility of closing them. The reason is fairly simple: if we do not believe something is possible, it would be hard to fear failing to accomplish it. Indeed, while acknowledging the limits of his ability to capture the subtle secrets of literary creation, he expresses the hope that someday his essay "will be known for revealing all the subtleties of writing." In light of these fundamental differences, it seems safe to argue that Lu Ji's *yi-yan* paradigm is grounded not in Zhuangzi's antiessentialist view but in the affirmative view of language articulated in *Commentary on the Attached Phrases* (see §21). Lu's debt to this *Commentary* will become clearer as we examine the essay proper.

In the "Spirit-Thinking" chapter, Liu Xie also reflects on the broad *yi-yan* paradigm used for conceptualizing the creative process. If Lu Ji sets up this paradigm to introduce his exploration of the creative process, Liu utilizes the same paradigm to recapitulate what he has said about all but the last phase of literary creation:

§38
Thus conception [*yi*] is received from spirit thinking [*si*], words [*yan*] from conception. They can be tightly matched, leaving no space between them, or

they can be far apart from each other by a thousand miles. Sometimes the principle [*li*] [to expound] lies within a speck of mind, yet we search for it beyond the world's boundaries; sometimes the meaning [to be expressed] lies only a foot away, but we search for it beyond mountains and rivers.

是以意授於思，言授於意；密則無際，疏則千里；或理在方寸而求之域表，或義在咫尺而思隔山河。（*WXDL*, chap. 26, sentences 18–19 [hereafter 26/18–19]）

This passage sums up what Liu Xie has just said in terms of a development through *si*, *yi*, and *yan*. The term *si* 思 denotes not conscious rational exercise of the mind but its unconscious transcendent flight or "spirit thinking" described at the beginning of the chapter. Liu's first statement, "conception [*yi*] is received from thought [*si*]," underscores the crucial importance of the initial transcendent flight of the mind. Like Lu Ji, Liu believes that "spirit-thinking" (*shensi* 神思) ushers in a plenitude of emotions, images, and words and fuses them as one. To Liu, this fusion of emotion, image, and words marks the formation of *yixiang* 意象 or "conception-image" of a work-to-be. The next statement, "Words in turn are received from conception," underscores the crucial importance of creative conception to the birth of a fine literary work. While acknowledging the chances of their being far apart, Liu expresses his abiding faith in *yi* and *yan* being seamlessly merged by a good writer: "They [conception and words] may be so close that there is no boundary between them." This statement leaves no doubt about Liu Xie's debt to the essentialist *yi→xiang→yan* paradigm of *Commentary on the Attached Phrases* (Xici zhuan 繫辭傳). Just as the author of the *Commentary* conceives of *yi*, *xiang*, *yan* as one producing another, Liu Xie traces a similar progressive chain of causation. As well, just as the *Commentary* regards *yi* as capable of full expression by *yan* (through the intermediary *xiang*), Liu contends that *yi* and *yan* could become one in the hand of a literary master. It seems inevitable that Liu Xie, as well as Lu Ji, would adopt this essentialist *yi→xiang→yan* paradigm to theorize the creative process. Unless they look to a perfect fusion of *yi* and *yan* into a great work of art, their theorization of the creative process simply becomes meaningless. The same holds for later critics who theorize the creative process in the vein of Lu and Liu. Indeed, many of them faithfully adhere to the route charted by Lu and Liu, with eyes set on the ideal fusion of *yi* and *yan*.

The Physical and Psychological Preparedness
In thinking about literary creation, many Chinese critics take the writer's physical and psychological preparedness as the starting point. This body-mind approach to literary creation stands in sharp contrast to the Western tradition, where, until the romantic era, the author was largely left out of the discussion.

Even today, a writer's physical condition rarely appears in Western works on literary creation. The dualistic worldview of the West posits an unbridgeable chasm between flesh and spirit, so why bother with the relationship between the body and creative mind? By contrast, thanks to the nondualistic yin-yang worldview held by native Chinese thinkers, body and spirit are regarded by most Chinese as complementary and inseparable. It is only natural that the writer's physical and psychological conditions figure as a prominent topic in Chinese writings on literary creation.

Lu Ji's *Exposition* contains a long passage in which he mentions the writer's bodily and psychological conditions as the cause of what we call writer's block.

§39

235	But when six emotions are stalled and hampered,	及其六情底滯
236	When mind strains toward something, but spirit remains unmoved,	志往神留
237	One is immobile as a bare, leafless tree.	兀若枯木
238	Gaping empty like a dried up stream.	豁若涸流
239	One draws the soul to search secret recesses,	攬營魂以探賾
240	Gathers vital forces to seek from oneself;	頓精爽於自求
241	But natural principle is hidden and sinks away ever farther,	理翳翳而愈伏
242	Thought struggles to emerge, as if dragged.	思乙乙其若抽
243	Thus at times I wear out my feelings, and much is regretted.	是以或竭情而多悔
244	At other times I follow the bent of my thoughts with few transgressions.	或率意而寡尤
245	Although this thing is in the self,	雖茲物之在我
246	It is not within the scope of my concentrated forces.	非余力之所戮
247	At times I consider the emptiness in my heart and turn against myself,	故時撫空懷而自惋
248	That I do not know the means to open this blockage.[5]	吾未識夫開塞之所由 (*WFJS*, 1)

Here, Lu describes writer's block in terms of the inability of his creative mind ("spirit" 神 on line 236 and "thought" 思 on line 242) to express what he wishes to convey ("intent" 志 on line 236 and "this thing" 茲物 on line 245). Why does this block occur? Lu argues that it is the writer's poor psychological condition—"the six emotions are stalled and hampered" (line 235) and "wearing out feelings" (line 243)—that causes the block. Then he considers why the writer is unable to overcome it; the reason, Lu explains, is the insufficient bodily vital energy (the body-bound "soul" 營魂 on line 239 and "refined essence" 精爽 on line 240).

If Lu makes only brief references to the body in literary creation, Liu Xie devotes an entire chapter, titled "Nourishing Lifebreath" (Yangqi 養氣) to explore physical factors' effect on literary creation. It opens:

§40

In the past Wang Chong wrote a chapter on the nourishing of lifebreath and it was based on his personal experience. How could it be a fictional account? Ears, eyes, nose, and mouth are instruments of one's life; the mind, thought, words, and phrase are the acts of one's consciousness [*shen*]. When one follows where the heart goes and abides the harmony [of lifebreath], the principles [he explains] cohere and [his expression of] emotions move unhindered. But if one overexerts oneself, his consciousness will be worn out and his lifebreath will wither. This is the proven rule of our natural disposition.

昔王充著述，製養氣之篇，驗己而作，豈虛造哉！夫耳目鼻口，生之役也；心慮言辭，神之用也。率志委和，則理融而情暢；鑽礪過分，則神疲而氣衰；此性情之數也。(*WXDL*, 42/1–22)

Here Liu Xie begins by citing Wang Chong's 王充 (27–ca. 97) equivalent view of spirit and form (see §34) as the foundation of his argument. His ensuing reasoning, however, is modeled on an earlier source: Sima Tan's 司馬談 (ca. 169–110 BCE) evaluation of the merits and demerits of Confucian and Daoist doctrines of government. Indeed, if we compare this passage with Sima's (see §32), we find it is simply an appropriation of the latter for a literary purpose. Liu's critique of a writer's overexertion corresponds to Sima's disapproval of a Confucian ruler's proactive agendas. These two negative cases point to the same life-threatening harm, to say nothing of the certain failure of their respective endeavors. Likewise, Liu's praise of a writer "following the intent and abide by harmony" 率志委和 corresponds with Sima's homage to the Daoist ruler's all-harmonizing turn of mind. These positive cases are lauded for the same double benefits: success in their respective enterprises while protecting their own lives.

After elaborating on his argument with concrete historical examples, Liu ends the chapter with an eloquent recapitulation and more insights of his own:

§41

Thus, to bring forth literature and art, one must refrain from venting, must make the mind pure and tranquil, and must ensure a smooth flow of one's lifebreath. When feeling vexed, you should stop thinking to avoid getting stuck. Whenever a conception emerges, give expression to what's in your mind and ply your writing brush. When principles elude you, put the brush down and let go of your thought. Carefree wandering is a good cure for exhaustion, and jokes and laughter can relieve your fatigue. You may, in leisure, sharpen your talent and expend your surplus energy cultivating literary boldness. When your thinking is honed like a sharp blade, [your lifebreath] will flow through your veins without the slightest hindrance. Even if this does not amount to the wondrous skill of embryonic breathing, it is a good method for preserving your lifebreath.

是以吐納文藝，務在節宣，清和其心，調暢其氣，煩而即捨，勿使壅滯，意得則舒懷以命筆，理伏則投筆以卷懷，逍遙以針勞，談笑以藥勸，常弄閑於才鋒，賈餘於文勇，使刃發如新，湊理無滯，雖非胎息之邁術，斯亦衛氣之一方也。 (*WXDL*, 42/77–92)

In this passage, Liu Xie has used two terms borrowed from Daoist sources: *couli* 湊理 and *taixi* 胎息. *Taixi* or "embryonic breathing" refers to a religious Daoist's exercise of internal alchemy as a means of achieving immortality. *Couli* depicts the perfect running of lifebreath throughout a perfected Daoist body. Liu's use of these two terms shows how, in expounding the importance of the body for literary writing, he goes beyond "highbrow" philosophical traditions to absorb ideas from popular religious Daoism. By aligning the act of writing with embryonic breathing, Liu formulates a truly original proposition on the therapeutic function of literary creation: properly executed, it not only does no harm to health but actually protects and prolongs the writer's life. Discussion of literature's therapeutic effects is not new in China or the West; think, for example, of Aristotle's theory of catharsis in *Poetics*. But the notion of writing literature as a means of prolonging one's life is extremely rare. Even in the Chinese tradition, it stands out as Liu Xie's unique invention, scarcely seen before or after him.

Affective Response to Things

To Lu Ji, Liu Xie, and other Six Dynasties critics, an "affective response to things" (*ganwu* 感物, or, literally, being "moved by things") is the immediate, primary stimulus for literary creation. Belief in the emotive origin of literature, however, was not pioneered by these critics. From time immemorial, the earliest statement on poetry, "Poetry expresses the heart's intent," clearly conveys such a belief. What is unique in Six Dynasties discussions of "affective response" is the shift in attention from sociopolitical events and conditions to the world of nature. The "things" arousing affective responses for them are first and foremost the sensuous appearances of nature, especially scenes of seasonal change. At the start of his *Exposition*, Lu Ji articulates this new Six Dynasties idea of affective response:

§42

	He stands in the very center, observes in the darkness	佇中區以玄覽
2	Nourishing feeling and intent in the ancient canons.	頤情志於典墳
	He moves along with the four seasons and sighs at their passing,	遵四時以嘆逝
4	Peers on all the things of the world, broods on their profusion,	瞻萬物而思紛
	Grieves for the falling leaves in strong autumn,	悲落葉於勁秋
6	Rejoices in the pliant branches in sweet spring;	喜柔條於芳春
	His mind shivers, taking the frost to heart;	心懍懍以懷霜
8	His intent is remote, looking down the clouds.	志眇眇而臨雲
	He sings of the blazing splendor of moral power inherited by this age,	詠世德之駿烈
10	Chants of the pure fragrance of predecessors,	誦先人之清芬
	Roams in the groves and treasure houses of literary works,	遊文章之林府
12	Admires the perfect balance of their intricate and lovely craft	嘉麗藻之彬彬
	With strong feeling he puts aside the book and takes up his writing brush	慨投篇而援筆
14	To make it manifest in literature.[6]	聊宣之乎
		(*WFJS*, 20)

This opening section depicts what a good writer needs to do in preparation for literary creation. The first two lines identify two primary "requisites": extensive observation of the universe and immersion in the classic canons. Spelling out the first requisite, lines 3–6 depict how changing scenes of nature move a writer to sadness and joy; lines 7–8 show, conversely, how the poet's inner feelings affect his observation of external scenes. Apparently, Lu Ji conceives of affective response as a dynamic two-way interaction. Lines 9–14 describe how, like observing nature, reading literary masterworks also motivates one to write. These six lines detail what the writer gains by immersion in the classics: cultivation of moral sentiment and perfecting the art of writing. It is also important to note Lu Ji's new concept of *qing* 情 or emotions expressed in these lines. Unlike the author of the "Great Preface to the *Book of Poetry*" (*Shi* da xu 詩大序), he does not identify *qing* as a direct response to specific sociopolitical realities, nor does he equate an unmediated expression of crude emotions with the making of literature. To him, *qing* or *qing-zhi* 情志 is merely the raw material that needs to be immersed and nourished in classical canons. In other words, the expression of *qing* must be mediated through refined literary language before the birth of a literary work.

Liu Xie attaches even more importance to affective response, to which he devotes an entire chapter, titled "Sensuous Appearances of Things" (Wuse 物色). This chapter elaborates on the essential issue in Lu Ji's passage just cited: How do changing scenes of nature stir up a writer's emotions and stimulate him to create?

Liu Xie begins by asking, "When summoned by sensuous appearances of things, who could be at peace?" 物色相召，人獲誰安 (*WXDL*, 46/11–12). He follows by depicting the poets' affective responses and their categorical associations in the *Book of Poetry*. Using selected examples of reduplicative binomes (*lianmian zi* 連綿字) from the *Book of Poetry*, he demonstrates the process where "as the eye moves forward and backward, the mind also receives and gives" 目既往返，心亦吐納 (*WXDL*, 46/118–19) and "emotions go forth as if giving a gift, and inspiration comes as if in response" 情往似贈，興來如答 (*WXDL*, 46/122–23). Liu Xie is clearly stressing here how the affective response actually entails mutual interaction between scenes and feelings, heralding their eventual fusion.

The Two-Way Journey of "Spirit-Thinking"

Although Lu Ji and Liu Xie give considerable attention to the first two creative stages—the writer's physical and psychological preparedness and his affective response—they do not make explicit connections between these stages and the next. To Lu Ji and Liu Xie, creative activities per se begin with the third stage: the writer's transcendent mental flight, or "spirit-thinking" (*shensi* 神思), as Liu Xie calls it. Their discussions of spirit-thinking have much in common, with the same emphasis on the following three points. First, spirit-thinking arises from a state of tranquil void with the suspension of all sensory organs. Second, spirit-thinking is a wondrous two-way journey: an outbound transcendent flight from the phenomenal world to the metaphysical realm, followed by its return to the world of senses. Third, this return journey is a dynamic process of introspection where images, emotions, and words move and interact until they fuse into what Liu Xie calls *yixiang* 意象 (conception-image), or the envisagement of the work-to-be. What follows is a summary of their elucidation of these three points.

Tranquil Contemplation and Transcendent Flight of the Mind

According to Lu Ji, literary creation begins with a self-conscious effect, which, ironically, is a self-forgetting tranquil contemplation.

§43

	This is how it begins: perception is held back and listening is reverted.	其始也，皆收視反聽
16	Engrossed in thought, one searches all sides.	耽思傍訊
	His essence galloping to the world's eight boundaries,	精騖八極
18	One's mind roaming across ten thousand yards.[7]	心遊萬仞 (WFJS, 20)

In the state of tranquil contemplation, Lu Ji tells us all sense perceptions are suspended, thus allowing one's essence or innermost spirit to take off in transcendent flight or, in his words, embark on a "roaming of the mind" 心遊 (xinyou). Notably, Lu's phase xinyou is an inversion of Zhuangzi's phrase youxin 游心, with essentially the same meaning. "Just go along with things and let your mind roam freely [youxin]," writes Zhuangzi. "Resign yourself to what cannot be avoided and nourish what is within you—this is best."[8] Commenting on the effects of youxin, Zhuangzi says, "Let your mind roam in simplicity and blend your qi with the vastness, follow along with things the way they are, and make no room for personal views—then the world will be governed."[9] There is little doubt that Lu Ji's description of the literary mind's transcendent flight is modeled on Zhuangzi's account of xinyou. Like Zhuangzi, Lu stresses that such mind-roaming is primed by one's well-concentrated essence and that it transcends all limitations of time and space to reach the ends of the universe.

Like Lu Ji, Liu Xie begins by depicting a writer's tranquil contemplation. After a writer has reached the state of "emptiness and stillness" (xujing 虛靜),[10] Liu maintains, his innermost spirit will wander off to meet things (wu) beyond the limit of time and space:

§44

An ancient said, "While one's body is on the rivers and lakes, his mind remains at the foot of the palace towers of Wei." This is what is called "spirit-thinking." In the thought process of literature, the spirit goes afar. As one silently reaches the state of mental concentration, his thought traces back one thousand years. As one shows the slightest movement in his countenance, his vision reaches ten thousand li.

古人云：形在江海之上，心存魏闕之下。神思之謂也。文之思也，其神遠矣！故寂然凝慮，思接千載；悄焉動容，視通万里。(WXDL, 26/1–10)

This account of the spirit's transcendent flight strikes me as a borrowing of Lu Ji's (§43). The only difference is that Liu defines it with the term shensi 神思 (spirit-thinking).

Return Flight of the Mind: Fusion of Images, Emotions, and Words

Unlike a Daoist adept striving to perpetuate his blissful flight in the Great Empyrean (Taiqing 太清), both Lu Ji and Liu Xie maintain that a writer does not seek to achieve permanent transcendence of time and space. The transcendent flight of his mind is momentary: it always turns around and heads back to this world. Immediately after describing the outbound flight "to the world's eight boundaries," Lu describes how it returns to the world of emotions, images, and words:

§45

	And when it is attained, light gathers about moods [*qing*] and they grow in brightness,	其致也，情曈曨而彌鮮
20	Things [*wu*] become luminous and draw one another forward;	物昭晰而互進
	I quaff the word-hoard's spray of droplets,	傾群言之瀝液
22	And roll in my mouth the sweet moisture of the Classics;	漱六藝之芳潤
	. . .	
	Then, phrases from the depths emerge struggling as when the swimming fish, hooks in their mouths, emerge from the bottom of the deepest pool;	於是沉辭怫悅，若游魚銜鉤而出重淵之深
26	And drifting intricacies of craft flutter down, as when the winging bird, caught by stringed arrow, plummets from the tiered clouds.[11]	浮藻聯翩，若翰鳥嬰繳而墜曾云之峻 (*WFJS*, 36)

The *wu* (things) mentioned here are not real physical objects but their insubstantial or virtual existence as images of the mind. Likewise, *qing* (emotions) does not mean crude emotional responses to external stimuli but, rather, denotes feelings that have been sublimated by the contemplative mind. Again, the *yan* (phrases) described here are not actual words coming from the tip of a writing brush but their virtual existence in the writer's mind.

Like Lu Ji, Liu Xie believes that the outbound transcendent flight is followed by a return flight back to the world of emotions, images, and words. This conception of the mind's "double journey" becomes very clear as he next traces how the wandering spirit brings images of things (*wu*) from afar into the writer's ears and eyes:

§46

In the midst of his chanting and singing, the sounds of pearls and jade issue forth. Right before his brows and lashes, the spectacle of windblown clouds spreads out. All this is made possible by the principle of thought.

吟詠之間，吐納珠玉之聲；眉睫之前，卷舒風雲之色：其思理之致乎 (*WXDL*, 26/11–15)

Although he does not mention emotions here, he later adds that this influx of images always comes blended with emotions and thoughts: "the whole mountain is filled with his feelings; when one observes the seas, the seas will overflow with his expressive intent" [登山則] 情滿於山，觀海則意溢於海 (*WXDL*, 26/43–44). According to Liu, there are a few crucial factors affecting the flight:

§47

When the principle of thought is at its most miraculous, the spirit wanders off along with things. The spirit dwells in the bosom, intent [*zhi*] and vital breath [*qi*] control the pivot of its outlet. External things come along the ears and the eyes, and phrases control the hinge and trigger [for their influx]. When the hinge and trigger allow passage, no external things can hide their appearances. When the pivot of its outlet is blocked, the spirit is impeded.

故思理為妙，神与物游。神居胸臆，而志气統其關鍵；物沿耳目，而辭令管其樞機。樞機方通，則物無隱貌；關鍵將塞，則神有遯心。(*WXDL*, 26/16–25)

Liu tells us that the outbound flight is controlled by the physiological-moral process (*zhiqi*). With regard to the return flight, he identifies the perceptual process (the use of ear and eye) and the intellectual process (the conscious use of language) as crucial to mediating the influx of things from afar. To Liu, a well-coordinated operation of all these processes guarantees a smooth double journey and brings about a fusion of emotions, images, and words into what he calls "conception-image" (*yixiang* 意象), or the envisagement of the work-to-be.

Judging by Liu Xie's description of spirit-thinking and its end result, conception-image, we infer that he drew from far more intellectual sources than Lu Ji. Writing at the height of the Xuanxue learning, Lu Ji made scant use of the Han equalizing spirit-form paradigm already out of fashion in his time. Throughout the *Exposition* he doesn't give too much attention to the role of the body in literary creation. Lu conceptualizes the "roaming mind" largely within the hierarchical spirit-form paradigm grounded in the *Zhuangzi* (see §§28–30). By contrast, Liu Xie reveals a simultaneous embrace of the two alternate spirit-form paradigms. While lauding transcendent flight out of the body like Lu Ji, he gives full credit to the body for being "the pivot of its outlet." Stressing this pivotal role, he urges all writers to "dredge the five organs" 疏瀹五藏 (*WXDL*, 26/28). Also noteworthy is that Liu Xie's coinage "conception-image" reveals his debt to the essentialist *yi→xiang→yan* triad established in *Commentary on the Attached Phrases*, where the sages' *yi* (intuitive cognizance) is described as fully captured by *xiang* (images).

The Transformation of Conception-Image into Language

Translating the conception-image, fruit of spirit-thinking, into a work of language is the final phase of literary creation. Both Lu Ji and Liu Xie ardently hail this compositional execution as a transformation from nonbeing to being. Lu Ji writes, "One probes empty nonbeing and brings forth being from therein, and one knocks on tranquil silence in search for tones" 課虛無以責有，叩寂寞而求音 (*WFJS*, 89). In the same vein, Liu Xie writes, "Unoccupied positions are given rules and norms; what is formless takes shape for carving and sculpturing" 規矩虛位，刻鏤無形 (*WXDL*, 26/42–43).

To perform well this final act of literary creation, Liu urges the writer to "observe the conception-image to wield the axe" 窺意象而運斤 (*WXDL*, 26/37).[12] The metaphor of wielding the axe alludes to various tales told in the *Zhuangzi* about the miraculous execution of an artisan's work. First and foremost, it makes us think of Zhuangzi' famous story of Butcher Ding:

> **§48**
> Cook Ding was cutting up an ox for Lord Wenhui. At every touch of his hand, every heave of his shoulder, every move of his feet, every thrust of his knee—zip! zoop! He slithered the knife along with a zing, and all was in perfect rhythm, as though he were performing the dance of the Mulberry Grove or keeping time to the Jingshou music.
>
> "Ah, this is marvelous!" said Lord Wenhui. "Imagine skill reaching such heights!"
>
> Cook Ding laid down his knife and replied, "What I care about is the Way, which goes beyond skill. When I first began cutting up oxen, all I could see was the ox itself. After three years I no longer saw the whole ox—now I go at it by spirit and don't look with my eyes. Perception and understanding have come to a stop and spirit moves where it wants. I go along with the natural makeup, strike in the big hollows, guide the knife through the big openings, and follow things as they are. So I never touch the smallest ligament or tendon, much less a main joint."[13]

This tale conveys what is demanded for the perfect execution of a literary work: years of strenuous technical training and the guidance of spontaneous creativity.

In view of these two demands, Liu Xie stresses the final composition as the greatest challenge facing a writer:

§49

Upon picking up the writing brush, he finds that his creative energy is doubly charged prior to writing. But upon completing a work, he finds only half of what's in his mind has gotten conveyed. Why so? The conception is virtual and therefore can easily be extraordinary; words have actual qualities and therefore are hard to skillfully employ.

方其搦翰，氣倍辭前，暨乎篇成，半折心始。何則?意翻空而易奇，言徵實而難巧也。(WXDL, 26/48–54)

Compared to the challenge described, Lu and Liu have set themselves the still harder task of capturing and explaining all the subtleties in the transformation from virtual to real. How to tackle this greatest of challenges? Lu Ji describes what the writer, after all the emotions, images, and phrases fuse in his mind, does next:

§50

	Only afterward he selects ideas, setting out categories,	然後選義按部
34	Tests phrases, putting them in their ranks,	考辭就班
	Striking open all that contains light,	抱暑者咸叩
36	Plucking everything that embraces sound within.[14]	懷響者畢彈
		(WFJS, 60)

With the transitional phrase *ranhou* 然後 ("only afterward," "thereupon"), Lu Ji clearly indicates the creative process has entered its final stage, that of compositional execution. The writer must now work hard to transform his insubstantial envisagement into an actual text. If the preceding stage of envisagement involves only the use of *yan* on a rarefied mental level, this compositional stage entails a conscious handling of *yan* in all its practical aspects—structure, phrasing, rhetoric, style, and so forth. To Lu Ji, this self-conscious endeavor must leave no stone unturned: "Striking open all that contains light, / Plucking everything that embraces sound within." To begin with, Lu Ji maintains that a writer must reflect on the meaning of his envisagement and accordingly lay out the structure of his work. Next he must carefully examine his chosen words and set them in proper order. Ironically, just as we expect Lu to be more precise in dealing with the subjects of structure and sentence, he waxes lyrical and vague. Instead of laying down concrete rules, he presents us with a series of metaphorical descriptions.

He may rely on the branches to shake the leaves,	或因枝以振葉
38 Or follow the waves upstream to find the source.	或沿波而討源
He may trace what is hidden as the root and reach the manifest,	或本隱以之顯
40 Or seek the simple and obtain the difficult.	或求易而得難
It may be that the tiger shows its stripes and beasts are thrown into agitation,	或虎變而獸擾
42 Or a dragon may appear and birds fly off in waves around it,	或龍見而鳥瀾
It may be steady and sure, simply enacted,	或妥帖而易施
44 Or tortuously hard, no ease in it.[15]	或岨峿而不安
	(*WFJS*, 60)

Such descriptive lines provide no clear instruction on what the writer should do with regard to structure and phrasing. This sudden weakening of logical connection has long baffled traditional and modern scholars. Although abundant textual notes and explanations have been offered, none is particularly convincing. It seems better just to take this "disconnection" as indicating the insurmountable difficulty Lu Ji faces in depicting the transformation of the intangible conception (*yi*) into the substantial words of a text (*yan*). Such a transformation simply allows no fixed rules. Seen in this light, the disconnection serves as a reminder of the extreme difficulty of describing this transformation in discursive terms. In what other terms, then, does Lu Ji want us to think of it? In my view, he may intend to steer us to think of the transformation as being propelled by dynamic thrusts and counterthrusts of thought.

Those descriptive lines are neatly paired to indicate such thrusts and counterthrusts: (1) from general to particular versus from particular to general (lines 37–38); (2) from hidden to obscure versus from straightforward to abstruse (lines 39–40); (3) from center to peripheral versus from peripheral to center (lines 41–42); and (4) a smooth flow of words versus an impeded and disturbed run of words (lines 43–44). By listing these four pairs of thrusts and counterthrusts, Lu seems intent to underscore this important point: artistic envisagement has to be transmitted through a dynamic structuring of sentences and words in a unique way that befits it.

Lu Ji also stresses that a successful transmission of artistic envisagement depends in no small measure on the attainment of a tranquil state of mind, in which the writer can assimilate "ten thousand finest thoughts" to produce a work that encompasses heaven and earth and brings all things under its sway (lines 45–50). After a lengthy discussion of all the technical issues of *yan*,

Lu once more returns, in the penultimate section, to examine the workings of poetic inspiration:

§52

	At the conjunction of stirring and response,	若夫應感之會
222	At the demarcation between blockage and passage,	通塞之紀
	What comes cannot be halted	來不可遏
224	What goes off cannot be stopped.	去不可止
	When it hides, it is like a shadow disappearing,	藏若景滅
226	When it moves, it is like an echo rising.	行猶響起
	When Heaven's motive impulses move swiftly on the best course,	方天機之駿利
228	What confusion is there that cannot be put in order?	夫何紛而不理
	Winds of thought rise in the breast,	思風發於胸臆
230	A stream of words flows through lips and teeth,	言泉流於唇齒
	Burgeoning in tumultuous succession,	紛威蕤以馺遝
232	Something only the writing brush and silk can imitate.	唯毫素之所擬
	Writing gleams, overflows the eyes:	文徽徽以溢目
234	The tones splash on, filling the ears.[16]	音冷冷而盈耳
		(WFJS, 241)

Why does Lu Ji wind up his long, quotidian discussion of technical issues with this sublime description of poetic inspiration? The abrupt switch of subjects may seem at first sight a compositional fault, but it actually signals a rhythmic interplay of sensory and suprasensory experiences, of conscious endeavor and spontaneity, and of learning and talent, throughout the creative process. None of these bipolarities alone, Lu Ji believes, could produce a great work of literature.

Although Liu Xie does not touch upon any technical issues of literary composition in the "Spirit-Thinking" chapter, he exhaustively examines them one by one elsewhere. To stress the point that by mastering language techniques alone a writer cannot produce a great work, he mentions Zhuangzi's story of Carpenter Bian's wheel making, in which "what is obtained in the mind, the hand follows" 得之於手而應於心.[17]

Unlike Lu Ji, Liu does not attempt to probe spontaneous creativity in final composition. Instead, he admits the impossibility of explaining how it guides the compositional act: "Yi Zhi cannot relay the [matters of the tripod] in words, nor Carpenter Bian the [workings of] the axe. This is subtle indeed!" 伊摯不能言鼎，輪扁不能語斤，其微矣乎 (WXDL, 26/123–25). Much to our regret, the great challenge of explaining how the creative mind works is not successfully met by Lu Ji despite all his efforts and is intentionally skipped by Liu Xie. But this lacuna in

Lu's and Liu's theory leaves room for original contributions by Wang Changling 王昌齡 (ca. 698–ca. 756) (see chap. 4) and Ming-Qing critics (see chap. 7).

The Finest Expository Essays on Literary Creation

In developing their comprehensive theories of literary creation, both Lu Ji and Liu Xie set their sights on "an immortal name," that is, recognition and remembrance by posterity. As noted above, Lu Ji explicitly states in the preface his cherished hope that his essay "will be known for exhausting all the subtleties of writing" (§37). Likewise, Liu speaks of entrusting his existence to literature: "If literature is indeed a vehicle for the mind, my mind has found a place to rest" 文果載心，余心有寄 (*WXDL*, 50/169–70).[18] By all measures, both Lu and Liu achieved their life goals splendidly.

The towering achievements of Lu Ji's and Liu Xie's theories inspire nothing less than awe. The first to introduce literary creation as a subject of inquiry, to appropriate the *yi→xiang→yan* paradigm and a host of key philosophical concepts for its exploration, and to explore the dynamic interplay of transcendent literary mind and tangible literary form, Lu Ji lays indisputable and unrivaled claim to being the most original Chinese literary theoretician. In drawing from broad intellectual sources to fill all the gaps in Lu Ji's thought, establishing a truly comprehensive theory of literary creation, and codifying this theory within his grand system of literary theory, Liu Xie earns his unparalleled reputation as the greatest of literary synthesizers, with no lack of original insights of his own.

In addition to their own unique achievements, they display the same extraordinary talent for combining intellectual rigor and literary flair at their best. Written in "rhymed prose," a form whose rhymed parallel phrasing normally served descriptive purposes, Lu Ji's *Exposition* effectively transforms it into a vehicle of broad and deep intellectual analysis while retaining all its poetic appeal. Liu Xie achieves a similar formal transformation with his fifty-chapter *Literary Mind*, written entirely in *pianwen* 駢文 or parallel prose, a form still more rigid and exacting than rhymed prose with its complex, interlocking modules of parallel phrasing. Yet, with incredible ingenuity, Liu turned the inordinate demands of parallel phrasing to advantage, using it as a convenient grid for probing the inherent relationship of countless bipolar terms and concepts.[19] By so doing, he launched the genre of expository parallel prose, leaving behind the finest of Chinese expository writings in parallel prose. Both Lu Ji's and Liu Xie's essays are indeed delightful to read as literary works.

Thanks to all the achievements noted, it is no surprise that Lu's *Exposition* and Liu's *Literary Mind* are seen by many as the pinnacle of Chinese theorization of literary creation. They are unsurpassed by later theories, at least in offering comprehensive discussions of the entire creative process, advancing rigorously analytical arguments, and blending theoretical and literary flair. After the Six Dynasties, many critics studied a particular creative phase within the *yi→xiang→yan* paradigm, borrowed, with or without modifications, from Lu and Liu. There were, of course, others who abandoned this paradigm altogether and returned to the earlier *yangqi* 養氣 (nourishing lifebreath) or "Shi yan zhi" (Poetry expresses the heart's intent) tradition, or to the Zen language of sudden enlightenment to characterize literary creation. But for their followers and opposers alike, Lu's and Liu's theories remained the basic frame of reference.

////////////////////////////

Notes

1. For English-language studies of Liu Xie's theory of literary creation, see Egan, "Poet, Mind, and World"; and S. Lin, "Liu Xie on Imagination."
2. Yu and Zhang, *Wei Jin Nanbei chao wenlun xuan*, 14.
3. For a different translation, see Owen, *Readings in Chinese Literary Thought*, 77, 80, 84.
4. Xu Shen has listed *yi* right after *zhi*, glossing the latter as the former and vice versa; see Xu, *Shuowen jiezi*, 502.
5. Owen, *Readings in Chinese Literary Thought*, 176, 178; with slight modification.
6. Ibid., 87, 90, 92, 94.
7. Ibid., 96.
8. ZZJS, 1:4.160; Watson, *Complete Works of Chuang Tzu*, 61, with slight modifications.
9. ZZJS, 1:7.294; Watson, *Complete Works of Chuang Tzu*, 94, with slight modifications.
10. What Liu says about the state of "emptiness and stillness" is obviously modeled on Zhuangzi's account of the Butcher Ding's mental preparation: the closing of his eyes, his suspension of understanding, his suprasensory or intuitive union with the ox, and the free roaming of his mind. Liu's description of "emptiness and stillness" also echoes Laozi's and Xunzi's discussions of that thoughtless state; see Zhang S., *Zhongguo gudai wenxue chuangzuo lun*, 5–47.
11. Owen, *Readings in Chinese Literary Thought*, 98, 101.
12. This phrase alludes to both the story of Butcher Ding (see below) and that of Carpenter Shi, who had such an intuitive skill that he could wield his ax effortlessly to remove a speck of plaster from his friend's nose (ZZJS, 4:24.843). Both stories are meant to illustrate the miraculous execution of an artisan's work achieved through suprasensory union with the Dao. Additionally, Liu's phrase "shaping and turning [as on a potter's wheel] literary thought" (*taojun wensi* 陶鈞文思; WXDL, 26/26) brings to mind yet another *Zhuangzi* story, that of Wheelwright Bian, who reached a divine-like skill in his trade through decades of conscious endeavor (ZZJS, 2:13.491).
13. ZZJS, 1:2.117–19; Watson, *Complete Works of Chuang Tzu*, 50–51. I have changed the style of romanization from the Wade-Giles to the pinyin system.
14. Owen, *Readings in Chinese Literary Thought*, 104.
15. Ibid., 107.
16. Ibid., 173–75.
17. See the "Heavenly Operations" 天運 chapter of *Zhuangzi* in ZZJS, 2.491).
18. Shih, *Literary Mind and the Carving of Dragons*, 11.
19. See Cai, "Six Dynasties Parallel Prose," 221–25.

Chapter 3

The Rise of a Buddhist-Inspired Theory of Art
Zhou Yong and Zong Bing on Visualization and Transcendence

En route to the next major theory of literary creation, by the Tang poet-critic Wang Changling 王昌齡 (ca. 698–ca. 756), this chapter makes a detour to examine Zhou Yong's 周顒 (?–493) and Zong Bing's 宗炳 (375–443) Buddhist reconceptualizations of visual objects and visualization, with a view to illuminate the intellectual foundation for the transition from Lu Ji's 陸機 (261–303) and Liu Xie's 劉勰 (ca. 465–532?) indigenous theories (chap. 2) to Wang Changling's Buddhist-inspired theory of literary creation (chap. 4). I begin with a review of the previously unnoticed philosophical proposition "A Piercing Glance Elevates the Mind" by Zhou Yong in his debate with Zhang Rong 張融 (444–497) over the similarities and differences between Daoism and Buddhism. The appearance of this proposition shows that as early as the Liu-Song dynasty (420–479), writers already went beyond the limitations of the native Chinese conception of "image" (*xiang* 象) and consciously applied Buddhist concepts to come to new understandings of the objects, methods, and effects of the visual sense and to probe their transcendental religious significance.

Utilizing this proposition as a framework of analysis, I next reread Zong Bing's famous essay "A Preface to the Painting of Landscape" in terms of the visual sense, to show how the terms, concepts, propositions, and discourse of the text's five sections form a logically coherent, fully systematic Buddhist exposition on painting. Support for the validity of Buddhist interpretations of all of its terms and concepts is provided by intertextual readings of Zong Bing's "Elucidating Buddhism" (Ming fo lun 明佛論), and the poetry and prose by the Buddhist monks of Mount Lu 廬山僧人集團. I also adumbrate how Zong's Buddhist theory of painting served as a firm foundation over which Wang Changling built his Buddhist-inspired theory, particularly noted for its discourse on the "inscape of physical objects" (*wujing* 物境).

A Buddhist Reconfiguration of Sight

According to the Buddhist anthology *Hongmingji* 弘明集 (Collected Writings on the Propagation and Clarification of Buddhism) compiled by Sengyou 僧祐

PRISM: THEORY AND MODERN CHINESE LITERATURE • 20 (ANNUAL SUPPL.) • DECEMBER 2023
DOI 10.1215/25783491-11080865 • © 2023 LINGNAN UNIVERSITY

(445–518), in the debate between Zhou Yong and Zhang Rong over the differences and similarities between Buddhism and Daoism, Zhang Rong employed a phrase he borrowed from *Zhuangzi* 莊子, "a piercing glance reveals the Dao here" 目擊道斯存, to explain how the superficial differences between the two doctrines are similar to the traces one can perceive at a glance. When those who possess wisdom perceive and intuitively grasp what lies behind "traces" (*ji* 跡), they can understand the Dao as a unity that is shared by both Buddha and Laozi. Repudiating his opponent's belief that Buddha's and Laozi's doctrines are identical, Zhou Yong coined the phrase "a piercing glance elevates the mind or emotions" (*Muji gaoqing* 目擊高情) to challenge Zhang's position that "a piercing glance reveals the Dao here." He believed that the Buddhist understanding of both "a piercing glance" and that which is perceived by such is completely distinct from that of Daoists. "A piercing glance" is regarded by Daoists as the instrument with which to reach a profound understanding of the Dao, and to them neither the object of visual perception nor the act of visual perception itself has an independent or unique significance. To Buddhists, however, and especially for the adherents of the Lesser Vehicle (Nikaya or Theravada) sects that flourished during that era, seeing had an extraordinary or transcendent significance. When taken as the objects of such visual perception, Buddhist icons and landscapes, both of which possess material forms, were precisely the sites within which the Buddha resided; through their conscious and sustained observation of these objects by means of such piercing glances, believers could transcend phenomenal reality and achieve spiritual communion with Buddha and other deities and thus attain what Zhou Yong called an "elevated mind or emotions." From Zhou Yong's perspective, the difference between "a piercing glance that elevates the mind" and "a piercing glance [that] reveals the Dao here" not only reveals the inherent differences between Buddhism and Daoism but also can serve as a theoretical basis for praising Buddhism while denigrating Daoism. Zhou Yong's explication of "a piercing glance [that] elevates the mind" proceeds on a theoretical philosophical plane, which amply justifies calling it a philosophical proposition. This philosophical proposition not only provided a high degree of theoretical consistency to the production of Buddhist icons and the contemplation of landscape or other related activities but also established standards for the understanding of phenomena and the visual sense by which to judge the respective merits of Buddhism and Daoism.

According to historical accounts, Zhang Rong lamented the contentiousness that plagued relations between Buddhists and Daoists and wrote "Discipline for the Gate" 門律 (Menlü) to advocate for the unity of the two creeds. He held a syncretic position and felt that the two were not fundamentally distinct from each other. He sent this work to He Yin 何胤 (446–531), He Dian 何點 (437–504), Zhou Yong, and others to elicit their responses.[1] Arguing from the position that

Buddhism was the more important of the two, and emphasizing the unique features of Buddhism, Zhou Yong thought Buddhism to be of a higher order than Daoism, and it was out of this disagreement that his dispute with Zhang Rong unfolded. "Zhou Yan [Yong] Criticizes Zhang Changshi's [Rong] 'Discipline for the Gate'" 周剡顒難張長史融門律 (Zhou Yan [Yong] nan Zhang Changshi [Rong] menlü), found in *Hongmingji juan* 6, records the following passage about the dispute between Zhou Yong and Zhang Rong:

§53

"Reaching the Source"[2] states: "When times change, customs cannot remain the same. In different eras, meanings diverge. I have seen that Daoists and men of the Dao do battle. Men of the Dao of Confucius or of Mozi dispute right and wrong with Daoists. In ancient times, there was a goose that flew to the heights of heaven. As it grew more distant, it became difficult to make it out clearly. People of Yue thought it was a *fu*, while people in Chu thought it was a *yi*. People identify themselves as from Chu or Yue, but the goose is invariably the same goose. The root of purity may be the same, but I always revere the origin of both. Since the traces of the goose have separated, I have risen to the place where they have flocked together."

Zhou asked, "The *Analects* says, 'When times change, customs cannot remain the same.' This is why Buddhism is different from Daoism. When the world changes, we cannot hold to the same thought. Therefore, Daoist teaching is at variance with Buddhist teaching. Daoism and Buddhism differ from each other just as *fu* and *yi* birds do. But tracing them to a single origin, you have taken them to be one object, the goose. Chasing after both Buddhism and Daoism can only lead to losing both. I do not know how in your superior judgment you have found a way to recognize their origin. Is there any good reason why you so casually trace [both] to this?"

通源曰。殊時故不同其風。異世故不一其義。吾見道士與道人戰。儒墨道人與道士獄是非。昔有鴻飛天首。積遠難亮。越人以為鳧。楚人以為乙。人自楚越耳。鴻常一鴻乎。夫澄本雖一。吾自俱宗其本。鴻跡既分。吾已翔其所集。

周之問曰。論云。時殊故不同其風。是佛教之異於道也。世異故不一其義。是道言之乖於佛也。道佛兩殊。非鳧則乙。唯足下所宗之本。一物為鴻耳。驅馳佛道無免二失。未知高鑒。緣何識本。輕而宗之。其有旨乎。[3]

Zhang Rong believes that the distinction between Buddhism and Daoism is equivalent to the difference between the names *fu* 鳧 and *yi* 乙: while Yue people call the goose *fu* and Chu people call it *yi*, both refer to the same bird.[4] When people in different places view the same thing, they may use different names for it, but the concept to which they refer is the same. Zhang Rong holds that the difference between Buddhism and Daoism is a matter of applying different names to the same object. Zhou Yong takes a diametrically opposite view and quotes Zhang Rong's own words to attack his position. Saying "'When times change, customs cannot remain the same,'" he really means that Buddhism differs from Daoism. "When the world changes, we cannot hold to the same thought" means that Daoism's doctrines are at odds with Buddhism. By saying that the times are different, customs diverge, and thought and meaning are different, too, Zhang actually implies that Buddhism and Daoism are necessarily at variance with each other. To Zhou Yong, Zhang Rong's belabored use of the analogy of the *fu* and *yi* to illustrate the relationship between Buddhism and Daoism actually misconstrues the doctrines of both creeds. Zhang Rong replies to these remarks of Zhou Yong as follows:

§54

In "Tracing the Source," [Zhang Rong] replied, "It is true that, as traces, [the bird you talked about] must be either a *fu* or a *yi* bird, and I will not respond further." But he adds: "Our understanding of Daoism and Buddhism is simply a matter of 'a piercing glance [that] reveals the Dao here.'" He also says that the ground for obtaining the essential truth is the same, so why should we say this is derived from one particular doctrine?

通源曰。非鳧則乙。跡固然矣。跡固其然。吾不復答。又曰。吾與老釋相識正如此。正復是目擊道斯存。又曰。得意有本。何至取教。[5]

Zhang Rong turned the tables and, based on the relationship between root and traces, argued that looking at their outward "traces," the *fu* and the *yi* are of course different. "Their traces are definitely so, and I need not answer you on that score," but the differences between these outer traces do not represent differences in the root that lies behind such appearances. Zhang Rong quoted Zhuangzi's 莊子 (ca. 369–286 BCE) remark, "A piercing glance reveals the Dao here," to explain the path by which he had come to understand the ways of Buddha and Laozi. The object of visual perception is the trace, while behind the trace exists the Dao, which is both Laozi's and Śākyamuni's Way, both of which are mutually consistent. As recorded in *Zhuangzi*, Confucius had long wished to see Wenbo Xuezi 溫伯雪子, but when they met, he said nothing. Since Zilu 子路 (542–480) did not understand the reason for this, Confucius explained his silence as follows: "As for people, when one sees them with one's eyes, the Dao remains, so how could there be room for making a sound" 若夫人者，目擊而道存矣，亦不可以容聲矣 (ZZJS, 7.706). In other words, once he had seen this person, there was no need for speech. "A piercing glance reveals the Dao here" means in this case that as soon as one's eyes make contact, one can understand the inner aspirations and moral attainment of the other party. The same sort of usage is found in *Shishuo xinyu* 世說新語 (A New Account of Tales of the World), which claims that the "great man" in Ruan Ji's 阮籍 (210–263) "Biography of a Great Man" is none other than Ruan Ji himself. "Seeing how his extended bellowing harmonizes with others, it approaches 'the piercing glance [that] reveals the Dao here'" 觀其長嘯相和，亦近乎目擊道存矣. When one sees such a person, one can understand that person's character and temperament.[6] Zhang Rong employs the "piercing glance [that] reveals the Dao here" to expound the principle that "seeing with the eyes" is merely a means, and an external method, and does not influence the fundamental presence of the Dao. In the same way, he also cites the idea that "there is a root for obtaining the essential meaning," and since the root of meaning is consistent, why would one need to distinguish them based on different verbiage? Hence, he implies, the original meanings of Buddhism and Daoism are fully consistent with each other. Zhou Yong shot back as follows:

§55

Your remark "A piercing glance reveals the Dao here [and thereby obtains the essential truth]" seems in truth to refer to the original mind or dharma-nature. If this is what you speak of, we have it in Buddhism. If what you say is not this, why should you talk about it being derived from a particular doctrine? The essence of what you set your eye upon is the traces of [Buddhist] teaching. If you call these traces the *fu* and the *yi*, then how can the goose become manifest? The myriad phenomena contain the true nature: the *Laozi* does not entertain such an idea. Setting your eye upon [divine traces] and thereby achieving a transcendental state of mind: there is no trace of this idea in the *Laozi*. Both the idea and its traces are lost, and no way can be found to search for their sources.

足下之所目擊道存。得意有本。想法性之真義。是其此地乎。佛教有之。足下所取非所以。何至取教也。目擊之本。即在教跡。謂之鳧乙。則其鴻安漸哉。諸法真性。老無其旨。目擊高情。無存老跡。旨跡兩亡。索宗無所。[7]

Zhou Yong appropriated the proposition "a piercing glance reveals the Dao here" to explicate his point of view one step further. First, he linked the phrase "a piercing glance reveals the Dao here" in *Zhuangzi* to the true meaning of the dharma-nature of Buddhism, followed by an attack on the basis of Zhang Rong's argument. "The basis of seeing lies in the traces of the teachings," and that with which the eyes make contact, is in fact "traces of the teachings." But if these traces of the teachings are taken as merely superficial *fu* and *yi*, how can the eye recognize the goose or the dharma-nature? The "true nature of the myriad dharmas" represented by the traces of Buddhist teachings does not exist in Lao-Zhuang Daoism; moreover, there is no trace of Lao-Zhuang thought within the Buddhist doctrine of "a piercing glance elevates the mind," either. Zhou Yong inserted "traces of the teachings" into the proposition of "a piercing glance reveals the Dao here," as "the basis for the glance." And, he linked the "traces" together with the "basis," namely, the object and the basic nature of sight, contending that to cast aside their traces to seek their "essential meaning" resulted in losing both meaning and traces and leaving no way to search for their source.

Zhou Yong has apparently appropriated Zhuangzi's remark "a piercing glance reveals the Dao here" and reconstructed it as an important proposition of Buddhist philosophy. Within the context of the *Zhuangzi*, "a piercing glance reveals the Dao here" mainly emphasizes an intuitive understanding that does not rely on language. Sight is only a kind of catalyst or stimulus. In Zhou Yong's understanding and application, "sight" (a piercing glance) becomes a deliberate focus of attention, its object the dharma-nature. From Zhang Rong's "a piercing glance reveals the Dao here" to Zhou Yong's "a piercing glance elevates the mind" lies the process of evolution from a general descriptive account to a philosophical proposition. The rise of this proposition demonstrates that thinkers of the Liu-Song period already transcended the limitations of the Daoist traditional view of the "image" and consciously applied Buddhist concepts to reach new understandings of the objects, means, and effects of the sense of sight, to explore their transcendental religious significance. The formulation of the philosophical proposition "a piercing glance elevates the mind" also provides us a new framework with which to reexamine and reinterpret Zong Bing's "Preface" and to unravel its profound theoretical significance.

A Buddhist Conception of Sages, the Dao, and Landscape

"A Preface to the Painting of Landscapes" (hereafter "Preface") also mostly deals with the objects, means, and effects of the sense of sight and consists of five sections that explicate and extrapolate in different dimensions the topic of "a piercing glance [that] elevates the mind." In the following sections, I engage in a close reading of "Preface" and link it to the writings and other Buddhist activities of the monks at Mount Lu during the same period. This will entail contrasting the different intellectual systems of Buddhism and Daoism and both analyzing and tracing the theoretical sources and intellectual contexts of the key concepts in the text, in order to explore the theoretical and historical significance of "Preface."

"Preface" may not be terribly long, but it draws on quite a number of terms shared by Buddhism and Daoism, and even Confucianism as well, such as the sage (*sheng* 聖), worthies (*xian* 賢), Dao 道 (Way), the numinous (*ling* 靈), response (*ying* 應), spirit (*shen* 神), and image (*xiang* 象). It also juxtaposes and applies these to formulate propositions never seen before, for example, "The sage enters the Dao to respond to things, the worthy purifies his breast to savor images."

Alongside these terms, concepts, and propositions, in a number of unique and unprecedented passages Zong Bing further expounds his views regarding the observation, painting, and then further observation of landscape. As a consequence, analyses of the philosophical sources and provenance of the views of literary arts developed in "Preface" have almost inexorably been characterized by open-ended and seemingly unresolvable debate. Expressing divergent opinions toward these various issues, art and literary critics have failed to reach consensus, instead tending to base their interpretations on whichever sections of the text they find attractive and ignoring those sections that are inconsistent with their particular views.[8]

To go beyond the traditional readings of "Preface" and overcome the tendency to reach conclusions based on narrow or incomplete readings that lead to empty generalizations, I engage in a close reading of the entire text and subject the key terms, concepts, propositions, and modes of expression of each of its five sections to in-depth interpretation. The first stage of this interpretative process is to ascertain the conceptual content of the key terms used by Zong Bing. Key terms can express different concepts depending on the contexts in which they are used, such as by different philosophical schools or in different time periods. Hence, we must return them to their original intellectual and other related contexts in order to determine their proper significance. To do this, I compare and distinguish the meanings of terms, concepts, and expressions used in both Daoist and Buddhist canonical texts, respectively. I analyze each case to determine if a Daoist or a Buddhist reading is more appropriate to the textual flow of "Preface" and maintains the highest degree of consistency with other concepts, propositions, and expressions in the text. I also draw corroborative examples from Zong Bing's "Elucidating Buddhism," as well as poetry and prose by Mount Lu–based clerics, to prove that a Buddhist interpretation of the entire preface has firm textual support. Finally, I analyze the overall structural coherence of the text and show how the terms, concepts, propositions, and expressions in the preface's five main sections form a logically integrated, fully systematic Buddhist view of art, laying the groundwork for Wang Changling's Buddhist-inspired theory of literary creation.

The first section of the "Preface" lays out its central perspective and forms the basis for understanding the entire work:

§56

[First Section of "Preface"]

The sage encompasses the Dao and responds to things; worthies purify their minds and savor iconic images. As far as mountains and rivers are concerned, they have the substance of existence and yet tend toward the numinous. Therefore, the likes of Xuanyuan, Yao, Kong, Guangcheng, Dakui, Xu You, and [the brothers of Boyi and Shuqi of] Guzhu took to roaming in the mountains of

Kongtong, Juci, Miaogu, Ji, Shou, and Taimeng. Their roaming has also been described as the delight of the virtuous and the wise. The sages establish the spirit as the law of the Dao, so that worthies can commune with it. Mountains and rivers beautify the Dao with their forms, and thus the virtuous can take delight in them. Aren't these two alike?

聖人含道應物，賢者澄懷味像。至於山水，質有而趣靈，是以軒轅、堯、孔、廣成、大隗、許由、孤竹之流，必有崆峒、具茨、藐姑、箕、首、大蒙之游焉。又稱仁智之樂焉。夫聖人以神法道，而賢者通；山水以形媚道，而仁者樂。不亦幾乎。[9]

The two simple lines of its opening, "The sage encompasses the Dao and responds to things; worthies purify their minds and savor iconic images," include the main terms and concepts used in this work. Structurally, the subject-predicate construction of these two parallel lines is divided into the subjects, the "sage" and "worthies," followed by two predicates: "encompasses the Dao and responds to things" and "purify their minds and savor iconic images," respectively. The subject, verb, and object of each sentence all require detailed explication. First, while the terms *sage* and *worthy* may have been borrowed from Confucian vocabulary, their actual meanings are completely different from those of Confucian canonical texts.[10] In the writings of Zong Bing as well as in documents that survive from the monks of Mount Lu of the same era, *sage* and *worthy* often refer to Buddhas or venerable monks at different stages of spiritual cultivation.[11] "Those who had practiced the root of goodness with anāsrava-jñāna [untainted wisdom]" 以有漏智修善根者 were praised as worthies, while those who had "proven the correct reason through anāsrava-jñāna" 以無漏智證見正理者 were praised as sages.[12] The first verb-object construction is "encompasses the Dao," contrasting the relationship between sages and the Dao in native Confucian and Daoist sources. The implied significance of this expression is quite extraordinary. In Daoist canonical texts, the phrase *encompasses the Dao* appears only very rarely, but the relationship between sages and the Dao is quite clearly spelled out in the chapter "Tracing the Dao as the Source" (Yuan Dao 原道) of Liu Xie's *Literary Mind*: "The Dao is handed down in writing through the sages; sages make the Dao manifest in their writings" 道沿聖以垂文，聖因文而明道.[13] In "The Dao is handed down in writing through the sages," the sage is the instrument for transmitting the Dao; the Dao is the subject, while the sage is the medium of transmission from the Dao to writing, placing him in the position of passively facilitating such a transmission. This type of primary and secondary relationship manifests in a spatial relationship through "being handed down": the Dao is above while the sage is below; the Dao descends into "writing" along the path composed by the sage. The sage's relationship with Dao is that of passive reception, not that of possession. By contrast, in Zong Bing's statement "the sage encompasses the Dao," the sage is the subject that encompasses the Dao. Zong Bing often employs the word "encompass" in his essay "Elucidating Buddhism," where it appears in explanations of the relationship between Buddhist deities and native Chinese mythological figures and between Buddhist sutras and native canonical texts. For example, his remark "The knowledge that Yao hated death is usually held by spirits" 知堯惡亡之識，常含於神矣 means that Yao's individual knowledge was encompassed within the omnipresent Buddhist deities. In discussing the Buddhist sutras, Zong Bing also uses the term "encompass": "Those Buddhist sutras . . . encompass the Daoist vacuity, and add the idea that all ends in emptiness" 彼佛經也. . . . . .含老莊之虛，而重增皆空之盡.[14] These examples corroborate a Buddhist reading of the term sage (*sheng*) in the statement "the sage encompasses the Dao."

Now let us consider the next key term, *ying* 應 (respond to), that follows "encompassing the Dao." Does this term express a Daoist or a Buddhist view of responding to things? In native Daoist texts, "response" 應 usually refers to "being moved to respond" 感應 or "respond in reaction" 回應.[15] In Buddhist canonical works, however, although they borrow the same vocabulary to describe the relationship of sages to things according to Buddhist doctrines, they do so within a completely different semantic range. In "Elucidating Buddhism," Zong Bing discusses "response" as follows:

§57

Buddhism is none other than the Dao of the sages. It is not simply the amelioration of customs by the ruler, or the extension of the transformation of the world in its outward manifestation. Now we can talk about the unique responsiveness through which [the Buddha] lets all things realize themselves without claiming credit in the way reminiscent of Yao. By means of categorical resonance through similarity, the rhythm of bells can mysteriously find a resonant chord within the mind, to say nothing of the categorical resonance between the numinous sages and the divine principle. Those whose body and soul reach the Buddhist kingdom all have lofty goals and pure spirit as they bring light to the accumulated cycles of suffering. They are all capable of achieving complete communion with the absolute. This will enable Śākyamuni to cast a brilliant *vajra* light that illuminates the Lamp King's entry into the chamber. How could it be only Buddha who appears?

夫佛也者非他也。蓋聖人之道。不盡於濟主之俗。敷化於外生之世者耳。至於因而不為功自物成直堯之殊應者。夫鍾律感類由心玄會。況夫靈聖以神理為類乎。凡厥相與冥遘於佛國者。皆其烈志清神積劫增明。故能感詣洞徹。致使釋迦發暉十方交映多寶踊見鐙王入室。豈佛之獨顯乎哉。[16]

In native Chinese texts, "response" means a kind of process by which one is passive toward, quietly awaits, and responds to the Dao. In this case, however, what is described is decidedly different. First of all, Zong Bing explains that the Buddhist "response" transcends Yao's "differential response" and points toward an individual response to a concrete object. "By means of categorical resonance through similarity, the rhythm of bells can mysteriously find a resonant chord within the mind" means that sound and mental response are linked through similarity, such that the mind is the vessel with which one responds to sound and musical modes. Through its communion with the spiritual Dao, Buddha "finds commonality with spiritual patterns," to actively respond to and be linked to the myriad things. The subsequent statement that "those whose body and soul reach the Buddhist kingdom all have lofty goals and pure spirit as they bring light to the accumulated cycles of suffering. They are all capable of achieving complete communion with the absolute," means that anyone who can find himself in the Buddhist kingdom, namely, those who have reached the Buddhist Pure Land and entered Nirvana, will have transformed their minds into a state of purity and achieved a state of enlightened perspicacity through which they can "achieve a state of complete communion with the absolute." They then dissolve into the myriad things, illuminating the world so that they can see the *vajra* Buddha emerge, and the Lamp King of Sumeru enters (Vimalakirti's) chamber.[17]

"How could it be only Buddha who appears?" means that the dharma body will not appear singly but will come forth through multiple different physical transformations. Hence, the "response" here is a type of active response and transformation. In this way, when Zong Bing describes the Buddhist activities of response, he often uses verbs like "brighten" (*guang* 光) or "shine" (*zhao* 照) to describe this, words that indicate the act of illumination. This can be corroborated by the fact that the word "reflect" (*ying* 應) is written in editions of "The Secret Book of Reaching the Ford" (Jindai mishu 津逮秘書) and "Searching for the Origin of Studying the Ford" (Xuejin Taoyuan 學津討原) as the (homophonous) graph for "reflect" (*ying* 暎). This latter *ying* (a variant of the standard form of *ying* 映) means to shine or reflect and through such illumination to make visible the original form of a thing. In the phrase "encompassing the Dao, responding to things," these two characters (應 and 暎) coexist in different editions, demonstrating that the semantic genealogy of the concept of response is rich with Buddhist connotations.

Buddhism transforms the essence of deities or spirits into the world of physical objects, and this viewpoint of Zong Bing originated from his teacher Huiyuan 慧遠 (334–416).[18] In "Monks Do Not Bow to the King; Though Forms Disappear, Spirit Is Not Extinguished, Number 5" 沙門不敬王者論·形盡神不滅第五, Huiyuan explicates this clearly: "The spirit responds fully without a master, its mystery ends namelessly. Moved by things, it moves; borrowing numbers, it goes forward. It is moved by things yet is not a thing; hence, when as a thing it transforms, it is not extinguished. It borrows numbers yet is not a number; hence, when as a number it concludes, it is not exhausted" 神也者圓應無主妙盡無名。感物而動。假數而行。感物而非物。故物化而不滅。假數而非數。故數盡而不窮。[19] Huiyuan describes the response of the spirit as a "full response," a visible response that is all-penetrating and without distinctions. On the one hand, the spirit comes into contact with things, is moved by them, and then moves, meaning that it makes contact with a physical form and comes into motion according to the laws of the physical world. However, because it is an entity that "is moved by things yet is not a thing," it does not disappear with its physical transformation, and its spirit exists eternally, as before. Buddha's "full response" is in reality the process by which he transforms his physical body, namely, the spiritualization of that body, to manifest within a concrete phenomenon.

This viewpoint is given alternative expression in Xie Lingyun's 謝靈運 (385–433) "Inscription for a Buddhist Image" (Foying ming 佛影銘): "The great merciful, vast form, is moved to make contact; the bonds that form from contacting things, divide into multiple strands; its forms are difficult to sort through, but its principles are easy to surmise" 夫大慈弘物。因感而接。接物之緣。端緒不一。難以形揽。易以理測。[20] The Buddha follows the characteristics of things and, in the process of responding to the myriad things, comes into contact with them and, through convergence with varied karmic connections, transforms into physical form among them. The phenomenon of Buddha transforming and responding received much attention in the Buddhism of that era and again after the Tang dynasty, as well. The chapter "Buddha's Virtue" (Fode pian 佛德篇) in *Expanded Collected Writings on the Propagation and Clarification of Buddhism* (Guang Hongmingji 廣弘明集) adduces dozens of examples of "responding to things" and, as "responding to a Buddhist image," explains how the Buddha transforms himself physically into the form of a Buddhist image.[21] These examples from texts of the same era show that Zong Bing's explanation of "responding to things" in the introduction to "Preface" should be recognized as a response within the ambit of Buddhist doctrine, which explains how Buddha can be embodied within concrete, visible phenomena. We must understand "encompassing the Dao and responding to things" within the conceptual system of the Buddhism of that era before we can piece together the semantic continuity of the entire work and, with that, grasp the philosophical content that lies behind such statements.

The next statement, "Worthies purify their minds and savor iconic images," speaks of transcendental realization from the perspective of visual objects. "Savoring iconic images" is the tasting, pondering, and contemplation of the visual object. We must link this to the attitude toward physical Buddhist images of that time. As an important feature of this stage in the development of Buddhism, a large number of encomia of Buddhist images appeared during this era.

For instance, Zhidun's 支遁 (ca. 313–366) "Encomium and Preface to an Image of Amitābha" states: "Recite the *Amitābha Sutra*, and vow to be born in that other land. Those whose sincerity does not falter will at the end of their lives be transformed and pass to that land, where they will see the Buddha and, spiritually enlightened, achieve the Dao" 諷誦阿彌陀經。誓生彼國。不替誠心者。命終靈逝化往之彼。見佛神悟。即得道矣.[22] In the practice of recitation of the *Amitābha Sutra*, "seeing the Buddha and, spiritually enlightened, achieve the Dao" means that by seeing a Buddhist image, one can achieve enlightenment and the Dao. The "Dao" here refers to the Buddhist path. Creating an image, viewing an image, and pondering an image of Amitābha were important components of the religious activities of the monks at Mount Lu during that era.[23]

In some editions of Zong Bing's "Preface" the character for "image" (*xiang* 象) is substituted by *xiang* 像, a nearly identical character for "iconic image."[24] We should not attribute the interchangeability of these two characters simply to errors in the transcription of the text. Instead, this manifestation of variability among written characters reveals the relationship between iconic image and natural image that appeared in the thought of Zong Bing as well as the Buddhists of that time. In their descriptions of the image of the Buddha, a particularly significant feature of both Huiyuan's and Zong Bing's texts is the mutual convergence of Buddhist iconic images with the images of natural scenery.[25] This differs from Zhidun's descriptions of Buddhist images, in whose encomium images from nature have no place. But Huiyuan's "Inscription for a Buddhist Image" describes a Buddhist image as follows:

§58

Broad is the great image, its patterns mysterious and nameless. When the body's spirit begins its transformation, it sheds its shadow and leaves its form. Circling in the radiance over the layered precipice, it congeals onto an empty pavilion. In the shade, it is not darkened, and in the dark, light intrudes. Stepping delicately, it molts from its shell, and pays respect to the hundred spirits. Responding in a different mode, its traces vanish and grow dark.

廓矣大象。理玄無名。體神入化。落影離形。迴暉層巖。凝映虛亭。在陰不昧。處暗逾明。婉步蟬蛻。朝宗百靈。應不同方。跡絕而冥。[26]

The opening lines, "Broad is the great image, its patterns mysterious and nameless," obviously incorporates the description of the "great image" of Lao-Zhuang verbiage, but "When the body's spirit begins its transformation, it sheds its shadow and leaves its form" transitions to Huiyuan's Buddhist view, converting Buddha into an eternal deity or spirit who takes form amidst the myriad things, yet also exists in a state that transcends physical form. After describing the physical image,

Huiyuan follows with a description of natural phenomena: "Circling in the radiance over the layered precipice, it congeals onto an empty pavilion. In the shade, it is not darkened, and in the dark, light intrudes." Here, he views the image of nature and the image of the Buddha as sharing a common existence.

Having uncovered the Buddhist import of the key terms in the two opening statements, we find ourselves confronting what seems a conundrum: the two Buddhistic statements are immediately followed by a lengthy mention of ancient Daoist hermits and their environs. The principal figures brought up there, like Dawei, Guangchengzi, and Xu You, are all immortals and deities found in native Chinese legends. Since the locations they are associated with, such as Kongtong and Juci, are also areas where Daoist spirits and immortals are said to reside, they appear to have no connection to Buddhist sacred geographies. But precisely for that reason, this passage often serves as a kind of red herring, leading readers astray by diverting their attention away from its Buddhist underpinnings. And because of this, many people have understood Zong's "Preface" as a theory of art established within the intellectual system of Daoism. However, appropriating Daoist terms and concepts does not imply that its underlying logic can be fully attributed to the Daoist philosophical system. The similarity of its vocabulary may unavoidably suggest linkages to their original Daoist contexts, but such superficial resemblances do not imply theoretical identity between them. If we understand this passage only in terms of its surface meaning, this will result in a contradiction with the opening passage, "The sage encompasses the Dao and responds to things, worthies clarify their hearts to savor natural images." But if we compare it to a similar passage in Zong Bing's "Elucidating Buddhism," its Buddhist underpinnings become clear:

§59

Sima Qian's descriptions of the Five [legendary] Emperors say as follows about them: They all were born with numinous powers. Some could speak while still very young, some could say their own names at birth. Their virtue was profound, their minds penetrating, and they were as wise as deities. And thus, they resembled Bodhisattvas of the Great Vehicle, who took human form to be born in the world. Dwelling *on the hills of Xuanyuan, they climbed Kongtong and ascended multiple peaks. They wandered among obscure hills and dense woods, hiding their traces and leaping over waves. How do we know they did not follow the path of the Tathagata [Gautama Buddha] . . . Guangchengzi, Dawei, Hongya, Chao Xue, Xu You, Zhifu huaren, the Four Masters of Gushe,* and others like them. . . . [The italicized words are identical to a passage in "A Preface to Landscape Painting."] How can we not find written traces of the heyday of these exemplary men of the Dao, even in fragmentary forms? Must we take them all to be empty, fictitious legend? Now, a perspicacious lord travels over a pure world, and taking seven sages by the hand to Juci, he sees a godly person in Gushe. Transforming in a single body hardly merits comment.... Guangchengzi says: The essence of the highest Dao is dark and mysterious. It is Śūraṃgama samādhi. The highest of those who attain our way become emperors, and those below them become kings. Successively transforming, rising and falling, they become flying celestial emperors, reincarnated sagely emperors, and the like.

史遷之述五帝也。皆云。生而神靈。或弱而能言。或自言其名。懿淵疏通。其智如神。既以類夫大乘菩薩化見而生者矣。居軒轅之丘。登崆峒陟几岱。幽陵蟠木之遊。逸跡超浪。何以知其不由從如來之道哉......廣成大隗鴻崖巢許支父化人姑射四子之流......豈至道之盛不見于殘缺之篇。便當皆虛妄哉。今以神明之君。遊浩然之世。攜七聖於具茨。見神人於姑射。一化之生復何足多談......廣成之言曰。至道之精窈窈冥冥。即首楞嚴三昧矣。得吾道者上為皇下為王。即亦隨化升降為飛行皇帝轉輪聖王之類也。[27]

In Zong Bing's understanding, the Three Celestial Emperors and Five Emperors were the "living beings" into which Great Vehicle bodhisattvas had transformed, and although they wandered in the legendary mountains of the gods, they followed the Way of the Tathagata. Appropriating the Daoist figure Guangchengzi's phrase, "The essence of the highest Dao is dark and mysterious," Zong Bing believes this to be the Buddhist doctrine of Śūraṃgama samādhi. Zong Bing places the Buddhist path in the highest position and infuses it with the Dao of Confucians and Daoists. Hence, in the conclusion of this passage, he says that those who follow the Buddhist path are emperors, while those below are kings, "successively transforming, rising and falling, becoming flying celestial emperors, reincarnated sagely emperors, and the like." Flying celestial emperors and reincarnated sagely kings are the rulers who bring order to the world in Buddhist narratives,[28] and in Zong Bing's understanding, Buddhism is the highest truth, while the celestial emperors of the Confucians and the gods and immortals of the Daoists are merely all reincarnations of this absolute Buddhist spirit (*foshen* 佛神). It is apparent that the ancient Daoist sages, hermits, and their haunts that appear in "Preface" are co-opted in the same way by Buddhist doctrines.

The last key term to investigate in the first section is *shen* 神 (spirit) as employed in these two parallel sentences: "The sage orders the Dao with spirits, and worthies fully penetrate it; landscapes embellish the Dao with their forms, and the humane delight in them."[29] The relationship between spirit and the Dao delineated here is completely distinct from the understanding of the relationship between these two in Daoism. As to the spirit and the Dao in Daoist thought, the "Commentary on the Attached Phrases" chapter (Xici zhuan 繫辭傳) in the *Book of Changes* (Yijing 易經) gives a clear description: "The alternation between yin and yang is called the Dao.... When yin and yang are unpredictable, this is called the spirit" 一陰一陽之謂道，陰陽不測之謂神.[30] But in his "Elucidating Buddhism," Zong Bing cites this passage to explain the relationship between spirits and the Dao of Buddhism and reinterprets the understanding of this doctrine in Buddhist terms:

§60

Today we say that the alternation between and combination of yin and yang is called the Dao, and when yin and yang are unpredictable, this is called the spirit. This explains that the Dao of supreme nonaction and of yin and yang are mixed together, and thus it is said that yin and yang alternate and combine. Since the Dao has descended, the essential spirit has entered and often exists on the surface of yin and yang. As it cannot be plumbed by yin and yang, it is said that yin and yang cannot predict it. This is what Junping described as when one gives birth to two, it is called spiritual luminescence. If we do not understand these two lines, how do we clarify the essential spirit? Although the spirits of the multitude living beings eventually reach their zenith, they follow their respective karmic destinies to separate into the [five different] gradations of crude and miraculous understanding, but their root is not extinguishable.

今稱一陰一陽之謂道，陰陽不測之謂神者。蓋謂至無為道陰陽兩渾。故曰一陰一陽也。自道而降便入精神。常有於陰陽之表。非二儀所究。故曰陰陽不測耳。君平之說一生二謂神明是也。若此二句皆以無明。則以何明精神乎？然群生之神其極雖齊。而隨緣遷流成麄妙之識。而與本不滅矣。[31]

First of all, when Zong Bing explains that "when yin and yang are unpredictable, this is called spirit," he applies this to a description of spirits that have the inscrutable power to change things, thus linking this idea to the Buddhist spirit. The spirit spoken of by Buddhists is the root of the spirits of all living beings, which follow their karmic destinies to appear in physical forms as individual spirits and which are called "knowledge." Such knowledge can be distinguished as crude or refined, and it is not the final transcendental reality of the Buddhist spirit, which is eternal and indestructible. Hence, the relationship between spirit and the Dao in Daoism is completely different from that of Buddhism. The spirits of Daoism describe the mysterious spirits by which the Dao operates, but in Zong Bing's discussion of the relation between spirit and Dao, spirit lies above the Dao and controls it. This understanding is explained in a passage in "Elucidating Buddhism," as follows:

§61

Only Buddha regulates the Dao with the spirit. Hence, virtue and the Dao are one. When spirit and the Dao are two, then there is reflection between them, enabling them to penetrate each other in transformation. Because they are single, they often follow one another without constructing anything. The ten thousand transformations each follow their own karmic destinies. Naturally, each lies within the Great Dao.

唯佛則以神法道，故德與道為一，神與道為二。二故有照以通化，一故常因而無造。夫萬化者固各隨因緣，自於大道之中矣。[32]

Zong Bing pointedly differentiates spirit from Dao as two separate entities, explaining that the relationship between spirit and Dao in Buddhism is that of "regulating the Dao with the spirit." Spirit is the underlying reality that controls the Dao, and in Buddhist dharma it pervades all transformations and exists eternally. This view can be compared with that of Huiyuan's "Monks Do Not Bow before a King": "The Dao of Heaven and Earth fully manifests its merit in transformation. The principle of rulers' virtue is fully realized in unimpeded circulation. If we set it beside the unmatched teachings and unchanging doctrines [of Buddhism], their relative strengths and weaknesses cannot be spoken of in the same breath" 天地之道功盡於運化。帝王之德理極於順通。若以對夫獨絕之教不變之宗，故不得同年而語其優劣。[33] Here, Huiyuan clearly distinguishes between the thought systems of Buddhism, on the one hand, and Confucianism and Daoism on the other, placing Buddhism in the highest position and recognizing it as "unmatched teachings" and "unchanging doctrines." It cannot be lumped into the same category as Confucianism and Daoism. In short, both Huiyuan and Zong Bing clearly imbue Buddhist teachings with a power that both orders and transcends the spirits, which are delegated the responsibility of ordering the Dao itself.

Spiritual Superiority of Landscape Painting over Writing
The second section of Zong Bing's "Preface" forms a sort of transition, moving from the more abstract topics of the first section into a discussion of Zong's own activity as a painter of landscapes.

§62

[Second Section of "Preface"]
I was so fond of the Lu and Heng mountains and so attached to the Jing and Wu peaks that I was unaware that old age was fast approaching. I felt ashamed that I could not concentrate my vital breath and keep up or even just limp along with others at the Stone Gate. Therefore, I paint images and spread colors to construct these cloudy peaks. Principles lost after middle antiquity can be sought through the conceptions of the mind; and the subtle meaning beyond

words and images can be obtained by the mind from books. This is to say nothing of what involves the movement of one's body and engagement of one's eyes, or where forms can be described with forms, and colors with colors!

余眷戀廬、衡，契闊荊、巫，不知老之將至。愧不能凝氣怡身，傷砧石門之流，於是畫象布色，構茲雲嶺。夫理絕於中古之上者，可意求於千載之下。旨微於言象之外者，可心取於書策之內。況乎身所盤桓，目所綢繆，以形寫形，以色貌色也。

Published research on Zong Bing rarely discusses this section, and the few that do regard it as a straightforward description of his painterly craft. Yet this passage actually contains evidence of a major turning point in the treatment of the visual sense, as well as a new evaluation and understanding of the visual object. To clarify Zong Bing's understanding of the visual object, we must first analyze native Chinese canonical works' descriptions of the "image," including concrete visual objects and other forms of images.

In typical works of Daoism, the images that are able to gain the viewer entry into the highest reality of the Dao are not concrete physical images but instead are abstract, vague, and indistinct images, such as those described in *Laozi*: "When the Dao becomes an object, it is vague and indistinct. Vague and indistinct, it encompasses a natural image within it. Indistinct and vague, there are objects within it. Mysterious and dark, it encompasses the essence within it" 道之為物，惟恍惟惚。惚兮恍兮，其中有象。恍兮惚兮，其中有物。窈兮冥兮，其中有精; and "The great sound has sparse sound, the great image has no form" 大音希聲，大象無形.[34] The "great image" does not have an actually existing formal image. In fact, Daoist philosophy does not regard the tangible object of the visual sense as important. This point of view manifests in Zhuangzi's parables of Li Zhu 離珠 and Xiangwang 象罔: Li Zhu has a very keen sense of sight and can bring events into clear perspective, but this sort of visual acuity does not enable him to perceive dark pearls or to reach the Dao. Blurry and imprecise, without the images of forms and traces, it is through this that Xiangwang can seek the Dao.[35] The difference between Li Zhu and Xiangwang is implied in the metaphor of the image with or without form, respectively. This is consistent with Laozi's description of the "Dao as a vague and intangible thing," and with slight variation in *Zhuangzi*, which approaches the realization of the Dao epistemologically: through a vague, formless, symbolic image, one can obtain the dark pearl, which is to say, to reach an intuitive understanding of the Dao. In the "Understanding *Laozi*" (Jielao 解老) chapter of Han Fei's 韓非 (ca. 280–233 BCE) *Hanfeizi jijie* 韓非子集解 (Works of Master Han Fei, with Collected Commentaries), there is also a similar description of a formless image:

§63

People rarely see a living elephant, but they can retrieve the bones of a dead elephant and reconstruct its living form. Hence, that which many people construct in their own minds is called an image. Today, although the Dao cannot be heard or seen, sages have persisted in holding on to their achievements in order to perceive its form, saying "the form which has no form and the image which has no physical existence is devoid."

人希見生象也，而得死象之骨，案其圖以想其生也，故諸人之所以意想者皆謂之象也。今道雖不可得聞見，聖人執其見功以處見其形，故曰：「無狀之狀，無物之象。」[36]

Objective images that have physical forms are the bones of a dead elephant, which are only able to stimulate people's imaginations of it. This symbolic type of image is often identified as the trigrams or as written characters in native Chinese texts, and the deification of such abstract images is very common. The chapter "On the Origin of the Dao" (Yuan Dao 原道) in *Wenxin diaolong* 文心雕龍 brings up formless images, including primitive images of trigrams on prognostication slips, and as for written characters, it provides a genealogy that places them at the origin of civilization itself.

§64

Human pattern originated in the Supreme, the Ultimate. "Mysteriously assisting the gods," the images of the Changes are the earliest expressions of this pattern. Paoxi began by drawing [their trigrams], drew their origins, and Confucius completed it by writing the "Wings." The words with pattern were written to explain Qian and Kun. . . . From the Yellow River Map were born the eight trigrams, and from the writing of the River Luo came the nine categories. For these and for the fruits contained in the jade and gold decorated tablets and the flowers blooming in red words and green strips [was anyone responsible]. . . . *The Book of Changes* says: The stimulation of all movements in the world depends upon the oracular judgments, and their power to stimulate the celestial world is derived from the power of the Dao.

人文之元，肇自太極。幽贊神明，易象惟先。庖犧畫其始，仲尼翼其終。而乾坤兩位，獨制文言......若迺河圖孕乎八卦，洛書韞乎九疇，玉版金鏤之實，丹文綠牒之華，易曰：鼓天下之動者存乎辭，辭之所以能鼓天下者，乃道之文也。[37]

Linking written characters to Paoxi's hexagrams and the images of the Yellow River and Luo River writing, Liu Xie believed that writing was the progeny of formless images and on this basis established a comprehensive genealogy of culture and civilization. In Liu Xie's telling, these images without outer forms are "the patterns of the Dao" that can animate the world and serve to represent civilization itself.

And thus, the workings of literary imagination are the manifestation of a visual sense that is suprasensory rather than sensory. Lu Ji's "Wenfu" 文賦 (Rhyme Prose on Literature) describes creative inspiration thusly: "Taking one's eyes away from and closing one's ears to [the world], plunging into profound thoughts, seeking tangential leads, one surges forth in the eight directions, and wanders into the depths of the mind" 收視反聽，耽思傍訊，精騖八極，心游萬仞.[38] "Taking one's eyes away from and closing one's ears to [the world]" is to turn one's resources inward and use suprasensory visualization to reveal inner images, to "wander with the mind" among formless images. It is not to direct one's awareness outward to physical objects. In addition to literary composition, Wang Wei 王微 (415–443) also spoke of suprasensory visualization and suprasensory inner images in the creation of painting and calligraphy: "A Humble Reply to Yan Guanglu's [Yan Yanzhi 顏延之 (384–456)] Letter. Pictures and paintings are not merely the exercise of artistic skill, but when done properly, should share the same forms as the images of the *Book of Changes*. Those who excel in the seal and clerical scripts believe their calligraphic skills to be very high. I wish they would be equally discriminating in the application of color, to discern what [painting and calligraphy] share in common" 辱顏光祿書，以圖畫非止藝行，成當與易象同體。而工篆隸者，自以書巧為高。欲其並辨藻繪，核其攸同.[39] Wang Wei thinks that painting and calligraphy can be spoken of in the same terms and subsumes painting under the category of abstract images, so that it can realize what he thinks is the loftier significance of painting and not merely showcase the skill of creating physical likenesses.

However, Buddhists in the Six Dynasties understood the painting of images in a completely opposite sense. In his "Encomium for an Image of Amitābha" (Emituofo xiang zan 阿弥陀佛像贊), Zhidun states: "Canonical texts have not projected [what exists] beyond the known universe. The way of spirits is inscrutable to the world, so how can we make guesses based on mental concepts?" 夫六合之外，非典籍所模，神道詭世，豈意者所測?。 The spiritual power of Buddhist images is not that of canonical texts, that is, something that can manifest through the written word. The mental concepts that are obtained from formless images in the native Chinese tradition cannot reveal the Buddhist spiritual path. And he continues with reference to the transcendental power of concrete Buddhist images as follows:

§65
Reciting the *Amitābha Sutra*, pledging to be reborn in that [paradisal] land, those whose sincere hearts do not waver will be transformed into spirit at their life's end, to make their way there. To see the Buddha and awaken to the spirit

is to achieve the Dao. In the final moments of life, treating what's left of life as shameful waste, with the heart racing toward the spirits' domain—this is not what I dare to hope for. Nonetheless, because a master craftsman erected a banner and made spirit manifest, I could look upward to gaze at its lofty appearance, and to inquire of Heaven.

諷誦阿彌陀經。誓生彼國。不替誠心者。命終靈逝化往之彼。見佛神悟即得道矣。遁生末蹤忝廁殘跡。馳心神國。非所敢望。乃因匠人。圖立神表。仰瞻高儀。以質所天。[40]

For those who recite sutras and whose faith is firm, on the verge of death they will see the image of Amitābha, and awakening spiritually, they will achieve the Dao. Because he longed for the Pure Land of the Buddhist realm, Zhidun asked others to erect a spirit banner, that is, an image of the Buddha, to serve as the physical realization of the spiritual Dao, toward which he could gaze in admiration.

In his "Monks Do Not Bow to the King," Huiyuan also deliberately distinguishes the "images" of Buddhism from the Daoist theory of trigrams, that is, abstract and symbolic images, as follows: "What is the spirit? It is when the essence reaches its maximum extent and becomes numinous. This supreme essence cannot be represented by the images of trigrams" 夫神者何耶。精極而為靈者也。精極則非卦象之所圖.[41] What Huiyuan calls "supreme essence" is none other than the spirit of Buddha that cannot be indicated by trigrams and images. In these lines Huiyuan's criticism of the limitations of the *Yijing* trigrams and images is particularly lucid: that which can contain and reveal the highest spiritual Dao is the physical Buddhist image and not a symbolic trigram or image. Undoubtedly, concerning the transcendental significance of images, Huiyuan ranked Buddhist images or icons above the images of the *Book of Changes* and criticized the limitations of native Daoist theories of the image.

Why, we may ask, can concrete visual objects surpass abstract images from the *Book of Changes* in manifesting the divine Dao? What element distinguishes the images that are taken in by the eyes? Where are their unique latent powers? In this section, Zong Bing offers a cogent explanation. The reason that concrete visual objects surpass abstract verbal images and written documents is that they use unlimited substantiation, and they employ concrete images to directly stimulate the viewer's emotions, as evidenced by "the movement of the body, and the engagement of the eyes." The superiority of landscape painting also lies in its "forms that can be described with forms, and colors with colors," imbuing concrete visual images with abstract spiritual principles that enable their viewers to viscerally receive and experience abstract spirit. His use of the expression "what is more" to push his argument further tells us that, in Zong Bing's religious and artistic thought, visual images possess a special capacity to transcend both abstract images from the *Book of Changes* and writing itself. This is diametrically opposite to the Daoist disdain for concrete physical images.

The Buddhist Discovery of Scale

The third section transitions from the power of the visual sense to discussing methods of visualization, methods of observing things, and also the mechanism for turning landscape into landscape painting—that is, a transparent principle of scale.[42] The mystery of the sense of sight is that it can turn an expansive phenomenon into something small, enclosing it within the inch occupied by the eyeball, so that the mountain peaks of Kunlun, Mount Lang, Mount Song, and Mount Hua can all be brought into a painting of a few feet or inches in size:

§66

[Third Section of "Preface"]

The Kunlun Mountains are so large and the eye's pupils so small that, if the former impress themselves upon the eye from a distance of inches, they cannot be seen. But if they are a few miles away, they can be encompassed by the inch-size eye. This is because the farther off they are, the smaller they appear. If we now spread fine silk to reflect things afar, the form of the Kunlun Mountains and Lang Peak can be encompassed within a square inch. A vertical stroke of three inches equals the height of a thousand feet; a horizontal ink-dab of several feet signifies a distance of several hundred miles. Therefore, the beholders of paintings only worry about the awkwardness in correspondence with the original, and do not consider a diminutive scale an impediment to verisimilitude—this is the propensity of nature. Given this, the magnificence of Mount Song and Mount Hua and the numen of the mysterious valleys can all be captured in a painting.

且夫昆崙山之大，瞳子之小，迫目以寸，則其形莫睹，迥以數里，則可圍於寸眸。誠由去之稍闊，則其見彌小。今張絹素以遠暎，則昆、閬之形，可圍於方寸之內。豎劃三寸，當千仞之高；橫墨數尺，體百里之迥。是以觀畫圖者，徒患類之不巧，不以制小而累其似，此自然之勢。如是，則嵩、華之秀，玄牝之靈，皆可得之於一圖矣。

This viewpoint is very different from the view of scale or proportion found in traditional painting theory. In Wang Wei's theory of painting, although he does not clearly bring up the question of scale, his vaguely derisory comments hint that he regards it as a simplistic technique lacking in vitality: "When the ancients created paintings, they did not do so by mapping out walled districts, marking prefectural boundaries, noting garrison towns, or tracing fluvial courses. Rather, they based them on merging form with spirit, and they made changes [rooted] in their minds. When the spirit is lost in what is seen, [the images] entrusted are not dynamic; when the eyes limit [one's view], then what is seen is incomplete. . . . Through sweeping changes and profound transformation, dynamism comes to life" 且古人之作畫也，非以案城域，辨方州，標鎮阜，劃浸流。本乎形者融靈，而動變者心也。靈亡所見，故所託不動；目有所極，故所見不周。. . . . . . 橫變縱化，故動生焉。[43] Wang Wei believes that creating a painting is not merely the coloring in of a map, as in "mapping out walled districts, marking prefectural boundaries, noting garrison towns, or tracing fluvial courses." While creating a map does indeed entail the reduction of the view of a large geographical space onto a sheet of paper through the use of scale, Wang Wei criticizes this sort of depiction of scenery as mere form, a lifeless object devoid of the power to move us emotionally. To infuse emotion into landscape, one must rely on brushwork and ink, show the lifeblood that circulates within all natural phenomena, and bring out the spirit of the landscape. This sort of abstract deployment of brush and ink is not emphasized in Zong Bing's theory of painting; to the contrary, he provides detailed explication of and much emphasis on the very principles of scale that are denigrated by Wang Wei.

As for the Buddhist method of observing images, a very important discussion of this can be found in Huang Jingjin's article on the subject.[44] In his analysis he brings up two examples. One is the mustard seed that can hold Mount Sumeru within it: "Even the vastness of Mount Sumeru does not change the size of the mustard seed that encompasses it" 以須彌之高廣，內芥子中亦無增減。[45] The other is the Bodhisattva who holds an infinite number of worlds inside his palm: "Śāriputra, the unfathomable liberating bodhisattva, took hold of three thousand great worlds, and like a potter's wheel, placed them in the palm of his right hand" 又舍利弗。住不可思議解脫菩薩。斷取三千大千世界。如陶家輪。著右掌中。[46] He inserts the gigantic Mount Sumeru into a single tiny mustard seed, without shrinking Mount Sumeru and without enlarging the seed. That gigantic worlds can be placed in the bodhisattva's palm, with these worlds' appearance remaining unchanged, is clear and self-evident. These two examples both touch on the unimpeded transition between large and small that is a special feature of Buddhist thought. In particular, many Buddhist sects make frequent use of the metaphor of the mustard seed that encompasses Mount Sumeru to explain the relationship between ultimate truth and the phenomenal world. When he discusses landscape and landscape painting, Zong Bing puts particular emphasis on the idea that the vastness of the world can be placed within a canvas of a foot in width, which accords with the method of observing images that convert large to small in Buddhist thought.

Another problem requiring resolution is the concluding sentence of this section: "The delicate beauty of Mount Song and Mount Hua is the spirit of the dark female. One can find them within a single painting." These references to Mount Song and Mount Hua, and to the dark female, are clearly borrowed from Daoist terminology and concepts. Daoist deities and immortals that appear within the landscape can be found in the same pattern in Huiyuan's "Miscellaneous Poems of the Eastern Forest of Mount Lu" (Lushan Donglin zashi 廬山東林雜詩):

§67

Lofty rocks exude clear vapors,	崇岩吐清氣,
Secluded gullies bear the traces of gods.	幽岫棲神跡。
Infrequent voices strum the symphony of natural sounds,	希聲奏群籟,
Echoing from the mountains, they pool and drip.	響出山溜滴。
A visitor wanders alone in darkness,	有客獨冥游,
And forgets where he is headed.	徑然忘所適。
Waving his hand, he runs it over the Cloudy Gate,	揮手撫雲門,
At the Spirit Pass, he rests his tired feet.	靈關安足辟。
His mind flowing, he knocks on the dark door,	流心叩玄扃,
Feeling at no remove from the utmost patterns.	感至理弗隔。
Which ones rise up to the nine skies?	孰是騰九霄,
Without struggle, fowl break into the heavens.	不奮沖天翮。
When their mystery is the same, meaning is naturally equal,	妙同趣自均,
One flash of enlightenment exceeds the three benefits.	一悟超三益。[47]

In the first half of this poem, landscape is identical to the realm of Daoist immortals: the "cloudy gate" and "spirit pass" are both alternative names for the immortal realm in religious Daoism. In adhering to the general structure of poems about wandering immortals, the line "He rests his feet at the spirit pass" is followed by a transition to describing the illumination to the truths of the spiritual way. While as elsewhere the vocabulary is drawn from esoteric Daoism, "His mind flowing, he knocks on the dark door / Feeling at no remove from the utmost patterns" actually refers to the spiritual truths of Buddhism. In "When their mystery is the same, meaning is naturally equal / One flash of enlightenment exceeds the three benefits," "three benefits" is a direct translation of Buddhist terminology, meaning the three different benefits of spiritual cultivation.[48] This line refers to the enlightenment to the Dao that is achieved in wandering through the mountains and can enable one to bypass the three stages of spiritual cultivation. The structure of the whole poem is representative of the process by which the theme of Daoist wandering immortals is turned into the realization of Buddhist truths. Huiyuan's description of Mount Lu as an "abode of gods and immortals"[49] in his "Record of Mount Lu" (Lushan ji 廬山記) demonstrates how the enlightenment toward Buddhist truth did not reject the Daoist tradition of the wandering immortal but instead brought the latter within its fold. Landscape is the immortal domain of religious Daoism, and at the same time, it is also the Pure Land of Buddhism; the final realization of Buddhism is not a Daoist-style wandering immortal but the spiritual illumination of Nirvana. Like his teacher Huiyuan, Zong Bing follows this line of thought, incorporating the Daoist imagination of wandering immortals and turning at the end of this third section from Daoist gods and immortals to the Buddhist realm that predominates in the fourth section.

Religion and Aesthetics within Landscape

The opening of the fourth section closely follows the conclusion of the third section, and from the Daoist immortal realm contained in landscape painting, it moves into the higher dimension of Buddhist "transcendence of the spirit to find the truth":

§68

[Fourth Section of "Preface"]

The [transcendent] principle in landscape is what we respond to with the eye and meet with the mind. If a painting has deftly achieved correspondence with a landscape, we can engage it with eye and mind in the same fashion. Through such a response, one communes with the spirit, achieves a transcendence of one's own spirit, and attains the [absolute] principle. Even though one can again search for the invisible amongst remote rocks, what else can be found? Infinite as it is by nature, the spirit dwells in forms and resonates with things by category, to the effect that the [transcendent] principle enters even reflections and traces. If a painting is executed to truly marvelous effect, the same will surely occur in it.

夫以應目會心為理者，類之成巧，則目亦同應，心亦俱會。應會感神，神超理得。雖復虛求幽岩，何以加焉？又神本亡端，棲形感類，理入影跡，誠能妙寫，亦誠盡矣。

"Responding with the eye" is to make contact with and perceive a visual object using one's line of sight, and "to meet with the mind" is for the physical image taken from the exterior by one's sight to be reflected within the mind. "Responding with the eye and meeting with the mind" thus means that the eye makes contact while the mind feels and responds to things. Subject and object are in harmony. When a painter views a landscape, he responds to things with the eye and meets with the mind. Then, he skillfully gives it form in his painting, such that those who view the painting "also respond with their eyes, and meet [it] with their minds"; that is, viewers of the painting can experience the landscape as the painter did, and the painter's experience of depicting the landscape can be transmitted to viewers thanks to the painting. The painter and the viewer can both create and appreciate the landscape painting through responding with the eye and meeting with the mind, in the end reaching the religious and aesthetic ideal state: "Through such a response, one communes with the spirit, achieves a transcendence of one's own spirit, and attains the [absolute] principle." "Through such a response, to commune with the spirit," one in the mind's eye can connect with and understand the spirit that appears during engagement with the landscape. Then, one "achieves a transcendence of one's own spirit, and attains the [absolute] principle": one's spirit transcends physical forms, and one understands the truth of the Buddhist path.

How, we might ask, can landscape painting not only express the "delicate beauty of Mount Song and Mount Lu, and the spirit of the mysterious female" but also make both its creator and a viewer "achieve a transcendence of their own spirit, and attain the [absolute] principle?" Out of what does the "spirit" of the landscape arise within the eye of the painter? Zong Bing says that "infinite as it is by nature, the spirit dwells in forms and resonates with things by category, to the effect that the [transcendent] principle enters even reflections and traces." This is to say that the Buddhas and spirits possess no embodied form and are not limited to any temporal or spatial existence. They lodge within physical forms and resonate with them, and at the same time, the principles of Buddhas and spirits enter into "shadowy traces" that can be seen and turned into forms. There is no particular or categorical distinction here between form and shadow (that is, image), and this is meant simply as a contrast with the formless spirit to indicate how spirit lodges in objects that possess form and, by transforming into a concrete image, reveals itself. Whether form or image, they are all the transformations of Buddha's spirit. In terms of Buddha's spiritual power to transform the myriad things, "spirit" transforms to manifest in the myriad things, while at the same time thanks to its spiritual luminescence, it is able to illuminate the myriad things. These myriad things naturally include the landscape, and through painters' marvelous depictions of landscapes, spirit also can enter into the world of paintings.

Zong Bing's understanding of this topic originates in the discussion of the relationship between spirit and image in Buddhist thought, with which the following discussion in Huiyuan's "Inscription for a Buddhist Image" is very closely connected:

§69
There is no fixed abode for the spirit's way; it makes contact with images
and lodges in them. The convergence of a hundred worries is not an ephem-
eral feeling. To thoroughly illuminate its truths, its position should be deeply
grounded. Supporting those who share the same commitments, they issue their
true intent. Thus, for the worthies who have performed good deeds, we portray
them and add inscriptions.

然後驗神道無方，觸像而寄。百慮所會非一時之感。於是悟徹其誠應深其位。將
援同契發其真趣。故與夫隨喜之賢。圖而銘焉。[50]

After Huiyuan heard the legend about Buddhist images,[51] he convened his fellow devotees and erected a Platform for Buddha's Shadow devoted to painting Buddhist images. "Buddha's Shadow" means a Buddhist image that exhibits Buddha's likeness in human form. In the above passage where Huiyuan describes the reasons for creating images, his terminology and line of thought herald Zong Bing's description of the reasons for painting landscapes. The statement, "There is no fixed abode for the spirit's way; it makes contact with images and lodges in them," is echoed by Zong Bing's remark, "Infinite as it is by nature, the spirit dwells in forms and resonates with things by category, to the effect that the [transcendent] principle enters even reflections and traces." Contemplating a Buddhist image is taken as one link in the practice of cultivating *samadhi*, and the conceptual basis behind this is the idea that the Buddha's dharma body 法身 (Skt: *dharma-kāya*) and spiritual luminescence transform and appear among the myriad forms. All of the objects in the world are the shadowy traces of Buddha, and thus to see the Buddha's dharma body while viewing an image is to come into resonance with the Buddha and to receive his spirit.

The Spiritual Efficacy of Contemplating Paintings

The fifth and final section of "Preface" turns to a discussion of viewing paintings. It describes the author's observation of his own landscape paintings and the aesthetic and religious experience of transcending the self that he gained from this:

§70

[Fifth Section of "Preface"]

Therefore, I live a leisurely life, controlling my vital breath, waving my cup, and strumming my lute. As I unroll paintings and face them in solitude, I probe far into the four desolate corners, not avoiding the overgrowth at the world's fringes, and confront the uninhabited wilderness by myself. The peaks and grottoes soar high, and the cloudy forests stretch deep into the distance. The sages and worthies cast their reflections from time immemorial, and the myriad things of interest are infused with their spirit and thought. What then should I do? Nothing but let my spirit expand untrammeled. Speaking of the expansion of one's spirit, how could there be an order of who was before whom?

於是閒居理氣，拂觴鳴琴，披圖幽對，坐究四荒，不違天勵之藂，獨應無人之野。峰岫嶢嶷，雲林森眇。聖賢暎於絕代，萬趣融其神思。余復何為哉，暢神而已。神之所暢，熟有先焉?

The first question we face in trying to understand this final section is whether this method of observation is "facing landscape with an esoteric Daoist [frame of mind],"[52] or instead a Buddhist encounter with landscape? The opening phrases,

"I live a leisurely life, controlling my vital breath, waving my cup, and strumming my lute," describe a Daoist-style cultivation of the breath (*qi*), but does "As I unroll paintings and face them in solitude, I probe far into the four desolate corners" follow from those previous sentences, and as part of the activity of cultivating the breath, should it be placed within the frame of "facing landscape with an esoteric Daoist [frame of mind]" 以玄對山水?[53] To accurately situate the philosophical foundations and Zong Bing's thinking that lie behind this passage and fully understand it, we must return it to its relevant linguistic and intellectual contexts. As for contemporaneous descriptions of observing paintings and iconic images, we can refer to typical discourses in neo-Daoist and Buddhist texts, respectively. One is the excursion in and observation of landscape in Sun Chuo's 孫綽 (320–377) "Rhyme Prose on Wandering on Mount Tiantai" (You Tiantaishan fu 遊天台山賦); the other, the contemplation of iconic images in Huiyuan's "Inscription for a Buddhist Image." According to Li Han's 李翰 (fl. 760) annotations, Sun Chuo never visited Mount Tiantai, but after hearing an account of the area, he longed to see it and ordered someone to paint its general appearance. It was for this painting that he wrote his rhyme prose.[54] Nonetheless, Sun Chuo does not speak of "observing a painting" anywhere in the piece, nor does he pay special attention to its landscape. Instead, he adopts the imaginative pose of a wandering immortal and, in imagining the stages of his travels, develops his descriptions of the landscape and the immortal realm within it, bringing the two of them into unity. Sun Chuo's observation of the landscape is that of dynamic roaming and observing and not a quietist, static act of contemplation.

The contrasting Buddhist style of observation is described by Huiyuan in the fifth poem of his series, "Inscription for a Buddhist Image," as follows:

§71

Inscribing it, picturing it,	銘之圖之，
How do we bring it about, how do we seek it.	曷營曷求。
We deify it, we listen to it,	神之聽之，
And looking inward, we cultivate it.	鑒爾所修。
Following its tracks, faithful to it,	庶茲臣軌，
We reflect its dark currents.	映彼玄流。
Rinsing away our desires in the numinous pond,	漱情靈沼，
We imbibe its gentlest softness.	飲和至柔。
Reflecting the void, responding with simplicity,	照虛應簡，
When wisdom descends, we are full.	智落乃周。
Deeply embracing, darkly holding,	深懷冥托，
Our thoughts rise to the skies, and our spirit wanders.	霄想神游。
Fulfilling our destiny to one and both,	畢命一對，
We cast off forever the hundred worries.	長謝百憂。[55]

The opening lines "Inscribing it, picturing it / How do we bring it about, how do we seek it" pose the question of what purpose is served by painting or carving iconic images. "We deify it, we listen to it" is saying that the viewer of the image must see the Buddhist image as a deity and listen to the Buddhist Dao that it encompasses and transmits. Although Buddhist images come into being through the work of many artisans, as soon as they have fully taken shape they immediately exhibit the spirit's traces. Hence, viewers must "look inward to cultivate themselves" while observing the image and, in the process, reflect on their own practice of self-cultivation. The subsequent sentences, "Reflecting the void, responding with simplicity / When wisdom descends, we are full. Deeply embracing, darkly holding / Our thoughts rise to the skies, and our spirit wanders" similarly recount the self-reflection and philosophizing of this experience of viewing an iconic image. With Huiyuan, contemplating an image becomes itself a form of self-cultivation that is the realization of an ideal spiritual world.

Read alongside Huiyuan's poem, we can clearly see how Zong Bing perceives the transcendental significance in his own landscape paintings in a way reminiscent of Huiyuan's perception of the same in his painting of, and his inscription on, Buddhist images. As he himself says, Zong Bing "responds to things with his eyes and meets them with his mind" until he reaches the state of "transcending the spirit and obtaining the principles." Zong Bing's debt to Huiyuan becomes even clearer if we compare the last section of "Preface" with Huiyuan's "Preface to the Poetry of the Men of the Dao Who Roam at Stone Gate on Mount Lu" (Lushan zhudaoren you Shimen shi xu 廬山諸道人遊石門詩序). The latter preface begins by recounting the uninhibited joy of roaming across the landscape, followed immediately by the imagining of Daoist immortals among hills and streams:

§72
Imagining the appearance of Daoist immortals as they alight, their plaintive voices rising in harmony, as if a mysterious sound had lodged in them. Though appearing to listen, through them the spirits expanded untrammeled. Though rejoicing we did not anticipate great pleasure, and celebrated till the end of the day.

想羽人之來儀，哀聲相和，若玄音之有寄。雖仿佛猶聞，而神以之暢。雖樂不期歡，而欣以永日。[56]

Following his typical spiritual ascendance from Daoism to Buddhism—a trait already noted above in his "Miscellaneous Poems of the Eastern Forest of Mount Lu," Huiyuan next speaks of a more profound Buddhist contemplation of landscape:

§73

Moments later, the sun fell into twilight, and stragglers soon left. Then, we understood the mysterious gazing of those who had renounced the world, and the expansive feelings for eternal things. Could such spiritual bliss come from landscape alone? Holy Eagle [Vulture] Peak grows distant, the forsaken path becomes more impassable as each day passes. Yet, if not for the presence of a great being, how could his divine traces have remained? His responsiveness must be profound and his enlightenment far reaching. Deeply moved, we reflected for a long time.

俄而太陽告夕，所存已往，乃悟幽人之玄覽，達恆物之大情，其為神趣，豈山水而已哉！......靈鷲邈矣，荒途日隔。不有哲人，風跡誰存？應深悟遠，慨焉長懷。[57]

Holy Eagle Peak is a geographical location described in Buddhist sutras, and also is a Pure Land toward which Buddhist devotees aspire. Although Holy Eagle Peak is too far away to visit, the spiritual traces of the Buddha have transformed into material forms that are dispersed throughout the entire world, and thus by contemplating landscapes we can glimpse the Buddha's traces. In Huiyuan's telling, landscape and the Pure Land merge into each other, as the visible reflections of spirit's traces. This contemplation goes beyond the imagination of the Daoist immortal and possesses significance as the actualization of Buddhist religious ideals.

The last section of Zong Bing's essay surely has many echoes of this preface by Huiyuan. First of all, if Huiyuan explicitly traces the progression from Daoist imagining to Buddhist contemplation, Zong Bing moves from the lifestyle of the Daoist hermit to a Buddhist act of contemplating a landscape painting. Then, while Huiyuan discerns the traces of Buddha in the Mount Lu peaks before their eyes, Zong Bing observes the same in his own painting even though he does not make an explicit allusion like "Holy Eagle Peak." He declares, "The sages and worthies cast their reflections from time immemorial, and the myriad things of interest are infused with their spirit and thought." Here the word *ying* (cast their reflections) is not primarily what we normally understand by "reflection." Rather, it conveys the sense of a sagely radiance actively shining on, penetrating into, and eventually transforming myriad things into embodiments of the divine spirit. As a result, Zong Bing frequently uses expressions like "spiritual transcendence" (*shentong* 神通) and "spiritual reflection" (*shenying* 神映).[58] The spiritual transformation of Buddha appears throughout the myriad things, and thus the following sentence, "The myriad things of interest are infused with their spirit and thought," echoes this with the spiritual thoughts of sages and worthies that flow throughout the myriad things. Finally, just as Huiyuan describes his pleasurable expansion of spirit, Zong Bing ends his essay with a salute to the same notion: "What then should I do? Nothing but let my spirit expand untrammeled. Speaking of the expansion of one's spirit, how could there be an order of who was before whom?" 余複何為哉？暢神而已。神之所暢，熟有先焉？ To him as to Huiyuan, the notion "expanding the untrammeled spirit" unites with the religious and aesthetic experience of self-transcendence. Notably, this notion also anticipates the rise of Zhou Yong's Buddhist proposition "a piercing glance [that] elevates the mind."

Conclusion: Essay Structure and Historical Significance

The last section of "Preface" reveals the circular structure of its composition, bringing its opening and closing passages into full, seamless agreement. The concluding sentences of the piece reflect back to the opening sentences almost line for line:

Section 5	Section 1
"Unrolling paintings and facing them in solitude"	"Worthies clarify their hearts to savor the image"
"The sages and worthies cast their reflections from time immemorial, and the myriad things of interest are infused with their spirit and thought"	"The Sage encompasses the Dao and responds to things, and as far as mountains and rivers are concerned, they have the substance of existence and yet tend toward the numinous"
"What then should I do? Nothing but let my spirit expand untrammeled. Speaking of the expansion of one's spirit, how could there be an order of who was before whom?"	"Sages regulate the Dao with spirit and worthies learn it. Mountains and rivers beautify the Dao with their forms, and thus the virtuous can take delight in them. Aren't these two alike?"

Moreover, Zong Bing's reference to his personal experience at the end of the preface echoes the description of the worthies at its opening: the painter's unrolling of his paintings and facing them in solitude corresponds to the worthies' purifying their minds and savoring the image, and Zong Bing's painter's "untrammeled expansion of the spirit" corresponds to the worthies' unimpeded spirit. In the creation and contemplation of landscape painting, Zong Bing's "untrammeled expansion of the spirit" explains how he elevated himself into the ideal realm of sages and worthies. "Preface" ends with a question, and the first section also concludes with a question. The arrangement of sentence patterns here exhibits a clever, deliberately constructed, seamless conclusion to the entire work.

The structure of "Preface" is both meticulous and striking, clearly unfolding in a four-part logical sequence comprising an opening statement, an elaboration, a shift, and then a resolution. The first section, as an opening, identifies the transcendental significance of the visual object, taking this as the transformed traces of the spirit, a landscape that "has the substance of existence and yet tends toward the numinous" and "beautifies the Dao with its forms, and thus the virtuous can take delight in them." The second and third sections are the elaboration, in which contemplation of the landscape then transitions to the author's own painting of landscape, where he speaks of the methods of viewing landscape and the reasons and methods for how landscape can be given form on the canvas. Zong Bing's method of "the piercing glance" is not the casual and unintentional observation in *Zhuangzi* but is in fact an intentionally performed observation or contemplation that is the result of training. The fourth stage, the "shift," covers the process by which the subject transitions from the creation to the reception of landscape. It describes the transcendental aesthetic experience of intently observing the landscape: "If a painting has deftly achieved correspondence with a landscape, we can engage it with eye and mind in the same fashion. Through such a response, one communes with the spirit, achieves a transcendence of one's own spirit, and attains the [absolute] principle." The fifth section is the resolution. With its structurally seamless linking of opening and conclusion, Zong Bing's "elevated mind" observing landscape painting reverberates with the "elevated mind" of the ancient sages and worthies who encompassed the Dao while responding to things, forming a single, integrated whole. And in doing so, Zong Bing rather unobtrusively elevates himself to the level of the sages and worthies.

Zong Bing's "Preface" can be seen as a precursor of the four-part structure: beginning, continuation, turning, and converging [with the beginning] (*qi cheng zhuan he* 起承轉合) in recent-style poetry of the Tang and Song, as well as in Ming and Qing examination prose. In terms of style, his work strikes me as a premier example of Six Dynasties parallel prose. Lu Ji's "Rhyme Prose on Literature" and Liu Xie's *The Literary Mind and the Carving of Dragons* both strictly adhere to the principles of parallelism, and hence, their thought is lucid, and their diction stately and elegant, but at the same time they suffer from a certain monotony. Although "Preface" mostly employs parallel constructions of four- and six-character lines, it also inserts nonparallel and ancient-style prose elements, which make it both lively and natural sounding. Moreover, Zong Bing also broke the convention that expository prose not touch on the author himself by interjecting his own life into the second and last sections, where he introduces his own experiences and relates the aesthetic and religious awakening he gains from observing landscape, painting landscape, and observing his own landscape paintings. These elements help the reader feel a sense of intimacy and vividness in the writing. Over the history of Chinese literary theory, it is rare to see the kind of expository style combined with personal lyricism found in "Preface." Here I should emphasize that my reconstruction of the four-part structure of "Preface" and evaluation of its aesthetic appeal are based entirely on a Buddhist reading of its key terms, concepts, propositions, and exposition. This reading reveals a high degree of consistency among these constituent elements, showing that Zong Bing, having absorbed the newly ascendant Buddhist view of perception, continued to develop his ideas toward the three topics of visual objects, visual methods, and visual effects; to probe the aesthetic and religious significance of the creation and reception of landscape painting; and thereby to attain an unprecedented depth and systematism. But if we had subjected this work to a Daoist or Confucian reading of its key terms, concepts, propositions, and exposition, would we have been able to find textual support for each of these, and could these various elements be said to achieve the consistency, depth, and seamlessness approaching perfection as demonstrated here? Looking over the existing body of research on "Preface," it is surely difficult, if not impossible, to make such a case for a Daoist or Confucian reading of it. The arguments presented above should be sufficient to confirm that Zong Bing's "Preface" constitutes an unprecedented theory of art informed primarily by Buddhist thought.

Although we can view Zong Bing's "Preface" as a forerunner of Zhou Yong's philosophical proposition, it did not elicit a major reaction in the field of calligraphy and painting during the (Liu) Song, Qi, and Liang dynasties. Nonetheless, by the time of Wang Changling in the Tang, Zong Bing's theoretical ideas were applied and further developed and became an important influence on theories of poetry. Even if all the words in Wang Changling's "Poetic Rules" (Shige 詩格) are easy to understand, reading it without reference to "Preface" makes its exact meaning and referents somewhat hazy. In fact, the particular theoretical significance of the terms employed in "Poetic Rules" has been lost in overgeneralized explanations of Wang's expositions on "the inscape of physical objects" (*wujing* 物境), "the inscape of emotions" (*qingjing* 情境), and "the inscape of ideation" (*yijing* 意境).[59] But if read against the systematic analysis of "Preface" given here, we can see that the internal logic of Wang Changling's theory of "the inscape of physical objects" in fact follows from the relevant passages on "a piercing glance elevates the mind" in "Preface." Elaborating on his theory of three inscapes, Wang writes:

§74

To set one's mind on writing a poem, one must concentrate the mind, and direct the eye toward this object, probing deeply into its circumstances, just as when climbing to the top of a high mountain one looks down over the myriad things below as if they were in the palm of one's hand. Viewing images in this way, grasping them from within the heart, this should be of use.

Poetry Has Three Inscapes

One is called the inscape of physical objects. The second is called the inscape of emotions. The third is called the inscape of ideation. The inscape of objects is the first. If one wishes to create landscape poems, then one opens up the inscape of spring pebbles and cloudy peaks, and for the extremely beautiful and most delicate places, one imbues it with spirit from the mind. Setting oneself within this inscape, and viewing it from the mind, then it appears from within the palm of one's hand. Then, applying one's thoughts, one fully intuits the images of this inscape, and therefore can create a likeness.

夫置意作詩，即須凝心，目擊其物，便以心擊之，深穿其境。如登高山絕頂，下臨萬象，如在掌中。以此見象，心中了見，當此即用。
　　詩有三境
　　一日物境。二日情境。三日意境。物境一。欲為山水詩，則張泉石雲峰之境，極麗絕秀者，神之於心。處身於境，視境於心，瑩然掌中，然後用思，了然境象，故得形似。[60]

When a poet writes a poem, "he must concentrate his mind, and direct the eye toward this object, probing deeply into its circumstances." Through such concentration, which means delving into the mind and purifying one's thoughts to reach a state of pure concentration, the poet can bring about an inner clarity that enables one to reflect the objective world. These remarks strike us as logically consistent with Zong Bing's statement "purifying the heart to savor natural images." Similarly, Wang's notion of casting a "piercing glance" (*muji* 目擊) reminds us of Zong Bing's remarks on how to observe landscape and landscape painting: "We can engage it with the eye and mind in the same fashion." This sort of process of an interiorized visual sense is what Wang Changling calls "concentrating the mind and engaging the eye." In the process of engaging both eye and mind, "deeply penetrating this world" means that concrete objects are observed through a concentrated mind. These are not single, isolated objects but are an entire "world." As is said in the *Vimalakirti Sutra*, the bodhisattva places the gigantic world in the palm of his right hand, and the entire world is contained within an object that is being intently observed in a concrete form. Hence, Wang states that "looking down below to the myriad things, they seem as if they are in the palm of one's hand," or "viewing images in this way, one will clearly understand them within one's heart." This is a reworking of the miraculous power of sight to transcend differences in size that is found in "Preface" and an even more direct expression of this Buddhist parable. "Poetic Rules" does contain the words "world of physical objects" and places particular emphasis on the body located in the midst of scenery, as in "situating oneself in a setting, and visualizing the setting through the mind." In his discussion of the painter's contemplation of landscape, Zong Bing says that it is necessary to "respond with the eye and meet with the mind," and in his discussion of the unique potential of landscape painting, he deliberately stresses "the movement of one's body and engagement of one's eyes, and where forms can be described with forms, and colors with colors!" There is no doubt that this emphasis on direct visual experience contributed to Wang Changling's theory of the inscape of physical objects.

At the same time, the philosophical and aesthetic proposition "a piercing glance elevates the mind" can also prompt us to take up the perspective of visuality to investigate the history of landscape poetry from the Eastern Jin through the Tang dynasties. Daoist descriptions of the landscape are dynamic: Sun Chuo's contemplation of the landscape is that of the subgenre of wandering immortal poetry, whose poet roams as he views; Tao Qian's 陶潛 (365–427) landscape of the farmstead portrays the harmony between human and natural rhythms; and Xie Lingyun's landscape shows a new view with each step taken by the poet, namely, the progression of natural scenery as the perspective changes. Wang Wei 王維 (692–761), however, is the complete opposite. In his poems, and especially in his pentasyllabic quatrains, the poet observes the world from a fixed vantage point, and gazing while in a state of quietude and stasis, he sees the changes occurring in the myriad things. Through such a view of natural phenomena, and within the limited range of images contained in these short poems, he unfolds a limitless world. With "a piercing glance [that] elevates the mind," Wang Wei employs in a single poem the image of a concrete object; unlike calligraphy, which relies on the flourish of the brush to create a mental construct or image, he produces a universal image of form out of singularity and particularity, in order to reveal a Chan-inspired state of awareness. This type of transcendental, focused glance can be seen as the realization within the domain of poetry of the artistic ideal of "piercing glance elevates the mind" pursued by Zong Bing and Zhou Yong.

////////////////////////////////

Notes

1. Sengyou, *Hongmingji*, 38.
2. This is the name of a chapter within "Discipline for the Gate."
3. Sengyou, *Hongmingji*, 39–40.
4. Li Y., *Nanshi*, 1879.
5. Sengyou, *Hongmingji*, 6.41.
6. Yu, Zhou, and Yu, *Shishuo xinyu jianshu*, 2.762.
7. Sengyou, *Hongmingji*, 6.41.
8. Hurvitz, "Tsung Ping's Comments," 153.
9. Wang Shizhen, *Wangshi huayuan*, 3.20–21. All subsequent references to "Preface" are to this edition. Other versions, such as the *Jindai mishu* 津逮秘书 and *Siku quanshu* 四庫全書 editions, use the characters 暎 or 映; the Wang text as well as Sun Y. et al., *Peiwenzhai shuhuapu* (15.4–5) write it as the homophonous 應 (as in the above quotation).
10. Susan Bush has coined the phrase *Confucian Buddhism* to describe Zong Bing's use of such terminology. See Bush, "Tsung Ping's Essay on Painting Landscape," 133.
11. Sengyou, *Hongmingji*, 2.17.
12. *Foguang dacidian*, 6.5577.
13. Shih, *Literary Mind*, 10, with modification.
14. Sengyou, *Hongmingji*, 2.9.
15. *ZZJS*, 196, 5.513, 6.539.
16. Sengyou, *Hongmingji*, 2.13.
17. On the *vajra* Buddha, see *Foguang dacidian*, 3.2337. On the Lamp King, see ibid., 7.6258.

18. Shen, *Songshu*, 8.2278.
19. Sengyou, *Hongmingji*, 31.
20. Daoxuan, *Guang Hongmingji*, 199.
21. Ibid., 201–3.
22. Ibid., 196.
23. Chen C., *Hua shanshui xu dianjiao zhuyi*, 164–80.
24. The 1586 edition of this text reverses the position of the words *wu ming* (no light) to *ming wu* (clearly absent). See the Guojia tushuguan 國家圖書館 edition (vol. 2, p. 73) or the Taiwan xinxingshuju 新興書局 edition (vol. 2, p. 24).
25. Miranda Shaw notes that the association of likenesses of the Buddha with landscapes may have been inspired by a particular image at the Donglin monastery that had been made in imitation of the Shadow Cave of Nagarahāra near Jelalabad in Afghanistan. It was said that its coloring gave the impression of mountain mists enshrouding the Buddha. Shaw, "Buddhist and Taoist Influences," 197. Eugene Wang also discusses the importance of Huiyuan's cave at Mount Lu for establishing a "new pictorial mode as opposed to the traditional surface-oriented curvilinear painting," a mode that approximates chiaroscuro. See E. Y. Wang, *Shaping the Lotus Sutra*, 246.
26. Sengyou, *Hongmingji*, 13.
27. Ibid., 12.
28. *Foguang dacidian*, 7.6624.
29. Sengyou, *Hongmingji*, 12.
30. Wang B., *Zhouyi zhengyi*, 150–51.
31. Sengyou, *Hongmingji*, 2.13.
32. Ibid., 2.13.
33. Ibid., 5.31.
34. Wang B., *Zhouyi zhengyi*, 1.52, 112.
35. *ZZJS*, 2.414.
36. Wang X., *Han Feizi*, 20.148.
37. Shih, *Literary Mind*, 9, 11, with modification.
38. *WFJS*, 20, 36.
39. Yu J., *Zhongguo lidai hualun leibian*, 585.
40. Daoxuan, *Guang Hongmingji*, 15.196.
41. Sengyou, *Hongmingji*, 5.31.
42. Reading "Preface" in terms of Western perspective, Zong Baihua believes that Zong Bing proposes the principle of scale as found in single-point (vanishing) perspective. See Zong, *Meixue yu yijing* 169. This view of single-point perspective has been challenged by Huang Jingjin in "Chongdu *Jingtuzong sanjing*," 230–31. My use of *perspective* here is not equivalent to the single-point perspective of Western painting theory but refers to the special methods of observation of landscape painters.
43. Yu J., *Zhongguo lidai hualun leibian*, 585.
44. Huang J., "Chongdu *Jingtuzong sanjing*," 236–39.
45. *Weimojiesuoshuojing*, 546.
46. Ibid.
47. Lu Q., *Xian-Qin Han Wei Jin Nanbei chao shi*, 1085.
48. Yan, *Quan Jin wen*, 162.1778.
49. Daoxuan, *Guang Hongmingji*, 15.198.
50. Fan X., *Luoyang qielan ji*, 5.341; also Xiao, "Dacheng fojiao de shourong," 39.
51. Daoxuan, *Guang Hongmingji*, 198.

52. Yu, Zhou, and Yu, *Shishuo xinyu jianshu*, 618.
53. Ibid., 727.
54. This incident is recorded in Li Shan, *Liuchenzhu wenxuan*, 209.
55. Daoxuan, *Guang Hongmingji*, 198.
56. Lu Q., *Xian-Qin Han Wei Jin Nanbei chao shi*, 20.1086.
57. Ibid.
58. Sengyou, *Hongmingji*, 19, 12.
59. Although I note the prevailing convention of rendering *jing* as "world" (as in *wujing*, the "world of [physical] objects"), I suggest that "inscape" might better convey some of the nuances of this term, and hence have adopted it for the majority of most instances in the remainder of this chapter. See Varsano, "Worlds of Meaning and the Meaning of Worlds."
60. Zhang B., *Quan Tang wudai shige jiaokao*, 139, 149.

Chapter 4

A Tang Reconstructed Comprehensive Theory of Literary Creation
Wang Changling

For a long time now, the study of Chinese theories of literary creation has needed a fresh look to uncover perspectives and treasures from all periods. The immense prestige of Lu Ji 陸機 (261–303) and Liu Xie 劉勰 (ca. 465–ca. 522) has meant that their theories, with their emphasis on creativity, have largely dominated the discussion. The formal expository style of their work has been prized, especially by modern critics, over less systematic forms, such as cataloguing critical terms and categories or the random collection of short comments. The upshot is that profound theoretical insights expressed in these unsystematic forms have gone unappreciated, if not totally neglected. Wang Changling's 王昌齡 (ca. 698–ca. 756) writings on literary creation are a case in point. To date, crucial misreadings of Wang's writing—partly due to neglect of the influence exerted upon it by Tathāgatagarbha and Yogācāra Buddhism—have prevented us from seeing it as a radically innovative work.. But with current interest in the cultural matrix from which traditional Chinese literary thought emerged, it's time to change all that.

This chapter examines Wang Changling's loosely organized writings and reconstructs his comprehensive theory of literary creation, largely hidden within the multivalent term *yi*. Close, intertextual reading demonstrates how Wang deftly appropriates Daoist and Buddhist notions of *yi* 意 to illuminate different phases of literary creation. Comparisons with the term's adaptations by earlier literary and calligraphy critics further accentuate Wang's unique and innovative approach. Looking into a hitherto neglected Buddhist source, I uncover the Buddhistic *yi→xiang→yan* 意→象→言 (conception→image→word) paradigm that allows Wang to move beyond Lu Ji and Liu Xie. Drawing on the Buddhist sense of *yi* and *yishi* 意識, Wang demonstrates the creative mind's receptivity to the world's richness and nuances, followed by the dynamic transformation of all it has absorbed in quietude. The result is a much more detailed view of the different phases of the creative process—one that leads to a new appreciation of its poetic results.

PRISM: THEORY AND MODERN CHINESE LITERATURE • 20 (ANNUAL SUPPL.) • DECEMBER 2023
DOI 10.1215/25783491-11080875 • © 2023 LINGNAN UNIVERSITY

"Lun Wen Yi": The Multivalence of *Yi* 意

Wang Changling's writings on literary creation are collected in "Lun Wen Yi" 論文意 (On the Roles of *Yi* in Refined Writing), along with a few important passages from his *Shige* 詩格 (The Norm of Poetry).[1] "Lun Wen Yi" occupies a prominent place in *Bunkyō Hifuron* 文鏡秘府論 (The Literary Mirror and the Secret Repository of Literature), a collection of Tang texts on poetry assembled by the eminent Japanese monk Kūkai 空海 (774–835) during his stay in the Tang capital Chang'an (today's Xi'an) and published after his return to Japan. Specifically, "Lun Wen Yi" consists of writings by two leading Tang poet-critics, Wang Changling and Jiaoran 皎然 (720?–798?). The first half—which also appears in the *Shige* 詩格 (The Norm of Poetry)—comprises Wang Changling's theoretical discussion on poetry. The second half presents Jiaoran's comments on various technical issues of composition, also published in his *Shiyi* 詩議 (Comments on Poetry). My discussion of "Lun Wen Yi" focuses exclusively on Wang Changling.[2]

The section titled "Lun Wen Yi" aptly underscores the ubiquity and importance of *yi* in Wang's writings.[3] The central importance of this term has been noted but not seriously studied by modern Chinese scholars.[4] Instead of investigating Wang's exploitation of its multivalence, they focus on his purported combination of *yi* 意 with *jing* 境 (inscape) to create *yijing* 意境,[5] a *yi*-compound that will grow in importance in Chinese literary thought until it is enshrined by some modern scholars as the highest Chinese aesthetic principle.[6]

In my view, the importance of "Lun Wen Yi" should be assessed in light of Wang's own use of the term *yi*, not the future significance of *yijing* that never appears in "Lun Wen Yi." Assuming his readers' familiarity with *yi*'s multivalence, Wang Changling freely moves from one meaning to another without explanation. He apparently believes that his readers will correctly contextualize his *yi* and follow him without difficulty. With a similar assumption of readers' fairly sophisticated understanding, neither traditional nor modern Chinese critics feel the need to probe and sort out the multivalence of *yi* in "Lun Wen Yi." But for anyone writing about "Lun Wen Yi" in English, the multivalence of *yi* presents a challenge from the very outset: how to translate the title? *Wen yi* 文意 is a set compound made up of two nouns, *wen* 文 (writing) and *yi* 意 (meaning), which literally means "the meaning of refined writing." But the translation "On the Meaning of Refined Writing" simply does not work. While he sometimes talks about *yi* with its nominal sense of "meaning," Wang far more frequently uses *yi* in a verbal sense, denoting the mind's different activities during the creative process. Given this, it seems best to leave *yi* untranslated and render the title "On the Roles of *Yi* in Refined Writing."

Confusing as it may be, *yi*'s multivalence provides a unique opportunity to discover the coherent theory of literary creation hidden in "Lun Wen Yi." To probe Wang's exploiting of *yi*'s multivalence for this purpose, I carefully read both textually and intertextually. First I contextualize all noteworthy occurrences of *yi* within "Lun Wen Yi" itself to determine which particular concept it is most likely to convey in each. Then I contextualize Wang's use of *yi* within the broader philosophical and aesthetic discourses. I hope to demonstrate how he deftly appropriates various Daoist or Daoist-inspired notions of *yi* to illuminate different phases of literary creation. Comparisons with earlier adaptations of the term by literary and calligraphy critics reveal Wang's unique and innovative use. Finally, looking at a hitherto neglected Buddhist source for Wang, I uncover a partially Buddhistic *yi→xiang→yan* paradigm for thinking about the creative process, one that allows Wang to give a more cogent account of the creative process than his predecessors (Lu Ji and Liu Xie) were able to do.[7]

The Paradigmatic Significance of *Yi* 意

"Lun Wen Yi" is the first work of literary criticism in which the term *yi* assumes full paradigmatic significance. Although Lu Ji and Liu Xie had conceptualized the creative process through the *yi→xiang→yan* paradigm, they used *yi* very sparingly. But with Wang Changling, *yi* becomes a kind of all-purpose term, through which he conceptualizes and describes all phases of literary creation. Its new paradigmatic significance is made clear at the very beginning of "Lun Wen Yi":

§75
With regard to the nature of poetic composition, *yi* constitutes the norm and sound of prosody. If *yi* is lofty, so is the norm; when sound is well differentiated, prosody becomes pure. When the norm and prosody become complete, we can speak of tonality.[8]

凡作詩之體，意是格，聲是律，意高則格高，聲辨則律清，格律全，然後始有調。(*WJMFL*, 3:1299)

Wang begins by identifying *yi* as the norm or *ge* of poetry. *Shige* 詩格 is not only the title of Wang's work from which "Lun Wen Yi" is purportedly taken but also appears in the titles of many other Tang writings on poetry.[9] In stating that "*Yi* is the norm," Wang seems to be establishing *yi* (creative conception) as the highest principle of poetry. Here *yi* cannot possibly be glossed as "meaning" because "meaning is the norm" is a nonsensical statement. This conception of *yi* as "creative conception" is confirmed by the next sentence, where Wang explains the decisive impact of *yongyi* 用意, namely, a poet's activation of his creative process. In establishing *yi* as the norm of poetry, he transcends his contemporaries' petty concerns with technical rules of composition to make the creative process the central topic of discussion.[10] Elaborating on the impact of *yi*, he writes:

§76

If a poet transcends ancients in using *yi*, the vision of heaven and earth may be keenly observed [in his works].

用意於古人之上，則天地之境，洞焉可觀。(*WJMFL*, 3:1299)

Here Wang focuses on the transition from transcendent contemplation to the resulting mediation of the external world. "Transcending the ancients in using *yi*" primarily refers to a transcendence of time and space at the initial creative stage, a point that is even clearer in several instances below. With "the vision of heaven and earth may be keenly observed [in his works]," Wang speaks to the ensuing mediation of external realities by the creative mind. In the next sentence, he skips the remaining creative phases to describe instead perceiving the power of *yi* in a finished work.

§77

Ancient writings adhere to a lofty norm. The workings of *yi* can be observed in a single line such as "Good like his own flesh and blood," in two lines such as "'Guan, guan,' cry the ospreys / On the islet in the river," or in four lines such as "Green, green is the cypress on the hillside / Piles and piles of rocks in the valley; / Between heaven and earth lives man / Like a sojourner on a long journey."

古文格高，一句見意，則"股肱良哉"是也。其次兩句見意，則「關關雎鳩，在河之洲」是也。其次古詩，四句見意，則「青青陵上柏，磊磊澗中石，人生天地間，忽如遠行客」是也。(*WJMFL*, 3:1299)

Reflecting this shift to an observational angle, he now talks about *jianyi* 見意 (perceiving the *yi*) as opposed to *zuoyi* 作意 (activating *yi*; see §80). Because *yi* is often used as "meaning," many might read *jianyi* as "to see the meaning" of poetic lines. However, if we contextualize *jianyi* with Wang's preceding remarks, we realize that he is actually talking about the end result of the creative process: a crystallization of a poet's creative conception in poetic lines, and thus we should read 見意 synonymously with *xianyi* 現意 (making *yi* manifest). To dispel any doubt about this reading of *jianyi* 見意, we have only to turn to Wang's own corroborating evidence:

§78

When composing a piece of refined writing, one must look at how ancients and contemporary masters activated their creative thinking and discern if there is novel prosody to learn from.

凡作文，必須看古人及當時高手用意處，有新奇調學之。(*WJMFL*, 3:1365)

The expression "look at how . . . activated *yi*" 看. . . . . . 用意處 strikes me as very similar if not identical to the expression "seeing *yi*" 見意. We know that Wang intended to illustrate the ways ancient masters exercised their creative mind; it follows that he does the same in the latter. Their similarity lends strong support to my interpretation of *jianyi* as an act of perceiving the crystallization of creative conception in a finished work.

Transcendent Initiation of the Creative Process: *Zuoyi* 作意 and *Liyi* 立意

Having adumbrated the pivotal roles of *yi*, Wang proceeds to illuminate these roles in the remainder of "Lun Wen Yi." We first consider how he describes his notions of *zuoyi* 作意 and *liyi* 立意 as an initiation of transcendent contemplation:

§79
One's creative thinking (*yi*) must transcend the world of ten thousand people. One must look at the ancients placed under his own norm and must gather the heaven and sea within the speck of one's heart. This ought to be the way a poet uses his mind.

意須出萬人之境，望古人於格下，攢天海於方寸。詩人用心，當於此
也。(*WJMFL*, 3:1315)

Wang stresses that a great poet must begin the creative process from a transcendent vantage point, where he can gather human worlds, past and present, heaven and sea in his mind. Characterizing this initial transcendent contemplation as "a poet's use of the mind" 詩人用心, he simply calls it *zuoyi* 作意 (activating *yi*) in the following passage:

§80
Those who compose literary writings must activate *yi*. He should focus his mind beyond heaven and seas, and unfold his thought in the world before the rise of primal energy. And then he should adroitly employ words and phrases while refining the essence of his creative conception.

凡屬文之人，常須作意。凝心天海之外，用思元氣之前，巧運言詞，精練意
魄。(*WJMFL*, 3:1327)

Liyi 立意 (enacting *yi*) is an alternative *yi*-compound Wang uses to describe the transcendent initiation of literary creation, stressing an unconscious, self-forgetting state of mind as the precondition for its enactment:

§81

In composing a refined piece of writing, you should set store by the enactment of *yi*. Before you search through your mind and exert yourself to think, you must forget your own existence and free yourself from all constraints.

夫作文章，但多立意。令左穿右穴，苦心竭智，必須忘身，不可拘束。(*WJMFL*, 3:1309)

For Wang, a sound sleep is the best way to reach an optimal mental state for the enactment of *yi*:

§82

A poet should set a lamp by his bedside. If he lets himself sleep as long as he likes, he will rise up immediately after waking and feel inspired to write, begetting *yi* in his mind. With his spirit pure and fresh, everything becomes crystal clear to him.

凡詩人，夜間床頭，明置一盞燈。若睡來任睡，睡覺即起，興發意生，精神清爽,了了明白。(*WJMFL*, 3:1329)

Combined, these passages illustrate Wang's *yi* and *yi*-compounds like *zuoyi* and *liyi* to denote his pathways to creative thinking.

Wang's transcendent conception of *yi* represents a major development in Chinese literary and art criticism. The cosmological-epistemological paradigm of *yi→xiang→yan* established by Wang Bi 王弼 (226–249), master of Abstruse Learning (Xuanxue 玄學), definitely granted *yi* a transcendent dimension (see §§21–22), but in appropriating this paradigm to explore the creative process, neither Lu Ji nor Liu Xie applied *yi* to the initial transcendent phase of literary creation. Instead, Lu Ji uses the phrase "roaming of the mind" (*xinyou* 心遊) to describe a transcendent flight of the mind, along with poetic images and hyperbolic statements (see §§43–44). Liu Xie introduces the compound *shensi* 神思 (spirit-thinking) to name the transcendent flight of the mind.[11] In theorizing about the creative process, both Lu and Liu do use the term *yi*, but in a much less sublime sense. While Lu identifies it with an author's general intent, Liu uses the compound *yixing* 意象 to describe the outcome of transcendent flight: an inner image of a work-to-be. It is not until Wang Changling's time that the term takes on a clear transcendent import in calligraphy criticism. Zhang Huaiguan 張懷瓘 (fl. 713–741), for instance, gives this intriguing account of *yi*'s transcendent power:

§83

Then, [a calligrapher's] *yi* communes with the numinous being and his strokes move with mysterious force. The spirit folds and unfolds as it brings forth changes out of nowhere. The Dragon Uncle, for all his valor, cannot match its strength. The Divine Diagram and Talismanic Characters, though they empower an emperor, cannot surpass its height. Subtle thought penetrates every interstice, the air of abandon overflows the universe, ghost and spirit come and go—no words or image, fish trap or hare snare can capture the existence of all this!

及乎意與靈通，筆與冥運，神將化合，變出無方，雖龍伯挈鼇之勇，不能量其力；雄圖應籙之帝，不能抑其高。幽思入於毫間，逸氣瀰於宇內，鬼出神入，追虛捕微，則非言象筌蹄，所能存亡也。[12]

Wang Changling and Zhang Huaiguan are close contemporaries, and the direction of influence (if any) is impossible to determine. This passage by Zhang is full of explicit Daoist references, such as "the Divine Diagram," "Talismanic Characters," "fish trap," and "hare snare." By contrast, Wang Changling's use of *yi* when referring to the initial transcendent contemplation is completely free of such references. Notwithstanding his debt to earlier calligraphy critics, Wang is likely inspired by a different source's transcendent notion of *yi*. In fact, Wang Changling's work betrays the strong imprint of Buddhist influence—an issue further explored later in this chapter.

A Mirror-like Mediation of the Outer World: Emergence of Inscape 境

Like Lu Ji and Liu Xie, Wang Changling believes that initial transcendent contemplation naturally ushers in the second creative phase: a representation of the outer world in the mind. To Lu and Liu, the second creative phrase is as dynamic as the first; if transcendent contemplation consists in an out-of-body mental flight, Lu and Liu see a representation of the outer world as a dynamic influx of nature's images, blended with emotions and words, in the mind.[13] But to Wang Changling, both creative phases are tranquil by nature. He ceases to characterize the initial phase as a transcendent flight and envisions its outcome as a quiet mirroring of the outer world:

§84

If your thought does not arise, you must let your feelings subside and get relaxed so that an inscape may emerge in the mind. Looking at the mirror of this inscape, your thought may come and then you can begin your composition. If the inscape-inspired thinking does not arise, you cannot begin to write.

思若不來，即須放情卻寬之，令境生。然後以境照之，思則便來，來即作文。如其境思不來，不可作也。(*WJMFL*, 3:1309–10)

The term *jing* 境 (inscape) is crucial to our understanding of this passage. Judging by the context, it refers to the outer world as perceived or mirrored in the mind.

This notion of *jing* is definitely of Buddhist origin. While pre-Buddhist Chinese thinkers use *jing* as an objective, descriptive word in the sense of a "realm," physical or mental, Buddhist thinkers use it to denote the outer world as the object of the mind, a referent that is at once physical and mental.[14] In fact, Buddhists use *jing* to label six categories of phenomena (*liujing* 六境) brought into existence by six corresponding senses (*liugen* 六根).[15] By adding this *jing* label, Buddhists express a worldview different from those held by Confucians and Daoists. To Buddhists, all so-called objective phenomena are mere illusion. Given this strong subjective connotation, "inscape" seems an ideal translation of *jing* as it resonates with the Buddhist worldview underlying the term. Moreover, it is the intended meaning of *jing* in this particular context: Wang Changling is actually talking about the mediation of the outer world following the initial creative phase. The all-embracing denoting of "inscape" (in relation to "landscape") nicely captures Wang's idea of a total mirroring of the external world. For him, what emerges from transcendent contemplation is not a stream of specific images (as with Lu Ji and Liu Xie) but a motionless, mirror-like vision or inscape of all things. In the following passage, he recounts how transcendent contemplation gives rise to such an inscape:

§85

To initiate creative conception and write poetry, one must concentrate his mind and set his eyes upon things. Next he penetrates things with his mind and reaches into the depth of the landscape. This is like climbing to the summit, looking at the ten thousand things down below as if they were just within his palm. Envisaging in such a way, one will have a crystal clear view of things in the mind and can immediately put it to use.

夫置意作詩，即須疑心，目擊其物，便以心擊之，深穿其境。 如登高山絕
頂，下臨萬象，如在掌中。 以此見象，心中了見，當此即用。(*WJMFL*, 3:1312)

In this context, *zhiyi* 置意 strikes me as synonymous with *zuoyi* 作意, both referring to an initiation of transcendent contemplation. To Wang, gazing at things is merely a way of inducing the mind to penetrate the objective world to gain a clear inscape of it in its totality—"like climbing to the summit, looking at the ten thousand things down below as if they were within his palm." For Wang, this mirror-like mediation of the outer world thus becomes available to the poet as he proceeds to the next creative phase.

Envisaging a Work-to-Be: *Si* 思 and *Yixiang* 意象

For Wang Changling, envisaging a work constitutes the second creative phase. If the first phase is largely unconscious mental activity, the second is a process of conscious thinking that Wang consistently describes with the word *si* 思 (think-ing). In "Lun Wen Yi," *si* appears fourteen times, each time denoting a conscious act of thinking. In his *Shige*, Wang Changling presents us with a list of "three *si*" (*sansi* 三思) or three modes of conscious thinking:

§86

The first is spontaneously inspired thinking. After a long exertion of meticu-lous thinking, one still could not form an envisagement [*yixiang*] [of a work]. Feeling physically worn out and mentally exhausted, one relaxes and calms his spirit and thought. Then, unexpectedly, one catches a reflection of an inscape in his mind and thinking spontaneously arises.

生思一。久用精思，未契意象。力疲智竭，放安神思。心偶照境，率然而生。[16]

In this passage, Wang is making two crucial points about the second creative phase. The first is that *si*, a conscious mental effort, usually arises in response to an inscape in the mind, reaffirming his notion of "inscape-inspired thinking" (*jingsi* 境思) expressed in "Lun Wen Yi" (see §84). The second point is that this inscape-inspired thinking aims to bring forth *yixiang* 意象 (conception-image). So what is meant by *yixiang*? The compound itself gives us a good clue. Its sec-ond character, *xiang*, carries the straightforward meaning of "image" and here denotes the virtual image or "envisagement" based on artistic imagination rather than physical realities. But the first character, *yi*, is harder to decipher. To figure out the import of *yi* in this particular compound, we need to trace back to Liu Xie's original coinage. In conceiving *yixiang*, Liu sought to link virtual "image" with two different referents of the term *yi*: visual imagination and refined feeling. Liu's linkage of visual imagination (*yi*) with virtual image (*xiang*) may have been inspired by Han Fei's 韓非 (ca. 280–ca. 233 BCE) account of how Laozi's sages, by virtue of intuitive envisagement, perceived the Dao:

§87

People rarely see a living elephant. When they got the bones of a dead elephant, they used them as visual hints to imagine how it looked when alive. Therefore what those people conjured up was called an image [*xiang*]. Now even though the Dao cannot be heard or seen, the sage dwells on things acctomplished by the Dao to envisage its shape. Therefore, [Laozi] says "the shape without shape, the image without image."

人希見生像也，而得死像之骨，案其圖以想其生也，故諸人之所以意想者皆謂之像。今道雖不可得聞見，聖人執其見功以處見其形，故曰："無狀之狀，無物之像。"[17]

In explaining Laozi's idea of "shape without shape and image without image," Han Fei stresses the dynamic role of *yi* 意 or *yixiang* 意想,[18] an act of conjuring up or imagining something absent—the shape of an elephant never seen. In a similar vein, Liu Xie credits "spirit-thinking" for the rise of a virtual envisagement of a work-to-be. The difference is that Liu not only talks about the relation between *yi* (creative conception) and *xiang* (virtual image) but actually combines them into a new compound, *yixiang* 意象 (see *WXDL*, chap. 26, sentence 37 [hereafter 26/37]).

Liu's coinage of *yixiang* also subtly denotes a fusion of feelings and images in a poet's mind, thanks to *yi*'s newly acquired meaning as "refined" feeling as opposed to crude emotions (see §90 below). There is no doubt this new meaning of *yi* looms large in Liu's mind. Immediately after introducing his coinage of *yixiang*, Liu explicitly uses *yi* as synonymous with, if not identical to, feeling (*qing* 情) when he depicts the fusion of feelings and images in a poet's mind: "When one ascends a mountain [in his envisioning]," Liu writes, "the whole mountain is filled with his feelings [*qing*]; when one observes the seas, the seas will overflow with his expressive intent [*yi*]" 登山則情滿於山,觀海則意溢於海 (*WXDL*, 26/43–44). In these two strictly parallel sentences *yi* is paired with *qing*, both meaning "feelings." For Liu Xie as for Wang Changling roughly two hundred years later, the compound *yixiang* epitomizes an optimal outcome of dynamic interaction between subject and object, between feelings and nature images in the second creative phase. Wang Changling's emphasis on the role of feelings in this phase is explicit in his next comment on the second mode of conscious thinking:

§88

The second is feeling-inspired thinking. As one ruminates the words of ancients, chants, and allegorizes in the ancient way, one feels moved to begin thinking.

感思二:尋味前言, 吟諷古制, 感而生思。[20]

Here, *gansi* 感思 (feeling-inspired thinking) seems congruent with *jingsi* 境思 (inscape-inspired thinking). In using this pair of compounds, Wang suggests there are two alternative ways of activating a poet's conscious thinking to create an ideal *yixiang* (conception-image). Ruminating, chanting, and allegorizing ancients' words may be just as powerful for inspiring conscious acts of thinking. In describing this so-called feeling-inspired thinking, Wang employs the term *yi* as well:

§89

A poet must project his own self into poetic feelings (*yi*). If there is no self in poetry, how can we possibly have poetry? If not to depict one's own self and mind, what's the point of composing poetry? So poetry is the envoy of the heart and an outlet of anger and grievances of the time. When a poet feels the flow of his emotions being impeded or that what's in his heart couldn't be conveyed, he would resort to one of these acts—satirizing those above him, edifying those below him, giving expression to his own feelings, or giving an account of events. All these acts arise from displeasures and unhappiness of the heart and the frustration of not being understood by others. If one speaks of poetry this way, one knows the foundation of the ancients.

皆須身在意中。若詩中無身，即詩從何有。若不書身心，何以為詩。是故詩者，書身心之行李，序當時之憤氣。氣來不適，心事不達，或以刺上，或以化下，或以申心，或以序事，皆為中心不決，眾不我知。由是言之，方識古人之本也。(*WJMFL*, 3:1329)

Here *yi* can be taken to mean "conception-image," connoting both "envisagement" and "refined feelings." By Liu Xie's time, the term had already come to mean "refined feelings." Expounding this new notion of *yi*, Fan Ye 范曄 (398–445) writes:

§90

It is often said that in giving expression to emotion and intent, a writer ought to foreground his conception and use refined writing to convey it. If his conception is foregrounded, his intended meaning will be surely perceived. As he uses refined writing to convey his conception, his phrasing will not be flippant and therefore his works will exude fragrance and resound like instruments of metals and stone.

常謂情志所托，故當以意為主，以文傳意。以意為主，則其旨必見；以文傳意，則其詞不流。然後抽其芬芳，振其金石耳。[21]

Here, to justify a self-projection into *yixiang* or conception-image, Wang deftly reinvents the Confucian concept of poetry by establishing the individual self as its foundation.[22] Contrary to Wang's claim, the feelings of an individual poet are never foregrounded in such Confucian texts on literature as the "Great Preface to the Mao Text of the *Book of Poetry*."[23] Discussing the third mode of conscious thinking, Wang returns to the issue of selecting nature images:

§91

The third is thinking in quest of [images]. Searching in the world of images, one's mind penetrates an inscape and has a spiritual communion with things. All is acquired through the mind.

取思三。搜求於象，心入於境，神會於物，因心而得。[24]

Consistent with his ideal of *yixiang* (conception-image), Wang stresses that the quest for poetic images is in effect a process of communion between mind and landscape, between one's spirit and external things.[25] In the following passage Wang explicitly mentions the role of subjective feelings in this process:

§92

The vapor and hues of spring, summer, autumn, and winter may at any time induce feelings [*yi*]. Speaking of the use of these feelings, you must calm your spirit and purify your thought when using them. Seeing things, you must let them enter your mind and let the mind commune with them. When things and the mind are in communion, you can begin to write.

春夏秋冬氣色，隨時生意。取用之意，用之時，必須安神淨慮。目覩其物，即入於心。心通其物，物通即言。(*WJMFL*, 3:1365)

Here we have yet another verbal *yi*-compound: *shengyi* 生意 (evoking *yi*). While the *yi* in *zuoyi* 作意 and *zhiyi* 置意 suggests transcendent contemplation, here *shengying* seems to denote feelings to be fused with images or, in Wang's own words, "feelings for use" 取用之意. For Wang, to use these feelings means fusing them with nature images. To achieve the best effect of such fusion, Wang urges poets to strive for a true communion between the mind and things.

Dynamic Envisagement and Compositional Execution

For Wang Changling as well as Lu Ji and Liu Xie, the final creative phase involves translating an artistic envisagement into a work of language. Liu Xie sees in this last phase the greatest challenge to the poet due to the huge gap between virtual envisagement and actual language. He writes:

§93

At the moment a writer picks up his brush, before anything is written, he feels doubly invigorated. But when the piece is completed, he finds only half of what he first had in his mind has been conveyed. What's construed [*yi*] is virtual and therefore easily extraordinary, but language is actual and therefore it's hard to be dexterous using it. So conception is derived from thinking, and words from conception—they can be seamlessly blended or apart from one another by a thousand miles.

方其搦翰，氣倍辭前；暨乎篇成，半折心始。何則？意翻空而易奇，言徵實而難巧也。是以意授於思，言授於意，密則無際，疏則千里。(*WXDL*, 26/48–54)

Though the main thrust of this passage underscores the author's difficulty in capturing the mind's creations (*yi*) in actual language (*yan*), Liu gives an abstract affirmation of the possibility of bridging the two. Apparently, it is just as challenging for a critic to explain how virtual envisagement is translated into actual language as it is for an author to complete such a translation. Indeed, in Lu Ji's *Wen fu* 文賦 (An Exposition on Literature), we find two large, distinctly separate parts: an exposition on how a poet construes an artistic envisagement and a laborious discussion on all language matters crucial to compositional execution, without an earnest effort by Lu to address the *yi-yan* gap. In his "Shensi" 神思 (Spirit-Thinking) chapter, Liu also fails to give a cogent description of how artistic envisagement is translated into a work of language. He says only that "looking at the conception image, one wields the axe [of language to carve it]" 闚意象而運斤 (*WXDL*, 26/37), as if to suggest such a conception-image (*yixiang*) constitutes a static, finished product of artistic envisagement to be observed and recast through the axe of language. In other words, conception-image is a self-contained entity, and language is extraneous to it. With Liu Xie, then, the issue of how virtual envisagement is translated into a poetic text remains unexplored.

To reveal how the virtual envisagement gets translated into an actual work of language, one must not consider the former as a completed process before compositional execution begins. Instead, it has to be reconceptualized as a force that actually drives all stages of compositional execution. This is exactly what Wang Changling has done in "Lun Wen Yi":

§94

Poetry has its basis in the heart's intent. What lies in the heart is intent and when intent is uttered it becomes poetry. Emotion stirs inside and finds form in words. A masterful poet can create momentum, bringing forth an envisagement [*yi*] in the first line. Next comes the one who brings forth an envisagement in the first two lines. Envisagement is like swirling smoke, rising from the ground higher and higher into the sky and leaving no trace of stages. An inferior poet writes progressively weaker lines, with no consideration of back-and-forth movement. His works do not espouse the principle of envisagement and are unbearable to read.

詩本志也，在心為志，發言為詩，情動於中，而形於言，然後書之於紙也。高手作勢，一句更別起意；其次兩句起意，意如湧煙，從地昇天，向後漸高漸高，不可階上也。下手下句弱於句，不看向背，不立意宗，皆不堪也。(*WJMFL*, 3:1304)

This passage is all about mind-to-language movement. First, Wang Changling articulates the traditional view of poetry as an expressive process from the heart's intent to spoken words. Next, skipping the first two creative phases (transcendent contemplation and the formation of envisagement), he turns to probe the translation of envisagement into a poetic text. Here, unlike any critic before him, he conceptualizes *yi* as the dynamic force that propels and unifies the entire compositional process. In writing poetry, Wang contends that a fine poet creates great momentum by evoking artistic envisagement in the first or second line and letting it surge higher and higher. This upward thrust of *yi*, which Wang terms *qiyi* 起意, is at once that of the poet's cerebral activities and of his act of writing out poetic lines. To Wang, these two parallel movements are essentially inseparable from each other, if not one and the same. In contrast to such a dynamic upward movement, Wang deplores an inferior poet's steady downward movement—a production of weaker and weaker lines. In failing to build momentum, Wang contends that these lines have forsaken the cardinal principle of "espousing *yi*," and hence he cannot bear to look at them.

By reconceptualizing envisagement (*yi*) as the dynamic force of compositional execution, Wang Changling has clearly surpassed Lu Ji and Liu in theorizing the final creative phase. However, his linking of envisagement (*yi*) with compositional execution is not entirely original when considered in the broader context of earlier and contemporary aesthetic discourse. In earlier calligraphy criticism, we can trace a similar notion of *yi* and compositional execution. Wang Xizhi 王羲之 (303–361), for instance, embraces *yi* as the highest principle of calligraphic execution:

§95
Calligraphy values quietude. The calligrapher's act of envisaging (*yi*) comes before moving one's writing brush. The writing of characters must come after the mind's effort. Before the act of writing, the calligrapher should complete his thought process.

凡書貴乎沉靜，令意在筆前，字居心後，未作之始，結思成矣。[26]

This privileging of *yi* by Wang Xizhi most likely inspired Wang Changling's pronouncement that "*yi* is the norm of poetry." In these remarks by Wang Xizhi, *yi* cannot possibly be mistaken for the static "meaning" of a text. The great calligrapher-critic is instead describing a dynamic act of inward visualization or envisagement just before calligraphic execution. In the following passage, he explains how *yi* or an act of envisaging breathes life and energy into all aspects of calligraphy:

§96
To write in calligraphy, one must first grind the inkstick without water and focus his mind and engross himself in quiet thought. One must preconceive the varied shapes and sizes of characters, as well as their movements downward or upward, straight or fluctuating, so that they are joined as if by veins and

sinews. This inward visualization or envisagement [*yi*] must occur before one sets brush to paper, and only then does one proceed to write out the characters. If the characters are all similar in their linear dimensions like beads of an abacus and are all uniformly aligned, top and bottom, front and back, that is merely dots and strokes, not calligraphy.

夫欲書者，先乾研墨，凝神靜思，預想字形大小、偃仰、平直、振動，令筋脈相連，意在筆前，然後作字。若平直相似，狀如算子，上下方整，前後齊平，便不是書，但得其點畫耳。[27]

While he talks about a dynamic movement of characters envisaged by a calligrapher, Wang Xizhi falls short of conceptualizing a calligrapher's envisagement itself as a dynamic process. For a dynamic notion of calligraphic envisagement, we need to wait until shortly before Wang Changling's time. Sun Guoting 孫過庭 (646–691), a great calligraphy critic who died just about when Wang Changling was born, writes:

§97

Envisagement [*yi*] comes first and strokes follow. They fly gracefully and swiftly, a writing brush moves unimpeded, and spirit unfurls its flight. This is like the mind of Hongyang finding delight in the boundless realm and like the eye of the Butcher Ding not seeing the whole ox. I had some interested students seeking to study under me. I gave them a brief outline and then proceeded to teach them. They all had an awakening of the mind, followed by the execution of a masterful hand. They have all forgotten the word and attained *yi*. Even if they had not thoroughly observed various calligraphic methods, they were sure to achieve perfection in this art.

意先筆後，瀟灑流落，翰逸神飛。亦猶弘羊之心，豫乎無際；庖丁之目，不見全牛。嘗有好事，就吾求習，吾乃㩐舉綱要，隨而授之，無不心悟手從，言忘意得；縱未窺於眾術，斷可極於所詣矣。[28]

Inspired by Zhuangzi's tale of the Butcher Ding, Sun Guoting compares the simultaneous movement of his envisagement and his writing brush to a miraculous flight. To Sun, such synchronized movement of mind and hand is the key to ultimate success in calligraphy. In some ways, Wang Changling's conception of envisagement (*yi*) propelling the compositional process strikes me as a literary adaptation of Sun's notion of dynamic calligraphic envisagement. Indeed, Wang's comparison of poetic envisagement to rising smoke recalls Sun's hyperbolic figure of a miraculous flight.

The Birth of a Poetical Text: Fusing Expressive Tenor and Scenes

Having identified *yi* as the driving force of compositional execution, Wang Chang-ling needs to demonstrate how it shapes different aspects of a composition. In tackling this task, Wang again seems to have found inspiration in Wang Xizhi's remarks on the impact of *yi* (envisagement) on *zi* (characters). For Wang Xizhi, calligraphic envisagement gives life to characters, turning them into symbols pregnant with energy and movement, and integrates them into an organic whole. Probably influenced by Wang Xizhi's animating notion of *yi*, Wang Changling stresses the primary role of the dynamic *yi* in activating and intensifying subject-object interaction on all levels of poetic composition, from overall structure to line formation. In configuring a poem, Wang advocates a balanced, orderly presentation of expressive tenor and scenes:

§98

One should see to it that both scenes seen by the eye and expressive tenor (*yi*) that yields delights are presented. If one exclusively presents expressive tenor, a poem will not have anything marvelous and will be tasteless. Likewise, if a poem has too much scene depiction not tightly integrated with expressive tenor, it will also be tasteless even though it bears on principles of things. Scenes of morning and dusk, and the atmospheres of the four seasons should all be arranged in accord with the expressive tenor. If scenes appear in such an orderly fashion and are depicted in tandem with expressive tenor, the effect will be miraculous.

然看當所見景物與意愜者相兼道。若一向言意，詩中不妙及無味。景語若多，與意相兼不緊，雖理道亦無味。昏旦景色，四時氣象，皆以意排之，令有次序，令兼意說之為妙。(*WJMFL*, 3:1365)

It's important to note that *yi* is used here as a noun meaning "expressive tenor." As noted earlier, when appearing in conjunction with "scenes" or "images," this nominal *yi* often denotes "refined feeling," namely, feelings that have been processed by the creative mind, as opposed to crude, uncontemplated emotions. Wang Changling's notion of expressive tenor and nature images as two basic components of poetic composition might even be said to anticipate T. S. Eliot's conception of artistic feelings versus "objective correlatives." It is also noteworthy that, by using *yi* instead of *qing* (emotions) to indicate subject-object interaction, Wang achieves a subtle resonance with the sense of *yi* as dynamic envisagement. The subject-object interaction also informs Wang Changling's more specific discussion of poetic structure:

§99

A poem may begin by presenting its expressive tenor. If its expressive tenor is exhaustively conveyed, a poem will have a large belly-like body. Having a belly-like body, a poem can accommodate a lot, allowing a dazzling display of appearances and sensuous colors. But when it ends, it should revert back to the expressive tenor and, furthermore, there should be resonance of the tenor in each and every section of the poem.

夫詩，入頭即論其意，意盡則肚寬，肚寬則詩得容預，物色亂下，至尾則卻收前意，節節仍須有分付。(*WJMFL*, 3:1317)

Wang maintains that a poem's beginning is particularly important and can be either an external scene or an emotive expression:

§100

As for the beginning of a poem, it could be a depiction of sensuous colors, the poet's experiential self, or self-expressive tenor. There are countless ways to begin a poem, but there is no fixed rule. Whatever arises spontaneously and runs smoothly can be the beginning of a poem.

凡詩頭，或以物色為頭，或以身為頭，或以身意為頭，百般無定，任意以興來安穩，即任為詩頭也。(*WJMFL*, 3:1335)

On the level of couplet construction, Wang also sets store by an interplay of nature images and expressive tenor:

§101

In a poem, [a couplet] may articulate expressive tenor in the first line and depict appearances of things in the second or, conversely, depict appearances of things in the first line and articulate expressive tenor in the second.

詩有上句言意，下句言狀；上句言狀，下句言意。(*WJMFL*, 3:1338)

Even when composing a single line, Wang holds that the poet should strive to blend scenes with expressive tenor:

§102

In a poem, it's best to have sensuous appearances of things along with expressive tenor. If a poem presents only sensuous appearances, uninspired by expressive tenor, it is not of much use even if dexterously composed. A line like "The sounds of bamboo are the first to know autumn's advent" can be said to have both.

凡詩，物色兼意下為好，若有物色，無意興，雖巧亦無處用之。如「竹聲先知秋」，此名兼也。(*WJMFL*, 3:1339)

Wang contends that the ideal blending of images and expressive tenor often leaves no trace of the latter: "Under a superior hand, external things and expressive content do not depend on each other" 凡高手，言物及意皆不相倚傍 (*WJMFL*, 3:1340). Among examples given of such traceless fusions, we discover Xie Lingyun's 謝靈運 (385–433) famous couplet "Pond banks grow spring grass, / Garden willows change singing birds" 池塘生春草，園柳變鳴禽.[29]

These and other passages reveal how Wang Changling envisioned a gestalt of subject-object interaction on all levels of composition, from the structure of a work down to the crafting of a single line.[30] By his own description, what activates and sustains the poet's process is just the dynamic *yi* that, like "swirling smoke, rising . . . higher and higher," propels the final compositional act toward the birth of a finished text (see §94). By envisioning this seamless fusion, Wang has managed to accomplish what eluded his predecessors Lu Ji and Liu Xie: provide a cogent account of the translation of virtual envisagement into poetic text.

The Imprint of Buddhist Concepts of *Yi* 意 and *Yishi* 意識

With Wang Changling's radical reconceptualization of the creative process in mind, I now explore how Buddhist notions of *yi* might have contributed to his thinking. By Wang's time, *yi* had been widely used in Chinese translations of the Buddhist sutras, especially those focused on the analysis of consciousnesses. Of course, this includes both *yi* and *yi*-compounds, so it makes sense to consider what distinctively Buddhist concepts of the mind *yi* and *yi*-compounds convey in these texts. In this section, I show how Wang Changling might have been inspired by these Buddhist concepts to rethink the creative process.

Yi's Buddhist connection is very conspicuous in "Lun Wen Yi." The string of *yi*-compounds like *zuoyi* 作意, *jianyi* 見意, *zhiyi* 置意, and *qiyi* 起意 discussed above carry a strong Buddhist flavor. In indigenous Chinese philosophical texts, we seldom come across such *yi*-compounds, much less so many of them in so short a text. But *yi*-compounds are a staple in Buddhist texts, especially those with a verb + *yi* structure. It seems rather strange that, when probing the Buddhist influence on Wang Changling's literary thought, Chinese scholars have overlooked *yi* and *yi*-compounds and focused on less important terms like *jing* and *zuoyong* 作用. In terms of their impact on Wang's literary thought, I consider *yi* and *yi*-compounds to be far more important than the other terms because they introduce an entirely new way of looking at the workings of the mind and its virtual reproduction of the world. In some ways, terms like *jing* (inscape) often merely signify aspects of that reproduced world.

The Chinese term *yi* has a long and complex history of application to express different Buddhist concepts about the mind. In his translation of *Saṃyuktāgama* 雜阿含經, the eminent Indian monk Gunabhadra 求那跋陀羅 (394–468) uses the term *yi*, together with *xin* and *shi*, to describe the changeable, insubstantial nature of mental activities:

§103

Those activities of the mind change every moment, day and night. They neither have life nor die. They are like monkeys bouncing among trees in a wood. They cling to tree branches every moment, releasing one only to catch another.

彼心、意、識日夜時刻，須臾轉變，異生、異滅。猶如獼猴遊林樹間，須臾處處，攀捉枝條,放一取一。(*T* 2n99_012)

In translating this passage, Gunabhadra was probably using the terms *xin, yi,* and *shi* as rough equivalents of Buddhist terms *citta, manas,* and *vijñāna,* which as Yoshito S. Hakeda notes, "are synonymous in the earliest phase of Buddhism, indicating 'mind' in the ordinary sense of the word."[31] But in later translations of the Tathāgatagarbha and Yogācāra sutras, these three terms become clearly distinguished. For instance, in translating *Laṅkāvatāra-sūtra* 入楞伽經, Bodhiruci 菩提流支 (?–527) uses the term *yi* 意 and its derivative *yishi* 意識 to denote two of the eight consciousnesses:

§104

Again, Mahamati, the talk of good or bad methods of cultivation is about the eight consciousnesses. What are the eight consciousnesses? The first is *ālaya-vijñāna* (storehouse consciousness), the second *manas-vijñāna* (ego-consciousness); the third *mano-vijñāna* (thinking consciousness); the fourth *cakṣur-vijñāna* (eye consciousness), the fifth *śrotra-vijñāna* (ear consciousness), the sixth the nose consciousness, the seventh the tongue consciousness, and the eighth the body consciousness.

復次，大慧！言善不善法者，所謂八識。何等為八？一者、阿梨耶識；二者、意；三者、意識；四者、眼識；五者、耳識；六者、鼻識；七者、舌識；八者、身識。(*T* 16n671_16)

Eight consciousnesses also figure prominently in Yogācāra sutras, although they are usually listed in reverse order, with *ālaya-vijñāna* the eighth rather than the first consciousness. In Chinese translations of Yogācāra sutras, the terms *yi* and *yishi* are also respectively used to denote the *manas-vijñāna* and *mano-vijñāna.* Alternatively, *manas-vijñāna* is often transliterated as *mona* 末那, probably for the purpose of avoiding confusion between *yi* and *yishi.*

To determine whether any connection exists between this Buddhist reconceptualization of *yi* and Wang Changling's use of the term, we first need a clear understanding of the nature and function of the two key consciousnesses called *yi* and *yishi* by various Buddhist schools. For this purpose, let us turn to the elucidation in *Dacheng qixin lun* 大乘起信論 (Awakening of Mahāyāna Faith), a very popular and influential Chinese Buddhist text in Wang's time that has no extant Sanskrit version but has been attributed, problematically according some scholars, to Aśvaghoṣa 馬鳴 (ca. 80–ca. 150).

§105

That a man is in samsara results from the transformation of his Storehouse Consciousness [*citta*], his mind [*manas*] and his consciousness [*vijñāna*]. This means that the Storehouse Consciousness, thanks to the unconscious rise of a nonenlightenment aspect, perceives, reproduces, and possesses the world of objects [as real], and these [deluded] thoughts continue on. This is what we call mind [*manas; yi* 意].[32]

生滅因緣者，所謂眾生依心、意、意識轉故。此義云何？以依阿梨耶識說有無明不覺而起，能見，能現，能取境界，起念相續，故說為意。(*T* 32n.1666_001)

This passage offers a detailed description of *manas*. First it is defined in terms of its origin in and dependence upon the storehouse consciousness. It comes into being as a result of an unconscious rise of the storehouse consciousness and becomes capable of perceiving, reproducing, and possessing the world of objects. What follows is a discussion of the five names given to *manas*:

§106

This mind has five names. The first is called the "activating mind," because the force of ignorance stirs up the mind unawares. The second is called the "evolving mind" because it emerges as a result of the agitated mind and becomes capable of perceiving phenomena. The third is called the "reproducing mind" because it reproduces the entire world of objects just as a bright mirror presents all material images. When confronted with the objects of the five senses, it reproduces them at once. It arrives spontaneously at all times and exists forever [reproducing the world of objects] in front of the subject. The fourth is the "analytical mind" for it differentiates what is defiled and what is undefiled. The fifth is the "continuing mind," for it united with [deluded] thoughts and continues uninterrupted. It retains the entire karma, good and bad, accumulated in the immeasurable lives of the past, and does not permit any loss.[33]

此意復有五種名：云何為五？一者、名為業識，謂無明力，不覺心動故。二者、名為轉識，依於動心能見相故。三者、名為現識，所謂能現一切境界，猶如明鏡現於色像；現識亦爾，隨其五塵對至即現，無有前後，以一切時，任運而起，常在前故。四者、名為智識，謂分別染淨法故。五者、名為相續識，以念相應不斷故；住持過去無量世等善惡之業，令不失故。(*T* 32n.1666_001)

The first two names, "activating mind" and "evolving mind," essentially repeat the preceding definition, reiterating its origin in storehouse consciousness and its endowed capacities. The third and the fourth names, "reproducing mind" and "analytical mind," throw light on its totalistic, mirror-like reproduction of the world and its dichotomous differentiation of the defiled and undefiled. The last, "continuing mind," elaborates on its karmic effects.

If we reread Wang's remarks on transcendent contemplation and mediation of the outer world (see §§79–85) against the passages just examined, we notice three conspicuous parallels. First, both Aśvaghoṣa and Wang Changling emphasize the unconscious transcendent beginning of the mental processes they investigate. While Aśvaghoṣa speaks of *manas* unconsciously arising from ignorance (*wuming* 無明), Wang repeatedly emphasizes the unconscious mental conditions under which transcendent contemplation begins. Second, in describing the phenomenal world subsequently emerging in the mind, they both emphasize its all-encompassing nature. Aśvaghoṣa talks about the *yi* 意 as capable of "reproducing the entire world of objects" 能現一切境界; Wang argues that an initiation of transcendent contemplation 用意 could bring forth "an inscape of heaven and earth" (*tiandi zhijing* 天地之境) in a poem. When used alone, *jing* 境 (inscape) often denotes the totality of the phenomenal world as mediated in the poet's mind, while *xing* 象, *wu* 物, and *jing* 景 are reserved for specific parts of that world. Third, in foregrounding a total reproduction or mediation of the phenomenal world by the mind, they both use the Buddhist mirror metaphor. While Aśvaghoṣa explicitly compares *yi* to "a bright mirror showing the image of the phenomenal world" 明鏡現於色像, Wang employs *zhaojing* 照境 (mirroring an inscape) that may be taken as a homonymic play on *zhaojing* 照鏡 (holding a mirror to). The discussion that follows of *mano-vijñāna* 意識 by Aśvaghoṣa invites similar comparisons with Wang's use of *yi*.

§107
What is called "consciousness" (*vijñāna*, 意識) is the "continuing mind."
Because of their deep-rooted attachment, ordinary men imagine that I and Mine are real and cling to them in their illusions. As soon as objects are presented, this consciousness rests on them and discriminates between the objects of the five senses and the mind. This is called "*vijñāna* [i.e., the differentiating consciousness]" or the "separating consciousness." Or, again, it is called the "object-discriminating consciousness."[34]

復次，言意識者，即此相續識。依諸凡夫取著轉深計我我所，種種妄執隨事攀緣，分別六塵名為意識，亦名分離識，又復說名分別事識。(*T* 32n.1666_001)

Here, Aśvaghoṣa discusses *mano-vijñāna*, the sixth consciousness in the Yogācāra scheme of eight consciousness, and we see it in its standard Chinese translation *yishi* 意識. The addition of *shi* 識 to *yi* 意 is apparently intended to distinguish it from *manas-vijñāna* 意, the seventh consciousness. In Chinese, *shi* 識 means cognition or knowledge and aptly indicates the difference between *mano-vijñāna* 意識 from *manas-vijñāna* 意. Although Aśvaghoṣa called it "analytical mind," *manas-vijñāna* is not all that analytical: its conception of self-ego and dichotomy of the defiled and undefiled indicate differentiation only of the broadest kind. By contrast, *mano-vijñāna* 意識 is a true intellectual process that can arise either in tandem with or disassociated from the five sense consciousnesses to form differentiation and cognitive knowledge. Hence its English translations also indicate its intellectual character: "thinking consciousness," "conceptual consciousness," "intellectual consciousness," among others. If *manas-vijñāna* 意 unconsciously reproduces the entire world of objects like a clear mirror, *mano-vijñāna* 意識, according to Aśvaghoṣa, represents a conscious, sustained process of "discriminat[ing] the objects of the five senses and of the mind" and "cling[ing] to them in their illusions."

In Wang Changling's "Lun Wen Yi," we find a parallel progression from unconscious transcendent contemplation to the conscious process of *si* 思 or thinking. In their modus operandi, *yishi* 意識 (*mano-vijñāna*) and *si* 思 are strikingly similar: both perceive and reproduce not the phenomenal world as a whole but its specific, differentiated objects. While *yishi* arises in tandem with objects of the five senses, Wang's *si* enacts a search for images (*souxiang* 搜象) in both nature and the human world. It is in this context that Wang speaks of *jingsi* 境思 (inscape-directed thinking; see §84) and *gansi* 感思 (feeling-inspired thinking; see §88). Moreover, the operation of both *yishi* and *si* entails an active play of emotions. In Buddhism, *yishi*'s coarising with the objects of the five senses and the mind is illusory and volitional as much as it is conceptual. Likewise, Wang Changling's *si* is very much a dynamic process of blending volitions or emotions with images on all levels of poetic composition.

It is at this point, though, that we notice a crucial disparity between Aśvaghoṣa's philosophy of consciousnesses and Wang's theory of literary creation. Rejecting the ultimately negative Buddhist view of *yi* and *yishi* as agents of illusion, Wang prefers to cast *yi* and *si* as indisputably positive processes of literary creation.[35] The basis for this preference, I would argue, is his firm allegiance to the world out there and his desire to incorporate it into the realm of poetry. Where Buddhism incorporates *yi* and *yishi* as agents of the illusory world from which detachment is the logical answer, Wang parts company with the Buddhist perspective. What he does, then, in effect, is *use* Buddhism to conceptualize the initial stages of literary creation. It gave him a new way of thinking about poetic receptivity: the Buddhist emphasis on passivity as a mental pose enabled Wang to envision a radical receptiveness to the world out there that would allow it to penetrate the mind in ways previously unimagined. And that, in turn, would give him a new basis for thinking about how the mind could infuse the world with its own emotion. In other words, it becomes necessary to receive the world in all its fullness with a kind of loving apprehension in order to inflect that world with one's own emotion or subjectivity. Thus, from Buddhist passivity, with its total receptivity to what is outside us, Wang arrived at a new form of poetic expressionism.

Conclusion: The Emergence of a *Yi*-Centered Theory of Literary Creation

In "Lun Wen Yi," Wang Changling's use of *yi* may seem confusing at first glance. Historically, in fact, his quickly shifting parade of *yi* and *yi*-compounds has baffled and confused readers even up to the present. Once sorted out, though, it becomes clear how Wang intended these complex terms to describe different phases of the creative process. In that respect, as in others, Wang broke new ground: seeing the creation of poetry as a mental process marked by distinct stages makes possible a new appreciation of the final result.

While both Lu Ji and Liu Xie theorized literary creation based on the *yi*→*xiang*→*yan* philosophical paradigm, neither ventured much on the role of *yi* at any creative phase. By contrast, Wang Changling stresses the primacy of *yi* at every creative phase and introduces a rich array of *yi*-compounds: *zuoyi* for initiating transcendent contemplation, *yixiang* for the ideal outcome of envisaging, and *qiyi* for the dynamic mental process behind compositional execution, among others. The underlying theme of this stress on *yi* points to a heightened visuality in his poetics. And that, in turn, we might see as a sign of his desire to make poetry more responsive to the richness and nuances of the world out there. Perhaps the most important breakthrough made by Wang is his use of a Buddhist perspective leading to a transformation of the *yi*→*xiang*→*yan* paradigm into a fourfold one: *yi*→*jing*→*xiang*→*yan*. His introduction of the Buddhist notion of *jing* (inscape) into critical discourse has a profound influence on subsequent development of Chinese poetic and aesthetic theories.

In examining the creative process, Wang follows in the footsteps of Lu Ji and Liu Xie, moving from initial transcendent contemplation (the *yi* phase) through artistic envisaging (the *xiang* phase) to compositional execution (the *yan* phase). Yet how Wang views the first two phases differs fundamentally from Lu and Liu. Regarding the first phase, Wang dispenses with the Daoist trope of transcendent roaming of mind favored by Lu and Liu. Instead, he sees it as an absolutely tranquil and unconscious state of mind, in which the entire object-world is mirrored. The second phase, too, he characterizes in a radically different way. While Lu and Liu contended that artistic envisaging arises from a dynamic interplay of image, feeling, and word in the mind, Wang posits two distinct, successive processes: first an unconscious reproduction of the entire phenomenal world, and then a conscious effort to search and commune with specific objects and images. Virtually all of this bears a clear imprint of Tathāgatagarbha and Yogācāra Buddhist ideas on the workings of the *yi* and *yishi* consciousnesses. By importing Buddhism into his thinking about the initial stages of the poetic process, Wang clearly wanted to bring the external world more into the picture: if poetry is to capture aspects of the world as we know it, that process would have to begin with something like a complete immersion in its phenomenological richness, the plenitude of existing things. By his use of a Buddhist take on *yi*, Wang attests to the Tang dynasty openness to foreign cultural influences, as well as its ability to use these creatively.

Nonetheless, Wang does not remain there. Instead he reverts to the traditional Daoist stance when explaining the last creative phase—translation of envisaging (*xiang*) into language (*yan*). This return to the indigenous Chinese tradition yields an equally important result. Drawing on traditional, Daoist-inspired calligraphy criticism, Wang accomplishes what Lu Ji and Liu Xie failed to do: he illuminates how *yi*, as a dynamic process of envisaging, propels the final compositional act and produces poetry marked by a fusion of feeling and image. This last phase, however, is made possible only by what preceded it, a complete absorption of the world. Only because the mind has absorbed the world, taken it into itself, can it then infuse the particular objects it wants to focus on with its own emotion. So Wang arrives finally at an expressionistic aesthetic, one for which images and the objects represented become expressive of a particular turn of mind.

By exploiting the multivalence of *yi* in such an ingenious fashion, Wang Changling has innovatively rethought all creative phases and cultivated a new appreciation of the final result. Thus we see a coherent *yi*-centered theory of literary creation gradually emerge, one never known before, even though reconstructed here rather than fully articulated by Wang Changling himself. Rivaling Lu Ji's and Liu Xie's theories in many ways, Wang's *yi*-centered theory of literary creation provides later critics, especially those of Ming and Qing times, with a productive competing model for theorizing literary creation.

////////////////////////////////

Notes

1. Wang Changling's authorship of a book titled *Shige* is almost indisputable thanks to the Japanese monk Kūkai, who stayed with and befriended Tang literati in the capital Chang'an, writing about how he came to have the book: "Wang Changling's one-volume *Shige* was obtained by chance from the author when I was in China" 王昌齡《詩格》一卷，此是在唐之日，於作者邊偶得此書 ("Shu Liu Xiyi ji xuan na biao" 書劉希夷集獻納表, in Kūkai, *Kōbō Daishi Kūkai zenshū*, 6:741). However, the existing edition of Wang Changling's *Shige*, collected in the Song anthology *Yinchuang zalu* 吟窗雜錄, is generally considered a mixture of authentic and spurious material. The part of this *Shige* preserved in "Lun Wen Yi" is widely considered Wang's authentic work. For a study on the authenticity of Wang Changling's *Shige*, see Li and Fu, "Tan Wang Changling de *Shi ge*," 85–97; and Luo, *Sui Tang wudai wenxue sixiang shi*.

2. I accept Japanese scholar Jin'ichi Konish's 小西甚一 view that the collection of Wang Changling's ends with a citation of Confucius that begins with "Therefore the *Analects* says" 故《論語》云. See *WJMFL*, 3:3:1286.

3. Wang Changling uses the character *yi* 意 sixty times, either as an independent term or in combination with other characters to form a *yi*-compound.

4. The ubiquity of *yi* prompts Jin'ichi Konish to argue that "Lun Wen Yi" presents a literary theory revolving around *yi*. However, when listing four major theoretical contributions made by this text, he does not relate any of them to *yi*; see *WJMFL*, 3:1393. Wang Yunxi, "Wang Changling de shige lilun," 24, takes note of two different meanings of *yi*, the author's expressive intent and the creative process, but does not investigate any particular instances of it.

5. On Wang Changling's view of *yijing*, see Luo, *Sui Tang wudai wenxue sixiang shi*, 179–83. For a summary of noteworthy studies on this subject, see Bi, *Wang Changling shige yu shixue yanjiu*, 317–20.

6. See Ye Lang, *Zhongguo meixue shi dagang*, 577–641; and Yuan X., *Zhongguo shige yishu yanjiu*, 26–74.

7. See Cai, "Early Philosophical Discourse," 494–510.

8. Unless otherwise indicated, English translations of all passages cited in this chapter are mine.

9. The term *Shige* appears in eleven of the twenty-nine titles collected in Zhang Bowei's *Quan Tang Wudai shige huikao* 全唐五代詩格彙考 (Complete Poetry Manuals of the Tang and Five Dynasties, with Collated Investigations), cited here as *QTWDSG*.

10. See Huang J., *Yijing lun de xingcheng*, 137–38; and Li L., "Wang Changling *Shige*," 94–96.

11. For English-language studies on Liu Xie's "Shensi" chapter, see Egan, "Poet, Mind, and World"; and S. Lin, "Liu Xie on Imagination."

12. Zhang Yanyuan, *Fashu yaolu*, 184.

13. See, e.g., these lines by Lu Ji:

> And when it is attained: light gathers about moods [*qing*] and they grow in brightness,
> Things [*wu*] become luminous and draw one another forward;
> I quaff the word-hoard's spray of droplets,
> And roll in my mouth the sweet moisture of the Classics;
>
> . . .
>
> Then, phrases from the depths emerge struggling as when the swimming fish, hooks in their mouths, emerge from the bottom of the deepest pool;
> And drifting intricacies of craft flutter down, as when the winging bird, caught by stringed arrow, plummets from the tiered clouds.
> (Owen, *Readings in Chinese Literary Thought*, 98, 101; see *WFJS*, 36)

14. For a careful study of the historical evolution of the term, see Huang J., *Yijing lun de xingcheng*, 1–134.

15. The six categories of phenomena are *se* 色, *sheng* 聲, *xiang* 香, *wei* 味, *chu* 觸, *fa* 法; the six corresponding senses are *yan* 眼, *er* 耳, *bi* 鼻, *she* 舌, *shen* 身, and *yi* 意. Wang Changling's adaptation of the sixth, or *yishi* 意識, for his theory of literary creation is discussed in the penultimate section of this chapter.

16. Wang Changling, *Shige*, in *QTWDSG*, 173.

17. *Hanfeizi jijie, juan* 20, 148.
18. This verbal compound, written as 意想 and meaning "to imagine," should not be confused with its homonym *yixiang* 意象, a nominal compound meaning "conception-image." Except for this case, *yixiang* discussed in this chapter pertains to "conception-image."
20. Wang Changling, *Shige*, in Zhang B., *Quan Tang wudi shige huikao*, 173.
21. Fan Ye, "Letter to My Nephews Written in Prison" 獄中與諸甥侄書, appended to Fan Y., *Hou Han shu*, vol. 12.
22. On the theoretical significance of this introduction of an individual self, see Zhang Jing, "Yijing yu shenti." On the complex relationship between the individual self and general subjectivity in Wang's own poetry, see Varsano, "Whose Voice Is It Anyway?," 1–25.
23. For an analysis of this important text on the *Book of Poetry*, see Cai, *Configurations of Comparative Poetics*, 44–49.
24. Wang C., *Shige*, 173.
25. This point has been noted in Huang J., *Yijing lun de xingcheng*, 147–72.
26. See Zhang C., *Shulun jiyao*, 15–16.
27. Wang Xizhi, "Diagram of the Battle Array of the Brush" 題衛夫人筆陣圖後, collected in *Zhongguo meixueshi ziliao xuanbian*, 1:173.
28. Sun Guoting, *Sun Guoting shupu jianzheng*, 91.
29. On the much praised appeal of this famous couplet, see Cai, "Synthesis Rhythm, Syntax, and Vision of Chinese Poetry," 385–86.
30. This gestalt not only guides Wang's own composition of recent-style poetry but also lays the groundwork for Ming-Qing critics' more sophisticated structural analysis of recent-style poetry. See Wen Shuang, "Jintishi de chengshu," 27–33; and Wang D., "Wang Changling yu," 99–104.
31. Aśvaghoṣa, *Awakening of Faith*, translated with commentary by Yoshito S. Hakeda, 47.
32. Ibid., 47–48; with a Chinese character added and some modification.
33. Ibid.; with modifications in the first half of the translated passage.
34. Ibid., 49.
35. Note that the term *yi* is also frequently used in a positive sense as a description of a Boddhisattva's transforming mind, as shown in the following remarks by Aśvaghoṣa:

> The Bodhisattvas in their first stage of aspiration [*fayi* 發意] and the others, because of their deep faith in Suchness, have a partial insight into [the nature of the influence of Suchness]. They know that the things [of the Bliss-body], such as its corporeal forms, major marks, adornments, etc., do not come from without or go away, that they are free from limitations, and that they are envisioned by the mind alone and are not independent of Suchness.
>
> 初發意菩薩等所見者，以深信真如法故，少分而見，知彼色相莊嚴等事，無來無去，離於分齊。唯依心現，不離真如。(*T* 32n1666_001; translation by Hakeda from Aśvaghoṣa, *Awakening of Faith*, 71, with two Chinese characters added to the translated passage).

In the compound *fayi* 發意, translated as "aspiration" by Hakeda, the character *yi* obviously refers to a stage of the mind that affords insight to Suchness, the Buddha nature. Such a laudatory use of *yi* encourages critics like Wang Changling to apply it when theorizing about literary creation.

Chapter 5

Qi- and Chan-Centered Theories of Literary Creation in the Tang-Song Period

The Tang-Song period (618–1279) saw the rise of both the *qi* 氣 (lifebreath)-centered theory, founded by Han Yu 韓愈 (768–824) in the mid-Tang, and the *chan* 禪 (enlightenment)-centered theory, pioneered by Su Shi 蘇軾 (1037–1101) in the late Northern Song. Blazing the trail for new ways to think about literary creation, they truncated Lu Ji's, Liu Xie's, and Wang Changling's comprehensive investigations (see chaps. 2 and 4), turning their attention almost exclusively to the first creative phase (the writer's physical and mental preparations), given least attention by Lu, Liu, and Wang. This shift reflects the profound changes in both literary practice and theory taking place in Han Yu's and Su Shi's times.

By the mid-Tang, the Six Dynasties' belletristic obsessions, particularly the pursuit of parallel phrasing and metrical patterning, had largely run its course. Divorced from ethico-sociopolitical concerns and dominated by literati from aristocratic clans, Six Dynasties literature was increasingly condemned by Tang Confucian scholars as a decadent tradition and even blamed for the successive downfalls within the Six Dynasties. Rather than take this radical Confucian approach and banish all literature, Han Yu sought to save the proverbial baby from the bathwater by launching a new literary tradition that simultaneously inculcates Confucian ethico-sociopolitical values and affords aesthetic pleasures. His point of breakthrough was prose, a genre where Six Dynasties' rigid yet florid formalism reached its extreme. By launching his Ancient-Style Prose movement (Guwen yundong 古文運動), Han aimed to create a competing kind of prose that emulates both the form and the content of ancient Confucian works. Exemplified by his own writings, this new ancient-style prose unambiguously expresses Confucian ethico-sociopolitical ideas while deploying natural language rhythms, marked by alternating long and short sentences. It is no surprise, then, that Han Yu would ditch Lu Ji's and Liu Xie's theories: with their *yi→xiang→yan* paradigm that largely shuns ethico-sociopolitical concerns, they were written in the rigid parallel forms Han Yu sought to demolish. Asked by a disciple how he mastered

PRISM: THEORY AND MODERN CHINESE LITERATURE • 20 (ANNUAL SUPPL.) • DECEMBER 2023
DOI 10.1215/25783491-11080885 • © 2023 LINGNAN UNIVERSITY

the art of writing, Han Yu's answer essentially constitutes a new theory of literary creation, one grounded in Mencius's famous remark on the "flood-like *qi*" (lifebreath) (see §27).[1]

Roughly three hundred years later, Su Shi engineered yet another shift in the theorizing of literary creation, namely, a turn toward the then flourishing Chan Buddhism. In rethinking art and literary creation from a Buddhist perspective, Su followed a tack quite different from that of Wang Changling, who made extensive use of Buddhist terms and concepts without openly acknowledging his Buddhist sources. Wang employed Buddhist terms and concepts almost surreptitiously within the traditional *yi→xiang→yan* paradigm. By contrast, Su Shi wrote to a Buddhist monk, sharing his thoughts on the Buddhist idea of Samadhi, a tranquil and transcendent mental state, and in the process elucidates the very essence of art and literary creation. This chapter explores how Su's notion of Chan differs from Han Yu's notion of spontaneous creativity.

The first person to perceive and elucidate the fundamental differences between their notions of spontaneous creativity is none other than Su Shi himself. The occasion for Su's elucidation was Han Yu's disparaging comments on Buddhism's ascetic lifestyle and its effect on the calligraphy of his monk-friend Gao Xian 高閑 (fl. late eighth century). Believing that art and literary creation are born of a flood-like surplus of lifebreath (*qi*), Han asserted that the monk's ascetic, quietist Buddhist lifestyle was bound to emaciate his body and dry up all his creative energy. In the poem "Seeing Off Canliao," written for his own monk-friend, Su repudiated Han's assertion by arguing that only the quietest contemplation can bring forth "ten thousand scenes," namely, reveal the true world or inscape of all worlds. Although Su did not explicitly reference Chan Buddhism in his poem, it was not lost on anyone that the transcendent state of the mind was none other than Chan. Historically speaking, Su's praise of Chan practically opened the floodgates for the voluminous statements on Chan enlightenment as the primary, even exclusive, factor for literary creation from his time through the end of the Southern Song. I show below how these statements eventually coalesced and evolved into a cogent Chan-centered theory of literary creation articulated in Yan Yu's 嚴羽 (?–ca. 1245) *Canglang's Remarks on Poetry* (Canglang shihua 滄浪詩話).

The *Qi*-Centered Theory of Literary Creation

To understand the intellectual background for Han Yu's *qi*-centered theory, we should bypass Wang Changling's *yi*-centered theory immediately preceding and trace it back first to Liu Xie's grand genealogy of *wen*, and then further back to Mencius's notion of the "flood-like *qi*" (lifebreath).

Han Yu very likely owes a debt to Liu Xie. His influential essay "Tracing the Dao as the Source" (Yuan Dao 原道) strikes me as heavily influenced by Liu Xie's *Literary Mind and the Carving of Dragons* 文心雕龍 (hereafter *Literary Mind*).

Not only did Han borrow his title from the *Literary Mind*'s first chapter, but he also mapped out a grand genealogy. In the first three chapters of *Literary Mind*, Liu Xie builds a massive genealogy of *wen* coterminous with the patterns of heaven and earth, on the one hand, and the history of human civilization, on the other. It encompasses all kinds of *wen* or cultural patternings through the ages: Paoxi's creation of the eight trigrams, the ritual and music of the Shang and Zhou, the classical texts from Qin and Han, all the way down to the belles lettres in the Six Dynasties. In his genealogy, sages occupy the pivotal position: "Dao is handed down in writing through the sages, and sages make Dao manifest in writing" 道沿聖以垂文，聖因文以明道 (*WXDL*, 1/110–11). The practice of literary writing, therefore, is inseparable from learning the sages' texts. Likely emulating Liu's endeavor, Han constructed a grand genealogy of Confucian sages from legendary antiquity to his own time.

While Han could not match Liu on the scale of his genealogy, he succeeded where Liu had conspicuously failed: he connected the sages' writing and the creative process. Despite all his emphasis on the sages' pivotal role, Liu Xie completely forgot the sages when discussing the creative process and analyzed the four creative phases from a purely aesthetic perspective (see §§40–41, 44, 46–47, 49). It sounds as if validating *wen* through the sages and reverence for the classics had become empty doctrines irrelevant to the actual writing process. But precisely for this reason, Liu Xie left ample room for later generations to develop a Confucian theory of literary creation. Han Yu would make perfect use of this space to successfully connect Confucian sages and literary creation.

To my mind, Han Yu owes a good deal of this success to his creative adoption of Mencius's notion of *yangqi* 養氣 (nourishing lifebreath). When asked what he is good at, Mencius says, "I have an insight into words. I am good at cultivating my 'flood-like *qi*.' . . . There is *qi* which, in the highest degree, is vast and unyielding. Nourish it with integrity and place no obstacle in its path and it will fill the space between Heaven and Earth. It is the *qi* which unites rightness and the Way."[2] Here, Mencius effectively transforms what the *Guanzi* compilers have said of Daoist sages' omnipotent and omniscient mind-lifebreath (*xinqi* 心氣) (see §§25–26) into a world-transforming force, which a living Confucian like himself could nourish by blending his lifebreath with Confucian moral ideals. To Mencius, the flood-like lifebreath is the integral unity among body, intellect (shown by an understanding of words), and morality. Mind and body, two distinct categories in Western philosophy, are inseparable in his Confucian thought.

In Mencius's account of this flood-like lifebreath as well as its association with words, Han Yu seems to find license for his reasoning: if Confucian sages' flood-like lifebreath infuses and perfects their writings, surely lifelong immersion in their works will not only endow writers with their moral qualities but also inspire great writing as well. Although Han Yu does not announce it, this reasoning clearly undergirds his account of his own growth as a master writer in his "Letter in Reply to Li Yi" 答李翊書:

§108

[1] Those aspiring to emulate the ancients to establish their [immortal] selves by means of words cannot expect quick success and cannot be seduced by power and gains. [As with plants], they must cultivate their roots and make them strong, must supply nutrients to make themselves shine. When roots are sturdy, good fruits will grow; when nutrients are abundantly applied, leaves will be luxuriant. This is how a man of benevolence and righteousness comes to have his amiable words.

將蘄至於古之立言者，則無望其速成，無誘於勢利，養其根竢其實，加其膏而希其光。根之茂者其實遂，膏之沃者其光煜，仁義之人，其言藹如也。

[2] To accomplish this is surely very difficult and, much as I endeavored, I am not sure if I have done it. Nonetheless, I tried to learn this [way of writing] for more than twenty years. When I first began, I dared not look at any books but those from three ancient dynasties and the Former and Later Han, and I dared not harbor any intent unworthy of the sages. When I stayed home, I felt as if I had grown forgetful; when I walked, I felt as if I had left things behind. I looked earnest and was lost in thought, and I seemed perplexed as if I had lost my way. When I sought to put what's in my mind into my writing hand, I sought to get rid of all clichés. I found how hard that was as I was grinding along. When I showed my writing to others, I did not know their opposition and mockeries were actually of no consequence.

抑又有難者，愈之所為，不自知其至猶未也。雖然，學之二十餘年矣。始者，非三代兩漢之書不敢觀，非聖人之志不敢存，處若忘，行若遺，儼乎其若思，茫乎其若迷。當其取於心而注於手也，惟陳言之務去，戛戛乎其難哉！其觀於人，不知其非笑之為非笑也。

[3] This persisted for a number of years, but I did not swerve. Then I learned how to tell true from spurious in ancient books. When things were clearly distinguished like black and white, I sought to remove [what's wrong] and gradually made progress. When I sought to put what's in my mind into my writing hand, I found all flowed smoothly like a swift stream. When I showed my writing to others, I took delight when they mocked me, but felt worried when hearing their praise, which showed that elements of their thought remained in my writing.

如是者亦有年，猶不改，然後識古書之正偽，與雖正而不至焉者，昭昭然白黑分矣，而務去之，乃徐有得也。當其取於心而注於手也，汩汩然來矣。其觀於人也，笑之則以為喜，譽之則以為憂，以其猶有人之說者存也。

[4] This persisted for more years, and then [my writing] came surging along like an expansive flood. As I still feared a mingling of impurities, I approached my writing from a distance and calmly observed it. When all was found to be pure, I give myself great abandon. Still, I cannot cease to cultivate myself. This is what I am resolved to do to the end of my life: to act on the path of benevolence and righteousness, and to journey through the sources of the *Book of Poetry* and the *Book of Documents*. I will never lose my way on that path and will never exhaust those sources.

如是者亦有年，然後浩乎其沛然矣。吾又懼其雜也，迎而距之，平心而察之，其皆醇也，然後肆焉。雖然，不可以不養也。行之乎仁義之途，遊之乎《詩》《書》之源，無迷其途，無絕其源，終吾身而已矣。

[5] Lifebreath is like water; and words, the objects that float on it. When water is vast, all floatable objects, big or small, stay afloat. This is what lifebreath is to words. When lifebreath is full and vast, all words fit with perfect variation in line length and tone pitch.

氣，水也；言，浮物也。水大而物之浮者大小畢浮。氣之與言猶是也。氣盛，則言之短長與聲之高下皆宜。[3]

For clearer analysis, I have divided this long passage into five sections. In section 1, Han tells us that lifelong devotion to moral cultivation is the secret of success of all the ancients who achieved immortal fame through writings. The next three sections depict specific activities: study of classics, spontaneous writing, and reflection on other's perceptions. Section 2 describes how Han immersed himself in the study of the classics for twenty years or so but still had trouble getting rid of clichés, even though he was spontaneously inspired to write. What is more, he still didn't know that other people's ridicule of his writing was actually of no consequence. Section 3 recounts progress in each of the three aforementioned activities. Han's immersive study of classics now becomes more analytical as he is able to distinguish right from spurious and even discern the imperfect within the right. When inspired to write, he finds that words well up like a vigorous flow. His attitude toward others' opinions of his writing, too, changes for the better: now he takes delight in other's mockery and grows worried about hearing praise for fear his writing still contains the unwholesome ideas of his contemporaries. Section 4 tells us how, as a result of sustained immersion in classics for years, he now writes vigorously, as if spurred by a vast, flood-like torrent, and with great abandon.

In section 5, we finally realize that Han is actually adopting Mencius's notion of flood-like lifebreath to characterize the source of his spontaneous creativity. He uses powerful images of flowing water ("smoothly like a swift stream" and "surging along like an expansive flood") to describe the powerful inspiration arising from long immersion in the ancient classics. All of this leads up to his announcement that a writer's spontaneous creativity is nothing but an overflow of *qi* or lifebreath. By comparing this lifebreath to water and words to objects floating on it, Han aims to make this emphatic point: excellent writings with natural, perfect line lengths and tone variations arise as inevitably and effortlessly as buoyant objects float. Once cultivated, our flood-like *qi* not only embodies morality but also produces naturally beautiful musical cadences—very different from the artificial tonal rules imposed on parallel prose.[4]

These insights of Han Yu inevitably invite comparison with Cao Pi's 曹丕 (187–226) famous remarks some six hundred years earlier. Cao Pi's notion of *qi* is one of pure aestheticism: by emphasizing a work's qualities as direct manifestations of the writer's unique lifebreath, Cao expresses an elitist belief in literary genius as neither inherited nor learned. By contrast, we might call Han Yu's *yangqi* a type of moral aestheticism intended to link moral cultivation and artistic pursuit. As much as Cao's notion is elitist, Han's is popular in that it stresses great literature may be produced by anyone willing to immerse themselves in Confucian classics to nourish sage-like lifebreath. For Tang-Song literati, this *qi*-centered theory of literary creation offers an ideal middle ground between the antibelletristic stance of neo-Confucian moralists and the fervent elitism of Six Dynasties literati. Han Yu's middle-of-the-road approach surely helped ensure the sustained, broad appeal of his *qi*-centered theory of literary creation throughout the Tang-Song period. To observe this lasting impact, we turn to its eloquent elucidation given more than two hundred years later by Su Che 蘇轍 (1039–1112), Su Shi's younger brother, in his "Letter to Grand Guardian Han of the Palace Secretariat":

§109

The Honorable Grand Guardian:

I, Che, am fond of refined writing and have some deep thought about it. I believe that refined writing is the manifestation of *qi* or lifebreath and therefore we can become good at it, not through learning but by cultivating our lifebreath. Mencius says, "I am good at nourishing my flood-like lifebreath." When we now look at his writings they are indeed broad, deep, and expansive, overflowing between heaven and earth, and thus do match the scale of his lifebreath. The Grand Historian traveled all over the world and viewed all famous mountains and great rivers within the four seas, and he befriended and journeyed with people of exceptional abilities in the regions of Yan and Zhao. As a result, his writings are vigorous and uninhibited and brim with a spectacular lifebreath. Did Mencius and the Grand Historian ever learn with a writing brush to compose such great writings? Their lifebreath is overflowing from within to their outer appearance, pulsating through their words and manifesting itself in their writings, without the writers being aware of it.

太尉執事：轍生好為文，思之至深。以為文者，氣之所形，然文不可以學而能，氣可以養而致。孟子曰："我善養吾浩然之氣。" 今觀其文章，寬厚宏博，充乎天地之間，稱其氣之小大。太史公行天下，周覽四海名山大川，與燕、趙間豪俊交遊，故其文疏蕩，頗有奇氣。此二子者，豈嘗執筆學為如此之文哉？其氣充乎其中而溢乎其貌，動乎其言而見乎其文，而不自知也。(*SCJ*, 381–82)

Su Che begins the letter by making three important statements on the relationship between lifebreath and literature that enable us to understand Han Yu's *yangqi* theory in a better light. The first, "I believe that refined writing is the manifestation of *qi* or lifebreath and therefore we can become good at it, not through learning but by cultivating our lifebreath," explains well the reason behind Han Yu's earlier eschewal of the *yi→xiang→yan* paradigm. Su Che's second statement, "Mencius says, 'I am good at nourishing my flood-like lifebreath.' When we now look at them, his writings are indeed broad, deep, and expansive, overflowing between heaven and earth, and thus do match the scale of his lifebreath," spells out another two points that Han Yu himself did not explain but are essential to understanding his lifelong *yangqi* practice. First, the lifebreath Han sought to nourish is none other than Mencius's flood-like lifebreath imbued with moral righteousness; second, Han urged a total immersion in the classics because these works are the embodiment of their authors' lifebreath, just as Su notes in the case of Mencius's writings. The third statement, "Their lifebreath is overflowing from within to their outer appearance, pulsating through their words and manifesting itself in their writings, without the writers being aware of it," is no doubt a poetic reaffirmation of Han Yu's belief that well-nourished lifebreath spontaneously gives birth to great literary works.

In this opening passage, Su Che also makes an important extrapolation: sublime natural scenery, too, has a way of imparting its own special lifebreath into one's writings, as in the prominent case of the Grand Historian Sima Qian 司馬遷 (145 or 135 BCE–?). Su Che goes on to broaden the scope of Han Yu's *qi*-centered theory as he recounts his own experience nourishing *qi* through the grand views of heaven and earth:

§110

Until I was nineteen years old, I stayed at home and made journeys only with folks in the neighborhood. The scope of my sightseeing was limited to an area of several hundred *li*. What's more, there are no high mountains or an expansive plain around for me to climb and stretch my horizons. Similarly, although I read books extensively and did not leave out any of the one hundred schools, they were merely traces left behind by ancients and are not sufficient to inspire my ambition or "intent-breath" [*zhiqi*]. Fearing that my life would be wasted away, I resolved to leave home to visit storied places and see grand views, hoping to know the greatness of heaven and earth. I passed through the ancient capitals of the Qin and Han, observed the heights of the Zhongnan, Song, and Hua mountains, looked northward toward the surging flow of the Yellow River, and there and then imagined seeing the great heroes of ancient times. Upon arriving at our capital, I looked up at the grandeur of the palaces of the Son of Heaven, marveled at the wealth and size of the granaries, court treasury, city walls and moats, and imperial gardens, and thus got to know the so-called colossal beauty [*juli*] of the world. Then, I met the Imperial Secretary, the Honorable Ouyang, listened to his eloquent elucidation of political discourses, and observed the grace of his appearance and demeanor, and made excursions with his following of disciples, worthies, and officials. After all this, I came to realize that this was where all the great refined writings of the world converged.

轍生十有九年矣。其居家所與遊者,不過其鄰里鄉黨之人,所見不過數百里之間,無高山大野,可登覽以自廣。百氏之書,雖無所不讀,然皆古人之陳跡,不足以激發其志氣。恐遂汩沒,故決然舍去,求天下奇聞壯觀,以知天地之廣大。過秦、漢之故都,恣觀終南、嵩、華之高,北顧黃河之奔流,慨然想見古之豪傑。至京師,仰觀天子宮闕之壯,與倉廩、府庫、城池、苑囿之富且大也,而後知天下之巨麗。見翰林歐陽公,聽其議論之宏辯,觀其容貌之秀偉,與其門人賢士大夫遊,而後知天下之文章聚乎此也。(*SCJ*, 381–82)

In this letter Su Che explicitly places Sima Qian's historical writings and Ouyang Xiu's 歐陽修 (1007–1072) prose alongside the Confucian canon as sources that nourish the lifebreath. Viewing spectacular nature and architecture complements this moral-aesthetic education as the writer imbibes the cosmic energy necessary for great writing. Through these remarks, Su Che makes the Tang-Song *qi*-centered theory of literature more well-rounded and inclusive. Strange, I note in passing, that so brilliantly conceived and energetically and beautifully written a letter ends so anticlimactically when the author shifts to embarrassing flattery of his powerful addressee, a top military commander at the time, with the hope of securing an appointment.

The Chan-Centered Theory of Literary Creation

If Su Che's "Letter to Grand Guardian Han of the Palace Secretariat" marks the culmination of *qi*-centered theory, his elder brother Su Shi's ancient-style poem, "Seeing Off Canliao," may be seen as ushering in a Chan-centered theory that will dominate Southern Song literary thought. On the historic significance of Su Shi's poem, Wang Shihan 汪師韓 (1707–1774) writes:

§111

Dwelling on the same theme as Han Yu's comments on the revered Gao Xian's cursive calligraphy, [this poem] reverses Han's stance and presents a counterview, attaining to the *samadhi* of the laws of poetry. Later Yan Yu consistently discusses poetry by drawing analogies between Chan and poetry, even dividing poetry schools in terms of [great vs. small] vehicles and sects. This poem illuminates the path for Yan Yu.

取韓愈論高閒上人草書之旨，而反其意以論詩，正得詩法三昧者。其後嚴羽遂專以禪喻詩，至為分別宗乘，此篇早已為之點出光明。[5]

With the phrase "reverses his [Han Yu's] stance" (*fan qiyi*), Wang registers Su Shi's strong opposition to the primacy Han gives *qishi* (lifebreath and momentum), a primacy noted above in discussing Han's "Letter to Li Yi" (see §108). Su Shi's poem is particularly illuminating here because it sets forth the essential differences between Han Yu's *qi*-centered theory and the Chan-centered theory he advocated, especially with regard to their respective understandings of successful literary creations' optimal conditions. Now let us closely examine this poem:

§112

Seeing Off Canliao		**送參寥詩**
	A revered monk practices extreme self-denying emptiness,	上人學苦空
2	All desires are reduced to cold ashes.	百念已灰冷
	Blowing through a hilt hole makes only a humming sound,	劍頭惟一吷
4	Burned millet puts forth no new bud.	焦穀無新穎
	How come you chase after men of our kind,	胡為逐吾輩
6	Striving to produce brilliant and luminous words?	文字爭蔚炳
	Your recent poems are like tiny pieces of jade,	新詩如玉屑
8	With expressions sharp and refreshing.	出語便清警
	Tuizhi commented on [Zhang Xu's] cursive script:	退之論草書
10	All worldly affairs have not been forsaken,	萬事未嘗屏
	Worry, sadness, and grievances	憂愁不平氣
12	Surge forward at the darting of the brush.	一寓筆所騁
	It's strange that [it is] by a Buddhist monk	頗怪浮屠人
14	Who sees his body as an empty well	視身如丘井
	And has kept his life plain and aloof from strife.	頹然寄淡泊
16	Who on earth lets loose this boldness and power for him?	誰與發豪猛
	Upon reflection, I see this thought is incorrect.	細思乃不然
18	True ingenuity is no delusion.	真巧非幻影
	If you want to make your poetic expressions wondrous,	欲令詩語妙
20	Don't be averse to emptiness and quietude.	無厭空且靜
	In quietude you comprehend all movements,	靜故了羣動

22	With emptiness you embrace ten thousand scenes.	空故納萬境
	You experience the world in the midst of men,	閱世走人間
24	You meditate by yourself, lying under a cloudy peak.	觀身臥雲嶺
	When the salty and sour are mixed with other tastes,	鹹酸雜眾好
26	Within them is a flavor perfect and lasting.	中有至味永
	Poetry and dharma do not impede each other,	詩法不相妨
28	This view I beg you to consider.	此語更當請[6]

Su Shi wrote this poem on the occasion of seeing off his friend, Canliao, courtesy name of the prominent Song monk Daoqian道潛 (1043–1106) Su Shi befriended during his exile in Huangzhou. Instead of writing about friendship and the sadness of parting typical of a farewell poem, Su presents a cogent exposition on the optimal conditions for producing great poetry.

The poem has a clear tripartite structure often seen in argument essays. The first part (lines 1–8) presents a question that has puzzled Su Shi: How is it that his revered friend, who has given up all desire, sees the world as light as a breeze through a sword hilt's tiny hole, and has a gaunt body like a scorched grain, can vie with literati like himself, producing poems refined as jade and with refreshing expressions? Does Canliao's Buddhist lifestyle have anything to do with his literary achievement?

The second part (lines 9–16) infers a likely neo-Confucian negative answer by citing Han Yu's farewell poem for his friend the Revered Gaoxian, in which he blames his friend's ascetic Buddhist lifestyle for sapping his lifebreath and the emotionally charged energy needed to produce great calligraphy. Han Yu holds up Zhang Xu as a positive example of someone driven by the force of emotions to produce his cursive script known for its dazzling display of dynamic force. Han's praise of Zhang Xu is obviously in sync with his *qi*-centered theory discussed above.

The third part (lines 17–28) presents a positive Buddhist answer to the question raised in the first lines. Here Su Shi argues that Buddhists in tranquil contemplation are able to reach this state: "With emptiness you embrace ten thousand scenes." In other words, they reveal the true reality (*shixiang* 實相) behind the phenomenal world. This description of Buddhism's penetrating, transcendent power strikes me as similar, almost identical, to Wang Changling's description of "inscape of physical things" (see §74), but there is an important difference: while Wang only surreptitiously employs Buddhist terms and concepts, Su Shi openly praises its quietist lifestyle as the unrivaled precondition for producing the greatest poetry. His unbounded admiration for Buddhism is powerfully communicated with his ending couplet: "Poetry and dharma do not impede each other, / This view I beg you to consider."

Su Shi's claim that "poetry and dharma do not impede each other" marks the formal entry of Buddhism into Chinese literary thought, especially with respect to theorizing literary creation. Soon *Chan*, the term for *samadhi* (enlightenment), became the catchphrase on everyone's lips, and the writing of doggerel-like quatrains with the generic title "Poems on Learning to Write Poetry" became a vogue lasting into the Ming. The plain vernacular language used in these quatrains was well suited for popular tastes and quickly became a style "delightful to the ear and eye" (*xiwen lejian* 喜聞樂見). Among famous examples of such quatrains are these written by Wu Ke 吳可 (fl. 1107–1110), active in the decade after Su Shi's passing.

§113

Learning to write poetry is just like learning to practice Chan,	學詩渾似學參禪
Countless years spent on bamboo floor and meditation mat.	竹榻蒲團不計年
Until one comes to a total understanding	直待自家都了得
and effortlessly brings forth a poem, with a sense of lofty detachment.	等閒拈出便超然
Learning to write poetry is just like learning to practice Chan,	學詩渾似學參禪
"Installing a head on the head" will not produce anything worthy of transmission.	頭上安頭不足傳
Breaking from the worn tropes of Shaoling,	跳出少陵窠臼外
The heroic breath of a great man will soar to the skies as destined.	丈夫志氣本沖天
Learning to write poetry is just like learning to practice Chan,	學詩渾似學參禪
How many perfect couplets are there since ancient times?	自古圓成有幾聯
The line "Spring grass [grows] on the pond"	春草池塘一句子
Astonishes heaven and moves the earth, as known to this day.	驚天動地至今傳
	(*ZGLDWLX*, 3:345)

If Su Shi uses serious philosophical terminology to explicate the identical nature of poetry-writing and Chan meditation, Wu Ke simply uses vernacular Chan witticisms to deliver two resounding messages. The first is that you should not waste countless years trying to write poetry because the finest poetry always comes to you spontaneously. The second is that you should break free from the entrenched practice of imitating Du Fu 杜甫 (712–770) and instead produce poetry spontaneously in the way of Chan meditation.

Gong Xiang's 龔相 (fl. 1153) "Poems on Learning to Write Poetry," written in the same style, launches a more vehement attack on the Jiangxi school, whose dictum "'transmuting iron into gold,'" he claims, is delusional. He directs his criticism at Huang Tingjian 黃庭堅 (1045–1105), founder of the Jiangxi school.

§114

Learning to write poetry is just like learning to practice Chan,	學詩渾似學參禪
Only when enlightened does one notice years gone by.	悟了方知歲是年
"Transmute iron into gold" is only a delusion,	點鐵成金猶是妄
Lofty mountains and flowing water are what they are by themselves.	高山流水自依然
Learning to write poetry is just like learning to practice Chan,	學詩渾似學參禪
Words can be arranged but *yi* cannot be communicated.	語可安排意莫傳
When *yi* is intuited all matters of prosody are transcended,	會意即超聲律界
There is no need to melt rocks to fix the broken blue skies.	不須煉石補青天
Learning to write poetry is just like learning to practice Chan,	學詩渾似學參禪
How many times have you wracked your brain to search for lines and couplets?	幾許搜腸覓句聯
If you want to know what is wondrous about Shaoling,	欲識少陵奇絕處
Seek where words and sentences were not yet formed or transmitted.	初無言句與人傳
	(*ZGLDWLX*, 3:348)

Examining this set of quatrains, we can see repeated emphases on three essential features of the finest poetry. The first is its transcendent tenor, described with the Chan Buddhist term *wu* 悟 ("awakening" or "enlightenment") in the first quatrain and with the Buddhistic term *yi* 意 in the second—here *yi* has outgrown its indigenous original sense and refers to a realization of Buddhist transcendent consciousness, as in Wang Changling's writings (see §§80–82, 103–6). Though less foreign sounding, the phrase 會意 (meeting or realizing the *yi*) is essentially identical with *zuoyi* 作意 and *qiyi* 起意 used by Wang Changling (see also §§103–6). The second, emphatic point is that the attainment of *yi* makes obsolete all linguistic efforts, especially the fruitless attempts to imitate Du Fu's lines, couplets, and prosody, as criticized in the second and third quatrains. The third point is that poems born of Chan awakening are as natural and perfect as "Lofty mountains and flowing waters in and of themselves." To borrow two famous lines from Southern Song poet Xia Yuanding 夏元鼎 (fl. 1200), "What cannot be found by a long hard search and after iron shoes are worn through / is obtained with no effort at all" 踏破鐵鞋無覓處，得來全不費工夫.[7] The finest poetry need not be sought from outside; it lies right in the poet's mind at the moment of enlightenment.

Dai Fugu 戴復古 (1167–1248) makes an analogy between Chan meditation and the process of poetry making in a set of poems bearing a long title or, rather, a de facto preface: "Wang Ziwen, Governor of Zhaowu Military Prefecture, reads one or two poets of the older generation as well as Late Tang poetry every day with Li Jia and Yan Yu. Thereupon, I wrote ten quatrains discussing poetry. Upon reading them, Ziwen commented, 'They contain nothing special, but provide rudimentary knowledge for beginning students of poetry'" 昭武太守王子文，日與李賈、嚴羽共觀前輩一兩家詩及晚唐詩，因有論詩十絕。子文見之，謂無甚高論，亦可作詩家小學須知：

§115

Deliberating on poetic prosody is like practicing Chan,	欲參詩律似參禪
Inspired interest cannot be communicated with words.	妙趣不由文字傳
Even if the meditative mind gets enlightened only a bit,	個裏稍關心有誤[悟]
Its expression in words displays lofty detachment.	發為言句自超然
Poetry is originally shapeless and exists in the dark and mysterious,	詩本無形在窈冥
enmeshing heaven and earth and enabling the chanting of emotions.	網絡天地運吟情
At times astounding lines are suddenly dashed out:	有時忽得驚人句
A feat that cannot be accomplished by wracking one's mind.	費盡心機做不成[8]

These two quatrains differ considerably from Wu Ke's and Gong Xiang's. In form, neither begins with the set line "Learning to write poetry is just like learning to practice Chan." In content, the difference is more significant. While Wu and Gong categorically dismiss the learning of poetic techniques, Dai's first quatrain begins by talking about learning prosody, arguably the most technical aspect of poetry writing. The phrase *miaoqu* 妙趣 (inspired interest) in the second line is often used by Buddhist-minded critics to describe the transcendent Buddhist tenor of a work of art, most often with an accompanying claim that tenor cannot be captured or transmitted by words. It seems the second couplet attempts to solve this contradiction: how can transcendent tenor reside in the words of a poem and yet cannot be transmitted by words? The poet devises a clear answer: it is by a minor slip that the transcendent mind lets itself appear in words. Nonetheless, the words flowing from such a transcendent mind, Dai claims, are perfectly natural and extraordinary. The second quatrain begins with a general statement that poetry, in its original, preexpressive form, is inseparable from mysterious cosmic processes operating in heaven and earth. The second couplet tells of a sudden, unself-conscious acquisition of a miraculous poetic line that no one can produce through conscious effort. This, Dai seems to say, is the way Chan enlightenment gives birth to great poetry.

Many scholars regard Yan Yu's *Canglang's Remarks on Poetry* as the crowning achievement in adopting Chan Buddhist ideas to develop a new theory of literary creation. Yan far surpasses the slogans of Wu's and Gong's "Poems on Learning to Write Poetry," instead employing more elegant language to present a cogent and thorough analysis of two aspects seen in both poetry and Chan practice, namely, "wondrous enlightenment" and "thorough deliberation":

§116

With regard to the development of Chan Buddhism, there is a distinction between the Great Vehicle and the Lesser Vehicle [in Buddhism as whole], between the Southern and Northern schools [in Chan Buddhism], and between correct and incorrect Ways. A Chan practitioner must follow the highest vehicle, possess the true dharma eye, and attain enlightenment of the first order. If one practices the Chan of the Small Vehicle with the aim of becoming a *shravaka* (who attains arhathood by hearing the Buddha's teachings) or a *pratyekabuddhas* (who attains arhathood by themselves), one is on the incorrect path. Discussing poetry is like discussing Chan. The poetry of the Han, Wei, Jin, and High Tang constitutes [enlightenment of] the first order. Poetry since the Dali reign is comparable to the Chan of the Lesser Vehicle and falls to the second order. Poetry of the late Tang is comparable to the attainment of a *shravaka* or a *pratyekabuddha*. Those who learn from the poetry of the Han, Wei, Jin, and High Tang are comparable to followers of the Linji sect [of Chan Buddhism]. Those who learn from poetry since the Dali reign are comparable to followers of the Caodong sect. Generally speaking, the way of Chan lies in wondrous awakening and the way of poetry, too, lies in wondrous awakening. Meng Haoran's scholarly abilities are inferior to Han Yu's, but his poetry is superior to Han's, and the reason is: Meng strives for nothing but wondrous enlightenment. Enlightenment is the sole pursuit and the original defining feature of poetry. Enlightenment can be shallow or deep. There is thorough enlightenment, limited enlightenment, and enlightenment of partial and incomplete understanding. Poetry of the Han and Wei is remote in time and does not depend on enlightenment. But Xie Lingyun and the High Tang masters attain thorough enlightenment, and as for others some may attain enlightenment, but not that of the first order.

禪家者流，乘有小大，宗有南北，道有邪正。學者須從最上乘、具正法眼，悟第一義，若小乘禪，聲聞辟支果，皆非正也。論詩如論禪，漢、魏、晉與盛唐之詩，則第一義也。大歷以還之詩，則小乘禪也，已落第二義矣；晚唐之詩，則聲聞、辟支果也。學漢、魏、晉與盛唐詩者，臨濟下也。學大歷以還之詩者，曹洞下也。大抵禪道惟在妙悟，詩道亦在妙悟，且孟襄陽學力下韓退之遠甚、而其詩獨出退之之上者，一味妙悟而已。惟悟乃為當行，乃為本色。然悟有淺深、有分限、有透徹之悟，有但得一知半解之悟。漢、魏尚矣，不假悟也。謝靈運至盛唐諸公，透徹之悟也。他雖有悟者，皆非第一義也。(*CLSHJJ*, 7, 27)

The word "enlightenment" (*wu* 悟) occurs ten times in the above passage. Yan divides enlightenment into two levels analogous to Mahayana and Hinayana Buddhism. He aligns the poetry from Han, Wei, Jin, and the High Tang with the former, and Dali- and post-Dali era poetry with the latter. But his analogy does not end here. He proceeds further to liken different kinds of poetry with Chan sects, claiming: "Those who learn from Han, Wei, Jin, and the High Tang are comparable to followers of the Linji sect, while those who learn from Dali and later poetry are comparable to the Caodong sect." Lastly, he posits three levels of enlightenment, thorough enlightenment, limited enlightenment, and enlightenment of partial understanding, and aligns the three levels with various poets of different periods.

Unlike Wu Ke and Gong Xiang, who entirely negate the necessity of study, Yan Yu does not reject learning from one's predecessors. If his friend Dai Fugu merely mentions prosody as a legitimate subject of study, Yan Yu goes one step further and argues that learning is necessary before one can attain enlightenment. Thus, after mentioning "enlightenment" ten times, Yan immediately follows with ten successive mentions of self-conscious "thorough deliberation" (*shoucan* 熟參):

§117
My commentaries are no transgressions, nor are my elucidations delusionary. In the world, there are people whom we can disparage, but there are no words [of theirs] that should be discarded. This is the way of poetry. If you do not think this way, it must be because you haven't read poetry widely and haven't deliberated on poetry. Why don't you select Han and Wei poems and thoroughly deliberate on them; and then select Ji and [Liu] Song poems and thoroughly deliberate on them; and then select poems from the Northern and Southern dynasties and thoroughly deliberate on them; and then select poems of Shen Quanqi, Song Zhiwen, Wang Bo, Yang Jiong, Lu Zhaolin, Luo Binwang, and Chen Zi'ang and thoroughly deliberate on them; and then select poems by various poets living during the Kaiyuan and Tianbao reigns and thoroughly deliberate on them; and then select poems of Li Bai and Du Fu alone and thoroughly deliberate on them; and then select poems of ten talented poets of the

Dali reign and thoroughly deliberate on them; and then select poems of the Yuanhe reign and thoroughly deliberate on them; and then exhaustively select poems of various Late Tang poets and thoroughly deliberate on them; and finally select poems of various poets of our dynasty after Su Shi and Huang Tingjian and thoroughly deliberate on them. Having done all this, the true right and wrong could not be hidden from him. If someone has done all this and still cannot form a perceptive view of his own, his judgment is sure to have been clouded by the deviant "wild fox way," and he is beyond cure and will never be enlightened.

吾評之非僭也，辯之非妄也。天下有可廢之人，無可廢之言。詩道如是也。若以為不然，則是見詩之不廣，參詩之不熟耳。試取漢、魏之詩而熟參之，次取晉、宋之詩而熟參之，次取南北朝之詩而熟參之，次取沈、宋、王、楊、盧、駱、陳拾遺之詩而熟參之，次取開元、天寶諸家之詩而熟參之，次獨取李、杜二公之詩而熟參之，又取大曆十才子之詩而熟參之，又取元和之詩而熟參之，又盡取晚唐諸家之詩而熟參之，又取本朝蘇、黃以下諸家之詩而熟參之，其真是非自有不能隱者。儻猶於此而無見焉，則是野狐外道，蒙蔽其真識，不可救藥，終不悟也。(*CLSHJJ*, 59–60)

Here Yan lists the must-read poets and poetry from Han and Wei and on down to the Song dynasty in the order in which they should be studied. After thorough deliberation on the poetry after *Chuci*, he maintains, one should be able to "receive broadly from the High Tang masters, ruminate over them in his bosom, and, over time, attain enlightenment in a natural way" 博取盛唐名家，醞釀胸中，久之自然悟入 (*CLSHJJ*, 73).

Yan Yu achieves a fair level of consistency in his discussions of "enlightenment" and "deliberation," but the same cannot be said for some of his other emphatic claims in *Canglang's Remarks on Poetry*. On the one hand, he claims that "insight is the central factor in learning poetry" 夫學詩者以識為主 (*CLSHJJ*, 65) and lists five rules of writing, nine categories of poetic style, and three areas that require effort in language. On the other hand, he also states, "Poetry requires a distinct talent that has little to do with books; poetry brings a distinct interest that has little to do with principles" 夫詩有別材，非關書也；詩有別趣，非關理也 (*CLSHJJ*, 129). To my mind, these seemingly contradictory claims reveal Yan Yu's use of the Buddhist "Middle Way" thinking in his treatment of the relationship between unconscious "enlightenment" and "thorough deliberation." The two sides are presented in an indeterminate relationship that may be considered coterminous or separable: coterminous because they may exist in harmonious compatibility and attain a dialectical unity, and separable because they may also be posited as separate and oppositional. To my mind, it is precisely this tension between coterminous and separable that caused *Canglang's Remarks on Poetry* to enjoy such sustained, profound influence in the Ming and Qing. As described in chapter 8, the Archaists subscribe to the coterminous aspect, believing in the attaining of "thorough enlightenment" like the Tang poets through deliberation on Tang poetry; the Anti-Archaists, in contrast, only take up the separable aspect, insisting that "enlightenment," which they define as the realization of one's natural disposition or in-born spirit, cannot be attained through deliberation or imitation.

Further Reflections

Having noted various divergences between the *qi*-centered and the Chan-centered theories, I now reflect on several important similarities. First, proponents of these two theories, notably Han Yu, Su Che, Su Shi, and Yan Yu, brushed aside the *yi→xiang→yan* paradigm and instead focused on the writer's physical and mental preparation, the least treated of the four creative phases covered by Lu Ji's and Liu Xie's comprehensive theories. The leading advocates of *qi*-centered and Chan-centered theories set store by self-conscious, long-time endeavors as a precondition for successful literary creation. For instance, both Han Yu and Yan Yu stress total immersion in the study of canonical writings, a practice Yan describes with the Buddhist phrase "thorough deliberation" (*shucan* 熟參). Of course, the canonical writings the two cherish are very different: the Confucian canon for Han Yu, belletristic poetry for Yan Yu. Their valorization of these different canons speaks to their respective pursuits of moral aestheticism and pure aestheticism.

A concomitant similarity is that both theories believe that the writer's immersive preparation culminates in a sudden burst of creativity and the birth of great literary works. Of course, their conceptions of this spontaneous creativity are quite different. For Han Yu, Su Che, and other Confucian-minded critics, it consists in a *dynamic* overflowing of the moral-cosmic lifebreath through the writer into literary work. But for Yan Yu and other Buddhist-minded critics, it is a *quietist* "wondrous awakening" (*miaowu* 妙悟), a transcendent experience akin to Chan enlightenment. A further related similarity is that, in privileging spontaneous creativity, the *qi*- and Chan-centered theories have shared basically the same aim: to counter the widespread practice of self-conscious imitative writing in their own times. While Han Yu and other Tang-Song masters of ancient-style prose direct their criticism at Qi-Liang parallel prose, Yan Yu and other Buddhist-minded critics relentlessly castigate Huang Tingjian and his followers' efforts to imitate Du Fu.

Assessing the impact of these theories on later periods, however, reveals a conspicuous difference. The *qi*-centered theory declined after the Northern Song as fewer and fewer critics opted to describe the creative process in terms of an unleashing of flood-like lifebreath. By contrast, the Chan-centered theory advanced by Yan Yu exerted a profound influence during the Ming-Qing period thanks in large measure to Yan Yu's "Middle Way" approach noted above. In

Canglang's Remarks on Poetry, Yan Yu endorses, in the same breath and with the same enthusiasm, two diametrically opposite concepts—sustained, self-conscious "thorough deliberation" and spontaneous, momentary, "wondrous awakening"— but offers no explanation on the relationship between them. Ironically, his simultaneous endorsements of two mutually opposing concepts creates the overarching dichotomous paradigm in which Ming-Qing critics will theorize all aspects of literature, including literary creation. As discussed in chapters 6–8, Ming critics fall into two broad camps: the Archaists, who value "thorough deliberation," and the Anti-Archaists, who value spontaneous creativity akin to "miraculous awakening." From late Ming onward, we see the rise of a third camp of critics who undertake to reconcile the two opposing stances in various ways. To my mind, no critical text has a broader and longer-lasting influence on later eras than Yan's *Canglang's Remarks on Poetry*.

///////////////////////////

Notes
1. See Pollard, "*Ch'I* in Chinese Literary Theory."
2. Lau, *Mencius*, 1:57; with modifications.
3. Dong et al., *Quan Tang wen*, 2474–75.
4. For a study on the form of Six Dynasties parallel prose, see Cai, "Six Dynasties Parallel Prose."
5. Wang Shihan, *Su shi xuanping jianshi*.
6. Su, *Su Shi shiji*, 905–7.
7. *Quan Song shi*, 56:2958.35236.
8. Dai Fugu, *Dai Fugu shiji*, 228.

Chapter 6

Transcendent Mind-Centered Theory of Literary Creation

In an interesting way, the historical development of Chinese theorizing about literary creation—and, arguably, Chinese literary theory as a whole—appears to follow a counterintuitive path. Instead of a more natural progression from the fragmentary to the systematic, we observe a development from the systematic toward the fragmentary. Thinking about the creative process begins with Lu Ji's and Liu Xie's comprehensive theories (see chap. 2), often praised as "vast in scope and refined in thinking" (*tida sijing* 體大思精). Although Wang Changling explores an equally broad range of topics (see chap. 4), his mode of writing marks a shift from systematic exposition to random remarks. In Han Yu, Su Che, and Yan Yu (see chap. 5) we find discussions a bit more cogent than those of Wang Changling, but expressed in letters or extended entries rather than well-rounded essays.

The Yuan, Ming, and Qing dynasties (1279–1911) display yet another interesting shift: even fewer sustained expositions regarding literary creation by a single critic, but an abundance of scattered insights from different sources. These remarks are like glittering gems waiting to be pieced together as a reconstructed theory. Feeling impelled to undertake this task, I read through various compendia of *shihua* 詩話 (poetry talks) and collected the finest excerpts. After combing through and classifying them according to four creative phases—physical and psychological preparedness, affective response to things, transcendent flight of the mind, and the transformation of conception-image into language (see chap. 2)—I found three distinct theory types emerged: a transcendent mind-centered theory focused on the third phase, a *yi*-centered theory focused on the final creative phase, and a *qing* (emotion)-centered theories focused on the second phase. This chapter discusses the first theory type; chapters 7 and 8 take up the other two.

In Yuan, Ming, and Qing poetry criticism, the transcendent literary mind is depicted as induced variously by the cosmic process of creation, physical landscapes, literary canon, and human emotions. Accordingly, its modus operandi is conceived as dynamic roaming, quietist contemplation, spiritual communion with ancient authors, and intuition prompted by tender affections. Of these, the first three reflect influences from Zhuangzi's 莊子 (ca. 369–286 BCE) Daoist philosophy, Buddhism, and Tang-Song Confucianism, respectively, while the last stems from the poet's own life and writing experiences.

The Mind's Dynamic Flight: Roaming with Creation

The notion of transcendent mind-roaming may be traced to Lu Ji's and Liu Xie's accounts of transcendent initiation of the creative process per se (see §§43–44), which are in turn rooted in Zhuangzi's idea of "letting the mind roam." "Cosmic Creation" or just "Creation" (*zaohua* 造化) as used here refers to the Dao of the Supreme Ultimate or the One that generates the Two (Heaven or *qian*, and Earth or *kun*) and, through interaction of the Two, also generates myriad things. As this process has no physical form and cannot be cognized by physical perception, one must first retract sight and hearing in order to follow it with the transcendental mind. The process of Creation is perpetually continuous and changing, and the transcendental mind must move in tandem with its transformations. Thus Zhuangzi's "let the mind roam" in his "Normal Course for Rulers and Kings" 應帝王 chapter describes the transcendental mind united and moving along with the Dao: "Roam your mind in blandness, let your lifebreath blend with the undifferentiated, follow the natural course of things, allowing no room for partiality, and the whole world will be well-governed" 汝遊心於淡，合氣於漠，順物自然而無容私焉，而天下治矣 (*ZZJS*, 1/294).

Inspired by Zhuangzi, Lu Ji posits that literary writing is similarly initiated by transcendent experience, emphasizing that suspension of the senses and spiritual focus are necessary preconditions for a mind-roaming that transcends all temporal and spatial limits. Of course, "mind-roaming" for literary writing has a different objective from Zhuangzi's: its goal is not eternal spiritual transcendence but the production of outstanding literature by returning to the world of emotions and things. Lu Ji provides this description of what results from such mind-roaming: "Emotions rise out of obscurity and grow ever brighter; things are illuminated and propel one another forward. One pours the sap of the word repository and savors the sweet dews of the Six Classics" 情瞳曨而彌鮮，物昭晰而互進。傾羣言之瀝液，漱六藝之芳潤 (*WFJS*, 36).

Liu Xie's notion of "spirit-thinking" is in fact identical with Lu Ji's "mind-roaming." They describe the same transcendent flight of the mind: with the first half an out-of-the-body flight toward the Dao of heaven and earth, transcending time and space, while the second half depicts the return to the phenomenal world. The difference is that Liu also mentions the decisive factors for the success or failure of this journey: the physical and moral conditions ("resolve and life-breath" 志氣) that control the "latch" for the first part; and talent, learning, and thinking ("rhetoric" and "deliberating on reason") that function as the "trigger" of the second (see §47).

Lu's and Liu's descriptions of the transcendent mind suffer from a lack of detail, which left ample space for Yuan, Ming, and Qing critics to interpret, substantiate, and even develop new views. In his essay "Inner Journey," Hao Jing 郝 經 (1223–1275) of the Yuan dynasty provides a more powerful, detailed, and profound discussion of the transcendent "inner journey" 內遊 of literary creation:[1]

§118

There are those who, following Sima Qian's example, wish to make journeys and seek help [with writing] from the external world. Why don't they also try an inner journey? While the body does not even leave where one sits and sleeps, the mind can travel beyond the six directions. Although one was born far away from high antiquity, one could journey back to high antiquity and beyond. How can this feat be performed by those who can only reach where their feet take them and can only observe what their eyes show? But one may abide by their mind and ride on lifebreath, cherishing rightness, retaining the essence inside, yet being not stranded inside. He is showered with blessings [from the external] but does not chase after the external. He constantly adheres in action to what's right, constantly pursues action while obeying quietude, constantly manifests sincerity with nothing amiss, constantly maintains harmony without aberration. He is unstoppable just as flowing water cannot be held back despite all efforts. He is like a bright mirror from which nothing can hide itself. He is like a balance scale, measuring everything without any partiality. Untainted, unhindered, and unperturbed, he has a steady and expansive reach, always entrusting himself to things and roaming together with them.

故欲學遷之遊，而求助於外者，曷亦內遊乎？身不離於衽席之上，而遊於六合之外，生乎千古之下，而遊於千古之上，豈區區於足跡之餘、觀覽之末者所能也？持心御氣，明正精遷於內而不滯於內，應於沐而不逐於外，常正而行，常動而靜，常誠而不妄，常和而不悖，如止水眾止不能易，如明鏡眾形不能逃，如平衡之權輕重在我，無偏仙倚。如汙無滯無撓州蕩，每寓於物而遊焉。

As for the classics, especially the making of the River Diagram and the Luo Script, he partakes in cleaving open remote antiquity, controlling the trigger of heaven and earth, disclosing heaven and earth's stores, exhaustively presenting the transformations of heaven and earth, and revealing the traces of ghosts and spirits. Thus, the Great Ultimate is made manifest and shows its face to the world—appearing in the manifold transformations of the myriad things and brimming over all rugged caves and ravines. Through my own mind, I see the mind of heaven, earth, ghosts, and spirits, and through my own journey, I see the journey of heaven, earth, ghosts, and spirits.

於經也則河圖、洛書劐劃太古，挈天地之幾，發天地之蘊，盡天地之變，見鬼神之跡。太極出形，面目於世，萬化萬象，張皇其中，而瀰茫洞豁，嶠嶇充溢；因吾之心，見天地鬼神之心；因吾之遊，見天地鬼神之遊。[2]

This passage, here divided into two parts for clarity, has a profound significance grossly overlooked in current scholarship. Its significance is also historic, achieved through Hao's brilliant engagement with his theorist predecessors. It begins by taking issue with Su Che's claim that the greatness of the Grand Historian Sima Qian's writings stems from his lifelong roaming about the world (see §109). Attempting to write great works by imitating Sima Qian's external roaming is, for Hao, unquestionably inferior to embarking on an internal journey. By stressing the transcendence of time and space through inner roaming, Hao undoubtedly appropriates Zhuangzi and, more directly, Lu Ji's "mind-roaming" and Liu Xie's "spirit-thinking," as evidenced by the phrase "always entrusting himself to things and roaming together with them."

At the same time, Hao Jing clearly diverges from Zhuangzi by stressing that this roaming should not be confined to Zhuangzian pure interiority but should respond to the external world as well. While Zhuangzi became celebrated for cultivating an indifference to the mundane world, Hao takes up a different posture: "He is showered with blessings [from the external] but does not chase after the external." For Zhuangzi, the material world exerts pressure on mind or consciousness, diverting it from its effort of spiritual transcendence. For Hao, by contrast, being "showered with blessings [from the external]" would suggest a distinct effort not only not to refuse or resist the world but also to achieve a heightened receptivity to what that world might have to give, namely, its showering of blessings. To Hao, such an external "outreach" becomes a mental journey reenacting the creation of human civilization by a long line of Confucian sages, from the makers of the River Diagram and the Luo Script to the Three Sovereigns, Five Emperors, King Tang of Shang, King Wen and Wu of Zhou, Duke Zhou, and Confucius. This blending of the Zhuangzian internal roaming with the Confucian narrative of the making of civilization formations surely attests to the syncretic spirit of the Yuan.

Turning now specifically to literary creation, Hao surpasses Lu Ji and Liu Xie in two respects, each representing a major breakthrough. First, Hao provides a more detailed and thorough description of the author's "mind-roaming" (Lu Ji) or "spirit-thinking" (Liu Xie). If Lu and Liu merely sketched out the reflexive journey of the writer's mind, Hao innovatively offers a more detailed account of what this process comprises. He believes its most significant characteristic is that it retains "the essence inside and yet is not stranded inside . . . showered with blessings [from without] but does not chase after the external." Here the key lies in how the mind on the one hand "is not stranded inside" as its roaming returns to the physical world. On the other hand, it "does not chase after the external." To do that would be, in effect, equivalent to getting absorbed in external detail, in materiality. Instead, Hao believes, by cultivating the receptivity of the mirror (which simply passively takes in what the world has to give), the mind avoids any kind of slavishness to that world, any obsession with materiality.

Hao Jing's second major breakthrough emerges in linking the two disparate paradigms developed by Liu Xie: "tracing the Dao as the source" (yuan Dao 原道) and "spirit-thinking" (shensi 神思). Specifically, we might see this as a linking of nature and culture. Hao says: "As for the Classics, especially the making of the River Diagram and the Luo Script, he partakes in cleaving open remote antiquity." But how exactly does this "cleaving of remote antiquity" come about? In fact, by a process very much like the mirroring described earlier. By simply opening himself to cultural influences in the same way that he had opened himself to natural influences before, Hao is able to feel or intuit the process by which the making of the River Diagram and the Luo Script have come about. Absorbing these works passively like a mirror leads to the same kind of image formation we've seen before. But now, because we're dealing with culture, the same sort of image formation can lead to insight into the "making" of the River Diagram and the Luo Script. And this is how Hao achieves his "cleaving open remote antiquity": by grasping the process by which the River Diagram and Luo Script have come about.

Liu Xie's first paradigm is fashioned to demonstrate a grand genealogy of refined writing, enabled by sages' transmission of the Dao through writing, but it does not describe any mental activities involved in the creation of graphic symbols, culture, Confucian classics, or belles lettres. Conversely, Liu's other paradigm, that of spirit thinking, is constructed solely for the purpose of illuminating the mental processes in the creation of belles lettres, with no connections whatsoever made with the sage's founding of writing and civilization. But with Hao Jing, the spirit-thinking of literary creation is no different from repeating the ancient sage's mental processes in founding human writing and civilization. By bridging Liu's two distinct paradigms, Hao Jing in fact resolves the problem that Han Yu tackled with only partial success. By adopting Mencius's notion of nourishing the flood-like lifebreath to explain the driving force of literary creation, Han succeeded in connecting literary creation with study of the Confucian sages. However, Han did not explain the grounds for this connection. Only with Hao Jing, roughly three hundred years later, do we find a convincing explanation: because receptively opening yourself to the remote cultural past yields insight into the creative process by which that cultural past was formed, it can also yield insight equally into what poets write about and accomplish the act of literary creation.

In subsequent Ming and Qing times Lu Ji's "mind-roaming" and Liu Xie's "spirit-thinking" no longer attract serious attention or inspire new conceptions like Hao Jing's. The one noteworthy exception is Xie Zhen's 謝榛 (1495–1575) succinct summary of the transcendent mind's journey:

§119

What poetry values is being at once far away and close by. In "Expositions on Literature," Lu Ji writes "This is how it begins: perception is held back and listening is reverted /Engrossed in thought, one searches all sides. / His essence galloping to the world's eight boundaries, / One's mind roaming across the ten thousand yards."[3] But these lines only depict the mind searching in the mysterious realm. The Tang poet Liu Zhaoyu has written this line: "Poetic lines are found in the depth of night, / The mind returns from beyond heaven." This idea originates from Shiheng [Lu Ji] and he knows well the method of "correlation between distance and closeness." Sitting in a quiet room and searching for poetic lines, the mind's spirit becomes shadowy, journeying west to the Indian kingdom but eventually returning to the Zhaojue Temple in Shangdang. This is the so-called "Method of Being at Once Far and Close-by."

詩貴乎遠而近。然思不可偏，偏則不能無弊。陸士衡《文賦》曰："其始也收視反聽，耽思傍訊，精騖八極，心游萬仞。" 此但寫冥搜之狀爾。唐劉昭禹詩云："句向夜深得，心從天外歸。" 此作祖於士衡，尤知遠近相應之法。凡靜室索詩，心神渺然，西游天竺國，仍歸上黨昭覺寺，此所謂 "遠而近" 之法也。[4]

Here Xie begins by stating his belief that "poetry sets store by going far away, only to be nearby" and then identifies Lu Ji's "mind-roaming" as the source of his belief. Xie goes on to quote the Tang poet Liu Zhaoyu 劉昭禹 (fl. 909), "The line of poetry is begotten late into the night / as my mind returns from beyond the skies," to illuminate the extraordinary, transformative journey implied in Lu Ji's "mind-roaming" and Liu Xie's "spirit-thinking." The flight toward the cosmic Dao is always followed by a return, enriched with new insights and capabilities, back to the present moment from the edges of the world and High Antiquity. For Xie, Lu's and Liu's expositions on the transcendent mind are not abstract theorizing but something like practical guides for writing poetry, showing him "the method of 'being afar and yet close by.'" Though less original than Hao Jing's, Xie's remarks give a cogent summary of Lu's and Liu's insights into the transcendent flight of the creative mind.

The Mind Mirroring the Ultimate Reality: Wondrous Encounter with Landscapes

On the highest philosophical level, the biggest difference among Buddhism and Confucian and Daoist thought lies in their different conceptions of the ultimate cosmic reality. Confucianism and Daoism uphold a Dao that is the perpetual, nonstop process of yin-yang transformations; it is physical rather than spiritual in its original form, although historical development has injected into it various spiritual elements such as Confucian moral ethics. By contrast, the Buddhist Dao is fundamentally of tranquil mental state, called the *Trikāya*, Buddha nature, *tathata*, and so on. Its name may change and vary, but it does not deviate from its spiritual character. The different Confucian, Daoist, and Buddhist understandings of ultimate reality naturally call for different ways to attain it. Indeed, these three schools each give a different description of the enlightened Dao. In the Confucian and the Daoist canon, we often see the dynamic transformations of yin and yang in bipolar unity, while in the Buddhist canon, we often see tranquil religious contemplation, with the mirror and the lamp as its most commonly used metaphors. Only in texts that lean toward synthesizing the three teachings do we find the opposition weakens and disappears between the material and the spiritual, movement and stillness.

The descriptions of transcendent experiences through the ages naturally reflect the Confucian, Daoist, and Buddhist influences in their respective understandings and accounts of the ultimate reality. Just as Lu Ji and Liu Xie drew from Zhuangzi's account of the "Ultimate Being roaming his mind in Dao" to imbue their descriptions of "mind-roaming" and "spirit-thinking" with dynamic movement, Zong Bing 宗炳 (375–443). modeled his account on the notion of awakening to the Spirit from Hinayana Pure Land sect, as he described in detail how a painter should "purify the mind and savor iconic images," connect with the indwelling Spirit (i.e., Buddha) of undying spirit of the blessed landscape, and produce superb paintings (see §§56–73). Wang Changling's account of "initiating *yi* and generate inscape" shows deep Buddhist influence, especially Yogâcāra Buddhism, in his notion of the seventh consciousness *manas-vijñāna* reproducing "the entire phenomenal world," and in the Yogâcāra's "three types of inscape." The *yi* he describes is a transcendental, tranquil state of mind, presenting the true reality of the universe and attained by contemplating on specific phenomena. Thus, Wang Changling provided detailed discussion and recommendations on the selection of landscapes and natural scenery, as well as the optimal time and spatial perspective of observing and contemplating nature. Such contemplation of objects and scenery—done with intense self-awareness—is the conscious act of "deliberation." But Wang does not mention "enlightenment" or the time needed to "mentally penetrate" objects and scenery.[5]

Yu Ji 虞集 (1272–1348) of the Yuan dynasty embraced Wang Changling's idea of landscape contemplation leading to spontaneous enlightenment—an intuitive grasp of the reality of the myriad things. Thus, his statement, "With one glance, the myriad realms return to the origin" 一視而萬境歸 is similar to Wang Changling's statement, "Situate oneself in the inscape, and observe it in the mind till it shines [like a gem] in one's palm" 處身於境，視境於心，瑩然掌中，然後用思 (*QTWDSG*, 172–73). His approach to landscape contemplation differs from

Wang Changling's mainly in the extent to which they focus on "deliberation" (*can* 參) and "enlightenment" (*wu* 悟). Yu and Ming-Qing Buddhist-minded critics seldom discuss the conscious selection of objects for contemplation, but they repeatedly emphasize the involuntary and instantaneous character of enlightenment induced by encountering a scene in nature. Yu Ji's description of "poetic observation 詩觀" in the former preface to *One-Finger Chan for Poets* (Shijia yizhi 詩家一指) illustrates this nicely:

§120

Here is the equivalent of Chan in poetry: equipped with Mahêśvara's eye, in one glance, the myriad realms return to their origin; with one movement, the tracks of all demons are swept clean. To transcend the boundaries of words and images and possess that which is prior to Creation—only the such-like have the capacity to observe [poetry].

詩有禪宗具摩醯眼，一視而萬境歸元，一舉而羣魔蕩跡，超言象之表，得造化之先。夫如是始有觀。[6]

"Equipped with Mahêśvara's eye in Chan" indicates Yan Yu's influence over Yu Ji and Ming-Qing poetry critics: when discussing poetry in terms of "wondrous enlightenment," they tend to emphasize "enlightenment" over "deliberation" in contemplating natural landscapes. Following the Buddhist canon, they believe that "traces of all demons are swept clean in one stroke," all phenomena are illusory, and only by entering into the intuitive state of *prajñā*, a state that "transcends the boundaries of words and images and precedes the start of Creation," can one observe the transformations of spirit and affections and the pervasive flow of inscapes in heaven and earth's infinitude and temporal successions. Only then can one start the actual composition process. The prominent Qing critic Wang Fuzhi's usage of the Buddhist term "direct perception" (*xianliang* 現量, Skt. *pratyakṣasamyak*) in his poetic commentary is another obvious example:

§121

The line "The monk knocks on the door in moonlight" is born of delusionary imitation. It is like talking about someone else's dream. The line may look like real, but does it have anything to do with the creative mind? Those who have insight know that the self-murmuring over the choice between the words "push" and "knock" is evidence of deliberate thinking. If the mind spontaneously meets a scene, a word is naturally chosen, either "push" or "knock." Written in response to scenes and emotions, a poem is naturally miraculous; why would it need any belaboring? The line "Long river, the setting sun—so round" did come from a preconceived scene; the line "Calling aloud to a woodcutter across the water" was not born of conscious thinking. [These two lines] are what Chan practitioners call "direct perception."

"僧敲月下門"，祗是妄想揣摩，如說他人夢，縱令形容酷似，何嘗毫髮關心？知然者，以其沈吟 "推敲" 二字，就他作想也。若即景會心，則或 "推" 或 "敲"，必居其一，因景因情，自然靈妙，何勞擬議哉？ "長河落日圓"，初無定景；"隔水問樵夫"，初非想得。則禪家所謂 "現量" 也。(*QSH*, 9)

"Direct perception" is a term of Buddhist epistemology in the Consciousness-Only school (see §77). In contrast with "inference" (*biliang* 比量), which involves thinking and demonstration stressing logical inferences and metaphors, "direct perception" emphasizes intuition in transcendent mental activities. It means to engage the external world directly through undifferentiating senses rather than through metaphors. As Wang believes poetry should be natural and spontaneous, he critiques Jiaoran's 皎然 (720?–798?) view that poetry writing requires hard thinking, which he regards as harmful to poetry's intuitive aesthetic. In addition, Yuan Mei's 袁枚 (1716–1798) *Sequel to the Grading of Poetry* (Xu shipin 續詩品) and Song Luo's 宋犖 (1634–1713) *Discussion of Poetry from the Brimming Hall* (Mantang shuoshi 漫堂說詩) both contain discussions on enlightenment through chance encounters with natural scenery. Influenced by the Daoist and Buddhist hermits' life of reclusion in nature, Yuan Mei's descriptions of natural scenery are casual and effortless (as opposed to intentional), reflecting his intuition of the true cosmic reality through visual experiences, just as he writes in *Sequel to Categories of Poetry*:

§122
The birds' chirping and flowers falling both commune with Spirit. But those who fail to get enlightened give them up to the drifting wind.

鳥啼花落，皆與神通。人不能悟，付之飄風。[7]

To Yuan Mei, "enlightenment" means "communion with Spirit." In poems written by an enlightened poet, one would, in Jiaoran's words, "only see his inborn nature and emotions as they are not shackled by language" 但見性情，不覩文字 (*QTWDSG*, 233). He advocates a mode of writing free of thinking and crafting— "to realize the charm of natural sceneries as they are encountered" 即景成趣. As for Song Luo, he emphasizes the importance of Chan enlightenment in writing poetry: "enlightenment" necessarily produces "inscape" or, in his words, the "post-enlightenment inscape" 悟後境. In such a mental state, fine writing flows effortlessly whether or not it involves the imitation of ancient classics, as he states in *Discussion of Poetry from the Brimming Hall*:

§123

After a long time, one gains insight into the source and naturally gets close to where true nature lies. One does not need to imitate the poetry of Tang, or antiquity, or Song, Yuan, and Ming poetry. My true poetry flows out as my eyes come into contact with a scene—this is what Buddhists call "casually picking it up by the hand" and what Zhuangzi says about [the Dao] lying in ants, barnyard grasses, and tiles, and everywhere. This is called "post-enlightenment inscape."

久之，源流洞然，自有得於性之所近，不必橅唐，不必橅古，亦不必橅宋、元、明，而吾之眞詩觸境流出，釋氏所謂信手拈來，莊子所謂螻蟻、稊稗、瓦甓無所不在，此之謂悟後境。(*QSH*, 416)

This passage provides a vantage point to review landscape-induced enlightenment in relation to Tang-Song Buddhist theories discussed in chapters 4 and 5. First, note a none-too-subtle rejection of Yan Yu's thoughts on "wondrous enlightenment" and "thorough deliberation" as Song Luo stresses that enlightenment has nothing to do with learning poetry of the past, whatever the period. Next, in advocating spontaneous poetry writing, we see a pronounced difference between the relaxed approach taken by these Yuan, Ming, and Qing critics and the slogan-mongering approach of Wu Ke, Gong Xiang, and others (see §§113–15). While the latter say nothing about how enlightenment comes about, the former identify landscape as the loci and inducement of enlightenment. Finally, the emphasis on landscape by these Yuan-Ming-Qing critics invites comparison with Wang Changling's remarks on "the inscape of physical things" (see §§85, 92). While Wang advocates intentional contemplation of landscape and, in fact, prescribes how to pursue such contemplation, Yuan-Ming-Qing critics stress just the opposite: it's the casual, unintentional encounter with landscape that brings forth enlightenment beyond thought and word, as captured in the finest landscape poems of Wang Wei and Meng Haoran 孟浩然 (689–740).

Creative Empathy: Catching an Author's Soul in a Text

Used in reference to reading, *empathy* generally denotes a reader's more or less automatic emotional identification with an author or, more often, a character. Neither English nor Chinese quite has a word for the reader's active borrowing of an author's creative mind in the course of reading. Accounts of such inspired experiences were probably unknown in Western literary theory until the rise of phenomenological criticism of consciousness.[8] In Ming-Qing discourse on literary creation, however, we find many accounts of writers achieving wondrous communion with great ancient literary minds through reading their masterworks. The appearance of such inspired reading experiences marks a new phase in the millennium-old endeavor to comprehend and harness texts as valuable sources of literary creation. Lu Ji opens his pioneering work "Exposition on Literature" by acknowledging the ancient canons, along with seasonal changes, as his primary stimulant for literary creation (see §42, line 2). For his part, Han Yu thinks of ancient canons, Confucian ones at that, as a veritable source of literary inspiration. His repeated syncing of progress between his immersive reading and his own growing volume of writing testify to their relation (see §108). Besides Han Yu, Zhu Xi 朱熹 (1130–1200) provides a systematic exposition on reading. Using Su Xun 蘇洵 (1009–1066), father of Su Shi and Su Che, as an example, Zhu argues that consistently studying the sage's works leads to sudden enlightenment that makes poetry writing a natural, spontaneous process.

§124

The elder Su tells that when he first learned how to write refined writing he would select the *Analects*, the *Mencius*, the *Hanfeizi*, and other writings by sages and worthies, unselfconsciously sit up straight, and read them the whole day. This he kept doing for seven or eight years. . . . Having done all this, he continued reading them until all of a sudden he found his own writing came so easily.

老蘇自言其初學爲文時，取《論語》、《孟子》、《韓子》及其他聖賢之文，而兀然端坐，終日以讀之者七八年，……已而再三讀之，渾渾乎覺其來之易矣。[9]

Yan Yu talks about "thorough deliberation" (i.e., immersive reading) and "wondrous enlightenment" in the same breath, suggesting a causal relation between the two (see §§116–17). His "deliberation" describes the intense act of reading and learning his predecessors' techniques, while his "enlightenment," as the unconscious, involuntary creative impulse arising from one's own spiritual being, is consequently accomplished. To establish a causal relationship between these activities, it would be necessary to describe the actual mental experience involved in the leap from the passive act of reading to the dynamic process of literary creation. This task is left to Ming-Qing critics.

Wang Tingxiang 王廷相 (1474–1544), one of the Former Seven Masters of the Ming, is among the first, if not the first, to take up this task. Like Yan Yu, Wang believes that studying the ancients involves a process of "deliberation" leading to "enlightenment":

§125

After long and thorough immersion, one spontaneously attains enlightenment. Spirituality illuminates one's insides, and numinosity penetrates what's seen and heard. The opening and closing, thrusting upward and down, changing of inward and outward movements—these miraculous methods of ancient masters all enter the gate of my mind. . . . Then one deploys phrases to convey what's in the mind. The splendor of the nine dynasties, the patterning of the *Book of Poetry*, the numinosity of immortals and sages, the essence of mountains and rivers—none would refrain from working in unison and providing divine aid. All this is not obtained from outside, but comes out of the self, through a self-transformation by learning. In this way, one transcends the imitation of forms and models and conceives a work in the void, as if begotten in spring and molded by nature, and leaves no trace of the past.

久焉純熟，自爾悟入。神情昭於肺腑，靈境徹于視聽。開闔起伏，出入變化，古師妙擬，悉歸我闥......敷辭以命意，則凡九代之英，《三百》之章，及夫仙聖之靈，山川之精，靡不會協，爲我神助。此非取自外者也，習而化於我者也。故能擺脫形模，凌虛構結，春育天成，不犯舊迹矣。(*QMSH*, 2993–94)

While assiduously learning from the ancients, Wang stresses, one should not be constrained by imitation but seek to attain enlightenment, one's own transcendent spiritual state: "Spirituality illuminates one's insides and numinosity penetrates what's seen and heard." In such a transcendent state of mind, one can produce a work that is "begotten in spring and molded by nature." Going one step further, Xie Zhen, one of the Latter Seven Masters of the Ming, argues that achieving such transcendence is tantamount to catching the soul of the author:

§126

Poetry without spirit-breath is like a painting of the sun and the moon without radiance. In learning from Li Bai and Du Fu, one should not get mired in sentences and words, and ought to read their works again and again until one attains it [Li Bai and Du Fu's poetic art] a long time later. This is the method of "extracting the hun-soul and catching the po-soul."

詩無神氣，猶繪日月而無光彩。學李、杜者，勿執於句字之間，當率意熟讀，久而得之。此提魂攝魄之法也。(*QMSH*, 1327)

The early Qing critic Jin Shengtan 金聖歎 (1608–1661) homes in on the optimal electrifying moment for such soul catching: the most exciting instant in the ancient's artistic creation. The capturing of the author's soul at this instant guarantees the birth of a work with lasting aesthetic appeal.

§127

In reading and discussing an ancient, one must shoot one's eyesight straight back a thousand years to meet the ancient's spirit at the very instant he picked up the writing brush on the day of composition—blending with his spirit like mixing water and milk. Only by so doing can one succeed. Otherwise, one's writing will be as tasteless as chewing a candlestick.

讀書尚論古人，須將自己眼光直射千百年上，與當日古人捉筆一剎那頃精神，融成水乳，方能有得，不然，真如嚼蠟矣![10]

If in the mid-Ming such a view of creative empathy was presented mainly by Archaists to justify and ennoble their practice of imitating the High-Tang poets, it gained wide acceptance by the late Ming. Even Zhong Xing 鍾惺 (1574–1624), prominent detractor of the Ming Archaists on many issues, adopted this view as his guiding principle in *The Ultimate of Poetry* (Shigui 詩歸), which became the bestselling poetry anthology of the time. In its preface, Zhong Xing writes:

§128

To bring the spirit of ancients to meet the minds and eyes of later generations, leading the latter to where they should go—this is all we wish to accomplish. . . . I and Tan Yuanchun of my hometown are worried and look into ourselves. We dare not first address the issue whether or not we should learn from ancients, and instead seek to find out where true poetry lies. True poetry comes from spirit. We observe their feelings of reclusion and loneliness—seeing how they acted alone and lived a life of quietude in the clamoring world and how they emptied their mind and exerted concentration for solitary roaming beyond boundless space. Rare is the visitor who has once met with them! Lucky is the seeker who has once found them! Happy any who but once joined their ranks. In haste, there occurred a sudden swap of minds between ancient past and present day, others and me, and I felt bewildered, uncertain where I was heading. What caused all this? It is because of the communion I had with the spirit of the ancients. All things, far or near, front or back, converged on this—toward which people cannot help gravitating.

引古人之精神以接後人之心目，使其心目有所止焉，如是而已矣......惺與同邑譚子元春憂之，內省諸心，不敢先有所謂學古不學古者，而第求古人真詩所在。真詩者，精神所為也。察其幽情單緒，孤行靜寄於喧雜之中；而乃以其虛懷定力，獨往冥遊於寥廓之外。如訪者之幾於一逢，求者之幸於一獲，入者之欣於一至......倉卒中，古今人我，心目為之一易，而茫無所止者，其故何也？正吾與古人之精神，遠近前後於此中，而若使人不得不有所止者也。[11]

For Zhong Xing and Tan Yuanchun 譚元春 (1586–1637), the primary goal of their anthology is to help readers connect with an ancient's spirit, preserved in their writings; to observe and contemplate such a spirit; and to partake in the power of open-minded concentration that enables a "solitary roaming beyond the boundless." While earlier critics such as Liu Xie, Han Yu, and Zhu Xi had discussed spiritual communion with the ancients through reading (Zhu, moreover, provided a systematic discussion in his "Discourse on Immersive Contemplation" 涵泳說), it is Zhong and Tan's innovation to explore the phenomenon specifically from the perspective of literary creation. Since the purpose of this spiritual communion is not to experience the ancients' feelings or become enlightened regarding their morality or aesthetics but to engage in literary creation for self-expression, the "self" naturally becomes the subject in this exchange, the ancients shifting to object position. Only by integrating the ancients' spirit with one's own—in other words, possessing the ancients' spirit—can one create fine writing equal to the ancients. From imitation via "deliberation," and taking possession of the best of the ancients' poetry, one proceeds to commune with the spirit embodied in ancient poetry, and then ultimately transcend it.

The Intuitive Sublimation of Emotions: A Solitary Poet's Discovery

In Chinese philosophical tradition, whether Confucian, Daoist, or Buddhist, Dao enlightenment is almost always realized in a state of tranquility. Emotions must be thoroughly purged before the mind can enter a transcendent state and unite with the Dao. Yet in literature, especially the dramatic genres, *qing* is often treated, seriously or playfully, as the object of deliberation-enlightenment. But in more serious and elegant poetry criticism, we only occasionally see discussions of enlightenment attained through deliberation on *qing*. The second of Wang Changling's "three inscapes," the "the inscape of *qing*," might be one of such uncommon cases. He writes of it: "Joy, happiness, sorrow, and grievances are all subjected to the *yi* and related to the self. Afterward, one lets the thoughts [*si*] run free and deeply grasp these emotions" 娛樂愁怨，皆張於意而處於身，然後馳思，深得其情 (*QTWDSG*, 173). As noted above, *yi* is frequently used to denote the transcendent state of the creative mind (see §§75–81). Thus, "subjected to *yi* and related to the self" may be seen as referring to a process of the transcendent mind sublimating personal emotions into an artistic inscape. But how precisely this sublimating process unfolds, Wang does not say. We must look to the late Qing to find an answer in Kuang Zhouyi's 況周頤 (1859–1926) *Huifeng Remarks on Poetry* (Huifeng cihua 蕙風詞話). There Kuang provides a thorough and original description of his own intuitive sublimation of emotions.

§129

When a thought arose, I immediately sought to dispel it by sound reasoning. Then, once the myriad phenomena were silent, my mind suddenly became crystal clear like the full moon and I felt a chill in my muscles and bones, not even knowing which world I am in. At this moment, nameless sadness and bitterness welled up and could not be held back. But when I try to observe them, all scenes and images disappear before my eyes, only a small window, a translucent curtain, a brush-holder, and an inkstone box. This is the inscape of *ci* poetry.

每一念起，輒設理想排遣之。乃至萬緣俱寂，吾心忽瑩然開朗如滿月，肌骨清涼，不知斯世何世也。斯時若有無端哀怨根觸於萬不得已；即而察之，一切境象全失，唯有小窗虛幌，筆床硯匣，一一在吾目前。此詞境也。[12]

The entry is titled "Account of *Ci* Inscapes I Have Experienced" and begins by describing the poet in the deep, silent night under a dim lamp, alert to the signs of autumn around him. Although he does not explicitly voice his emotions, the melancholy of autumnal thoughts seems to flow from his words. All kinds of thoughts arise in the poet's mind as he attempts to "dispel [them] by sound reasoning" until, in a moment of internal quiet, "all scenes and images are gone." Kuang calls this intuition, arising from sustained brooding over human affections, the "*ci* inscape." This description marks an important departure from what we have seen before. We recall Zong Bing: "Worthies purify their minds and savor iconic images" (§56); and Wang Changling: "To initiate creative conception [*yi*] and write poetry, one must concentrate his mind and set his eyes on things. Next he penetrates things with his mind and reaches into the depth of the landscape" (§85). For both, to "purify" or "concentrate one's mind" involves clearing the mind of all human affections and entering a state of purity or emptiness. In contrast, Kuang's enlightenment into *ci* inscape arises from longtime brooding over his sadness and bitterness—a sadness grounded in the world of experience, such that even after he attains enlightenment, the poet cannot remain "unsullied despite growing from the soil" (like a lotus flower) because "boundless sadness and bitterness" still well up spontaneously in his chest.

§130

I listened to wind and rain, viewed rivers and mountains, and often felt that, beyond wind and rain, rivers and mountains, there is something that inexorably exists. That which inexorably exists is the heart of *ci* poetry. I use my words to describe my mind—this is my *ci* poems. That which inexorably exists is brewed in my mind and is the true essence of my *ci* poems. It cannot be forced nor does it need to be sought—all depends on how the brewing of my mind goes. My mind is the foremost factor and books are only complementary.

吾聽風雨，吾覽江山，常覺風雨江山外有萬不得已者在。此萬不得已者，即詞心也。而能以吾言寫吾心，即吾詞也。此萬不得已者，由吾心醞釀而出，即吾詞之真也。非可強為，亦無庸強求，視吾心之醞釀何如耳。吾心為主，而書卷其輔也。[13]

Carrying the entry titled "Writing My Mind with My Own Words" 述所歷詞境, this passage presents a theoretical recapitulation of Kuang's earlier description of the *ci* inscape. It reveals the two most important characteristics of his proposition: first, the dialectical unity between "gradual deliberation" over emotions (or "brewing 醞釀") and "instantaneous enlightenment" or intuition (into "that which inexorably exists" 萬不得已者); and second, this intuition transcending the distinction between self and things and constituting what Kuang calls the "*ci* lyricist's mind." In addition, note that the phrase "rivers and mountains" 江山 is tinged with Confucian moral sentiment about the family and state.

Another entry, "Confided Meaning Is to Be Prized in *Ci*," discusses the relation between "entrusting of meaning" (*jituo* 寄託) and inborn nature and affections. It reveals the historical factors leading to Kuang's unique theory of intuition through deliberation-enlightenment over *qing*:

§131

Ci poetry values *jituo* or an entrusting [of moral tenor]. What is valued is this: all is revealed unselfconsciously and arises from what one cannot help oneself. The feelings over the vicissitudes of one's life penetrate one's inborn numinosity. Inborn numinosity is what *jituo* is. The latter is not an analogy drawn between two things. If one has a *jituo* lying across the mind before holding up the brush, or if one uses an object as an analogue to one's moral intent as has been uniformly done in hundreds of poems, one can produce only expressions of polite formality or clichés without the slightest change. Seeking changes from things that allow no change, this kind of *jituo* becomes all the more untrue. Commenting on the writings of Qu Yuan, past scholars liken them to alien spirits bouncing up and down as these writings vented the poet's bitter resentment. His poems cannot be explicated, and the changes they exhibit are anything but changes consciously sought after.

詞貴有寄託。所貴者流露於不自知，觸發於弗克自已。身世之感，通于性靈。即性靈，即寄託,非二物相比附也。橫亙一寄託于搦管之先，此物此志，千首一律，則是門面語耳，略無變化之陳言耳。於無變化中求變化，而其所謂寄託，乃益非真。昔賢論靈均書辭，或流於趺宕怪神，怨懟激發，而不可以為訓，必非求變化者之變化矣。[14]

First, Kuang's attention to *jituo* clearly signals his inheritance from the Changzhou school's Confucian poetics, which advocates *jituo* and moral transformation. To get beyond the entrenched Confucian penchant for moralistic allegorization, Zhou Ji had proposed that "one moves into [the realm of *ci*] by having invested meaning and moves out by being free of it." Thus he often described the mental process of "entrusting meaning" in deliberately vague and elusive language. But to Kuang, Zhou did not go far enough because he still allowed a concept to "lie across the mind"—that is, having a clear moral conception prior to writing. To counter this lingering element of allegorization, Kuang pulls out "inborn numinosity," a term enshrined by Ming Anti-Archaists and their Qing followers, to redefine *jituo*, through which he seeks to further aestheticize Confucian poetics.

In some sense, Kuang's expositions on intuitive sublimation of emotions may be seen as the pinnacle of many Qing critics' endeavors, especially the Changzhou school's, to idealize and aestheticize Confucian poetics. Although various Ming-Qing notions of "inborn numinosity" came under persistent, relentless attack by later Confucian-minded theorists, Kuang did not shrink from using this term to define the core Confucian poetic principle of *jituo*. This fully demonstrates the power of his original thinking and his courage to transcend the boundaries of doctrinal differences. For us, his example also shows that, in investigating the development of Ming-Qing theories of literary creation, we should pay attention not only to the opposition between the Archaists and Anti-Archaists, aestheticism and Confucian didacticism, but also to the reciprocal influence and integration of the two traditions.

////////////////////////////////

Notes

1. This Hao Jing should not be confused with late Ming scholar Hao Jing 郝敬 (1557–1639), whose works are extensively discussed in chapter 8.
2. Hao Jing, *Lingchuan ji*, in *Siku Quanshu*, 1192:215.
3. Owen, *Readings in Chinese Literary Thought*, 96.
4. I remember well my joy upon stumbling across this passage a few years ago. More than twenty years ago, when discussing Liu Xie's description of "spirit-thinking" in my contribution to the collection *A Chinese Literary Mind*, edited by myself, I pointed out that Liu Xie's "spirit-thinking" is distinguished by its unique two-way journey. For a long time, I thought I was the first one to note this defining feature until my discovery of this passage by Xie Zhen.
5. See Cai, "Weishi sanleijing," 49–59.
6. *One-Finger Chan for Poets* is traditionally attributed to the Ming monk Huai Yue 懷悅 and is listed as such in *QMSH*, 1:111–21. However, based on Zhang Jian's convincing textual studies, I have listed Yu Ji as the author of this text. Cf. Zhang Jian, "*Shijia yizhi* de chansheng."
7. Yuan M., *Xiaochangshan fang shiwen ji, juan* 20, 490.
8. See Lawall, *Critics of Consciousness*.
9. Zhu X., *Zhuzi quanshu, juan* 24, 3593.
10. Jin, *Jin Shengtan pingdian caizi quanji, juan* 1, 694.
11. Zhong, *Zhong Xing sanwen ji*, 27.
12. Kuang, *Huifeng cihua, juan* 1, 22.
13. Ibid., *juan* 1, 23.
14. Ibid., *juan* 5, 246.

Chapter 7

A *Yi*-Centered Theory of Literary Creation

Of all the theories of literary creation produced during the Ming and Qing, the *yi*-centered theory is the most significant in volume and coherence. In Ming-Qing poetry criticism we find a staggering number of expositions on *yi* as the cardinal principle of poetic composition. Such concerted attention on a single critical term is rare. Further, these expositions are unusually coherent in two ways. First, they largely focus on the last creative phase as they seek to illuminate the activity of the creative mind while composing, a challenge that thwarted Lu Ji and Liu Xie (see §§50–52). Second, the critics who penned these works, often Ming Archaists and their Qing followers and sympathizers, are critics who place a high value on learning poetic art from the Tang masters. To prepare for discussion of these expositions, I first review the rich array of meanings the term *yi* that had accrued by Ming-Qing times:

Six Different Senses of *Yi*

1. *Yi* as an indigenous metaphysical concept, mainly used as a verb or in a verbal sense: In the pre-Qin text *Commentary on the Appended Phrases*, *yi* denotes ancient sages' intuitive cognizance of the ultimate cosmic process (see §20), but in the writings of Wei-Jin thinker Wang Bi it evolves into the highest ontological-epistemological category (see §21). Both Lu Ji and Liu Xie appropriated this indigenous metaphysical concept and its concomitant *yi→xiang→yan* paradigm to analyze the creative process, even though they did not elucidate this concept itself (see §§37–38).

2. *Yi* as a metaphysical concept of Buddhist origin, also used as a verb or in a verbal sense: This originated from the Buddhist concept of *manas-vijñāna* (seventh consciousness) in the Yogācāra sutras (see §§103–7) and was introduced into critical discourse by Wang Changling to describe tranquil, transcendent contemplation at the initial phase of creation (see §§79–85).

3. *Yi* as an artistic conception: In literary criticism, this means bringing forth a mental image of a projected work; in calligraphy criticism, envisioning the shapes, size, ink shades, and movement of strokes prior to writing.

PRISM: THEORY AND MODERN CHINESE LITERATURE · 20 (ANNUAL SUPPL.) · DECEMBER 2023
DOI 10.1215/25783491-11080905 · © 2023 LINGNAN UNIVERSITY

Depending on the context, this artistic conception may carry a strong metaphysical connotation derived from the first sense or may be devoid of such connotation.

4 *Yi* as a nominal concept on the experiential level: In critical discourse, this denotes artistic sublimation of emotions as explained by Fan Ye (see §139) and deployed by Wang Changling in lieu of emotions (see §§98–102).

5 *Yi* as a nominal concept referring to the "idea" or "meaning" that language conveys, whether the meaning of a character, word, or sentence or the overall meaning of a piece of writing.

6 *Yi* as "intention," mainly used adjectivally or adverbially: In critical discourse, this conveys the sense of "with intent" 有意 or "without conscious intent" 無意. It is often used to differentiate self-conscious from spontaneous acts of literary creation.

In writings on literary creation, the first and second senses of *yi* have a paradigmatic function, as they set the general direction for exploring the creative process. While the indigenous metaphysical concept of *yi* has a lasting influence, the impact of the Buddhist metaphysical concept of *yi* is short-lived. As discussed in detail in chapter 4, Wang Changling borrowed the sense of *manas-vijñāna* from Yogācāra Buddhism to describe transcendent contemplation and used the term "inscape" (*jing* 境) for the totality of the universe's myriad things as presented by this *yi*. But after Wang, most Buddhist-minded critics in the Song and Yuan opted to borrow instead Zen terminology such as Chan or "Maheśvara's eye" (see §§113–16, 120). In Ming-Qing times, there are no examples of *yi* used in the second, Buddhist sense.

Generally speaking, what most concerned Ming-Qing critics was not the transcendent contemplation that initiates the creative process per se but the writer's mental activities in the last, compositional phase where the writer, according to Liu Xie, translates suprasensory *yi* that "turns in the void" (*fankong* 翻空) into language that "has veritable existence" (*zhengshi* 徵實). In probing the role of suprasensory *yi* in compositional execution, they follow two different routes. One route tends to abstract, theoretical inquiry with little reference to specific issues of composition. As with Yu Ji and Wang Fuzhi (see §§132–34), those taking this route seek to depict and extol *yi* as the mysterious force driving the entire compositional process. To this end, they trace this source to the cosmic process itself and then demonstrate how it primes more observable forces of nature: *shi* 勢 (momentum of things) and *qi* 氣 (lifebreath).

The other route is that of a practical quest for optimal compositional outcome. Critics taking this route explore the "deploying of *yi*" in various technical aspects of composition, arguing such a deployment endows a work with dynamic unity. For example, among Wang Tingxiang's "Four Tasks" 四務 ("deploying *yi*"

運意, "setting the norm" 定格, "structuring composition" 結篇, and "refining sentences" 鍊句), all of the last three tasks refer to compositional stages to be completed by "deploying *yi*" (see §138). This discussion of "deploying *yi*" encompasses the work of language on various levels, including structural arrangement, use of images and allusions, and selection of words and phrases.

The following six sections are organized along an abstract-to-concrete axis in sync with the compositional process itself. The first section examines the eulogies dedicated to the most abstract aspect of *yi* as a mysterious driving force of composition. The next four sections consider, respectively, the following themes: *yi* as the unifying principle of composition, *yi* and the sublimation of emotion, *yi* and the seeking of tones and images, and *yi* and the casting of words and phrases. Then, turning from the concrete back to the abstract, the last section discusses the dialectic dynamics between *yi* and the law of poetic composition.

Yi as the Mystical Force Driving the Compositional Process

Yuan, Ming, and Qing poetry criticism witnesses a frequent recurrence and steady "metaphysization" of the statement "*yi* or conception is of primary importance to writing," first made by Fan Ye 范曄 (398–445) and later appropriated by late Tang poet Du Mu 杜牧 (803–853) as the cardinal principle of refined writing. In arguing for *yi*'s precedence over *qi* (lifebreath), Du Mu apparently intended to challenge Cao Pi's 曹丕 (187–226) statement, made some six hundred years earlier, that "*qi* or lifebreath is of primary importance to writing." Judging by its context, Du Mu's *yi* belongs to the third sense noted above, denoting artistic conception that precedes the act of composition. While the term *yi* is largely devoid of metaphysical import in Du Mu's usage, it more often than not takes on a metaphysical dimension when used by Yuan, Ming, and Qing critics. In Yu Ji's *One-Finger Chan for Poets* (Shijia yizhi 詩家一指), for instance, we find probably the first conspicuous case of this "metaphysization":

§132

Yi. We form a conception before composing a poem. This is like building palaces and houses: we must have in mind all the measurements, forms, and devices before wielding axes and applying pincers. If we use a physical phenomenon as a metaphor, *yi* is what wind is to the empty sky and what spring is to the world: we find their traces but cannot pin them down as things; they reveal the transcendence of Creation and bring with ease all changes to completion. Even if conceptions are humble and ordinary, the emotions they convey are genuine and profound.

意 作詩先命意，如構宮室，必法度形制已備於胸中，始施斤鋏。此以實驗取譬，則風之於空，春之於世，雖暨有其迹，而無能得之於物者，是以造化超詣，變化易成，立意卑凡，情真愈遠。

Qu. What is not exhausted of *yi* is called *qu* or inspired interest. It is like the vague and subtle lingering sound from a struck bell. It is like the mind riding on the moon in boundless space. What is remote and obscure has true usefulness and flows with Creation—that is the inspired interest of *qu*!

趣 意之所不盡而有餘者之謂趣，是猶聽鐘而得其希微，乘月而思遊汗漫。窅然真用，將與造化者同流，此其趣也![1]

Here Yu Ji tries to mystify and "metaphysicize" *yi* or artistic conception in four steps: comparing it to intangible phenomena like wind and springtime, identifying it with the metaphysical process of change, likening its aesthetic effect—which he calls *qu* or inspired interest—to the faint but lingering sound of a struck bell, and lauding its union with Creation. All these hyperbolic metaphors and superlatives resemble panegyrics of the Dao in the Daoist classics.

Like Yu Ji, the early Qing critic Wang Fuzhi 王夫之 (1619–1692) accentuates the miraculous nature of *yi* by comparing it to external processes of change. But instead of lavishing superlatives on *yi* as an agent of Creation, Wang seeks to demonstrate how it brings about extraordinarily dynamic force and movement in poetry, as exemplified by powerful twists and turns, contraction and expansion, in Xie Lingyun's 謝靈運 (385–433) poems:

§133
Yi is of primary importance and momentum [*shi*] is second to it. *Shi* is the divine principle of *yi*. Xie Kangle [Lingyun] was the only person capable of mastering *shi*. His poems make subtle turns, contract and expand in order to fully convey the *yi*. Once the *yi* is fully conveyed, the poems end without any extra words. Moving gracefully and winding along, enveloped in drifting mists and clouds—such is [the movement of] a real dragon, not a painted one.

以意為主，勢次之。勢者，意中之神理也。唯謝康樂為能取勢，宛轉屈伸，以求盡其意，意已盡則止，殆無剩語；夭矯連蜷，煙雲繚繞，乃真龍，非畫龍也。[2]

If Wang Changling drew on the metaphor of rising smoke to describe the driving force of writing (see §94), Wang Fuzhi here uses the abstract term "momentum" (*shi* 勢) to characterize the miraculous transformation of artistic conception (*yi*) into a text's dynamic movement. According to Wang, it is by dexterously tapping *shi* that Xie Lingyun succeeds in creating a powerful movement comparable to the contracting and expanding, extending and rolling of a real dragon. To drive home the paramount importance of *yi*, he borrows the marshal-soldier comparison from early calligraphy criticism:

§134

Whether in poetry or writings made up of long lines, *yi* should be of primary importance. *Yi* is like a marshal or supreme commander. Troops without such a commander may be called just a chaotic mob. Li Bai and Du Fu are called great masters because in every ten poems they composed we can find just one or two poems that are not expressive of *yi*. Once endowed with *yi*, mists and clouds, spring and rocks, flowers and birds, mosses and woods, or gold-decorated mattresses and brocade bed curtains all become numinous.

無論詩歌與長行文字，俱以意為主。意猶帥也。無帥之兵，謂之烏合。李杜所以稱大家者，無意之詩十不得一二也。煙雲泉石，花鳥苔林，金鋪錦帳，寓意則靈。[3]

From mid-Qing through the late Qing, while abstract theoretical discussions on *yi* continued, they began to revolve around its relationship with *qi* (lifebreath), a physical force more concretely manifest than *shi* (momentum). During the Qianlong-Jiaqing reigns, a debate of sorts broke out between two contemporaries, Qian Yong 錢詠 (1759–1844) and Li Zhi 厲志 (1804–1861). Qian Yong sought to overturn the entrenched valorization of *yi* by contending that the predominant factor in composition is *qi* or lifebreath:

§135

Writers of poetry and prose must have three kinds of ampleness: ampleness in reason, ampleness in conception [*yi*], and ampleness in *qi* [lifebreath]. When reason is ample, one's work will possess essence-spirit; when conception is ample, it will be nuanced and subtle; when *qi* is ample, it will be a tour de force. Both reason and conception move in sync with *qi* as its auxiliaries. Therefore, *qi* must necessarily be of primary importance. With *qi* there is life [in a work] and without *qi* there is death.

詩文家俱有三足，言理足、意足、氣足也。蓋理足則精神，意足則蘊藉，氣足則生動。理與意皆輔氣而行，故尤必以氣為主，有氣即生，無氣則死。(*QSH*, 871)

Challenging Qian's view that "*Qi* is of primary importance," Li Zhi presents a counter argument in his "Discussions on Poetry from the Man of the Baihua Mount'" (Baihua shishuo 白華山人詩說):

§136

When people of our time write poetry, they let lifebreath [*qi*] take the lead, to be followed by *yi* or conception. But when the ancients wrote, they let *yi* take the lead and boosted its movement with lifebreath [*qi*]. If lifebreath takes the lead, all becomes subordinate to it. But if lifebreath arises in subordination to *yi*, naturally there will be no fault of ferociousness.

今人作詩，氣在前，以意尾之。古人作詩，意在前，以氣運之。氣在前，必為氣使，意在前，則氣附意而生，自然無猛戾之病。(*QSHXB*, 2283)

While Li Zhi put forth a polemic argument, Zhang Yuchao 張裕釗 (1823–1894) gave a clear and incisive analysis of the interplay between *yi* (conception) and *qi* (lifebreath) in compositional process:

§137
The ancients who discussed refined writing said, "*Yi* is of primary importance to refined writing." Phrasing is to match the *yi*, and *qi* (lifebreath) is to carry phrasing forward. If we compare this to chariot riding, *yi* is the rider, phrasing is the load, and *qi* is what drives it forward. Those wishing to study ancients' writings should begin by "following sounds to seek *qi*." When *qi* is acquired, *yi* and phrasing often become manifest, and methods are no exceptions to this.... Therefore, the idea of "Following the sounds to seek *qi*" advocated by Yao [Nai] and various others is invariably correct. This is how I seek help from ancients: I follow *qi* to reach their *yi* and their phrasing and methods as well, seeking to comprehend their profundity. As for how I myself compose writings, I consistently treat *yi* as of primary importance, to be followed by phrasing, *qi*, and methods.

古之論文者曰：文以意為主。而辭欲能副其意，氣欲能舉其辭。譬之車然，意為之禦，辭為之載，而氣則所以行也。欲學古人之文，其始在因聲以求氣，得其氣，則意與辭往因之而並顯，而法不外是矣。......故姚氏暨諸家 "因聲求氣" 之說，為不可易也。吾所求于古人者，由氣而通其意以及其辭與法，而喻乎其深。及吾所自為文，則一以意為主，而辭、氣與法胥從之矣。[4]

In seeking to link the mysterious operation of the transcendent *yi* with the actual deployment of language, Zhang Yuzhao 張裕釗 (1823–1894) followed a different approach from Wang Fuzhi and Li Zhi. Instead of using *shi* (momentum) or *qi* (lifebreath) as the intermediary, he adapted Yao Nai's 姚鼐 (1732–1815) sounds-lifebreath-words-spirit gestalt by replacing its highest category "spirit" with *yi*.[5] The following four sections show how Ming-Qing critics undertook to theorize the predominant role of *yi* in major aspects of composition.

Yi as the Unifying Principle of Composition
Moving from hyperbolic praise of *yi* to address its relation to specific issues of composition, the crucial first step, logically speaking, is to consider whether and how *yi* functions as a unifying principle of composition. This is what Wang

Tingxiang 王廷相 (1474–1544) seeks to accomplish in his "Letter to Guo Jiafu to Discuss Poetry" 與郭價夫論詩書:

§138

Alas! If words are bound by concrete referents, they leave no lingering taste. If emotions are directly expressed, they can hardly have affective impact on things. Therefore, conception-image [yixiang] comes into play, compelling us to dwell on it and moving us to commune with it. How far-reaching and deep this is! Such is the rough shape of a poem. Then, one raises his hands to wield the axe. Regarding how to follow rules to get into action, there are four tasks. . . . What are the four tasks? They are the transmission of yi, the setting of norms, the casting of a composition, and the refining of sentences. Yi is the spirit breath of poetry, and therefore one should value well-roundedness and seamlessness, and avoid blurriness and impediment. Norms represent the ambition of poetry, and one should value lofty antiquity and avoid disorderliness. Composition is the bodily substance of poetry, and one should value coherence and smooth flow, and avoid fragmentation. Sentences are the limbs of poetry, and one should value indirection and avoid being straightforward.

嗟乎！言徵實則寡餘味也，情直致而難動物也。故示以意象，使人思而咀之，感而契之，邈哉深矣。此詩之大致也。然措手施斤，以法而入者有四務……何謂四務？運意、定格、結篇、鍊句也。意者，詩之神氣，貴圓融而忌闇滯；格者，詩之志向，貴高古而忌蕪亂；篇者，詩之體質，貴貫通而忌支離；句者，詩之肢骸，貴委曲而忌直率。

Therefore, those who excel in yi command transcendent changes and cast forms and shapes in the same way as Creation. Those who excel in norms craft emotions in ancient antiquity, draw from the airs and odes of the Book of Poetry, and stay clear of the ordinary and shadow. Those who excel in compositional art arrange analogies and allusions and integrate loosely connected phrases like beads on a string. Those who excel in casting sentences employ diverse textures, express a wealth of meanings with sparse phrasing, and never err by being flippant. These four tasks are the principles and rules for a craftsman of art. If one falls short of them even a little bit, one cannot fly high on the path of writing and cannot gallop in the ancient gardens of writing. With the passage of time, he inevitably fades into obscurity.

是故超詣變化，隨模肖形，與造化同工者，精於意者也；搆情古始，侵風匹雅，不涉凡近者，精於格者也；比類攝故，辭斷意屬，如貫珠累累者，精於篇者也；機理混含，辭鮮意多，不犯輕佻者，精於句者也。夫是四務者，藝匠之節度也。一有不精，則不足以軒翥翰塗，馳迹古苑，終隨代汩没爾。(QMSH, 2993)

Taken in isolation, this long passage may be misperceived as having little theoretical significance. In fact, it has been so misunderstood to date. This may be due to the highly technical nature of the three described tasks: setting the norm, structuring a composition, and molding sentences. However, if carefully viewed in the historical development of Chinese theories of literary creation, this passage reveals an extraordinary theoretical significance. Poring over the first few lines, we find consistent reference to Liu Xie's "Spirit-Thinking" chapter. His phrases "words are bound by concrete referents" 言徵實, "conception-image" 意象, and "applying the axe" 施斤 are taken almost verbatim from Liu Xie's famous statements in §49. As I noted earlier, Liu Xie could not find a way to describe the transformation of conception-image into concrete words; or, to use his own metaphor, Liu could not explain how and where a writer should apply his axe. But here, Wang Tingxiang tells the writer how to exercise his *yi* or conception to guide his "axe wielding" to the three most important tasks of composition, in abstract-to-concrete order: norm, structure, and sentence. Connecting the rarefied conception with various aspects of composition was the task Lu Ji and Liu Xie tried but failed to accomplish (see §§50–52). Wang Changling makes significant headway when he compared the dynamic role of *yi* in poetic composition to rising smoke and intimated its effect on structures, couplets, and lines with the fourth sense (sublimated emotions) of *yi* (see §§98–102). However, he fell short of spelling out connections between *yi* and compositional aspects as Wang Tingxiang does here. Seen against Lu's and Liu's failures and Wang Changling's partial success, Wang Tingxiang's achievement in connecting *yi* with major compositional aspects is nothing less than a historic breakthrough. And this breakthrough has truly paradigmatic significance, as numerous later critics follow in his footsteps to explore the dynamics of composition with *yi* as its unifying principle. The sections below explore these dynamics.

Yi and the Sublimation of Emotions

Compositional execution, a process of translating the insubstantial conception-image (*yixiang*) into actual words, entails at the very outset a sublimation of emotions (*qing*) into artistic feelings. So-called artistic feelings are the *yi* of the fourth sense noted above. The affinities of *qing* with *yi* were noted long ago by Xu Shen 許慎 (Eastern Han), the compiler of China's first dictionary, *Explanations of Simple and Compound Characters* (Shuowen jiezi 說文解字). In that dictionary, Xu glosses *yi* with *zhi* (the heart's intent), treating the two characters as interchangeable synonyms (see §§1–2). Looking into the subtle differences between these two concepts, the [Liu] Song scholar Fan Ye 范曄 (398–445) writes:

§139

It is often said that emotions [*qing*] and intent [*zhi*] are mainly confided in *yi* and that refined writing should convey *yi*. When *yi* is predominant, the purport would certainly be manifest; when writing conveys *yi*, the words would not be adrift. Only then could we extract its fragrance and sound its metallic and jade tones. In such refined writings, the inborn nature and emotions, and the embedded purport and interests, fall into hundreds and thousands of categories; in their twists and windings there are established principles.

常謂情志所託，故當以意為主，以文傳意。以意為主，則其旨必見；以文傳意，則其詞不流。然後抽其芬芳，振其金石耳。此中情性旨趣，千條百品，屈曲有成理。[6]

Judging from this passage, Fan Ye clearly does not equate the two terms, because *qing* must be refined into *yi*, in other words, sublimated into an artistic or "patterned" feeling before it enters writing. Only then may this ideal aesthetic effect be achieved: "The inborn nature and emotions, and the embedded purport and interests fall into hundreds and thousands of categories." Reading these remarks by Fan, we cannot but be impressed with his critical insight. His view that *yi* (the fourth sense, sublimated emotions) results from *qing* (direct emotions) being filtered through or patterned by language and acquiring fine aesthetic efficacy strikes me as very modern and reminds me of what Susanne Langer has said about artistic feelings.[7]

Following Fan Ye's line of thought, many Qing critics offered more detailed and cogent discussions on the importance of establishing *yi* (sublimated emotion) in the compositional process. For example, the early Qing critic Huang Sheng 黃生 (1622–?) speaks of the primary importance of enacting *yi*:

§140
In writing poetry, one must first establish *yi*. *Yi* is the host of the entire body. For example, when [writing about] seeing someone off, you express the *yi* of separation and reluctance to part; in writing to someone afar, you express the *yi* of longing, unable to meet in person; in writing about flowers and trees, you deploy the *yi* of fragrant plants in *Lisao*. . . . When *yi* pertains to leisure, then express it with elegant and bland words throughout; when *yi* pertains to grief, then express it with sorrowful, tender feelings throughout; when *yi* pertains to meditation on the past, then express it with impassioned words throughout—this is being enlightened to *yi* in poetry.

作詩先須立意，意者，一身之主也。如送人，則言離別不忍相舍之意；寄贈，則言相思不得見之意；題詠花木之類，則用離騷芳草之意。......故意在於閒適，則全篇以雅淡之言發之；意在於哀傷，則全篇以悽婉之情發之；意在於懷古，則全篇以感慨之言發之。此詩之悟意也。(*QSHXB*, 1588–89)[8]

The "establishing yi" (*liyi* 立意) of the opening sentence may seem synonymous with Wang Changling's "*zuoyi* 作意, *zhiyi* 置意" (see §§76–77, 85), but it is fundamentally different. While Wang's phrases speak to the Buddhist transcendent state of mind that engenders inscape, Huang's "establishing *yi*" articulates the notion of *yi* as sublimated emotion. Here, he gives a subject-based typology of sublimated emotions and stresses the importance of letting these permeate and unify an entire poem. The final sentence, "This is being enlightened to *yi* in poetry," reveals the extraordinary premium Huang sets on the establishment of *yi* in poetic composition.

Expounding the significance of *yi* in this sense, the late Qing critic Zhu Tingzhen 朱庭珍 (1841–1903) adds to it an ethical dimension unseen in earlier discussions like Huang Sheng's:

§141

Poetry is that which expresses the heart's intent and also that which gives expression to our inner nature. Inner nature is still and resides inside. It moves when stirred and undergoes changes as we respond [to external stimuli] and develop emotions. With the rise of emotion, we have the formation of conception [*yi*]. Conception is what the heart's intent confides in while emotions flow within. It entrusts itself to sounds and manifests itself in words. When sound and meaning of words are interwoven like warp and weft, poetry is born. For this reason, poetry can manifest the heart's intent, foster moral values, refine inner dispositions, and convey emotions. So, poetry sets a premium on true conception. True conception relies on the heart's intent to form its backbone and on emotions to generate patterns. Such is the source and the heavenly endowment of all poets.

詩所以言志，又道性情之具也。性寂於中，有觸則動，有感遂遷，而情生矣。情生則意立，意者志之所寄，而情流行其中，因託於聲以見詞，聲與詞意相經緯以成詩，故可以章志貞教、怡性達情也。是以詩貴真意。真意者，本於志以樹骨，本於情以生文，乃詩家之源，即詩家之先天。

As for rhetorical endeavors, such as selecting sounds and images, they are all matters of embellishment that come afterwards and are the most insignificant. This is why poets attach primary importance to the molding of conception [*yi*]. Through painstaking effort of the mind, poets guide conception with thinking, aid conception with their talent, propel conception with lifebreath, and make conception manifest with writing, such that conception takes form in words and words are fully expressive of conception. Within or outside the *yi*, the heart's intent [*zhi*] emerges, half hidden and half manifest, and emotions [*qing*] are touchingly melancholic and profound. Such a work contains true substance and reveals the sincerest feelings in one's heart to the fullest.

至修詞工夫，如選聲配色之類，皆後起粉飾之事，特其末焉耳。詩人首重鍊意以此。慘淡經營於方寸之中，以思引意，以才輔意，以氣行意，以筆宣意，使意發為詞，詞足達意。而意中意外，志隱躍其欲現，情悱惻其莫窮，斯言之有物，衷懷幾若揭焉。(*QSHXB*, 2404–5)

This long passage appears in his *Xiaoyuan's Remarks on Poetry* (Xiaoyuan shihua 筱園詩話), a work highly regarded for its cogent expositions on important critical issues. It seeks to redefine the *yi* (sublimated emotions) by broadening it to encompass two dominant kinds of expressive tenor: *zhi* (the heart's intent) and *qing* (emotions). Though closely related and at times used interchangeably, the two have been taken by many as mutually opposing, especially by those following rigid Confucian thinking on literature. From antiquity, *zhi* almost always figures as a strongly positive term, referring to one's laudable sentiments or attitude toward ethico-sociopolitical realities. By contrast, *qing* (emotion) has, by turns, been praised by followers of an aesthetic approach, and condemned by adherents to a rigid didactic (Confucian) approach to literature. Here, Zhu ingeniously subsumes and integrates the two terms under the *yi*, comparing their integration to a perfect physical body, with sturdy bones under a pleasing outward appearance. To demonstrate the magical effect of this sublimation of both *zhi* (moral intent) and *qing* (emotions) by the *yi*, he writes, "Within or outside the *yi*, moral intent [*zhi*] seems to emerge, half hidden and half manifest, and emotions [*qing*] are touchingly melancholic and profound. Such a work contains true substance and reveals the sincerest feelings in one's heart to the fullest."

Inspired or not by Zhu Tingzhen forty-five years his senior, Huang Kan 黃侃 (1886–1935) employs a similar physiological metaphor to elucidate the significance of *yi* as sublimated emotions:

§142

It is said that literary phrasing depends on bones in much the same way as an upright body depends on the skeleton; emotions contain wind [airs in the *Book of Poetry*] in much the same way as a physical body is enveloped by *qi* or life-breath. So it is clear that a body stands erect thanks to the skeleton and a physical form possesses life thanks to *qi* or lifebreath. Literary phrasing is to writing what bones are to a body and, barring this, there is s no literary phrasing. By the same token, *yi* [sublimated emotion] is to writing what *qi* or lifebreath is to a physical body and, barring this, there is no *yi*.

其曰辭之待骨，如體之樹骸，情之含風，猶形之包氣者，明體待骸以立，形待氣以生；辭之於文，必如骨之於身，不然則不成為辭也，意之於文，必若氣之於形，不然則不成為意也。[9]

Here, Huang seems to paraphrase Liu Xie's abstruse expositions on wind and bone. In Liu's usage, "bone" refers to the actual employment of words and phrases that provide a textual basis or a skeleton (to stay with his metaphor) for generating meanings; "wind" is the lifebreath (*qi*) and energy breathed into a text by emotions. While recapitulating these points, however, Huang makes an important change: substituting *yi* for *qing*. This substitution indicates that Huang was keenly aware of the increasing usage of *yi* as sublimated feelings by Qing critics before him and that he shared their core belief that the expression of *yi* or sublimated feelings rather than raw emotions is what poetry is about.

Yi and the Seeking of Tones and Images

According to Lu Ji, compositional process begins with the selection of tones and images. Immediately after his poetic account of the reflexive journey of the transcendent mind, Lu writes "To investigate emptiness to bring things into existence; / to knock on tranquil silence in search of tones" 課虛無以責有，叩寂寞而求音 (*WFJS*, 89). The "existence [of things]" and "tones" spoken of here refers to the transformation of virtual mental images into actual words describing objects and sounds, not virtual images in the mind. To underscore this act of externalization, Lu adds "Capturing the remote in a foot of silk; / Pouring out the surging current of the mind" 函緜邈於尺素，吐滂沛乎寸心 (*WFJS*, 89). Wang Changling holds a similar view, but he conceptualizes this "surging current of mind" as dynamic *yi* (third sense, envisioning) and likens it to upward billowing smoke (see §94). But neither Lu Ji nor Wang Changling could overcome the seemingly unbridgeable chasm between the abstract *yi* and concrete images and tones. To resolve this tension, Qing critics ingeniously exploit *yi*'s sixth sense (intention) through a misinterpretation of this oft-quoted passage from the *New Accounts of the Tales of the World* (Shishuo Xinyu 世說新語):

§143
After Yu Zisong [Ai 敳] completed the "Poetic Exposition on Idea [*Yi*]," his clansman Wenkang [Yi 翼] saw it and asked, "If you have the Idea, can it be fully represented in a poetic exposition? If you have no Idea, then what did you write a poetic exposition on?" Yu answered, "I am just between having the Idea and not having it."

庾子嵩作《意賦》成。從子文康見，問曰：“若有意邪，非賦之所盡；若無意邪，復何所賦？” 答曰：“正在有意無意之間。”[10]

Judging by its immediate context and intellectual background, the *yi* of Yu Zisong's "*Fu* Exposition on *Yi*" is not "intent," though it has been widely misinterpreted as such to the present day. This is due to a failure to understand the use of *yi* in the context of Wei-Jin Abstruse Learning, where it means not "intent" but the highest onto-epistemological category, as articulated by Wang Bi (see §§21–22). Yu Yi's 庾翼 (305–345) point is that "having *yi*" (*youyi* 有意) takes place on an ontological level, which makes it inexpressible in words, while "not having *yi*" (*wuyi* 無意) means having no such lofty meaning and therefore not being worth the effort to write a poetic exposition on it. Yu Zisong, meanwhile, believes that there is room between "having *yi*" and "not having *yi*" for mind-roaming and verbal expression, which makes writing poetic expositions on *yi* still meaningful.

As his "Poetic Exposition on *Yi*" has not survived, it is impossible now to know how Yu Ai discussed the relationship between "having *yi*" and "not having *yi*." But for Ming-Qing critics, this play of having/not having *yi* comes in handy to explain the transformation of mental images (*yixiang*) into actual words. If *yi* is taken in its sixth sense (intention), having it suggests conscious endeavors, and not having it, more spontaneous acts of composition. This sixth sense of *yi* (intention) seems to be what many Ming-Qing critics have in mind when they use the expression "between having *yi* and not having *yi*" to explain the compositional process of "seeking tone and grasping image." Consider, for example, the late Ming critic Feng Fujing 馮復京 (1573–1622):

§144

When someone in the Jin wrote the "Poetic Exposition on *Yi*" and was quizzed about it, he answered, "In between having *yi* and not having *yi*." Alas! This in-between space is subtle indeed! When the reach of divine transformation is still unknown, one necessarily thinks forward to the next in sequence. This being the case, then "carving and gouging one's insides" [meaning an extremely painstaking effort] is indeed perfectly congenial to nature's truths; scrutinizing conditions and probing appearances also make wondrous fish weirs to capture *yi*.

晋人作《意》賦，被詰乃曰：“在有意無意之間。” 嗚呼,此間亦微矣哉。神化所至，未之或知, 必思其次，則刻腎鏤腸，固天真之司契，窺情鑽貌，亦得意之妙筌也。 (*QMSH*, 3842)

To Feng, the unconscious "reach of divine transformation" and the conscious "carving and gouging one's insides" are mutually complementary acts, and therefore, both make "wondrous fish weirs to capture *yi*." Precisely from this dialectical unity of opposites, Feng's discussion of "constructing *yi*" (*gouyi* 構意) simultaneously affirms Liu Xie's notion of "producing literature for the sake of emotions" 為情而造文 and his opposite notion of "generating emotions for the sake of literature" 為文而造情 (*WXDL*, 31/62, 74). In a similar vein, Feng equally emphasizes seeking images from both the metaphysical and the physical realms.

By the same token, in *Discussions of Poetry from the Zhenyi Studio* (Zhenyizhai shishuo 貞一齋詩說), the Qing critic Li Chonghua 李重華 (1682–1755) upholds "between having and not having *yi*" as the highest principle for composition. He claims, "*Yi*'s deployment of spirit cannot be conveyed by language. Those capable of it often stay between having *yi* and not having *yi*" 意之運神，難以言傳，其能者常在有意無意間 (*QSH*, 921). He designates the movements of *yi* as "*yi*'s deployment of spirit" and appends the following vivid description:

§145
For those skilled in depicting *yi*, when *yi* moves, spirit is poised to leap forth, and when *yi* is exhausted, spirit would disappear into boundless obscurity. This process is accomplished wordlessly and rests on the individual person. If asked, "Which of the three comes first?" I reply "When *yi* is enacted, images and tones follow." . . . As when a dancer dancing to music is moved to sing, all the pleasure of *yi* comes from the flying movement. Whether it's affective image, metaphor, or exposition, all contain what's striking to the mind and eye.

善寫意者，意動而其神躍然欲來，意盡而其神渺然無際，此默而成之，存乎其人矣。曰：是三者孰為先？曰：意立而象與音隨之......如舞曲者動容而歌，則意愜悉關飛動，無論興比與賦，皆有怳然心目者"。(*QSH*, 921)

Here, he introduces the concept of "depicting *yi*" from painting criticism into poetry criticism, emphasizing the importance of deploying *yi* in the compositional process and describing the rich, beautiful imagery as the product of deploying *yi*.

Yi and the Casting of Words and Phrases

Phrasing, the casting of words and phrases, is the final step in the compositional process. The relation between creative conception and phrasing is a topic that long challenged Chinese critics who devoted countless expositions to its understanding. The position a traditional Chinese critic takes on this topic largely depends on what he wants language to do. If language functions as an instrument of sociopolitical governance, he aims for maximum conceptual clarity and linguistic precision. A prime example is Confucius, as evidenced by his censure of speculative thinking (see §4) and imprecise use of language (see §3). The essentialist bent of Confucius and his followers' expositions on language is discussed in detail in chapter 1 (see §§3–9). If one uses language to generate aesthetic pleasure, a critic naturally appreciates a blurring of conceptual and linguistic boundaries for maximum aesthetic effect. A prime example of this counter view is what Su Shi Su Che 蘇轍 (1039–1112) says in his "Letter in Reply to Judge Xie Minshi" 答謝民師推官書:

§146

Confucius says, "Words without embellishment cannot travel far" and also, "All words are about is getting things across." Some people take the statement that words go no further than getting *yi* across as a dismissal of refined writing, [but] that is certainly not the case. To capture the wondrousness of things is as hard as tying down wind or catching scenery by the hand. Out of millions of people, only one has a luminous vision of things in the mind, to say nothing of the one who can transmit it to the mouth and hand. This is what "words getting things across" means. If words can get things across this way, the usefulness of writing cannot be exhausted.

孔子曰：“言之不文，行而不遠。” 又曰： “辭達而已矣。” 夫言止於達意，
即疑若不文，是大不然。求物之妙，如繫風捕景，能使是物瞭然於心者，蓋千
萬人而不一遇也。而況能使瞭然於口與手者乎？是之謂辭達。辭至於能達，則
文不可勝用矣。[11]

In this passage, Su Shi cleverly reappropriates Confucius's remarks to affirm the opposite stance. By aligning Confucius's statement, "There is nothing more to phrases than getting [things] across," with another remark by the master, "Without refinement, words cannot travel far," Su flips and appropriates Confucius's advocacy of unadorned use of language for ethico-sociopolitical purposes into an aesthetic principle for literary composition. He does this in three steps. First he adds *yi* as the missing object of the verb "getting across" in Confucius's statement. Then he conceptualizes this *yi* as the wondrousness of things, difficult to capture, like wind or shadow. Finally, he praises the finest literary phrasing (*ci*) as capable of "tying wind and catching shadow," an accomplishment of only the rarest person. Viewed from a still broader context, Su Shi's appropriation of Confucius's statement represents a refashioning of Zhuangzi's remark on the *yi-yan* polarity (see §13). As was surveyed in chapter 1, the Warring States and Han-Wei thinkers developed the Zhuangzian *yi-yan* polarity into the *yi→xiang→yan* onto-epistemological paradigm, which was later appropriated by Lu Ji and Liu Xie to develop their comprehensive theories of literary creation. But here, Su Shi refashions the Zhuangzian *yi-yan* polarity into a paradigm for judging compositional excellence—a paradigm that would be taken up and used by Ming-Qing critics in various ways.

In the late mid-Ming, for instance, the prominent Archaist Xie Zhen 謝榛 (1495–1575) made use of this new *yi-yan* paradigm to advance the Archaist campaign against Song poetry in favor of High Tang poetry. To advance this sectarian agenda, Xie set up a dichotomy between what he calls "Pre-phrasing *Yi*" and "Post-phrasing *Yi*," using the former to critique Song poetry and the latter to praise Tang poetry:

§147

Song poets always form a general idea [before writing], following the path of reason and utterly lacking the subtleties of thought.

宋人必先命意，涉於理路，殊無思致。

Master Siming says, "When people write poetry today, they first determine a main idea that becomes awkward as soon as it is bound by a line. Their language fails to convey meanings and their *yi* cannot be fully conveyed." The deficiency of this mode of writing is "like chiseling a pool to store the azure skies" or "raising a cup to collect sweet dew"—the amount that can be contained is limited. This is called the "pre-phrasing *yi*."

四溟子曰：“今人作詩，忽立許大意思，束之以句則窘，辭不能達，意不能悉。譬如鑿池貯青天，則所得不多；舉杯收甘露，則被澤不廣。此乃內出者有限，所謂 ‘辭前意’ 也。”

Alternately, when one cannot compose good lines, one does not allow his spirit thinking to be exhausted. He reads books and keeps a clear mind. Then he suddenly gets something, *yi* activates with the writing brush. Inspiration cannot be held back, and he partakes in spiritual transformation and achieves what one cannot achieve through deliberation. He gets a line by expanding from one word and completes the line with rhyme. Coming from nature, such lines and their contents are beautiful. They are like bamboo tubes bringing in spring water and sending off its melodious sounds. Reading them, we feel as if we are climbing the city wall and watching the sea, overwhelmed by its expansive view. This is the case of boundlessness coming from outside and this is called "post-phrasing *yi*."

或造句弗就，勿令疲其神思，且閱書醒心，忽然有得，意隨筆生，而興不可遏，入乎神化，殊非思慮所及。或因字得句，句由韻成，出乎天然，句意雙美。若接竹引泉而潺湲之聲在耳，登城望海而浩蕩之色盈目。此乃外來者無窮，所謂 ‘辭後意’ 也。” (*QMSH*, 1369)

By "pre-phrasing *yi*," Xie Zhen refers to Song poets' common tendency to first form a conceptual idea and then use words and phrases to express it. The problem, for Xie, with this compositional approach lies in the paucity of aesthetic response it can generate. Xie delivers this harsh judgment with two vivid metaphors: "Like chiseling a pool to store the azure skies" or "raising a cup to collect sweet dew . . . the amount that can be contained is limited." Conversely, by "post-phrasing *yi*," Xie refers to the high-Tang poet's spontaneous approach to composition: "He suddenly gets something and the writing brush activates the *yi*." If we compare Xie's remarks with Su Shi's passage, we clearly see Xie's debt to Su's notion of simultaneous syncing of the mind and the writing hand, a notion further traceable back to Zhuangzi's tale of the Butcher Ding (see §48). But compared with Su, Xie assigns more spiritual significance to the act of composition. With his notion of post-phrasing yi, Xie Zhen elevates the status of words to unprecedented heights—before, if not above, *yi*. Xie believes that in the unconscious deployment of language, transcendent *yi* arises spontaneously. This is highly original, and it is difficult to find a precedent in earlier discussions of literary creation. Outside this discourse, however, multiple sources might have inspired or at least provided support for Xie's reification of phrasing. These include the reification of written graphs in traditional accounts of their creation and in the treatment of written characters as embodiment of natural forces in calligraphy criticism.[12] But a more immediate source may be the rise of "Chan through words" (*wenzi Chan* 文字禪) in Song Buddhism.

Regardless of whether it was Xie Zhen's intention to do so, his notion of post-phrasing *yi* provided theoretical justification for the Archaists' imitation of High Tang poetry and at the same time inspired some Qing critics to probe the spiritual import of poetic words and phrases, as shown by Huang Sheng's grading of poetic lines:

§148

Poetic lines of the first level are obtained from nature and do not need cutting and polishing. They possess natural prosodic harmony as well as visual and spiritual appeal. Among them, what's extraordinary and unsurpassable is like a lone peak or a high cliff; what has the flavor of remote antiquity is like a temple bell or the Grand Bell; what's solemn and awesome is like battle banners and flags, armor and weaponry; what's grand and sublime is like thousands of troops and war horses; and what's magnificent is like precious rare flowers and beautiful women. All these are miraculous lines. The next level must exhibit fine compositional skill. If a line has some of these qualities—whether movement and quietude, large and small, true and false, life and death, near and far away, antiquity and present day, virtual and real, or intangible changes—it is an excellent line.

第一字句得於天然，不待雕琢， 律呂自諧，神色兼備，奇絕者如孤厓斷峯， 高古者如黃鐘大呂， 飄逸者如清風白雲， 森嚴者如旌旗甲兵， 雄壯者如千軍萬馬， 華麗者如奇花美女，如是為妙句。其次必須造語精工， 或動靜大小，眞假生死， 遠近古今，虛實有無， 或變化彷彿， 一句之中， 常具數節義， 乃為佳句. (*QSHXB*, 1589–90)

Here Huang establishes the highest levels of poetic lines: the first is for "marvelous lines" that are begotten naturally, while the next contains "excellent lines" that show fine skill and craft. Of the highest grade, he lists six major styles and compares each to a breathtaking sight in nature or the human world. After describing these lofty levels, he proceeds to designate five subcategories according to their content and aesthetic qualities: "Lines with penetrating views of heaven and earth" 洞觀天地之句; "lines that turn one's insides out" 剖出肺腑之句; "lines with thorough understanding of life and death" 了達生死之句; "lines invested with billowing inspirations" 寄興悠揚之句; "lines that depict scenes beyond a barrier" 隔關寫景之句. Close examination of Huang's organization reveals significant overlap with calligraphy critics' description of brush strokes, character shapes, and dynamic flow of lines. Clearly inheriting from calligraphy a belief in the dynamic brush's evocation of natural forces, Huang argues for a similar metaphysical evocation through the casting of poetic words and phrases.

Transcendent *Yi* and Compositional Law (*Fa*): Dialectical Interplay

As shown above, the shift in critical attention onto the compositional process was largely spearheaded by the Former and Latter Seven Masters of Ming and other Archaists. As ardent advocates of High Tang poetry, they were naturally burdened with two tasks. First, they had to extract methods from Tang poetry for structuring a composition, sublimating emotions, selecting tones and images, and casting words and phrases. Then they would need to demonstrate that all these methods can be appropriated through transcendent *yi*'s intervention so that students of Tang poetry could hope to produce beautiful poems to match the Tang masters. We have just seen the resourcefulness of Ming Archaists and their Qing followers in accomplishing this. By exploiting *yi*'s polysemy and appropriating "essentialist" notions of written characters in calligraphy criticism, they managed to bridge the seemingly unbridgeable gap between *yi* and language. Not content just to discuss methods of handling compositional material, mid-Qing critic Zhang Huiyan 張惠言 (1761–1802) and late Qing critic Zhu Tingzhen explored the relationship between transcendent *yi* and *fa* 法, or the general law of composition that encompasses all technical methods. Citing his friend Qian Lusi's experience appreciating and practicing calligraphy, Zhang Huiyan sheds light on this dialectical relationship:

§149

So, [Qian] Lusi said, "In the past I could only see methods in the calligraphy of ancients. But now when I look at what is printed from stone tablets, I can see what existed [in the calligrapher's mind] before the stone tablets were carved. The idea that '*Yi* comes before the writing brush' does not mean one consciously forms a conception and then picks up the brush. As I move the brush and let out the ink, I already know well the merits and demerits of various masters from Wei, Jin, Tang, and Song dynasties and have internalized them in my mind. So, when I pick up my brush, something seems to be out there far away, gently moving, now shadowy and now clear. When encountering it, I do not know why this happens. This is the working of *yi* or conception. Conception is not the law but is never separated from the law. There are sources for nourishing it and what comes out of it is something real. While law has limits, conception is inexhaustible. When I write poetry, I also see *yi* working in the same way. In fact, this is true, not just for poetry and calligraphy, but also for ancient-style prose."

魯斯遂言曰："吾曩於古人之書，見其法而已。今吾見拓於石者，則如見其未刻時；見其書也，則如見其未書時。夫意在筆先者，非作意而臨筆也。筆之所以入，墨之所以出，魏、晉、唐、宋諸家之所以得失，熟之於中而會之於心。當其執筆也，繇乎其若存，攸攸乎其若行，冥冥乎，成成乎，忽然遇之，而不知所以然，故曰意。意者，非法也，而未始離乎法。其養之也有源，其出之也有物，故法有盡而意無窮。吾於為詩，亦見其若是焉。豈惟詩與書，夫古文，亦若是則已耳。" [13]

Zhang Huiyan astutely notes this dialectical interplay between *yi* and *fa*. Using the term "law" (*fa* 法) to cover all aspects of poetic technique, he describes the relationship between *yi*, the creative mental activity so elusive to language, and *fa*, the law of composition under which all technical details such as structure, tone, and imagery are subsumed. Zhang believes that, in the compositional phase, "*yi* is not the law but never deviates from the law"—in other words, the deployment of the nonsubstantial *yi* never departs from the determinate law of poetry. He thus claims, "*Yi* is not *fa*, but never departs from it. Therefore, there are sources by which we nourish it; it has substance when it is expressed. For this reason, we say *fa* (compositional law) has limits, but *yi* is boundless."

While Zhang speaks of *yi-fa* relationship in general terms, Zhu Tingzhen seeks out this relationship with a fourfold scheme:

§150

A poet releases a flight of the mind's essence, encircling heaven and setting the earth's boundaries, traversing a thousand years, and crisscrossing ten thousand *li*. When his brush comes down, wind and rain are startled; when his composition is done, ghosts and spirits weep. How can there be a fixed law?

詩人一縷心精，蟠天際地，上下千年，縱橫萬里，筆落則風雨驚，篇成則鬼神泣，此豈有定法哉! (*QSHXB*, 2327)

Yet, among lofty mountains and soaring peaks, long rivers and grand rivers are nature's sinews, arteries, and veins—threading through like waves, appearing like a spider's web and the trail of a horse. These nodes run from beginning to end and form an integrated whole while each has its own organic structure. So, it is not necessarily the case that there are no laws.

然而重山峻嶺，長江、大河之中，自有天然筋節脈絡，鍼綫波瀾，若蛛絲馬迹，首尾貫注，各具精神結撰，則又未始無法。

Therefore, we speak of rising and falling, continuation and linkages; twists and turns and mutual correspondence; openings and closings; pauses and turns; capturing and releasing, suppressing and amplifying; contrastive shading of the positive and the negative; extension and contraction, and breakage and continuation. All these belong to the fixed law of poetry.

故起伏承接，轉折呼應，開闔頓挫，擒縱抑揚，反正烘染，伸縮斷續，此詩中有定之法也。

Being extraordinary at times and orthodox at times, appearing clear here and indistinct there—one just follows the mind's wish and achieves marvelousness wherever it goes. This is the law that has no fixities.

時奇時正，若明若滅，隨心所欲，無不入妙：此無定之法也。(*QSHXB*, 2327)

In the fourfold scheme sketched here, the first tier is an account of the transcendent flight of the mind, the likes of which we have seen many times and need no further comment here. Such a transcendent poetical mind is of course "without law" (*wufa* 無法)—is not subject to any law. The second tier is the wondrous configurations and appearances of nature that Zhu surmises "may not necessarily be without *fa*" 未始無法. The third is a host of dynamic rhetorical maneuvers: "rising and falling, etc. All these belong to the fixed law of poetry" (*youding zhifa* 有定之法). Finally, at the highest tier is a great poet's achievement of the intended results of all these rhetorical maneuvers by doing just the opposite, which Zhu calls "the law of having no fixities" (*wuding zhifa* 無定之法).

According to Zhu, when a poet operates through this law of having no fixities (the fourth tier), he essentially turns compositional maneuvers (third tier) into a process no different from the free flight of the transcendent mind (the first tier), or the processes of nature (second tier). In this way, he attains the perfect dialectic and unifying interplay of transcendent *yi* and compositional law:

§152
In poetry, it is through the self that laws are deployed, rather than the self being employed by the laws. Therefore, in the beginning, one takes laws as the law, but next, one takes having no law as the law. To be capable of not adhering to laws but also not deviating from the law—only this can be called success.

詩者以我運法，而不為法用。故始則以法為法，繼則以無法為法。能不守法，亦不離法，斯為得之。(*QSHXB*, 2327)

In devising this fourfold scheme, Zhu undertakes what other Ming-Qing critics attempted but never fully achieved: to bridge the seemingly unbridgeable gap between the transcendent mind and the physical act of composition with language. By presenting and unifying the four tiers as corresponding processes of a cosmic yin-yang operation, Zhu established a firm ground for linking or even equating a great poet's compositional process with his precomposition mental flight. Of all the traditional Chinese literary theory I've read, I can find no more innovative, systematic, or compelling explanation of how the transcendent mind makes the leap to literary composition.

* * * * *

We will fully appreciate the significance of *yi*-centered theory only when we grasp its breakthrough in the context of evolving literary thought. After Lu Ji's "Exposition on Literature," the challenge to describe the transformation from the conception-image (*yixiang*) to concrete language would have been on the mind of many critics. How does the author get from imaginative activity to actual composition? Despite Liu Xie's awareness that "spirit-thinking" must ultimately shape compositional structure, for which he lists "three standards" (*sanzhui* 三准), he is still unable to elucidate the relation between spirit-thinking and the practice of the three standards. The Tang critic Wang Changling makes innovative use of *yi* in the third sense (dynamic "envisagement" as used in calligraphic discourse) to describe the writer's mental activities during the phase of composition execution. Additionally, he uses *yi* in the fourth sense (its static noun usage) to refer to writing's emotive content and regards the latter's interplay with external scenes as the principle for organizing language. Ming-Qing discussants of *yi* followed the path pioneered by Wang Changling. By using the dynamic conception of *yi* as the paradigmatic principle linking all levels of compositions, they reformed the "law of poetry" from a set of rigid rules into a "living law." To a great extent, Ming-Qing critics may be said to have resolved the challenge to describe the process by which the writer's imagination is crystallized in language, thereby making compositional process an integral part in the theorization of literary creation.

If we further broaden our critical perspective, we may discern another significant contribution made by the *qi*-centered theory: its revitalization of the traditional "study of composition" (*wenzhang xue* 文章學). In Song studies of composition, the term *yi* is largely used in its fifth sense, referring to the "main idea" of a prose or poetic composition, rarely connected with the mental activities in the course of composition. Ming-Qing poetry critics no doubt propelled the study of composition to take a turn from compositional analysis toward theoretical examination of the impact of the creative mind on the compositional process. In this way, they must be recognized for breathing new life into that old branch of learning.

Notes

1. *One-Finger Chan for Poets* is traditionally attributed to the Ming monk Hui Yue 懷悅 and is collected in *QMSH*, 1:111–21. I agree with Zhang Jian's attribution of this text to Yu Ji and list Yu as its author; see Jian Zhang, *Shijia yizhi* de chansheng, 33–34.
2. Wang F., *Jiangzhai shihua*, 48.
3. Ibid., 44.
4. Zhang Yuzhao, *Zhang Yuzhao shiwen ji, juan* 4, 85.
5. See Cai, "Sound over Ideograph."
6. Shen, *Songshu, juan* 69, 1830.
7. See Langer, *Form and Feeling*.
8. This passage is traditionally attributed to Mao Chunrong 冒春榮 and is listed as such in *QSHXB*. Based on Jiang Yin's *Qing Shihua kao* (358), Huang Sheng is listed here as the author of this passage.
9. Huang K., *Wenxin diaolong zaji*, 101.
10. Liu, *Shishuo xinyu*, 140.
11. Su Shi, *Su Shi wenji*, 49:1418.
12. See Cai, *Configurations of Comparative Poetics*, chap. 6.
13. See Zhang H., *Mingke wenbian*, 70.

Chapter 8

Qing-Centered Theories of Literary Creation (I)
Ming through Mid-Qing

The Chinese poetic tradition has a long history of valuing emotions, or *qing* 情. Their importance is summed up in two statements: "Poetry expresses the heart's intent" (*Shi yan zhi* 詩言志), and "*Shi* poetry coarises with emotions" (*Shi yuan qing* 詩緣情). When "poetry expresses the heart's intent" first appeared in the *Book of Documents*, it pointed toward the author's emotive intent. Afterward, thanks to the Spring and Autumn–period practice of performing *Shijing* poems as analogs to state politics, the term *zhi* (heart's intent) gradually evolved to denote an emotive category with deep sociopolitical and moral implications. "Records of Music" (Yue ji 樂記) in the *Book of Rites* (Li ji 禮記) states that, when moved by external things, "*qing* stirs on the inside" and "manifests itself in words." During the Han, this view was fleshed out in the "Great Preface to the *Book of Poetry*" (*Shi da xu* 詩大序): "Poetry is where the *zhi* [the heart's intent] goes. When in the mind, it is intent; disclosed in words, it becomes poetry" 詩者，志之所之也。在心為志，發言為詩 (*ZGLDWLX*, 1:63) Yet in the Western Jin, when Lu Ji states, "*Shi* poetry arises alongside emotions and is thus exquisite and gentle" 詩緣情而綺靡 (*WFJS*, 99), the import of *qing* has shifted to indicate the literary-aesthetic nature of poetry and mainly involves an individual's private emotions with no obvious sociopolitical or moral implications. Inheriting Lu's notion that "poetry arises alongside emotions," Liu Xie then defines the nature of literature as the "patterning of emotions" (*qingwen* 情文). In discussing literary creation, however, Lu and Liu treat *qing* only as an inducive factor for writing and as raw material for the formation of conception-images (*yixiang* 意象). Although many scholars consider the lyrical tradition (*shuqing* 抒情, or the expression of *qing*) central to classical Chinese literature, *qing* did not figure prominently in the theorization of literary creation until the Ming and Qing dynasties. The Ming-Qing discourses on poetry offer an abundance of discussion on *qing* across a wide range of aspects. The traditional *yan zhi* 言志 versus *yuan qing* 緣情 divide is no longer sufficient to classify and analyze these discussions; we need a framework broad enough to encompass the vast scope of material, and analytical enough to comb through and classify richly diverse points of view. Such a framework I stumbled on when rereading two classic Western texts on poetic emotion: William Wordsworth's "Preface to the 1800 edition of *Lyrical Ballads*" and T. S. Eliot's "Tradition and the Individual Talent." I discovered that Wordsworth's and Eliot's theories of emotion could be best distinguished in terms of their antithetical expositions on five key issues along the creative process: the source of poetic emotion, optimal conditions for poetic expression, the interplay of emotions and images, use of language, and the functions of poetry. This discovery, in turn, led me to apply the same analytical framework to sort out primary material and reconstruct various *qing*-centered theories of literary creation. Before presenting my findings about these theories, let me briefly present Wordsworth's and Eliot's different views on poetic emotion. This short detour should afford a comparative perspective to perceive not only the individual uniqueness of various Ming-Qing *qing*-centered theories but also the complex web of interrelations between them.

Wordsworth and T. S. Eliot on Poetic Emotion

What Wordsworth and T. S. Eliot have to say about the expression of emotion in poetry revolves around five key critical issues. I explore these in some detail because they can help us to pinpoint the Ming-Qing theory of poetic emotion. I begin with the origin of poetic emotion. Wordsworth affirms poetry's emotive value is directly related to individual life experiences, especially those of rural life:

> Low and rustic life was generally chosen because in that situation the essential passions of the heart find a better soil in which they can attain their maturity, are less under restraint, and speak a plainer and more emphatic language; because in that situation our elementary feelings exist in a state of greater simplicity and consequently may be more accurately contemplated and more forcibly communicated; because the manners of rural life germinate from those elementary feelings; and from the necessary character of rural occupations are more easily comprehended; and are more durable; and lastly, because in that situation the passions of men are incorporated with the beautiful and permanent forms of nature.[1]

Wordsworth believes rural life offers the best source for poetry because, as he notes in the 1850 preface, "in that condition of life our elementary feelings exist in a state of greater simplicity." In other words, because the urban scene often involves more complex relationships among people, what people feel becomes more difficult to decipher and express. These elementary feelings, according to Wordsworth, find their best expression through human engagement with nature. Hence, his principal object is to "choose incidents and situations from common life, and to relate or describe them, throughout, as far as was possible in a selection of language really used by men."[2] In 1800 he firmly declares that good poetry necessarily originates from powerful feelings arising naturally in ordinary life: "For all good poetry is the spontaneous overflow of powerful feelings; but though this be true, Poems to which any value can be attached, were never produced on any variety of subjects but by a man who being possessed of more than usual organic sensibility had also thought long and deeply."[3] Nonetheless, a later passage from the 1800 preface complicates the picture: "I have said that Poetry is the spontaneous overflow of powerful feelings: it takes its origin from emotion recollected in tranquility: the emotion is contemplated till by a species of reaction the tranquility gradually disappears, and an emotion, similar to that which was before the subject of contemplation, is gradually produced, and does itself actually exist in the mind."[4] Finally, then, poetry isn't simply the "spontaneous overflow of powerful feelings" but something much closer to the thoughtful contemplation of that feeling (in other words, thought), which then leads to the reproducing of that emotion. In other words, not emotion but thought that itself engenders what we might call a *secondary* emotion. And this would be very much like the two-stage process of imaginative creation (primary and secondary imagination) described by Coleridge in the *Biographia Literaria*.[5]

Nonetheless, it is precisely this statement that Eliot would target in "Tradition and the Individual Talent." Facing Wordsworth, Eliot wants to maintain the following:

> For it is neither emotion, nor recollection, nor, without distortion of meaning, tranquility. It is a concentration, and a new thing resulting from the concentration, of a very great number of experiences . . . which would not seem to be experiences at all. . . . Of course, this is not quite the whole story. There is a great deal, in the writing of poetry, which must be conscious and deliberate. . . . Poetry is not a turning loose of emotion, but an escape from emotion; it is not the expression of personality, but an escape from personality.[6]

Eliot believes poetic emotions aren't the same as individual emotions; the former is impersonal and has nothing to do with the poet's life, personality, and passions. True poetic emotion must be the artistic transmutation of individual emotions in a process akin to that of a chemical reaction. Eliot considers this an artistic process approaching the condition of science.

The second issue involves the mode of lyrical expression: what are the optimal conditions that make it possible? Unlike Wordsworth, Eliot believes the whole process is one that gradually takes us further and further away from anything like individual feeling or consciousness: because it involves the "transmuting" of emotion, it is one where all individual feeling or consciousness finally completely disappears. And here he offers the ingenious analogy of a chemical catalyst: "When the two gases previously mentioned are mixed in the presence of a filament of platinum, they form sulphurous acid. This combination takes place only if the platinum is present; nevertheless the newly formed acid contains no trace of platinum, and the platinum itself is apparently unaffected; has remained inert, neutral, and unchanged. The mind of the poet is the shred of platinum."[7] Like the newly formed acid, then, Eliot claims poetry shouldn't contain any trace of the poet's personal experiences, emotions, or personality.

The third issue I want to discuss is the interplay of emotion with external object and image. How do emotions engage and blend with images? Wordsworth wants the poet to capture experiences from simple rural life, hoping by doing so to isolate emotion that because of its simplicity is not lost in the abysses of individual subjectivity:

> Such a language arising out of repeated experience and regular feelings is a more permanent and a far more philosophical language than that which is frequently substituted for it by Poets, who think that they are conferring honour upon themselves and their art in proportion as they separate themselves from the sympathies of men, and indulge in arbitrary and capricious habits of expression in order to furnish food for fickle tastes and fickle appetites of their own creation.[8]

Although Eliot is also highly intent on linking emotion to external object, he believes the latter—like the former—should be wholly distinct from the poet's personal life. In his essay on *Hamlet*, he advances the well-known concept of an "objective correlative." Emotion (even artistic emotion) should not be expressed directly but can only be successfully evoked by a kind of image, or objective correlative. It could be "a set of objects, a situation, a chain of events which shall be the formula of that particular emotion; such that when the external facts, which must terminate in sensory experience, are given, the emotion is immediately evoked."[9] Eliot argues that images that evoke artistic emotions do not exist in isolation: every image resumes or takes up all the significance with which past poets have endowed it, and a truly good poem is not a series of individually inflected or subjective images strung together but an intertextual tapestry woven by the poet out of different words, phrases, and images coming from a collective tradition.

My fourth point concerns the coming together of emotion and language. Wordsworth thinks that subject matter aptly chosen should naturally yield ideal poetic language conveying the appropriate passion. Eliot doesn't comment specifically on the transition from emotion to language but emphasizes that, because of the collective framework of tradition, any new expression must fit into an existing order that simultaneously transforms and is transformed by it: "The existing order is complete before the new work arrives; for order to persist after the supervention of novelty, the *whole* existing order must be, if ever so slightly, altered; and so the relations, proportions, values of each work of art toward the whole are readjusted; and this is conformity between the old and the new."[10] In other words, because every work of art acts upon the existing tradition, every element of that work of art must likewise act on all the elements of all the works comprising that tradition. This is what makes literary creation truly meaningful. For Eliot, then, literary creation involves a whole set of "intertextual moves." And indeed, his own High Modernist verse, like *The Waste Land*, is just that: with its plethora of allusions ranging all over Western tradition, he manages to create a sense of modernity that is essentially one of intertextuality.

The final issue I want to discuss is the function of poetry. For Wordsworth true poetry should reveal reality and truth by its beauty—not individual and local truth, but general and operative truth—making it the most philosophical form of writing: "Not standing upon external testimony, but carried alive into the heart by passion; truth which is its own testimony, which gives competence and confidence to the tribunal to which it appeals, and receives them from the same tribunal."[11] In other words, poetry should possess an autonomy by virtue of its giving significance to itself: since it is in effect its own tribunal, any value it possesses must obviously come exclusively from itself. And while Eliot professes a pure aesthetic view of poetic emotion, this could obviously be open to a different but equally strong version of poetic autonomy.

Like Wordsworth and Eliot, Ming-Qing criticism can also be assessed by looking at precisely the same critical issues: the origin and nature of poetic emotion, the mode of lyrical expression, the interplay of emotion and imagery, the usefulness of poetic craft, and the function of poetry. Indeed, the Ming Archaist discussion of poetic emotion would seem to anticipate Eliot's pure aestheticist approach in completely divorcing poetic emotion from the poet's life experiences, espousing a literary patterning of emotion through interplay with imagery, and seeking intertextual resonance with Tang masters by imitating their poetic craft. Their theory of poetic emotion can be called a "patterning-focused theory of emotion" (*qingwen shuo* 情文說). Conversely, the Ming Anti-Archaist position on emotion displays a critical stance akin to Wordsworth, with an abiding emphasis on the powerful overflow of personal emotion in response to real-life situations and a disdainful dismissal of contrived poetic craft. This theory of poetic emotion consists of an "event-focused theory of emotion" (*qingshi shuo* 情事說). In addition, Wordsworth and Chinese poetic belief both affirm an inherent bond between emotion and human nature, with the Chinese from antiquity considering emotion (*qing* 情) and inborn nature (*xing* 性) inseparably bound. In fact, these two terms are etymological cognates, the former evolving from the latter. Since the Warring States and the Han period, the binome formed from *xingqing* 性情 or *qingxing* 情性 has been used to denote moral disposition (primarily by Han-Tang Confucian-minded critics) or refined artistic sensibility (notably by the Six Dynasties practitioners of belles lettres). But from the late Ming through the mid-Qing, we see a new disposition-emotion theory (*xingqing shuo* 性情說), championed by Huang Zongxi 黃宗羲 (1610–1695), Shen Deqian 沈德潛 (1673–1769), the Changzhou school of *ci* lyrics, and others, characterized by a persistent endeavor to blend moral consciousness and aesthetic sensibility through a sophisticated aestheticization of traditional image-based allegorization. During the late Qing, we find two prominent instances of a rethinking of emotion's functions in the context of deepening sociopolitical crises brought on by China's successive defeats by Western powers. One is Gong Zizhen's 龔自珍 (1792–1841) transformation of the Ming Anti-Archaists' espousal of powerful, uninhibited, iconoclastic emotive expression into a more positive means of cultivating a bold free-thinking necessary for advancing a reformist agenda. The other is Lu Xun's 魯迅 (1881–1936) appropriation of Byron's "demonic" emotion as a means of fermenting a cultural and sociopolitical revolution that would uproot China's feudal ethico-sociopolitical order and thereby help build a modern China.

Having mapped out the complex, evolving relationships of *qing* with real-life circumstances, literary patterning, inborn nature, and sociopolitical reform, I now explore Ming-Qing critics' discussions of *qing* so as to reconstruct their five distinct *qing*-centered theories of literary creation. The remainder of this chapter covers from the Ming Archaists and Anti-Archaists through the mid-Qing; chapter 9 follows with discussions of the late Qing period.

Ming Archaists' Aestheticist Theory of *Qing* (Emotion)

In their understanding of literature, Ming critics fall into two camps: the Archaists and Anti-Archaists. Though following different approaches to literary creation, the two camps place equal emphasis on *qing* and did not engage in direct debate over it. Still, their views of *qing* can be differentiated with regard to the five dimensions noted above.

From a broad comparative perspective, we may say that the Archaist view of *qing* in poetry aligns with Eliot's impersonal, aestheticist, and historical/intertextual notion of poetic emotion. Both discuss emotions largely divorced from the real-life events that originally prompted them. Concomitant with this depersonalizing is their aestheticization of *qing* through an abiding emphasis on its interplay with *xiang* (imagery) or *jing* (scene), or what Eliot calls "objective correlatives."

Archaists seek to pattern and aestheticize *qing* along the historical/intertextual lines established by the great Tang masters—a move comparable to Eliot's advocacy of the poet's immersion in tradition. All these parallels with Eliot on poetic emotion, however, are not unique to Ming Archaists. Much the same can be said of Six Dynasties aestheticism of *qing* vis-à-vis Eliot.

So, what is unique about Ming Archaists' articulations of *qing*? What sets them apart from those by, say, Lu Ji and Liu Xie, as discussed in chapter 3? In my view, it is their unique prioritization of *qing* in accounts of the creative process, as here, by Xu Zhenqing 徐禎卿 (1479–1511), one of the Former Seven Masters:

§153

Qing is the essence of the mind. *Qing* does not have fixed dimensions and rises when one is moved. What stirs inside must take form in sounds. When happy, one bursts out laughing. When saddened, one sighs. Then [these feelings] are brought out in sounds, made possible by *qi* (lifebreath). Thanks to *qing*, *qi* is generated; thanks to *qi*, sounds are formed; thanks to sounds, words are wrought; thanks to words, rhymes are established—this is the origin of poetry.

情者，心之精也。情無定位，觸感而興，既動於中，必形于聲。故喜則為笑啞，憂則為吁戲，怒則為叱吒。然引而成音，氣實為佐；引音成詞，文實與功。蓋因情以發氣，因氣以成聲，因聲而繪詞，因詞而定韻，此詩之源也。(QMSH, 2988)

At first sight this passage from Xu's *Recorded Remarks on Art* (Tan yi lu 談藝錄) seems to just flesh out the famous statement, "*Qing* stirs inside and becomes manifest in words," made in the "Great Preface to the *Book of Poetry*." However, if carefully read against Liu Xie's statements on the origins of literature, a few things underscore its extraordinary significance. First, we can see a qualitative difference between the "Great Preface" statement and Xu's. The former merely describes the common experience of expressing emotions in words, but the latter is a logical exercise of causal inferences about the birth of poetry. Second, this exercise is likely inspired by Liu Xie's cosmological-philosophical argument about the origin of *wen* (written symbols, culture, cultivation, writing, and belles lettres) and Cai Pi's physiological-philosophical argument about the origin of poetry as Xu seems to co-opt the key terms "mind" and *qi* (lifebreath) from Liu and Cao, respectively. Third, even though Liu and Cao respectively regard "mind" and *qi* as the ultimate origins of literature, Xu places *qing* above both "mind" and *qi*. In the opening paragraph of "Tracing the Dao as the Source" (Yuan Dao 原道), the first chapter of Liu Xie's *Literary Mind*, Lu Xie claims that "[humans are] the florescence of the five elements and the mind of heaven and earth. When the mind comes into being, words are established and patterning becomes manifest. This is the way of nature" 為五行之秀， 實天地之心， 心生而言立， 言立而文明， 自然之道也 (*WXDL*, 1/17–21). Considering Liu's linkage of the creative mind with heaven and earth, Xu's claim that "*qing* or emotion is the essence of the mind" strikes me as all the more astounding. Similarly, with Cao Pi on *qi*'s primary importance for literary creation, Xu's claim that *qing* generates *qi* strikes me as equally ground-breaking. To my mind, no such claim for emotion had been made before.

Having so traced the origin of poetry, Xu proceeds to discuss what he calls "the flow of poetry" 詩之流:

§154

Qing is indeed profound and one must use thinking to exhaust its mysteries. *Qi* [lifebreath] can be crude or weak, one must use strength to correct its imbalance. Words are hard to suit perfectly, and one must use talent to bring them to perfection. Talent may easily run wild, and one must use substance to guard against its excess. This is the flow of poetry.

然情實眑眇， 必因思以窮其奧； 氣有粗弱， 必因力以奪其偏； 詞難妥帖， 必因才以致其極；才易飄揚， 必因質以御其侈。 此詩之流也。(*QMSH*, 2988)

Reading this passage on the "flow of poetry," we see how Xu wants to illuminate the key factors that make possible the smooth transformation of emotion (*qing*) into great poetry. To begin, Xu contends that the poet must "use thinking to exhaust the mysteries of *qing*." The next stage is *qing*'s generation of *qi* (lifebreath), and a smooth completion of this stage is contingent upon the poet's forceful intervention, should *qi* veer astray. The third stage is the generation of words and sounds by *qi*, powered by a forceful poetic talent and guided by substance to curb excess. To Xu, these three stages are not a process of emotion petering out but, rather, that of emotion performing its different operations:

§155

From dim vagueness it buds a sprout—this is the advent of emotion! A boundless overflow—this is how emotion flaunts its great abundance! A continuous stretch of intricate links—this is how emotion unifies all as one!

朦朧萌坼， 情之來也； 汪洋漫衍，情之沛也； 連翩絡屬， 情之一也。(*QMSH*, 2988)

Considering Xu's sense of emotion's decisive roles throughout literary creation, as well as his view of emotion as the mind's essence, it is little wonder he then claims: "Poetry is the spirit's finest flower and the Creator's undisclosed thoughts" 詩者乃精神之浮英， 造化之祕思也. His euphoric praise of emotion-unified poetry continues with this poetic description:

§156

So the poet miraculously gallops with his mind and makes flexible adaptations to tropes and rhythms. He may use concise ideas to expound meanings or write voluminously to describe what's in the mind—sometimes initiating gently like the zither's vermilion strings; sometimes triggering suddenly like a darting arrow; sometimes starting swiftly but halting midway; sometimes shifting pace from relaxed to hurrying; sometimes being passionate and unleashing heroic vigor, or being mournful and inducing people's tears; sometimes by being clumsy only to achieve technical perfection; or sometimes disclosing the marvelous, seemingly without effort.

若夫妙騁心機，隨方合節，或約旨以植義，或宏文以敘心，或緩發如朱絃，或急張如躍栝，或始迅以中留，或既優而後促，或慷慨以任壯，或悲悽以引泣，或因拙以得工，或發奇而似易。(*QMSH*, 2988)

He sums up his thoughts on emotion and poetry with, "Such is the gist of the grand strategy of establishing the norm by *qing* and maintaining hold over the essentials" 此乃因情立格，持守圜環之大略也 (*QMSH*, 2988). This stands in strong contrast with both Wang Changling's "*Yi* constitutes the norm" 意是格 (see §75) and Wang Tingxiang's (another of the Former Seven Masters) expositions on the pivotal roles of *yi* (see §138). In substituting *qing* for *yi* and establishing it as the all-unifying principle of poetry, Xu blazed a new trail to explore the sublime emotive mind as it operates through all the stages of composition.

Xie Zhen 謝榛 (1495–1575), one of the Latter Seven Masters, is another Ming Archaist known for his original expositions on *qing*. While Xu Zhenqing investigates how *qing* activates and unifies the compositional stages, Xie Zhen focuses on expounding the dynamic interplay between *qing* and *jing* (scenes). This difference comes to the fore when we read the following passage against Xu Zhenqing's, cited above:

§157

Poetry-making is based on *qing* and *jing*: neither can be [poetry] by itself and the two cannot go against each other. As one ascends on high and concentrates his thoughts, one's spirit communes with the ancients, reaching far and near, encountering happiness and worry. This happens by chance, by which one produces forms out of what's traceless and rouses sounds in silence. With regard to *qing* and *jing*, there are similarities and differences; and literary descriptions can be difficult or easy. There are two essential factors in poetry-making, and nothing is more important than them. We observe the same thing outside, but feelings aroused inside are different. A poet ought to exert his strength to render outside and inside the same, that is, there is no boundary between what comes into the mind and what the mind sends forth. Scenes [*jing*] are the medium of poetry while emotion [*qing*] is its embryo. When the two merge as poetry, a few words can encompass the myriad forms and generate primordial *qi* [lifebreath] that is expansive and boundless.

作詩本乎情景，孤不自成，兩不相背。凡登高致思,則神交古人，窮乎遐邇, 擊乎憂樂，此相因偶然，著形於絕迹，振響於無聲也。夫情景有異同，模寫有難易，詩有二要，莫切於斯者。觀則同於外，感則異於內，當自用其力, 使內外如一，出入此心而無間也。景乃詩之媒，情乃詩之胚，合而為詩，以數言而統萬形，元氣渾成，其浩無涯矣。(*QMSH*, 1340)

Long before Xie Zhen, Lu Ji and Liu Xie had described the interplay of emotion and objects in the two stages of literary creation: first in the emotions brought on by seasonal change that spark literary creation (see §42), and then the interplay of emotions and objects within the writer's mind during artistic conception (see §§45–46). But neither went so far as to claim that this emotion-object interplay alone could produce a work of art. In fact, to my knowledge, no one did, at least not with any theoretical rigor. Here, Xie Zhen not only conceptualizes *qing* and *jing* as the decisive essentials of literary creation but also theorizes their interplay and eventual fusion in abstract terms of internal-external bipolarity. This lays the groundwork for ever more sophisticated discussions of *qing-jing* exchange by Qing critics of different persuasions, including aesthetics-minded critics like Wang Fuzhi 王夫之 (1619–1692) and Ye Xie 葉燮 (1627–1703), as well as Confucian critics like Shen Deqian and the critics of the Changzhou school of *ci* lyrics.

In their discussions of *qing*, Ming Archaists are generally concerned with sublimating and refining it in order to endow it with an aesthetic quality, and they show no interest in emotions relating directly to an individual's life experience or sense of external reality. As we've seen, Xu Zhenqing's description of *qing* is generic, not pertaining to everyday reality or grounded in specific individual emotions. His paradigm of "establishing norms by *qing*" features processing and refining language and imagery in accordance with aesthetic sensibility and the normative standards of poetic tradition. Xie Zhen's approach to literary creation also emphasizes the procedural aspect in the artistic union of *jing* and *qing*, rather than simply a direct expression of what is on the author's mind or a description of external scenery. Exemplified by Xu's and Xie's expositions, the aesthetic theory of emotion championed by Ming Archaists strongly resonates with Eliot's understanding of poetic emotion and tradition.

Ming Anti-Archaists' Anti-Aestheticist Theory of Emotion

Although Ming Anti-Archaists did not engage in debate on *qing* or emotion with Archaists, their theory of emotion is diametrically opposed to the latter's aesthetic theory. They advocate precisely what Archaists oppose, and vice versa. The *qing* extolled by Ming Anti-Archaists is a direct response to one's life conditions, and they particularly prize instantaneous, volcanic outbursts of emotion. This seems to resonate with Wordsworth's concern with the naturalness, immediacy, and intensity of poetic emotion. Contrary to the Archaists' commitment to artistically processing *qing* for poetry, Anti-Archaists like Xu Wei 徐渭 (1521–1593) and Li Zhi 李贄 (1527–1602) value emotion from everyday life unchecked by traditional social, ethical, and literary norms and rules. They regard an unreflective, spontaneous burst of intense emotion as *zhiqing* 至情 (the perfect *qing*). Articulated in language without artistic processing, emotion yields *zhiwen* 至文 (perfect writing). Their proposition naturally renders irrelevant all discussions of poetic technique.

By presenting such unmediated *qing* in drama, fiction, and prose, they not only castigate artificial emotion and literary archaism but also break free of traditional norms of propriety in self-expression. In his "Preface to Selected North and South Drama from the Past and Present," Xu Wei declares:

§158
Ever since their birth into this world, humans have been driven by emotions. Even when people were little kids playing with sand and being calmed by their parents' tall tales of golden leaves, they fell under the sway of emotion. From then to the end of their lives, they encounter and experience situations and events of all kinds. When they could not dispel their sorrow or contain their joys, they'd write *shi* poetry, prose, *sao* and *fu* poetry that are brilliant and sublime, capable of making readers happy and laugh, or so angry they feel their eyes would burst, or so sad they cry and sob. Readers would feel as if they were right next to the author, dusting their clothes, teasing each other, laughing, or uttering mournful words hundreds of years old. Why so? There is no other reason than this: the truer the emotion being described, the more easily it touches people's heart, and the farther posterity it reaches. The northern and southern dramas particularly excel in this.

人生墮地，便爲情使。聚沙作戲，拈葉止啼，情昉此已。迨終身涉境觸事，夷拂悲愉，發爲詩文騷賦，璀璨偉麗，令人讀之喜而頤解，憤而眥裂，哀而鼻酸，恍若與其人即席揮塵，嬉笑悼唁於數千百載之上者，無他，摹情彌眞則動人彌易，傳世亦彌遠，而南北劇爲甚。(*XWJ*, 1296)

Expounding Xu's notion of genuine emotion, Li Zhi emphasizes that it must have such intensity that the writer cannot suppress it, must let it pour forth unrestrained:

§159

Of all who are truly good at writing in our world, none begins by consciously pursuing writing. They have strange and indescribable feelings in their chest, feel choked by things they wish but dare not spit out, and often have at the tip of their tongue many words they want to share but cannot. Pent up for too long, all this builds momentum that cannot be contained. Once their emotions arise in response to scenes, they can't help sighing as they catch sight of anything. They snatch others' wine cups to drown their own grievances and vent their feelings of injustice. Their emotions display a magnitude barely seen in a thousand years.

且夫世之真能文者，比其初皆非有意于為文也。其胸中有如許無狀可怪之事，其喉間有如許欲吐而不敢吐之物，其口頭又時時有許多欲語而莫可所以告語之處，蓄極積久，勢不能遏。一旦見景生情，觸目興嘆；奪他人之酒杯，澆自己之壘塊；訴心中之不平，感數奇於千載。(*FSXFS*, 97)

Li Zhi champions the poetry and prose resulting from such unimpeded outbursts of passion with its unsurpassable, natural affective power, and calls it "perfect writing." For him, all perfect writing is the product of the pure and genuine "childlike mind" that has not yet been disciplined by ethical norms: "As long as we always keep a childlike mind, we will not act by moralistic principles and from conventional wisdom, and in no time is *wen* not produced and no people fail to produce *wen*. Of words that don't follow uniform styles and norms, none fall short of *wen* or refined writing" 苟童心常存，則道理不行，聞見不立，無時不文，無人不文，無一樣創制體格文字而非文者 (*FSXFS*, 99). Nourished by the "childlike mind," one need not approach the writing of literature with an archaist mentality. The childlike mind renders the distinction between "ancient" and "present" totally irrelevant:

§160

Why should poetry [imitate] anthologized ancient poems? Why should prose [imitate] pre-Qin prose? Literature evolved from the Six Dynasties styles into recent-style poetry, and then further evolved into Tang *chuanqi* short stories, Jin drama, Yuan drama, the tunes of the Western Chamber, the novel *Water Margins*, and the writing of examination essays of our times. The perfect writings of ancient and our times cannot be evaluated in terms of which comes first. This is why I feel the sway of spontaneous writings from the childlike mind, and ask, what's the point of talking about the Six Classics, the *Analects*, and the *Mencius*?

詩何必古選，文何必先秦。降而為六朝，變而為近體；又變而為傳奇，變而為院本，為雜劇，為西廂曲，為水滸傳，為今之舉子業，皆古今至文，不可得而時勢先後論也。故吾因是而有感于童心者之自文也，更說甚麼六經，更說甚麼語、孟乎？(*FSXFS*, 99)

Using "childlike mind" as the ultimate criterion of literary judgment, Li Zhi not only undermines the ground for Archaists' slavish imitation of Tang poetry and pre-Qin prose but also elevates three new, low-status genres—vernacular Jin, Song, and Yuan dramas, vernacular fiction, and examination essays—to the pedestal of *zhiwen* or perfect writings. In this passage, Li Zhi also reveals his iconoclasm as he describes the Six Classics, *Analects*, and *Mencius* as incomparable to writings that come straight from the childlike mind. Alongside the momentous development of anti-aestheticist theories of emotion spearheaded by Xu Wei and Li Zhi, we witness this bold breaking of Confucian moral bondage in literary production, especially the suppression of erotic passions. A prime example is the romance plays written by Tang Xianzu 湯顯祖 (1550–1616), with his deeply held belief that "love is of source unknown, yet it grows ever deeper. The living may die of it, by its power the dead live again."[12] The late Qing celebration of uncensored passion was pervasive enough that even die-hard Confucian moralists like Hao Jing 郝敬 (1557–1639) find it necessary to acknowledge the validity and affective power of love as recorded in the *Book of Poetry*, notwithstanding his attempt to harness this fundamental human emotion within the Confucian allegorical framework.[13]

The Aestheticist-Individualist Theory of Poetic Emotion from Late Ming through Early Qing

The Gong'an school 公安派 and Jingling school 竟陵派 in the late Ming may have presented a united front against archaism, but their ideas about poetic emotion are more aligned with the Archaists than with Anti-Archaists like Xu Wei and Li Zhi. Like Archaists they advocate the aestheticization of *qing*, but they add a transcendent dimension by exalting the expression of one's "inborn nature and spirit" (*xingling* 性靈). The Gong'an and Jingling schools espouse transcendent artistic sensibility as a cure for the perceived flaws of coarseness, shallowness, vulgarity, and mundanity plaguing the Anti-Archaists. In this sense, their views are similar to Eliot's aestheticist view of poetic emotion, but they differ on the conditions and methods of the creative process. Rather than writing with deliberate intent, lyrical expression, they contend, is the natural overflow of "inborn nature and spirit," which brings them closer to Wordsworth as well as the Anti-Archaist emphasis on naturalness and spontaneity.

In the Yuan dynasty, Yu Ji 虞集 (1272–1348) in *One-Finger Chan for Poets* (Shijia yizhi 詩家一指) supplies the intermediate link between past and future critics by elucidating the connection between feeling (*qing*) and inborn nature (*xing*):

§161
Everyone knows the functions of poetry, but do not know how it can perform such functions. . . . They know that what enables poetry is *qing* [emotions] and *xing* [inborn nature]. *Qing* is born of the mind's engagement with phenomena.

Therefore heaven and earth, the sun and the moon, rivers and mountains, mists and clouds, humans, grass, and trees, people's back-and-forth interactions, awakening, encounters, bodily engagements all belong to *qing*: that which one randomly obtains is natural and that which one produces by endeavors is conscious work. What's natural is profound and tranquil and what's born of conscious work extends far and deep.

世皆知詩之為，而莫知其所以為。知所以為者情性，而莫知其所以為情性。．
．．．．．心之於色為情，天地、日月、星辰、江山、煙雲、人物、草木、響答、
動悟、履遇、形接，皆情也。拾而得之為自然，撫而出之為機造。自然者厚而
安，機造者往而深。(*QMSH*, 116–17)

This description of the relation of *qing* and *xing* recalls Shao Yong's 邵雍 (1012–1077) treatment of the same topic, but in contrast to the latter's total negation of *qing*, Yu Ji describes the *qing-xing* transition as a process to "purify the mind in reflective contemplation." His statement that the "mind's encounter with phenomena makes *qing*" is followed by a long list of *qing*: heaven and earth, the sun and the moon, stars, rivers and mountains, and so on—suggesting an amalgam of the pre-Qin notion of *qing* as the essential nature of things, physical or otherwise and the Buddhist notion "All things are only created by the mind," articulated in the *Flower Garland Sutra* (Avataṃsaka Sūtra 華嚴經). Reconceived in this way, *qing* transcends the dichotomy of subjective and objective, mental and physical, and becomes a conduit to the ultimate transcendent reality. Having thus expounded the spirituality of the natural scenes, Yu proceeds to depict how one can realize *xing* as the ultimate reality behind all phenomena. He begins by launching into an abstruse Madhyamaka Buddhist "deconstructive" interpretation:

§162
Xing [inborn nature] is emptiness to the mind; emptiness and *xing* are the same. It is not merely with *xing* that emptiness exists, neither does *xing* exist apart from emptiness. It must be [in the flux of] neither not-emptiness nor not-*xing* that *xing* is preserved.

性之於心為空，空與性等。空非惟性而有，亦不離空而性，必非空非性，而性
固存矣。(*QMSH*, 116–17)

Here, the play of "not-empty" and "not-*xing*" against each other is an exercise of Madhyamaka double-negative logic that preserves the Middle Way without attachment to either side.[13] For Yu Ji, it's only by taking this double-negative approach that one can "unimpededly encompass all and henceforth thoroughly attain one's *xing*." After this exercise of the Madhyamaka logic, Yu proceeds to explain how one actually attains *xing*:

Now someone walks amidst the shade of green trees on a balmy day, and before him are limpid water, crying fowls with beautiful feathers, musical tones of pine and bamboo groves, songs of woodcutters and herdsmen—coming to meet one another. So, as one's consciousness travels beyond heaven and earth to encompass all things and as his spirit is extended to the full, one obtains *xing* by hearing—this is what ultimately becomes of oneself. What the world calls the tone is derived from [physical] hearing, with no exception. *Xing* is that which nothing doesn't aspire to, but all those seeking to obtain *xing* through [physical] hearing is just like going to the inn to look for a long-departed visitor. Those who obtain it do so not because they grasp its form, or because they pry into its secret. They wander freely beyond the myriad things in the depth of clouds and jade-green skies, dense woods and green mountains, clearing up stones and the spring of greediness, cleansing their inner spirit, and solitarily returning to original purity. Just like the buds of spring flowers waiting for timely rains— why wouldn't they have in store the destined moment of awakening?

夫今有人行綠陰風日間，飛泉之清，鳴禽之美，松竹之韻，樵牧之音，互遇遞接，知別區字，省攝備至，暢然無遺，是有聞性者焉，自是而盡。世之所謂音者，無不得之於聞。性無一物不有欲求，其所以聞之而性者，猶即旅舍而覓過客往之久矣。故取之非有其方，得之非睹其竅，翛然萬物之外，雲翠之深，茂林青山，掃石酌泉，蕩滌神宇，獨還冲真，猶春花初胎，假之時雨，夫復不有一日性悟之分耶？(*QMSH*, 116–17)

Here he presents a Buddhist transcendent view markedly different from the indigenous Daoist transcendent views of nature. In the latter case, nature enables humans to achieve spiritual transcendence through an integration with the Dao's inherent rhythm. But here, Yu shows us how to achieve a transcendent awakening through hearing the sounds of nature or what lies behind the sounds of nature. The term *wen xing* 聞性 is an ingenious adaptation of the Buddhist notion of *sheng wen* 聲聞, a method of achieving through hearing Buddha's teaching. Along with this adaptation, Yu substitutes sounds of nature for the Buddha's speech as the medium of enlightenment and gives hearing a new transcendent dimension previously unknown. To forestall confusion of this transcendent hearing with ordinary hearing, he dismisses the latter as futile, like "going to the inn to look for a long-departed visitor." Yu's description of tranquil nature suggests his alternative: "attaining *xing* through hearing" through a kind of "supra-acoustic perception" or intuitive cognizance of the ultimate reality.

By redefining *qing* and *xing*, as well as their relationship in Buddhist terms, Yu Ji not only cleanses the two terms (whether used either separately or as a binome) of their ingrained Confucian moral import but also endows them with a new transcendent dimension. Such thinking about *qing* and *xing* seems to presage Yuan Hongdao's 袁宏道 (1568–1610) conception of "inborn nature and spirit" (*xingling* 性靈), with which he praises his younger brother Yuan Zhongdao's 袁中道 (1570–1623) poetry:

§164

These poems most uniquely express their inborn nature and spirit and are not constrained by norms and conventions. Unless he has something flowing out of his own bosom, he would not apply the brush to write. Sometimes, when emotion meets scene, thousands of words suddenly surge in the mind just like water dashing out to the east—capable of capturing the reader's soul. [In writings so produced], there are places of excellence as well as faults. The places of excellence need no comment and even places of faults contain many authentic and original expressions. However, it is regrettable that the places of excellence do not stay clear of embellishment and imitation as he cannot completely shed the entrenched practices of recent literati.

大都獨抒性靈，不拘格套，非從自己胸臆流出，不肯下筆。有時情與境會，頃刻千言，如水東注，令人奪魂。其間有佳處，亦有疵處，佳處自不必言，即疵處亦多本色獨造語。然予則極喜其疵處；而所謂佳者，尚不能不以粉飾蹈襲爲恨，以爲未能盡脫近代文人氣習故也。[14]

To "uniquely express one's inborn nature and spirit" means to naturally and spontaneously express one's true emotions without being constrained by conventional norms and rules. When one's inborn nature and spirit pour forth in response to a situation, even occasionally flawed language cannot detract from the expression. In fact, minor flaws may help accentuate the writer's true, unique character.

In a similar vein, the Jingling school critics, represented by Zhong Xing 鍾惺 (1574–1624) and Tan Yuanchun 譚元春 (1586–1637), insist on the predominance of spirit and true nature in poetry regardless of whether one chooses to model oneself on ancient authors. For instance, Tan Yuanchun stresses that writing is a direct expression of emotion: "The poet goes off alone with his *qing*, and the myriad phenomena open up before him. Unexpectedly, his mouth starts to chant and his hand starts to write. One's mouth and hand always obey what flows from one's own heart" 夫作詩者一情獨往，萬象俱開，口忽然吟，手忽然書。即手口原聽我胸中之所流。[15] In other words, the flow of emotions in the poet's heart is the sole lead for his mouth and hand, unconstrained by traditional methods or prescribed rules.

From late Ming to early Qing, Lu Shiyong 陸時雍 (fl. 1634), Wang Fuzhi 王夫之, and Pang Kai 龐凱 (1657–1725) continued to emphasize naturalness in lyrical expression as spontaneous response to immediate encounters. In his *Shijing zonglun*

(The Mirror of Poetry: Comprehensive Discussions 詩鏡總論), Lu Shiyong regards "writing with *yi*" as the very opposite of natural genuine emotion: "Poetry does not depend on *yi* or artistic conception—it is done of its own accord on encountering natural scenery; *yi* does not need to be sought after—it is none other than the stirring of emotions" 詩不待意，即景自成。意不待尋，興情卽是 (*QMSH*, 5120). Here the term *yi* also connotes deliberate intent, and Lu obviously uses the term pejoratively. "Wang Changling thought much of *yi* and deployed it often," he writes; "Li Bai thought little of *yi* and deployed it rarely." In other words, Wang Changling often writes with a clear intent, something rarely seen in Li Bai 李白 (701–762), who writes with freedom and spontaneity. Thus, Li Bai's poetry "springs from nature" while Wang Changling's "conception-images are profound indeed." Between *qing* and *yi*, Lu values the former over the latter through a series of oppositional binaries:

§165

What surges nonstop to the end is *qing* or emotion; what comes out of painstaking imitation is *yi* or conception. What appears across existence and nonexistence is *qing*; what distinguishes "this" from "not this" is *yi*. *Yi* is lifeless and *qing* is full of life; *yi* is merely a trace, but *qing* is spirit. *Yi* is shallow but *qing* is profound. *Yi* is artificial but *qing* is genuine. This is how *yi* and *qing* are distinguished from ancient to our times.

夫一往而至者，情也；苦摹而出者，意也；若有若無者，情也；必然必不然者，意也。意死而情活，意迹而情神，意近而情遠，意偽而情真。情意之分，古今所由判矣。(*LDSHXP*, 1414)

Like Lu Shiyong, Wang Fuzhi also explores aesthetic dimensions of *qing* while not neglecting its social and moral dimensions. Consider, for example, Wang Fuzhi's comments on Wang Shimao's 王世懋 (1536–1588) "Springtime Boating in Hengtang":

§166

The emotive purport is what distinguishes the elegant from the vulgar. That which has no emotive purport is inevitably vulgar even though it may look elegant. Yet it is not easy to truly have emotive purport. It is not that Zhong [Xing] and Tang [Yuanchun] do not pride themselves on having emotive purport, but they regard beggarly pedants' woes and marketplace gossip as emotions, with the worst kinds blended with vulgar affections. If emotions contain what is unworthy of emotive meaning, having them is the same as having no emotive meaning—how could they come to be valued?

關情是雅俗鴻溝，不關情者貌雅必俗。然關情亦大不易，鍾、譚亦未嘗不以關情自賞，乃以措大攢眉、市井附耳之情爲情，則插入酸俗中爲甚。情有非可關之情者，關焉而無當于關，又奚足貴哉![16]

Here Wang Fuzhi lays out a clear set of criteria for the artistic quality and aesthetic sensibility (elegant or vulgar) of the *qing* being presented in a poem. He considers it descending into "pedantry and vulgarity" when one writes about beggarly pedants' woes and marketplace gossip. In the third entry of his commentary on "East Mountain" from the "Airs of Bin," he elucidates two modes of the mind's engagement with external objects: the outward that moves from "a consciousness in the mind" to "extending it to objects"; and the inward mode, initiated when "an unexpected encounter with external objects arouses the mind." He emphasizes that poets must incorporate their perceptions, sensations, and experience into poetry and use their own language. Once the poet's movements, in body and mind alike, synchronize with the external, the charm of *qing* is "invigorated."

In contrast to the "high-brow" expositions of Lu Shiyong and Wang Fuzhi, Pang Kai uses popular Chan-style language to describe poetry writing and lyrical expression in his *Shiyi gushuo* 詩義固說 (Abiding Discussions on the Meanings of Poetry):

§167
Of recent poems written on an assigned topic, most merely revolve around what is set forth at the head of the scroll and have nothing to do with the poets themselves. What is the point of writing poems for others? One must write about oneself inside a poem and then the poem has emotion in it.

近時題咏詩，多就軸上冊頭，描模着語，於己毫無關涉，此詩作他何用？必須寫入自己，乃有情也。

If in writing poetry all comes out from one's true self, miraculous inscape emerges by itself. If one makes strained allusions, one will forgo the principle of naturalness, and the highest achievement one can boast is but an exercise of the wild-fox deviant way, driven by fads.

作詩任真而出，自有妙境，若一作穿鑿，失自然之旨，極其成就，不過野狐外道，風力所轉耳。(*QSHXB*, 739–40)

In these comments, Pang rejects poems of "embellished verbiage," consisting entirely of allusions and empty words. He repeatedly stresses poetry's relation to the self and to genuine feeling. We may regard this principle of naturalness, by which lyrical expression flows forth freely, complete with *jing* and *qing* in its original genuine form, as the continuation of Yuan Hongdao's ideal: "To uniquely express one's inborn nature and spirit without being constrained by rules and norms."

To my mind, the passages discussed above seem to exemplify an "aestheticist-individualist" approach to poetry writing. In contrast to the mid-Ming Archaists and Anti-Archaists, late Ming and early Qing critics like Lu Shiyong and Wang Fuzhi outgrew the sectarian hostility of the older generation and steadily turned eclectic if not syncretic. This tendency was already quite conspicuous in the poetry criticism of the Yuan brothers despite the label "Anti-Archaists" often attached to them. Their advocacy of true emotion, spontaneity, and individuality was not articulated as an impassioned, iconoclastic rebuke to prescribed mores or literary norms as in the case of Xu Wei and Li Zhi. Instead, it was more calmly advanced in the context of discussing poetic art and spoke to a shared desire to promote true emotions, spontaneity, and individuality as the key to poetic greatness.

The Theory of "Twofold Inborn Nature and Emotion" in the Late Ming through Mid-Qing

If Confucius really expurgated the text of the *Shijing*, why does it still contain so many explicit depictions of romantic love? This is a question of incessant debate among poetry critics since the Song dynasty. Not only were various interpretive methods invented to solve this mystery, but critics have also proposed new theories of "inborn nature and emotion" (*xingqing* 性情) as the conceptual basis for these interpretive methods. Mao's "Great Preface" avoids commenting on the issue altogether, noting only the poems' indirect sociopolitical criticism directed at historical events or figures. Zhu Xi's *Collected Commentaries on the Book of Poetry* (Shi jizhuan 詩集傳) is severely critical of Mao's preface for overlooking many explicitly racy poems, inventing lofty sociopolitical criticism for them while looking away from their lascivious content. Zhu himself takes them as the direct confession of "lewd elopers" (*yinben zhe* 淫奔者), which Confucius left in the canon only to serve as admonition.

The late Ming witnessed a surge of interest in depicting, appreciating, even glorifying romantic love in drama and fiction. As noted above, Tang Xianzu went so far as to elevate romantic love to a supreme status. Against this backdrop of growing cultural liberalism, it is not surprising that Zhu Xi's censure of the so-called lewd songs in the *Shijing* became the major target of relentless attack. In joining these attacks, Confucian-minded scholars who repudiated Zhu's reinterpretation of the *Book of Poetry* and defended Mao's "Great Preface" were in a seemingly hopeless position if they wanted to salvage romantic love while still maintaining Confucian mores. The late Ming scholar Hao Jing 郝敬 (1557–1639) devised a clever solution when he claimed the *Shijing* contains two categories of *qing*. The first is the emotions of a poem's subjects or personae, the most prominent of which is romantic love as expressed in the *Airs of the States* (Guofeng 國風) section in the *Shijing*. Giving his endorsement to the passions of love, he writes:

§168

There is a lot of singing between men and women in the *Book of Poetry*. Why? It is because husband and wife constitute the beginning of the human way. No passion and desire can surpass those between men and women. No sense of shame can be greater than what is felt inside a boudoir. The deepest rituals and righteousness are those cultivated inside a boudoir, and sounds uttered by men and women can most easily move people. For this reason, what the *Book of Poetry* expresses through affective men-women tropes is the sound of harmonious action and marks the beginning of "inborn nature and emotion." It is not all about love affairs between men and women.

《詩》多男女之詠，何也？曰：夫婦，人道之始也，故情欲莫甚于男女，廉恥莫大于中閫。禮義養于閨門者最深，而聲音發于男女者易感，故凡《詩》托興男女者，和動之音，性情之始，非盡男女之事也。[17]

Here Hao Jing praises romantic love represented in the *Shijing* as the "beginning of the human way" and affirms the affective impact of lyrical expressions of love on the audience. At the same time he stresses that love poems "are not all about affairs between men and women." According to Hao, these touching expressions contain an unmatched edifying power thanks to their subtle moral amelioration.

Hao goes on to reveal the agent(s) of such moral amelioration and explain why love poems were chosen as the means of moral edification:

§169

When living men and women, especially ordinary people of exceptional emotional sensitivity, harbor grievances in the heart, they express themselves through male and female personae and most often speak in the voice of a young woman. Men possess masculine strength and can be petulant. By contrast, women have feminine softness and quietly keep to themselves. So, regarding the secret of inborn nature and emotions, women have the deepest understanding. Women's words are precise, gentle, and capable of influencing people. Thus the sage(s) recorded their words and phrases, used pipes and strings to enhance their sounds and rhythms so that their desires are properly released. When what's suppressed is let out and what's excessive is curbed, human emotions are beneficially guided.

男女生人，至情恒人，心緒牢騷，則托詠男女，而為女子語常多。蓋男子陽剛躁擾，女子陰柔幽靜。性情之秘，鍾于女子最深，而辭切婦女，最悠柔可風。故聖人錄其辭，被諸管弦，協之音律，以平其躁，釋其慾，宣其壅，窒其淫，因人情而利導之也。[18]

Hao Jing argues that expressions of love, especially those by women, make the best guides and were thus strongly favored by the sages as a means of moral edification. By adding "(s)" to the word "sage," I want to alert the reader to two possible readings: it may refer to Confucius alone, as he is said to have expurgated the *Shijing* text, or, more likely in my opinion, may also include later Confucians who provided prefaces to individual poems to elucidate their meaning. With this active involvement by the sages, the love poems contain not only the original poets' feelings and thoughts but also the sages' moral sentiment and judgment. Given this, it seems appropriate to say that Hao Jing advanced a twofold theory of inborn nature and emotions.

In Hao Jing's view, the use of passionate love and the female voice, mediated by sages, constitutes the best means of achieving the principle of "mild, gentle, sincere, and generous" (*wenrou dunhou* 溫柔敦厚) long prized by Confucians. But where earlier Confucians mostly see this principle as prescribing moderation in ethico-sociopolitical criticism, Hao Jing discovers its aesthetic possibilities, especially as he moves beyond *Shijing* exegesis to explore literary creation. His unreserved privileging of *xing* 興, a related mode of expression, is an excellent case in point.

Challenging traditional treatments of *fu* 賦 (exposition), *bi* 比 (metaphor), and *xing* 興 (affective image) as rhetorical devices, Hao Jing casts them as characterizations of three different modes of engagement between emotions and literary language during creative and receptive processes. For him, *xing* as an associational mode of lyrical expression is the most important mode. In *A Vulgar Country Man's Talk in the Garden of Arts* (Yipu cangtan 藝圃傖談), Hao writes:

§170

Xing is the poem's emotive content [*qing*] and is all there is in the *Poetry*. The Six Principles of the *Poetry* begins with the "Airs" and ends with *xing*. Having a clear understanding of *xing* brings one close to understanding the *Poetry*.

興者，詩之情，詩盡乎興矣。故六義以風始，以興終。明乎風與興而詩幾矣。(*QMSH*, 2115)

Hao elevates *xing* or the associational mode above the expositional mode (*fu*) and the metaphorical mode (*bi*) on the grounds of its unrivaled aesthetic efficacy. Elaborating on this efficacy, Hao writes:

§171

In explicating the *Book of Poetry*, critics across the ages invariably take *xing* [affective images] in allegorical terms. The only exception is Zhong Rong's *Grading of Poets*, which says "Words are all said but meanings remain inexhaustible—such is *xing*." These remarks are right on the mark. The human mind leaves no shadow [to be traced] and, when moved to take flight, makes indistinct sounds to produce poetry. When sublimated into *zhi* [intent], emotions expand with twists and turns and are not fixed to any particular point. In response to events, they extend the scope of meanings and course along with changes. Therefore, they can be chanted but not precisely traced, what one can understand in the mind but cannot capture in words. All this belongs to *xing*. What is observed with eyes is shallow; what is received into ears is deep. While black and yellow patterns on ritual robes can be taken in with a glance, sounds of chanting and sighing expand our mind and lift up our spirit and are capable of moving heaven and earth, bringing ghosts and spirits to tears, and transforming customs and traditions. This is what's called *xing*.

從來說詩，以托物爲興，惟鍾嶸《詩品》云：「文已盡而義有餘者，興也。」
此語得之。蓋人心無影，感動發越，肸蠁而成詩。其攄情爲志，逶迤旁薄，
不主一端。即事引伸，變動周遊，可諷吟而不可切循，心能會而口不能言者，
皆興也。故目之所察者淺，耳之所入者深。玄黃黼黻，一覽無餘。惟聲音咏嘆，
使人心曠神怡，能動天地，泣鬼神，移風易俗者，興之所謂也。[19]

Here Hao Jing makes clear that Zhong Rong's 鍾嶸 (?–518) definition has inspired his rethinking of *xing* in terms of its unique aesthetic efficacy, characterized by its evocation of emotive associations that defy conceptualization. It is important to note that this passage ends with the standard Confucian panegyric of poetry's transformative power, a reminder that Hao's aestheticization of *xing* is not for the sake of aesthetics but an endeavor to chart a new of path of literary creation leading to the realization of the Confucian aesthetic-moral ideal of "mild, gentle, sincere, and generous."

Hao Jing's twofold theory of inborn nature and emotion and his reconceptualization of "mild, gentle, sincere, and generous" as the core aesthetic-moral ideal of poetry have profound paradigmatic significance for the development of Qing poetry and poetry criticism. In the theorization of literary creation, Huang Zongxi's debt to Hao's version of the inborn nature and emotion theory are clear, and there are traces of Hao's influence as well in Shen Deqian's expositions on "poetic character and tones" (*gediao* 格調) and the new notions of "metaphor and affective image" (*bixing* 比興) and "entrusted meaning" (*jituo* 寄託) advanced by Zhang Huiyan 張惠言 (1761–1802) and Zhou Ji 周濟 (1781–1839) from the Changzhou school of *ci* lyrics. The minor differences in these theories do not belie a shared conceptual foundation laid by Hao Jing.

Following in Hao Jing's footsteps, many Qing poetry critics consider past theories of *qing* crude and plebeian and emphasize instead the principle of "mild, gentle, sincere, and generous." It was a new trend in poetry criticism of the Kangxi-Qianlong reigns to steer discussions of *qing* back to the Confucian tradition of "teaching by poetry" (*shi jiao* 詩教). Shen Deqian and Zhang Huiyan both value *qing* with profound moral implications and at the same time emphasize the sublimation of this morally charged *qing* onto an aesthetic level. Shen surpasses his teacher Ye Xie 葉燮 (1627–1703), who discussed *jing* and *qing* solely from an aesthetic perspective, by developing a discourse centered on "character and tone" (*gediao* 格調) that accords with Confucian moral ideals. He states in *Gentle Discussions on Poetry* (Shuoshi cuiyu 說詩晬語):

§172

As it is impossible to openly relay matters and exhaustively explicate principles, we always describe them through objects and their categorical associations. When our pent-up emotions seek release, just as the heavenly mechanism is triggered, we always use objects to convey what's in our hearts. We deploy metaphor and affective image together, chanting and sighing over and again, and joy or sadness would be contained therein, indistinct yet ready to be conveyed. The words are simple, but the feeling is profound.

事難顯陳，理難言罄，每託物連類以形之；鬱情欲舒，天機隨觸，每借物引懷以抒之；比興互陳，反覆唱歎，而中藏之懽愉慘戚，隱躍欲傳，其言淺，其情深也。(*QSH*, 548–49)

Here Shen expounds on the principle that poetry effects moral transformation by being "mild, gentle, sincere, and generous." It is the same view as stated in the "Great Preface": "When an admonition is given that is government by patterning [*wen*], the one who speaks it has no culpability, yet it remains adequate to warn those to hear it."[20] Yet here, "mild, gentle, sincere, and generous" are no longer abstract concepts; they point to an artistic creative condition that governs the writing of poetry. What Shen seeks to achieve with *bixing* is a kind of profundity where artistic emotion is imbued with moral import.

Hao Jing's and Shen Deqian's new theories of *qing* also provided the conceptual foundation for the Changzhou school of *ci* lyrics in the Qing. Zhang Huiyan 張惠言 (1761–1802), Zhou Ji 周濟 (1781–1839), and Chen Tingzhuo 陳廷焯 (1853–1892) all upheld *yanshi* 艷詩 (poetry of sensual beauty and romantic love) as a model of writing, where a virtuous gentleman's moral nature and feeling are "entrusted in" the emotions of languishing husbands and wives. Zhang Huiyan writes:

§173

The *Commentary* [referring to *Explanations on Simple and Compound Characters* by Xu Shen] says, "What contains meaning inside and manifests in words is *ci*." It arises from emotion in the beginning and is conveyed by subtle words cast in the associational mode [*xing*]. It brings about empathy among people and exhausts the usefulness of folksongs. [With *ci* poetry] men and women living in alleys express their joys and sorrows, and worthies and gentlemen brood over and reveal to the fullest unspeakable grievances hidden in their hearts. In so doing, they come close to the ways of the *bixing* [metaphorical-associational] mode of expression in the *Book of Poetry*, the meanings of the changed airs, and the songs of the *Sao* poets.

《傳》曰：〝意內而言外，謂之詞。〞 其緣情造端，興於微言，以相感動，極命風謠。里巷男女，哀樂以道。賢人君子幽約怨悱不能自言之情，低徊要眇，以喻其致。蓋《詩》之比興，變風之義，騷人之歌，則近之矣。[21]

Zhang Huiyan grants equal status to the sadness and joy of men and women in love and the worthy gentlemen's private, ineffable emotions depicted in *ci* lyrics and maintains that these lyrics approximate the principles of *bixing* and "Changed Airs" in the *Shijing*. He advocates learning from the *Shijing* tradition of "speaking through another's voice"—in other words, to express a gentleman's feeling and resolve indirectly through the trope of love between ordinary men and women.

Following Zhang Huiyan, Zhou Ji highlights the nonconceptual content "entrusted" (*jituo*) in the *qing* of the *ci* lyric. Like Shen Deqian, he also stresses the importance of objects and their categorical associations as the medium for lyrical expression. Highlighting the importance of *jituo* 寄託 (entrusted meaning) to *ci* poetry, Zhou writes:

§174
As for *ci* poetry, we shouldn't enter into writing without entrusted meanings, nor should we exit with entrusted meanings alone. Encountering one object or one event, we extend the range of meanings and entertain a multitude of categorical associations. We exercise our mind in the way a spider spins its web to catch a snowflake; and we apply the writing brush the way the Ying craftsman wielded his axe to remove a speck as thin as a fly's wing, as if moving a very thin blade through small crevices. After sufficient practice, one is spontaneously inspired with conception as he reaches all categories of analogue, surveys hundreds of years leaving no stone unturned. This is what I call "entering [into writing]." . . . When we read his composition, we feel as if we are watching fish down a deep abyss: conception darts forth like a carp and we felt as if awakened by midnight lightning and left disoriented. [So electrifying] even an infant would laugh and cry with his mother and villagers would be overcome with joy and anger as the story unfolds. This can be considered capable of "exiting."

夫詞，非寄託不入，專寄託不出。一物一事，引而伸之，觸類多通，驅心若遊絲之罥飛英，含毫如郢斤之斲蠅翼，以無厚入有間，既習已，意感偶生，假類畢達，閱載千百，聲欬弗達，斯入矣。……讀其篇者，臨淵窺魚，意為魴鯉，中宵驚電，罔識東西，赤子隨母笑啼，鄉人緣劇喜怒，抑可謂能出矣。[22]

When writing in *bixng* and *jituo* modes, one encounters an object and entertains a multitude of categorical associations. The shift from love songs in the *Shijing* to the love-themed *ci* lyric in Ming and Qing poetics aptly demonstrates the continued development of the metaphorical and associational modes to integrate *qing* and *jing* (feeling and scene). Yet "entrusting meaning" as Zhou Ji illustrates it is a complex and even mystical imaginative process. The final product holds a wealth of deep feeling but appears wholly natural without a trace of human artifice. At the same time, Shen Deqian and the Changzhou school lyricists all believe that, in writing poetry, imbuing natural scenery with *qing* is a gradual and continuous process allowing one to produce poems layered with meaning and, ultimately, in Zhou Ji's words, transcending the boundaries of *ci* by breaking free from conceptualizable meanings.

Hao Jing's notion of *xing*, and Shen Deqian's and the Changzhou school's advocacy of *bixing* and *jituo* modes of writing all highlight the connection between objects (as vehicle) and moral feeling and artistic sensibility (as tenor). Moreover, through these new modes of writing, one transcends individual romantic love on the surface level and looks toward a virtuous gentleman's moral nature and feeling as the final reference. In a way, these views resonate with Eliot's notion of the objective correlative and depersonalization in the creative process.

///////////////////////////////

Notes

1. Wordsworth, *Prose Works of William Wordsworth*, 1:39–40.
2. Ibid., 1:123.
3. Ibid., 1:126.
4. Ibid., 1:148.
5. Coleridge, *Biographia Literaria*, 304.
6. Eliot, *Sacred Wood*, 58.
7. Ibid., 54.
8. Wordsworth, *Prose Works of William Wordsworth*, 1:124.
9. Eliot, *Sacred Wood*, 100.
10. Ibid., 50.
11. Wordsworth, *Prose Works of William Wordsworth*, 1:139.
12. Birch, *Peony Pavilion*, ix.
13. This Hao Jing should not be confused with the Yuan scholar Hao Jing 郝經 (1223–1275) discussed in chapter 6.
13. See Cai, *Configurations of Comparative Poetics*, chap. 7.
14. Yuan H., *Yuan Zhonglang quanji*, Ji section, vol. 174, *juan* 1, 415.
15. Tan Yuanchun, *Tan Yuanchun ji*, *juan* 23, 622.
16. Wang F., *Ming shi pingxuan*, *juan* 6, 1510.
17. Hao, *Maoshi yuanjie*.
18. Ibid., 2863.
19. Ibid., 2117.
20. Owen, *Readings in Chinese Literary Thought*, 46.
21. Zhang H., *Ci xuan*, 6–7.
22. Zhou, *Song sijia cixuan*, 2.

Chapter 9

Qing-Centered Theories of Literary Creation (II)
The Late Qing Period

Like their predecessors, many late Qing critics continued to place emotion at the center of their discussions of literary creation. Their views, however, were now forged in a radically different cultural context, marked by the onslaught of Western science and technologies, ideas and values; the Qing court's inability to embark on a meaningful program of modernization; and, above all, successive military defeats and territorial concessions to Western powers. As Chinese civilization faced existential threat, some late Qing scholars began to theorize literary creation in terms of how it could help reverse the course of China's rapidly accelerating decline. To many, literary creation could effect this salvation only if driven by new kinds of powerful emotion. Among proponents of this new thinking about emotion and literary creation, the most prominent are the reform-minded Gong Zizhen 龔自珍 (1792–1841) and the revolutionary Lu Xun 魯迅 (1881–1936). This chapter examines their theoretical work in relation to the *qing*-centered developments discussed in chapter 8.

A Reformist Theory of Emotion and Literary Creation: Gong Zizhen

Among major late Qing critics, Gong Zizhen was the first to try to revitalize literary traditions by rethinking the role of emotion in literature.[1] With great courage he challenged the then dominant imitative aesthetics of the Tongcheng prose school 桐城派 (Tongcheng pai) and Song poetry school 宋詩派 (Songshi pai), both informed by Cheng-Zhu neo-Confucian orthodoxy. He reconceptualized literary creation as the spontaneous expression of one's inner emotions and thoughts untutored by neo-Confucian orthodoxy. In "A Postscript Written for *The Collected Poetry of Tang Haiqiu*" (Shu *Tang Haiqiu shiji* hou 書湯海秋詩集後), Gong sets forth this new view:

§175

A man becomes known through his poetry. Poetry becomes known through its author. . . . In all these cases [referring to several leading Tang, Song, and Qing

PRISM: THEORY AND MODERN CHINESE LITERATURE • 20 (ANNUAL SUPPL.) • DECEMBER 2023
DOI 10.1215/25783491-11080925 • © 2023 LINGNAN UNIVERSITY

poets], poetry and its author are one. Outside the author there is no poetry; outside poetry there is no author the man—his countenance is completely revealed therein. Tang Peng of Yiyang County, courtesy name Haiqiu, wrote more than three thousand poems, of which two thousand-odd pieces remain after editing. Although the commentators on his poetry undoubtedly number in the dozens, I, Gong Gongzuo, am eventually asked to write a few words. What [I] Gongzuo would write is this one word: "complete." Why should his poetry be described as "complete"? Because therein is what Haiqiu cherished in his heart, what he wanted to say, what he did not want to say but could not help saying, what he did not want to say and eventually did not say, and what he did not say but others can infer. He simply would not pick up words from others and use them as his own. Take any of his poems as an example, whether or not you are familiar with them, you can say, "This is a poem by Tang Yiyang [Tang Peng]."

人以詩名，詩尤以人名。......皆詩與人為一，人外無詩，詩外無人，其面目也完。益陽湯鵬，海秋其字，有詩三千餘篇，芟而存之二千餘篇，評者無慮數十家，最後屬龔鞏祚一言，鞏祚亦一言而已，曰：完。何以謂之完也？海秋心迹盡在是，所欲言者在是，所不欲言而卒不能不言在是，所不欲言而竟不言，於所不言求其言亦在是。要不肯掊搚他人之言以為己言。任舉一篇，無論識與不識，曰：此湯益陽之詩。(*GZZQJ*, 241)

Gong Zizhen's ideal of literature, poetry in particular, consists in a complete expression of oneself. For him, Tang Peng could attain this ideal because he did not follow the centuries-old tradition of filtering out private feelings and bringing them in conformity with Confucian moral and ritualistic rules, a tradition begun by the "Great Preface to the *Book of Poetry*" (*Shi* da xu 詩大序) in the Han and vehemently pursued by didactically inclined critics from Song onward. Instead, Tang gave free rein to his personal emotions and thoughts in his works, expressing them voluntarily or involuntarily and always in his own words. Gong Zizhen's unabashed respect for individual feelings is undoubtedly a calculated act of defiance against the Tongcheng school and Cheng-Zhu neo-Confucian orthodoxy.

Gong's challenge to the dominant literary and cultural traditions becomes all the more conspicuous in his "Account of the Hall of Sick Plum Trees" (1839) (Bing mei guan ji 病梅館記; *GZZQJ*, 186). In this thinly disguised parable, he first recounts how literati writers and painters in the areas around Suzhou and Hangzhou took special delight in thwarting the growth of plum trees and contorting their branches into whatever shapes caught their fancy. Then, he tells us that he himself bought three hundred pots of such plum trees and found all of them sick from being bound and contorted. After three days of tearful lamentation, he resolved to cure them all, destroying the pots, planting them in the ground, and letting them grow naturally. The allegorical meaning of this piece is not terribly subtle. He's clearly targeting the enforcers of Cheng-Zhu neo-Confucian orthodoxy, who censured expression of private emotions in literature and other discourses. The sick plum trees he wants to save represent all whose emotions and thoughts are stifled by the prevailing literary and political orthodoxy. His pledge to plant the sick trees more naturally signals his determination to fight the oppressive literary and political establishment and champion free expression of individual feelings and thought.

Gong Zizhen directs the brunt of his attack at the two dominant literary schools of his time, the Tongcheng prose school and the Song poetry school, both espousing neo-Confucian views of emotion along Cheng-Zhu orthodox lines.[2] With their Theory of Principles and Methods (Yi fa shuo 義法說), the Tongcheng school advocated yi (borrowing from Cheng-Zhu neo-Confucianism) and fa, an imitation of Tang-Song compositional methods represented by Han Yu 韓愈 (768–824) and Liu Zongyuan 柳宗元 (773–819). For its part, the Song poetry school advanced the Theory of Sinews of Principles (Jili shuo 肌理說). By inventing the term "sinews of principles," the leader of this school, Weng Fanggang 翁方綱 (1733–1818), proposed a literary ideal organically merging two principles: the moral principle, or the Way, to be obtained through evidential scholarship (kaozheng 考證) or philological study of Confucian classics, and the principle of literary composition exemplified by Song poetry. According to Gong Zizhen, both schools adopted the negative, didactic, neo-Confucian view of emotion and sought to purge literature of any genuine expression of personal feelings and thoughts, thus reducing literature to a vehicle for moral indoctrination or a trivial exercise of evidential scholarship and literary imitation.[3] For Gong, poetry and prose works produced by these two schools were worse than useless: they stifled people's emotions and minds, lulled their conscience, and ultimately rendered them powerless against despotic rule. For these reasons, Gong openly condemned such works as "spurious forms" (weiti 偽體)[4] and advocated the free expression of spontaneous emotions as an antidote to such baneful influence.

This antiestablishment stance is undoubtedly the most important hallmark of Gong's works. When Wei Yuan 魏源 (1794–1857), another leading reformist thinker and close friend of Gong, wrote a preface to the Collected Works of Ding'an [Gong Zizhen] (Ding'an wen lu 定盦文錄), he used a single word to summarize the unique features of Gong's works just as Gong himself did for Tang Peng. The word he chose is ni 逆, meaning roughly "to go against" or "to resist." Wei Yuan praised Gong Zizhen's works for their free, spontaneous expression and compared his way of writing to the legendary swordsmanship of the Women of Yue, seeing both as evidence of inborn artistic genius. In the opinion of Wei Yuan, Gong's uninhibited style of self-expression demonstrates not only his artistic genius but also his defiance of literary and social conventions. "His is constantly the way that aims to rebel against the traditions—going against folk customs and local practices on the small scale and against the prevailing social trends on the large scale."[5]

Gong Zizhen wrote three other important essays with the express intent to justify and in fact sanctify the expression of individual feelings. In "Forgiving Emotion" (You qing 宥情), he depicts a heated discussion on the significance of emotion among five fictional characters named numerically. Character One imagines a scholar who is preoccupied with and never tires of talking about feelings of joy and sorrow, and One wants to know the reason for such an absorption with emotion. Following Cheng-Zhu neo-Confucian orthodoxy, Character Two replies that the scholar in question is a flippant man because he indulges in emotion, the undesirable *yin* lifebreath (*yinqi* 陰氣) of fleshly desires within man. A sage, Character Two continues, is one whose *yin* lifebreath of desires has been purged and whose *yang* lifebreath (*yangqi* 陽氣) of moral rectitude fills the heaven. Character Three disputes the view of Character Two by saying that the sage of the West (i.e., a Buddhist sage) regards emotion as the best of three kinds of desires and does not scorn it. Character Four takes issue with both views. He challenges Character Two's Cheng-Zhu neo-Confucian view of emotion, arguing that an oversimplified equation of emotion with fleshly desires leads to an erroneous censure of morally correct emotions that have nothing to do with fleshly desires. He holds that emotion, after all, is what distinguishes man from insentient beings. Meanwhile, he faults the alleged Buddhist view of Character Three, saying that it is equally undesirable to privilege desire and subsume all emotions under it. For him, emotions driven by fleshly desires are nothing but a source of obscenity and evil. Character Five dismisses all four views on the grounds that they are all simplistic wholesale negations or affirmations of emotion. Even though Character Four's view is quite as "centrist" as his, he attacks it anyway as yet another extremist view. After presenting these four views of emotion through his fictional characters, the author steps in to tell us that he felt *yin* lifebreath, namely, emotion, weighing heavily in his heart, and he wondered if he was ill. To trace its origin, he looked into his own heart and followed its traces, which led him back to his childhood. Even reaching back to his personal primordial state, before subjective consciousness and language, he found himself filled with *yin* lifebreath and realized what he mistook for illness had always been with him. Having thus traced the origin of his emotion, Gongs then asks himself:

§176

Now I am leading a leisured life and looking into myself in this manner. Don't I know what the sages of this land denounce? Don't I know what the sages of the West [i.e., India] denounce? Of Characters One, Two, Three, Four, and Five, who will be partial to me? Who will condemn me? For the time being, let me make my excuse for emotion and wait for someone to look into it again. Hereupon, I have written "Forgiving Emotion."

如今閒居時。如是鞠己，則不知此方聖人所訶歟？ 西方聖人所訶歟？ 甲、乙、丙、丁、戊五氏者，孰黨我歟？ 孰詬我歟？ 姑自宥也，以待夫覆鞠之者。作《宥情》。(*GZZQJ*, 90)

What Gong calls his forgiveness of emotion understates his complete endorsement of it. In seeing emotion as part of original or primordial human nature, he repudiates not only neo-Confucianism's direct denunciation of it (personified in Character Two) but also less negative views presented by the other characters. While Gong does not explicitly endorse emotion here, he goes further in his preface for a collection of his own *ci* 詞 poetry:

§177
I also tried to eradicate it [emotion]. I couldn't eradicate it, so I turned around and began to forgive it. As there is no end to my forgiving of emotion, I turned around and began to revere it. . . . Isn't it true that I want to revere emotion? Indeed, and for that reason I revere it. This is consistent with what I wrote in "Forgiving Emotion." Indeed, for that reason I made my excuse for emotion. That is, I had tried to eradicate emotion for fifteen years but ended in failure.

亦嘗有意乎鋤之矣；鋤之不能，而反宥之；宥之不已,而反尊之。. . . . . . 是非欲尊情者耶？且惟其尊之，是以為《宥情》之書一通；且惟其宥之，是以十五年鋤之而卒不克。(*GZZQJ*, 232)

The second essay, "On Partiality to the Self" (Lun si 論私), is framed as a dialogue with a disciple about the slogan "great public spirit and unselfishness" (*da gong wu shi* 大公無私). Enforcers of Cheng-Zhu neo-Confucian orthodoxy censured emotion as the link to fleshly desires that lead toward self-gratification and away from public interest. Their negation of emotion represents just one of their concerted efforts to eliminate the individual self and establish a selfless social-moral order. In this context, to justify free expression of one's emotion, Gong had no choice but to repulse their attacks of the self or individualism. This is the task he undertook in his second essay.

It begins with the disciple asking Gong about the origin of *si* 私 (selfishness or partiality); Gong then launches into a long list of examples of selfishness and public spirit. He first identifies the selfishness of heaven that allows itself an extra day in leap years, warm days in winter, and cool days in summer; the selfishness of the earth keeping to itself miscellaneous tracts of uncultivated land; the selfishness of sage-kings who love no countries but their own; the selfishness of ministers and officials loyal only to lords; and the selfishness of filial sons who are kind to their own parents and no one else's. Then, Gong gives two contrasting examples of "the utmost public spirit under heaven" (*tianxia zhigong* 天下至公): Zi Kuai 子噲

(r. 320–312 BCE), who wanted to give away of the eight-century-old Yan state to his prime minister Zi Zhi 子之 (d. 312 BCE), and Emperor Ai 哀帝 (r. 6–2 BCE) of Han, who did not treasure his own empire and intended to give it to his commander in chief, Dong Xian 董賢 (23–1 BCE). With these examples, Gong wants to show that self-interest should not be condemned or generosity lauded generally or in and of themselves. For him, the Cheng-Zhu neo-Confucian moralists who exhort others to "great public spirit" are none other than those "who use the principles of Mo [Zi 墨子's altruism] to expedite their practice of Yang [Zhu 楊朱's extreme egoism]" (*GZZQJ*, 92). The essay ends with a scathing mockery of such hypocrites. When we consider that birds and beasts mate in public while human beings exchange intimacies in private, Gong asked, "Are those who nowadays preach 'great public spirit' human beings? Or are they animals?" (*GZZQJ*, 92).

In the third essay, "An Observation on the [Cosmological] Origin Made between the Years of Ren and Gui (1823), No. 1" (Ren gui zhi ji tai guan di yi 壬癸之際胎觀第一; hereafter "Observation"), Gong lays the cosmological ground for his sanctification of emotion and the individual. Neo-Confucian condemnation of the same rests on the belief that they prevent people from internalizing the cosmological-moral principle *li* 理 and achieving sagehood. Gong must dismantle this assumption and found a new cosmological scheme centered on the individual self. Such a new cosmological scheme is mapped out in "Observation":

§178

Heaven and earth, they are what men have made. They were made by the multitude of men themselves, not by sages. Sages are the ones who stand in opposition to the multitude of men and for whom the multitude are an inexhaustible mass. The master of the multitude, who is neither the Dao nor the Ultimate, calls itself "I." The light of the "I" has made the sun and the moon. The force of the "I" has made mountains and rivers. The evolution of the "I" has made birds and insects. The reason of "I" has made written characters and spoken languages. The lifebreath of "I" has made heaven and earth; and the heaven and earth of the "I" in turn have made men. The "I" has discretely made human principles and orders. The multitude of men means those who go through transformations together and become human beings. None of them begins alone before others.

天地，人所造，眾人自造，非聖人所造。聖人也者，與眾人對立，與眾人為無盡。眾人之宰，非道非極，自名曰我。我光造日月，我力造山川，我變造毛羽肖翹，我理造文字言語，我氣造天地，我天地又造人，我分別造倫紀。眾人也者，駢化而群生，無獨始者。(*GZZQJ*, 12–13)

What distinguishes this cosmological scheme from traditional ones is the emergence of the "I" as the ultimate reality. As we all know, the Daoist Tao, the Confucian Tao, and the neo-Confucian *li* all betoken an ultimate reality into which all things, natural and human, dissolve and lose their individual identities. By contrast, this "I" emerges as the ultimate reality not through the elimination but through the full realization of the individuality of each and every man. The word *wo* 我, "I," is particularly well chosen to accentuate this direct, cognate relationship between the ultimate reality and the individuality of each man.[6] An English translation of it as "Individual Self" seems quite appropriate. On the ground of this direct, unmediated link with the ultimate reality, Gong emphasizes that the multitude of men can each claim that he himself, not the sages, is the maker of all things.

The relationship of this Individual Self with all things is revealed through a description of the cosmogonic process, which strikes me as very similar to the one described in chapter 25 of Lao Zi's 老子*Dao de jing* 道德經, despite the different name of the ultimate reality in the two texts. "Man is modeled on the earth," Lao Zi writes, "the earth is modeled on heaven, and heaven is modeled on the Dao, and the Dao is modeled on self-so-ness (*ziran* 自然)."[7] Apparently, Gong conceived of the cosmogonic process in fundamentally the same way, even though he traces it the other way round (from the "I" to the Dao or the Ultimate to heaven and earth to man) and substituted *wo*, or the Individual Self, for the nonhuman self-so-ness. Of course, this substitution of names is of profound philosophical significance and amounts to nothing less than a humanizing of the ultimate reality. By reconceiving the nonhuman self-so-ness in such humanistic terms, Gong apparently aimed to establish the philosophical foundation for sanctifying one's individual self and freely expressing one's own feelings and thoughts. Of course, Gong is not the first to do this. More than one and a half millennia earlier, neo-Daoists like Ji Kang 嵇康 (223–262) and Ruan Ji 阮籍 (210–263) reconceptualized Lao Zi's notion of *ziran* as synonymous with uninhibited human volition, thereby transforming it into the ultimate sanction for their iconoclastic feelings, thoughts, and behaviors.[8] However, they fell short of substituting Individual Self for *ziran* and consecrating individualism in its own name, that is, the "I."

Gong Zizhen undoubtedly owes an important debt to the Wei-Jin neo-Daoist individualists, but the immediate source of his individualistic ideas is Li Zhi 李贄 (1527–1602), echoes of whose literary and political views abound in Gong's works. His ideal of complete self-expression (*wan* 完) harks back to Li Zhi's conception of *wen* 文 or literature as an uninhibited, unstoppable overflow of emotion. His idea of the perdurance of childhood emotions is apparently inspired by Li Zhi's "Theory of the Childlike Heart [Tongxin shuo 童心說]" (see §§159–60). His piece about the sick plum trees reads like an allegorical elaboration of Li Zhi's "let people follow their own nature" (*shun qi xing* 順其性) and condemnation of attempts to "rein in emotion with rituals and morality" (*zhi hu liyi* 止乎禮儀).[9] His elevation of the multitude of individuals above a sage reminds us of Li Zhi's view that

"Yao, Shun, and a traveler are one and the same; sages and ordinary people are one and the same."[10] For both Li and Gong, the rethinking of emotion constitutes an attempt not only to revitalize the literary tradition but also, more important, to challenge the social establishment as a whole. Like Li Zhi, Gong Zizhen fought against the entrenched Cheng-Zhu neo-Confucian orthodoxy and advocated freedom of expression for individual emotion and thought in political as well as literary arenas. He shared with Li Zhi the same goal of liberating the people from the shackles of repressive neo-Confucian ritualism and state ideology. In pursuing this common goal, however, Gong is less iconoclastic than Li because he stopped short of openly dismissing, as Li had done, the six Confucian classics along with *Analects* and *Mencius* as the "source of the men of falsehood" (*jia ren zhi yuan sou* 假人之淵藪).[11] Nevertheless, both can be regarded as true Confucians at heart for their commitments to core Confucian ideas of loyalty (*zhong* 忠) and filial piety (*xiao* 孝). Gong is more of a reformist than Li in that he embraced the so-called *jingshi sixiang* 經世思想 or statecraft thought and committed himself to various social and political reform projects.[12] In all his endeavors, he sought to shatter human bondage surely because he believed only free-thinking individuals could accomplish the daunting task of reforming China. With this ultimate goal underlying his works, Gong is rightly regarded as the forerunner of late Qing reformist thinking and leading advocate of an individualist view of emotion.[13]

A Revolutionary Theory of Emotion and Literary Creation: Lu Xun

Unlike Gong Zizhen, Lu Xun did not rethink the role of emotion and literary creation for the sake of national reform. The cause he vigorously pursued was that of cultural revolution and national rebirth.[14] What distinguishes his goal from that of reformers like Gong, Liang Qichao 梁啟超 (1873–1929), and others is that he aimed to destroy the very foundations of traditional Chinese sociopolitical order and build a new China on the ruins of the old. In rethinking emotion and literary creation within the framework of such a radical cultural revolution, Lu Xun inevitably had to look at emotion and literary creation from beyond traditional Chinese literary criticism and launch an attack on various traditional views as well as general cultural values informing them. This is exactly what he sought to accomplish in his 1907 essay "On the Demonic Poetic Power" (Mo luo shi li shuo 摩羅詩力說).

   This long essay is divided into nine sections. Section 1 is an eloquent elucidation of the crucial importance of literary revitalization to the survival of the Chinese nation. He begins by examining the relationship between literature and the rise and fall of the world's oldest civilizations—the Hindu, Judaic, and Islamic Egyptian—observing that they were on the rise when their poets sang fresh, proud songs and wrote grand, sublime works. Conversely, they were set on a course of irreversible decline and extinction as the voices of their poets faded. From these historical examples, Lu Xun concludes that literature is the spirit of a nation and that China must reinvigorate its literature and spirit in order not to fall victim to the same fate. As an old, stagnant civilization, China must look to younger, not yet fully civilized nations and absorb what Nietzsche called the new, energizing force of a savage people:

§179

Alas, it is not that the inward voices and writings of the ancients aren't awesome, grand, and noble. But their breath does not reach down to the present. Did the ancients held up for our reverence leave to posterity anything but what we lovingly lay our hands on and what we chant? As we may only speak about our own past glories and feel lonesome next to them, wouldn't emerging nations—whose cultures, though not yet flowering, hold great promise for the future—be more worthy of our salute?

嗟夫，古民之心聲手澤，非不莊嚴，非不崇大，然呼吸不通于今，則取以供覽古之人，使摩挲詠嘆而外，更何物及其子孫？否亦僅自語其前此光榮，即以形邇來之寂寞，反不如新起之邦，縱文化未昌，而大有望于方來之足致敬也。(*LXQJ*, 57)

For Lu Xun, the emerging nations are European, and their spirits are what he calls poets of the "demonic school" (*moluo pai* 摩羅派). He explains that "the term 'moluo' 摩羅 [i.e., Mara, the Destroyer or Evil One] is borrowed from the Hindus, meaning the heavenly demon or what Europeans call 'Satan,' and is originally used as an appellation for Byron."[15] His "demonic school," then, refers to a group of European Romantic poets headed by Byron, with his "demonic" or destructive penchant and, at the other end, Hungarian poet Petőfi: "They are all bent on rebellion and aim to take action, and all those loathed by the world belong to their rank" (*LXQJ*, 59). Praising their spirit of rebellion, Lu Xun writes:

§180

They would not sing the notes of an orderly world and harmonious music. When they burst out shouting, all those who hear them rise up to fight the heaven and oppose vulgar customs. Their spirit profoundly touches the hearts of later generations and reaches far beyond to infinitude.

大都不為順世和樂之音，動吭一呼，聞者興起，爭天拒俗，而精神復深感後世人心，綿延至於無已。(*LXQJ*, 57)

In section 2, Lu Xun proceeds to explain why their calculated destruction of peace and harmony was beneficial for the development of human civilization in general and the transformation of the Chinese society specifically. Applying the social

Darwinian view of human history, he first praises their destruction of peace and harmony as a forward thrust by a new nation fiercely competing for dominance. Then he dismisses the ideal of peace and harmony as symptomatic of the complacency and stagnation of an old nation bound for defeat in the global struggle. Next, Lu Xun considers why European nations could dispense with the ideal of peace and harmony while China remained obsessed with it. Although all peoples have an instinctive fear of war and yearning for peace and harmony, he explained, Europeans and the Chinese adopted different approaches to dealing with these instincts. Ever since Plato's *Republic*, Western thinkers, realizing the inevitability of fierce battles for survival, envisioned various social utopias as a way to energize their people to fight and win. While Europeans obeyed the law of evolution and looked to the future, according to Lu Xun, the Chinese went against this law and looked back to the times of the legendary Yao and Shun or even earlier as the ideal era of peace and harmony. For Lu Xun, this idealization of an ancient golden age was disastrous because it induced "hope for non[action] [*wu* 無], to see non[action] as progress, and strive for non[action]" (*LXQJ*, 60). He offers an incisive analysis of how this idealization of an ancient golden age began and how it led to Chinese society embracing a vision of peace and harmony:

§181

Those who knew they themselves were weak and incapable of action sought only to escape from the dusty world. They yearned for an ancient world and let men fall to the level of insects and beasts. They ended their own lives as recluses. Such were the men of despondency. Society endorsed their retreat, calling them men of noble detachment; and they themselves said, "We [are] insects and beasts, we [are] insects and beasts." Those who were still not contented would commit themselves to words and phrases, hoping that others too would return with them to the simple, ancient world. Of those people, Lao Zi and his likes are the ringleaders. Lao Zi wrote five thousand words and his intention was to make sure that peoples' hearts would not be agitated. In order not to agitate other hearts, he would first turn his own heart into the state of withered wood, and establish nonaction as the principle of government. By transforming society through the action of nonaction, he sought to bring great peace to the world.

惟自知良懦無可為，乃獨圖脫屣塵埃，惝恍古國，任人群墮于蟲獸，而己身以隱逸終。思士如是，社會善之，咸謂之高蹈之人，而自云我蟲獸我蟲獸也。其不然者，乃立言辭，欲致人同歸于朴古，老子之輩，蓋其魁雄。老子書五千語，要在不攖人心；以不攖人心故，則必先自致槁木之心，立無為之治；以無為之為化社會，而世即于太平。(*LXQJ*, 60–61)

Lu Xun maintained that such a Daoist ideal of peace and harmony made sense only if "men could return to the biological state of birds, insects, flowers and plants and gradually become emotionless" (*LXQJ*, 61). Unfortunately, however, there has never been nor ever will there be a time when things do not compete for survival. The course of evolution may slow down or even pause, but living things cannot regress to their primordial state. To seek a Daoist ideal of peace and harmony, he felt, is "[like] hoping that an outgoing arrow will fly backward and return to the bow: the principle of things cannot allow such an occurrence" (*LXQJ*, 61).

After this scathing attack on the Daoist ideal of peace and harmony, he turns to condemn the same Confucian ideal in the social realm, observing, "In regard to governing China, the ideal has always been 'no agitation'" (*LXQJ*, 61). If Daoists pursued "no agitation" in hopes of eradicating competition, strife, and chaos, the emperors enforced "no agitation" for selfish reasons. "Supposing there are people trying to agitate others or people being agitated by others," Lu Xun writes, "these situations will be vehemently prohibited by an emperor for the purpose of protecting his own reign and ensuring its continuation by posterity for thousands of generations without end" (*LXQJ*, 61). So, whenever a genius emerges who might stir people's hearts, an emperor will exercise his power to eliminate the genius. Sadly enough, the populace would often do the same because they "want to make their lives safe and would rather bend and degrade themselves than strive for progress" (*LXQJ*, 61). Thus Lu Xun illustrates how the Confucian ideal of peace and harmony, however noble in appearance, functioned to legitimize the elimination of the genius who, through social revolution and overthrowing of feudal rulers, might deliver the people from ignorance and moral degradation.

For Lu Xun, such a genius is none other than the creative poet who can awaken our deepest emotions and guide us to heroic action for both self-liberation and social revolution. This poet possesses such power because he reminds people of what's already in their hearts and gives expression to what they wish to say but have no words for. Commenting on the potential of such a response, Lu Xun writes,

§182

What the poet says for us is like a plucking of the strings of our hearts, setting off sonorous notes that reach to the soul's innermost chamber and make all those endowed with emotion raise their head as if seeing the sunrise. Those people will now exert their great strength and display their noble spirit in their endeavors. Then the putrefying peace and harmony will be destroyed. Once such peace and harmony are destroyed, the way of man will rise.

詩人為之語，則握撥一彈，心弦立應，其聲激於靈府，令有情皆舉其首，如睹曉日，益為之美偉強力高尚發揚，而污濁之平和，以之將破。平和之破，人道蒸也。(*LXQJ*, 61–62)

Citing the example of Plato's banishment of poets from his ideal *Republic*, Lu Xun pointed out that all those wishing to maintain the status quo—ranging from the heavenly gods to the ignorant populace—always conspired to forbid the poet to express his emotions in such an agitating manner. What has happened to Chinese poets over the millennia is, Lu Xun contended, a poignant testimony to this brutal suppression of emotional expression. "Because poetry could not be thoroughly eradicated," he went on to say, "rules and norms were set up to imprison it." According to him, this is the sole purpose for which the entire system of traditional Chinese poetics was developed. Although the sage-king Shun stated that poetry expresses the heart's intent, later critics established the critical tenet that poetry "controls one's disposition and emotion" (*chi ren xingqing* 持人性情; *LXQJ*, 62) and adopted the principle of "no evils" (*wu xie* 無 邪) based on Confucius's comment on *The Book of Poetry*. Exposing the repressive motives behind these views, Lu Xun asked, "Since the statement goes that [poetry] expresses the heart's intents, why should one say that [poetry] controls the same? To impose the 'no evils' [principle] is to obliterate one's intents" (*LXQJ*, 62). The impact of such critical tenets and principles was truly debilitating. The majority of Chinese poets obeyed the restrictions on the contents and manners of emotional expression and limited themselves to writing about their gratitude to their powerful patrons or their refined sentiments for the mountains and streams. Even those who dared to go against the vulgar customs could not express their emotions in a way that would raise public agitation for social revolution. For instance, Qu Yuan's 屈原 (340?–278 BCE) works "abound in fragrant plants and pathetic notes, but there are no traces of defiance and rebellion to the very end. Thus, the influence of his works on later generations is none too strong" (*LXQJ*, 62). Surveying the rank of Chinese poets, Lu Xun sighed:

§183

Since the time written characters came into existence to this day, among all the masters of *shi* 詩 poetry and the practitioners of *ci* poetry, has there really been anyone who could spread his miraculous voice, impart his divine consciousness, perfect the disposition and sentiments of our people, and make noble the ideals of our people? There are practically none. (*LXQJ*, 63)

Believing that the spirit of a people was none other than its poetry, Lu Xun naturally assumed an inherent connection with China's lack of drive for change and progress and the taming of emotion in its poetry. For him, it is the critical tenets of "no agitation" and "no excess" that prevented a soul like Qu Yuan from venting his emotions uninhibitedly and turning them into a powerful force to change a corrupt world. This taming of emotion, Lu argued, practically deprived China of an energizing poetic spirit crucial to its drives for change and progress. He saw the notable absence of great poets capable of energizing national spirit as the ominous evidence of the decline of the Chinese civilization. Worse still, this taming of emotion virtually turned the Chinese masses into ignorant slaves. By habits of their long observance of "no agitation," they lost their desires and abilities to contemplate and express their own emotions, let alone think and act independently. Under such deplorable conditions, they could not but submit themselves to the tyranny of despotic rulers and become obedient, unthinking slaves. When rebellions arose, they would assist despotic rulers in crushing them rather than seek their own liberation. In this way, they became instrumental to the continuous existence of monarchical despotism in China. For Lu, this is the ultimate evil of the taming of emotion. So, the destruction of the repressive Chinese society must begin with the liberation of emotion and the nurture of "demonic" poets, who could break the bondage of traditional Chinese poetics and produce works that will stir up public passions for social changes and revolution.[16]

In sections 3–5, Lu Xun delineated the life and works of Byron the demonic poet par excellence, hoping that Chinese poets would emulate him and become demonic poets in his image. He first told us why Byron came to be condemned as demonic or Satanic:

§184
Then, there came Byron who transcended the traditional norms and expressed his beliefs outright. No single piece of his writings is not filled with the voices of strength, rebellion, destruction, and challenge. Could those of peaceful and harmonious disposition not fear him? So they called him Satan.

迨有裴倫，乃超脫古範，直抒所信，其文章無不函剛健抗拒破壞挑戰之聲。平和之人，能無懼乎？於是謂之撒但。(*LXQJ*, 67)

A man called Satan is, Lu Xun explained, as much an anathema to Christians as a man called "rebel against the Way" (*pandao* 叛道) is to the traditional Chinese society. Both are "cast out from the human society and find it hard to go on living. So, no one can bear to have this stigma unless one is strong, ferocious, belligerent, broad-minded, and intelligent" (*LXQJ*, 68). For Lu Xun, these attributes of a Satanic being—be he a fallen angel or a human rebel—are exactly the essential qualities the Chinese people need to develop in their struggles for self-liberation and national salvation. So, he ardently joined Byron in turning "Satanic" into an honorable term for eulogizing those who dare to challenge the absolute authority, to defy the social mores and public opinions, and to fight for the individual freedom of all. To manifest and glorify these three "Satanic" goals, Lu Xun believed there was no better way than to depict the works and life of Byron himself. In depicting the works of this quintessential demonic poet, Lu Xun recounted how

Byron sang praise of Lucifer's and Cain's challenges to God's absolute authority in *Don Juan* and *Manfred*, the pirate chief Conrad's defiance of laws and social mores in *The Corsair*, and Satan's assertion of his own will and power in *Heaven and Earth*. In describing the life of Byron himself, Lu Xun showed how he fearlessly pursued these same great goals at all costs. He mocked the morality of the British polite society with his romantic love affair with Lady Caroline Lamb and endured his virtual ostracization from aristocratic and literary England. As he treasured the freedom of not only himself but all individuals, not only his own people but all other peoples, he went to lead the Greek people in their fight for freedom and independence from the Turks and actually lay down his own life for their cause. In addition to these heroic actions, Lu Xun mentioned Byron's profound admiration for Napoleon's destruction of the Old World and Washington's construction of a new world free for all, and took this as emblematic of the two opposite yet equally laudable sides in Byron and all other demonic poets: the destructive and the constructive.

In sections 6–9, Lu Xun described how Byron inspired Shelley, Pushkin, Lermontov, and other demonic Romantic poets to help bring about social revolutions in various European nations. In concluding the essay, he returned to the issue of China's fate. While he credited the demonic Romantic poets with arousing the public passions for social revolution and bringing about the rebirth of European nations, he saw the dearth of such poets in China as responsible for the failures of various programs of national reform. He believed that only the demonic poets, whom he now called "warriors in the spiritual realm" (*jingshen jie zhi zhanshi* 精神界之戰士), could unleash revolutionary passions that are as "powerful as gigantic waves, and strike directly at the pillar of the old society" (*LXQJ*, 100). Only the clarion call of these warriors can awaken the spirit of the Chinese nation and herald the birth of a New China.

To sum up, Lu Xun sought in this essay to rethink the roles of emotion in the same way the demonic Romantics did decades earlier—taking it as the means of destroying old social, political orders and establishing new ones. This reconceptualization of emotion and poetic creation, the cornerstone of the demonic Romanticism, also lies at the heart of all literary, social, and political theses Lu Xun put forth in the essay. He attributed the rise of European nations to the ability of their poets to evoke the people's passions for social changes and revolution. Conversely, he ascribed the stagnation and decline of the Chinese nation to the inability of its poets to arouse the same in the people's hearts. He urged Chinese poets to expunge the basic tenets of traditional Chinese poetics such as "no excesses," "no evils," and "controlling one's emotions." What is more, he called upon them to uproot the Daoist and Confucian ideals of "peace and harmony"—the very cultural foundation on which traditional Chinese literary criticism, as well as the entire system of feudal state ideology and apparatus, was established.[17]

By describing the lives and works of Byron and other demonic Romantics, Lu Xun wished to teach Chinese how to unleash torrents of revolutionary passion that will topple the absolute authority (the Qing court, by insinuation), sweep away all feudal mores and customs, and pave the ground of the emergence of a new China free for all. As Lu Xun's rethinking of emotion and poetic creation leads to nothing less than cultural revolution and self-liberation, it seems fitting to call his theory of emotion and literary creation a revolutionary individualistic one.

/////////////////////////////////

Notes

1. For a brief English biography of Gong Zizhen, see Wong, *Kung Tzu-chen*. For Chinese- and Japanese-language publications on Gong's life and intellectual development, see Ch'ien, *Zhonguao jin sanbai nian xueshu shi*, 2:532–54; Zhu J., *Gong Ding'an yanjiu*; Guan, *Gong Zizhen yanjiu*; and Zou, *Gong Zizhen lungao*.
2. On Gong's attack on these two literary schools, see Zou, *Gong Zizhen lungao*, 88–109.
3. Gong explicitly criticized these two literary trends in "Yu ren jian yi" 與人箋一 (*GZZQJ*, 336–37) and in "Jixi Hu hubu wenji xu" 績溪胡戶部文集序 (*GZZQJ*, 207–8).
4. See his poem titled "Geyan you qi shu shang zhe" 歌筵有乞書扇者 (*GZZQJ*, 490).
5. Wei Yuan, "*Ding'an wenlu* xu" 定盦文錄序 (*GZZQJ*, 650).
6. Of course, insofar as this *wo* denotes the individuality of each and every man, it may carry the implications of "we" as well. However, the main thrust of Gong's argument is to glorify individuality by establishing it as a cosmological absolute above the sages and the Tao. So, it seems better to render *wo* as "I" or "Individual Self" rather than "we." Although the elements of "I" and "we," the individual and the collective, are closely intertwined in many popular terminologies of late Qing political discourse, it is generally possible to note the emphasis on one or the other side of the dyad. For instance, if we examine the term *qunzhi* 群治 (self-government of the collective group) used by Liang Qichao 梁啟超 (1873–1929), we will see that the emphasis is placed on group cohesiveness rather than the exercise of individual rights.
7. See Zhu Q., *Laozi jiaoshi*, 103.
8. See Mather, "Controversy over Conformity and Naturalness."
9. In condemning this Confucian view of emotion, Li Zhi says, 蓋聲色之來，發於情性，由乎自然，是可以牽合矯強而致乎？故自然發於情性，則自然止乎禮義，非情性之外復有禮義也 ("Du lü fu shuo" 讀律膚說, *Fenshu, juan* 3, collected in *Fenshu, Xu Fenshu*, 132).
10. Li Zhi and Liu Dongxing, *Daogu lu*, 11.30a, 439.
11. Li Zhi, "Tongxin shuo," *Fenshu, juan* 3, collected in *Fenshu, Xu fenshu*, 99. For examples of Li Zhi's iconoclastic remarks against Confucians, see his "Fu Zhou Nanshi" 復周南士, *Fenshu, juan* 1; "Da Geng Zhongcheng" 答耿中丞, *Fenshu, juan* 1; and "Da Liu Xie" 答劉諧, *Fenshu, juan* 3. These remarks can be found in *Fenshu, Xu Fenshu*, 14–15, 16–17, 130.
12. For a study of Gong Zizhen's statecraft thought, see Guangde Sun, "Gong Zizhen di jingshi sixiang."
13. The status of Gong as the forerunner of late Qing reformist thinking is most accurately observed by the following remarks by Liang Qichao: "Speaking of the herald of the freedom of thought in recent times, we must first think of Ding'an 定盦 [Gong Zizhen].

Among our contemporary worthies whom I have met, those who now shine in the realm of thought, all began by worshipping Ding'an. When they first read Ding'an's collection, none of them did not feel their minds stimulated by it" ("Lun Zhonguo xueshi sixiang bianqian zhi dashi" 論中國學術思想變遷之大勢 [On the Major Trends of Chinese Intellectual Thought, 1902], in Liang, *Yinbing shi heji*, 1:7.97); Hsü, *Intellectual Trends in the Ch'ing Period*, 88–89. See Liang's similar comments on Gong in *Qingdai xueshi gailun* 清代學術概論 (A Survey of Qing Intellectual Thought), in Liang, *Yinbing shi heji*, 8:34.54–56.

14. Leo Ou-fan Lee provides valuable insights into the genesis of Lu Xun's literary theories and practices in Lee "Genesis of a Writer"; and Lee, *Voices from the Iron House*, chaps. 1–2. See also Lyell, *Lu Hsün's Vision of Reality*.

15. *LXQJ*, 58. It is quite natural that Lu Xun found kindred spirits in the "demonic" Romantic poets as he not only embraced their sociopolitical views but also shared their fascination with darkness, death, destruction, and tales of supernatural phenomena. For an analysis of the dark, morbid side of Lu Xun's psyche, see Hsia, "Aspects of the Power of Darkness in Lu Hsün."

16. The inconsistency between Lu Xun's wholesale negation of traditional Chinese literary criticism and his masterly accomplishments in old-style poetry and prose has been the subject of numerous critical studies in both Chinese and English. Among these studies, see Yao Wang, *Lu Xun yu Zhongguo wenxue*, 1–59; Lee, "Tradition and Modernity in the Writings of Lu Xun"; and J. C. Y. Wang, "Lu Xun as a Scholar of Traditional Chinese Literature."

17. Lu Xun's denunciation of the entire system of traditional Chinese literary criticism is part of his totalistic iconoclasm directed against the traditional Chinese society and culture as a whole. On the nature and origins of the totalistic iconoclasm of Lu Xun and other May Fourth writers, see Y. Lin, *Crisis of Chinese Consciousness*, particularly chaps. 2, 3, and 6. On the historical background to the rise of the iconoclastic May Fourth Movement, see Y. C. Wang, *Chinese Intellectuals and the West*, esp. chaps. 2–5, 8–10.

Chapter 10

Literary Creation
Chinese versus Western Theories from a Comparative Perspective

Originating from a confluence of Confucianism, Daoism, and the Abstruse Learning dating from pre-Qin through the Wei-Jin period, the *yi→xiang→yan* paradigm offers a broad framework for examining Chinese thinking about literary creation in this book. By the late Warring States era, the philosophical import of three concepts, *yi*, *xiang*, and *yan*, had evolved into a protocosmological theory in *The Commentary on Appended Phrases* (§§14–15, 20–22). Subsequently the Wei philosopher Wang Bi would not only tease out ontological and epistemological aspects of these concepts but even establish a causative relationship between them. He thus founded the basic *yi→xiang→yan* paradigm, in which the three key terms engage each other bidirectionally. Thus *yi* gives rise to *xiang* which in turn gives rise to *yan*—myriad objects come into being from nonbeing, and from hidden to manifest. Meanwhile, human understanding operating on the phenomenal world traverses the same path in a reverse direction, proceeding from manifest to hidden, obtaining *xiang* from *yan*, capturing *yi* from *xiang*.

In at least one important way, the *yi→xiang→yan* paradigm is perfectly suited to reveal the process of literary creation. *Yi* refers to transcendent mental activity leading to creative conception or imagination; *xiang*, to the semi-suprasensory imagery born of creative conception; and *yan*, to the linguistic medium necessary for translating the *xiang* into tangible writing. Given this stepwise or progressive aspect, it's not surprising that the *yi→xiang→yan* paradigm was adapted by Lu Ji and Liu Xie (§§37–38). to explore the entire creative process, including the final act of composition. In turn, the adapted literary *yi→xiang→yan* paradigm of Lu and Liu provides a convenient vantage point for examining various theories of literary creation developed later. By using Lu and Liu on *yi*, *xiang*, and *yan* as reference points, we not only see continuity in later critics but also appreciate their innovations and breakthroughs vis-à-vis their predecessors. By tracing concepts to their sources and following their subsequent evolution, we see the complex, interactive dynamics by which traditional theories of literary creation

PRISM: THEORY AND MODERN CHINESE LITERATURE • 20 (ANNUAL SUPPL.) • DECEMBER 2023
DOI 10.1215/25783491-11080935 • © 2023 LINGNAN UNIVERSITY

were produced—hence my use of these concepts as a framework for studying the history of Chinese theorizing about literary creation.

To my mind, however, examining Chinese thinking about literary creation through the *yi→xiang→yan* paradigm offers another significant advantage as well: an optimal perspective for comparison with Western theorizing about the same topic. Comparing both traditions on transcendent mental activity, artistic conception, and language would highlight the cogency and uniqueness of Chinese thinking on these topics, in turn initiating an in-depth dialogue between the two traditions and thereby deepening our collective understanding of literary creation. Having studied Western literary theory for several decades, I can't help but feel it would require an entire monograph to compare Chinese and Western theories of literary creation comprehensively. In this chapter, I merely attempt to roughly delineate what distinguishes the two traditions from each other.

Transcendent Creative Activity

For both China and the West, transcendent creative activity is regarded as fundamental to producing great works of art. As ancient Chinese critics observed, the most magnificent works are necessarily "visited by spirit"—showing the influence of either spirit or some god. But what, exactly, is the artistic "spirit"? How does a writer commune with it? Here Chinese and Western critics differ fundamentally. In Western literary theory, spirit is intimately linked to imaginative activity. An early dialogue by Plato, the *Ion*, views the artist's creative act as induced by a form of spiritual possession in moments of ecstasy. But here spirit involved the gods of Greek mythology, possessing a specific body and form, rather than anything like the eternal Idea or a more basic, ontological reality. Later, in *The Republic*, Plato offered a very different view of art as the imitation of what was already an imitation of reality, and so as "thrice-removed" from what was "really real," a formulation that led him to treat art negatively and to banishing poets from his ideal republic. Although Plato's mimetic theory helped set the direction of Western literary discourse for the next two thousand years, his belief that art is unrelated to spirit at a deeper, more ontological level failed to exert much influence on later thinking about literary creation. One important reason for that is the conceptual turn taken by Plato's Neoplatonic successors. For Plotinus, the souls of creators of beauty represent extensions of the highest ontological reality, "the One." His conceptual scheme of three levels of ontological reality (in top-down hierarchical order) as the One, Nous or Divine Intellect, and the Universal Soul thereby narrowed the gap between ontological reality and the mind as a creative force. For Plotinus, all beautiful and sublime forms manifest ontological reality because the embodied souls, creators of beauty and sublimity, derive from the Universal Soul, the Divine Intellect, and ultimately the One. This sort of Neoplatonism not only induced Western poetics in the Renaissance and after to explore the subjective imagination but also became an important intellectual source for the Romantic theory of creative imagination in the early nineteenth century.

In different ways, Neoplatonism exerted an especially profound influence on English Romanticism. The lingering connection of the young mind to the immortal Soul—of which Wordsworth writes in his famous "Ode: Intimations of Immortality from Recollections of Early Childhood"—no doubt harks back to the Platonic theory of recollection in the *Meno*. For Wordsworth, this sort of memory formed an important passageway to spiritual communion and imagination. Another renowned English Romantic poet, Samuel Taylor Coleridge, equated art with what he called the activity of "secondary imagination." If primary imagination is "the living Power and prime Agent of all human Perception, and as a repetition in the finite mind of the eternal act of creation in the infinite I AM,"[1] secondary imagination or artistic activity, as an "echo" of that, displays an affinity with the Wordsworthian notion of memory/recollection as having ultimately a spiritual or divine source. In *A Defence of Poetry*, Percy Bysshe Shelly likewise proclaims that a poet "participates in the eternal, the infinite, and the one," enshrining poets in reverence and crowning them as "philosophers of the very loftiest power," "legislators of the world," and "prophets."[2]

German idealism offered another intellectual source for the Romantic theory of imaginative creation. Unlike Neoplatonists, Fichte, Schelling, and Hegel viewed external, objective reality as immanent in human cognitive capacity and activity, positing the former as an a priori for the latter's birth and development. Thus Hegel made innovative use of the subjective-objective opposition inherited from Kant, turning it into a movement from objective to subjective that could then be used to explain human history as a continual and necessary progression of Spirit toward freedom and self-realization. Schelling shifted attention away in a different direction from Kant's transcendental epistemology to aesthetics, attempting to close the gap between nature and subjectivity by seeing the subjective as having a formative capacity similar to that of Nature itself. Coleridge, well versed in German idealism, especially Schelling, deployed the latter's notion of a dialectical unity between concept and intuition (*Ineinsbildung*) to explain the creative imagination unique to great poets, coining the term *esemplastic* expressly for the purpose. This capacity to turn dialectal opposition into organic unity is perhaps the most important characteristic of "secondary imagination."

But while Western and Chinese thinking about literary creation shared a belief that the greatest, most successful works necessarily involved transcendent activity and spiritual communion, from the Chinese standpoint "spiritual communion" doesn't have to imply anything like absolute spirit in the Hegelian sense, or those Kantian epistemological categories existing a priori in the mind. Rather, it means comprehending the recondite cosmic Dao, the so-called unfathomable spirit of *yin* and *yang*. The spirit that ancient writers sought to evoke was not an embodiment of absolute Spirit but, rather, the highest principle of birth, growth, and change in the phenomenal world. While briefly used in the Six Dynasties Buddhist discourse to refer to an embodied divine essence such as the Buddha or dharmatā, "spirit" (*shen*) still differs from the Western notion in not involving any link to God as Creator. The transcendent experience of comprehending the Buddha spirit was also strikingly different from the activity of creative imagination described in Western literary discourse, even as the terms used in Chinese texts to describe transcendent creative activity continued to vary with time and critics' personal preferences.

For example, Lu Ji employs terms like "mind-roaming": "My essence galloping to the world's eight bounds / My mind roaming ten thousand yards, up and down"[3] 精騖八極，心游萬仞 (see §51), while Liu Xie calls it "spirit-thinking": "One's spirit roams with the world's objects" 神與物遊, "his thoughts traces back one thousand years" 思接千載, and "one's vision reaches ten thousand *li*" 視通萬里 (§§53–54). Though expressed differently, these terms both derive from the notion of "roaming the mind" in the *Zhuangzi* and the *Huainanzi* (see §§28–30). Unlike early philosophers, however, Lu and Liu both stress that such transcendent activity must end with a return to the phenomenal world. Wang Changling adopted the term *yi* from Yogācāra Buddhism to describe a transcendent mental activity going beyond temporal and spatial boundaries even as Hao Jing 郝經 (1223–1275) of the Yuan dynasty[4] considers transcendent creative activity as an "inner roaming" process where the writer journeys beyond his specific space-time limits, experiencing anew the ancient sage's creation of civilization (§118).

In describing transcendent imaginative activity, all these writers fall mainly into two categories: dynamic or tranquil. For the former, witness statements by Lu and Liu: "Withdraw one's vision and retract one's hearing" (*shoushi fanting* 收視反聽); "one's spirit roams with the world's objects"; and "one's mind roams beyond heaven and earth." Nonetheless, such dynamic mind roaming must begin from a "vacant and still" state of mind and a suspension of bodily perception. Such transcendent communion is obviously influenced by "spirit over form" philosophy (the *Zhuangzi* and the *Huainanzi*). As stated in the *Huainanzi*: "He [the sage] reaches the Three Springs below and searches nine levels of Heaven above; he encompasses the universe in all six directions and comprehends the myriad things" 下揆三泉，上尋九天，橫廓六合，撰貫萬物 (§30). In Lu Ji's essay "Exposition on Literature" and Liu Xie's "Spirit-Thinking" chapter, such dynamic transcendent activity induces a fusion of human emotions (*qing*), images (*xiang*), and words (*ci*), eventually forming a mental image of the work-to-be. The renowned calligrapher Wang Xizhi was the first to employ *yi* in his "Treatise on Calligraphy" to describe the calligrapher's imaginative activity, emphasizing that "*yi* must precede the brush"—in other words, before setting brush to paper, one must envision the movement and sequence of every dynamic stroke (see §§95–96). The transcendent tendency in such discussions became even more pronounced in the Tang, where every calligraphic *yi* involves the artist's encounter with divine spirit (see §97). Rather than the tranquil sense of *yi* from Yogācāra Buddhism, this dynamic sense of *yi* from indigenous calligraphic discourse informs Wang Changling's usage of the term in discussing the final compositional phase. Anchoring his discussion on *yi*, Wang seeks to reveal the writer's mental activity at the moment of producing a perfect line that achieves a fusion of emotion and external scenery. Du Mu 杜牧 (803–853) of the Late Tang also stressed the dynamic quality of *yi*, or its function as the driving force of composition, and used the concept *qi* to depict the dynamic transformation from *yi* to *yan*.

Buddhism exercised the greatest influence over descriptions of tranquil transcendent activity. The earliest case appears in Zong Bing's "Preface on Painting Landscapes" examined in chapter 3: here the myriad phenomena are physical transformations of the dharma body, to which the worthy man responds by tranquilly contemplating the landscape and landscape paintings and entering into communion with the indwelling Spirit. This type of transcendent activity follows the imperative "purify the mind and savor iconic images" to effect "expansion of one's spirit"—in other words, observing, savoring, and contemplating the visually perceived object (see §67). Later, with the advancement of Buddhism, the corresponding philosophical concepts evolved beyond the Six Dynasties' exegetical commentary, and critics were able to apply original terminology unique to Buddhism to explicate Buddhist philosophy. For example, Wang Changling in the Tang appropriated the concept *yi* from Yogācāra Buddhism to construct a paradigm of tranquil contemplation centered on *yi*. He appropriated phrases such as "initiating *yi*," "activating *yi*," and "deploying *yi*" to refer to transcendent mental activity at the initial stage of creativity. Wang believed *yi*—as in "feeling inspiration and begetting *yi*" in a state of tranquil contemplation—to be of an unconscious and instantaneous nature (§§79–81). Here, "inspiration" (*xing*) no longer refers to creative volition in native Chinese literary discourse but to the instant at which one is gazing on specific objects and scenery and begetting a transcendent conception (*yi*), whereby the true reality of myriad things is ultimately revealed through intuitive contemplation—in other words, crossing over to the realm beyond objective phenomena.

Compared to the tripartite *yi→xiang→yan* of Lu Ji and Liu Xie, Wang Changling with his fourfold *yi→jing→xiang→yan* (意→境→象→言) paradigm was able to offer a more complete and logically refined structure. To Wang, *yi* as the optimal mental state in creation underlies the entire creative process. His idea of transcendent activity differs from the out-of-the-body flight of the mind through the universe proposed by Lu Ji and Liu Xie. As a form of tranquil contemplation, Wang's vision bears the imprint of possible influence from Zong Bing. Yu Ji in the Yuan and Wang Fuzhi and Yuan Mei in the Qing were all inheritors of

Wang's legacy—specifically, of his "piercing glance and tranquil contemplation." Each, however, developed his own theory of enlightenment through deliberating on the natural landscape, by which one purifies one's mind and instantaneously comprehends the absolute reality of the phenomenal world (§§120–23). Wang Fuzhi also took the Buddhist term *pratyakṣa-pramāṇa* to emphasize the immediacy and instantaneousness of the mind's engagement with the external world in this kind of transcendent experience. On another front, Yan Yu of the Song borrowed a Chan concept, "wondrous enlightenment," to explicate transcendent mental activity during creation, with the result that "deliberation-enlightenment" and "wondrous enlightenment" both became fashionable catchphrases in literary criticism (§§116–17).

In sum, then, both Chinese and Western literary critics believe a transcendent spiritual act achieves comprehension of the ultimate reality, but they differ fundamentally in their view of what that "ultimate reality" is. The West took it as the embodiment of absolute Spirit, while in Chinese discourse it figures as the eternal principle (Dao) of cosmic transformation or of Buddha Nature transcending the subjective-objective split. In addition, both Chinese and Western tradition proposed two modes of comprehending ultimate reality: dynamic or tranquil. Neoplatonic literary sources usually held that during tranquil visual contemplation the writer may discover and activate traces of the highest Soul lingering in the self, and that spiritual communion with Nature produces the most beautiful poetry. Wordsworth's philosophical poems and Coleridge's "primary imagination" both offer evidence of that. At the same time, ardent followers of German idealism tend to emphasize the writer's agency in engaging the creative imagination (witness Coleridge's "secondary imagination") by actively transforming a priori categories of cognition already existing in the mind. In traditional Chinese creation discourse, likewise, literary critics who were also devout adherents of Buddhism all urged the writer to attain enlightenment through deliberation on natural objects and scenery—in other words, an awakening to cosmic reality by contemplating a natural landscape in tranquility. On the other hand, believers of the Daoist worldview stressed a suspension of physical sense perception—"withdraw sight and retract hearing"—as a way of inducing intense interaction among emotion, object phenomena, and language until the three fused into a perfect conception-image, the virtual blueprint of a work-to-be before its achieving linguistic expression.

The Mediating "Image" in the Creative Process

Since both Chinese and Western literary critics saw the "image" or envisagement as an important medium or intermediary for translating transcendent mental experience into language, it should come as no surprise that discussions of image or envisagement figure richly and prominently in both traditions. In the West, the core theme is the transcendent imagination, whose Latin root, *imaginari*, involves a picturing of oneself. For China, likewise, the internalized, virtual image also focused critical attention. For example, in the *Commentary on Appended Phrases*, the word *xiang* figures prominently: in the statement "the Sage created symbols to adequately convey their intent," *xiang* (translated as symbols) actually refers to the sage's mental image rather than images of external objects (see §15). Clearly, Daoist metaphysical thinkers have always assigned great significance to such virtual images. But does "image" in Chinese and Western discourse share more similarities or differences? To my mind, image within the two traditions connects to the highest reality in two fundamentally different ways. In the West, it offers a passage to absolute Spirit, while Chinese writers see it as leading to the highest cosmic principle of objective transformations. And while the Buddhist idea of a highest reality may seem tinged with subjectivity, the cosmic reality sought is still far from the realization of any absolute Spirit; rather, it means a transcending of the subjective-objective opposition.

The second reason for seeing *xiang* as differing from "image" has to do with different ways of understanding the relationship between mental image and ordinary sense-perception of the phenomenal world. In German idealist philosophy, vision is not so much a way of achieving cognition of external phenomena as an instrument for seeing how absolute Spirit manifests in the phenomenal world hence the primacy in Western criticism of the faculty of vision, extolled in Wordsworth's "Ode: Intimations of Immortality from Recollections of Early Childhood" and Coleridge's "primary imagination." Contrary to this apotheosizing tendency, Chinese Daoist thinkers have always held sight and hearing to be impediments to comprehending Dao, the highest cosmic principle. If the latter is to manifest, it would be the "Grand Image" to which Lao Zi refers (§§16–17). In *Zhuangzi*, such a manifestation would be invisible even to the superhuman eyesight of a fictional character like Lizhu (§18).

Precisely for this reason, Lu Ji emphasizes that at the initial stage of creation, only when the writer "withdraws sight and retracts hearing" can he "purify his mind and focus his thoughts," "encompass heaven and earth in the form [of his writing]" (see §43). In Liu Xie's "Spirit-Thinking" chapter, "spirit roaming with external objects" has nothing to do with vision, while the final product is a mental image of the work-to-be or a so-called conception-image—an intangible, imperceptible virtual blueprint of that work in the mind (§54). Thus Lu and Liu both take the virtual mental image to be a product of some transcendent flight of the mind. Such a mental image or conception-image, having fused emotion, external object, and language into one, would constitute ample preparation before setting brush to paper. Of course, this isn't to say Lu and Liu completely neglected external phenomena and visual perception, but no doubt the latter's function is limited to arousing authorial emotion and intent. As Lu Ji avers in "Exposition on Literature": "He moves along with the four seasons and sighs at their passing on, / Peers on all the things of the world, broods on their profusion" 遵四時以嘆逝，瞻萬物而紛披 (§42). Liu Xie also observes in the "Sensual Appearances of Things" chapter: "At the stirring of sensual appearance of things, the mind also sways" 物色之動，心亦搖焉 (WXDL, 46/3–4); "When summoned by sensual appearances of things, who could be at peace" 物色相召，人獲誰安 (WXDL, 46/11–12). In statements of this sort, however, external phenomena figure merely as factors inciting poetic inspiration but never as crucial determinants of the entire creative process.

Only in Zong Bing's "Preface to the Painting of Landscape" do external phenomena and visual perception begin to assume the important function of inducing some sort of transcendent epiphany. As Zong Bing and his Buddhist contemporaries see it, the iconic Buddha image (foxiang 佛像) and images of the natural scenery converge, likewise natural landscapes and the Pure Land, both being an embodiment and manifestation of the transcendent dharma spirit: "Infinite as it is by nature, the spirit dwells in forms and resonates with things by category, to the effect that the [transcendent] principle enters even reflections and traces" 神本亡端，棲形感類，理入影跡 (§68). Thus, as the dharma spirit imbues the myriad phenomena with "reflections and traces," the devotee could hope to awaken to the ultimate divine principle via specific, visually perceived iconic Buddha images and the natural landscape.

Based on this new understanding of how we perceive external phenomena, Zong Bing boldly elevates painting (which involves contemplation of the natural landscape) to paramount status, placing it above the apotheosized Yijing trigrams and hexagrams of Confucian and Daoist tradition. Zong's view in turn exerted an influence on Wang Changling's notion of wujing (object-inscape). Regarding the "object-inscape" in his Norms of Poetry, Wang urges the poet to "situate oneself in inscape and observe the inscape in one's mind" 處身於境，視境於心 (§79). He believes that by mentally concentrating on some perceived object, one may penetrate the phenomenal surface so as to grasp intuitively the cosmic reality transcending sensuous forms (§85).

At the same time, Wang Wei's poetry, steeped in Chan Buddhism, is fully in accord with Zong Bing's "Preface" on the level of practical composition. Wang Changling's ingress from tranquil contemplation of the object-inscape to a transcendent dimension offers a perfect theoretical recapitulation of Wang Wei's landscape poetry—not restricted to observation of object and scenes but representing a leap from the particular objects or scenes to the ultimate of all phenomena, dharma nature, tathātā, dharma body, nirvana, and Buddha nature.

Language in the Creative Process
Compared to what we've seen with "image" or envisagement, Chinese and Western views of the role of yan or language share far fewer affinities. If we think

of Romantic criticism as offering a two-stage view of the creative process (primary and secondary imagination as expounded by Coleridge), the reasons for this divergence become apparent: poetic language can only be part of the secondary process, echoing the initial act of creation. For eighteenth-century neoclassicism, more focused on poetic technique, literary language was indeed a central topic. For example, Alexander Pope discussed principles governing the imitation of classical poetry in *An Essay on Criticism*. Even so, the value of his essay appears to have been soon forgotten in at least some quarters, perhaps because he did not fully elucidate the relationship between language and the creative process. In the Romantic era, as exploration of the creative process becomes the dominant concern, discussion of language use enters into a more complex, mediated relationship to creativity: because it isn't part of the initial creative act, language lacks primacy, but on the other hand, without it realization or expression is impossible, hence the complex discourse on language in Romanticism, much of it involving the relation between language and an initial creative act, rather than between language and some external object. Unlike Romantic literary theory, its Chinese counterpart tended to treat the entire creative process as one seamless whole—from the initial transcendent mental activity to the final stage of composition. As a result, we can see the two traditions diverging.

Nevertheless, Chinese and Western literary critics are in closer accord on the chasm between virtual image and verbal expression. A passage from Shelley's "Defence of Poetry" bears a striking similarity to Liu Xie's statement in his "Spirit-Thinking" chapter:

Shelley's remarks, from *A Defence of Poetry*:	Liu Xie's remarks, from "Spirit-Thinking":
"When composition begins, inspiration is already on the decline, and the most glorious poetry that has ever been communicated to the world is probably a feeble shadow of the original conception of the poet. I appeal to the greatest Poets of the present day, whether it be not an error to assert that the finest passages of poetry are produced by labour and study."[5]	"When a writer picks up his brush, and right before writing anything, the breath of his creativity is doubly charged. But when the piece is completed, he finds only half of what he first had in the mind is conveyed. Why is this so? Conception [*yi*] turns in the void and therefore can easily be extraordinary; words are actual and therefore hard to be dexterously employed. Conception [*yi*] is derived from spirit thought, and words from conception. The two can be tightly matched, leaving no space between them; or they can be far apart from each another by a thousand miles." 方其搦翰，氣倍辭前；暨乎篇成，半折心始。何則？意翻空而易奇，言徵實而難巧也。是以意授於思，言授於意；密則無際，疏則千里. (*WXDL*, 26/48–58)

Here the two passages reveal an astonishing level of agreement on the wide gap between original conception and actual composition. The crucial term for Shelley, *conception*, is comparable to Liu Xie's *yi*, while Shelley's *original conception* renders perfectly Liu Xie's *yi* in "*yi* that turns in the void." But on the question of whether the poet is capable of closing the gap between conception and language by labor and study, Shelley and Liu go their separate ways. Shelley, like other Romantic writers, believes "labor and study" produced through "artificial toil" can't adequately represent the creative process because its only option is to try to re-create or reproduce something that's already occurred (the initial creative conception. By contrast, Liu Xie firmly believes that "words are derived from conception. The two can be closely matched, leaving no space between them" 言授於意，密則無際 (*WXDL*, 26/55–56). So just as the Western concept-language dichotomy might be seen as a variant of matter-spirit dualism, Liu Xie no doubt could base his *yan-yi* continuum on the belief in linguistic adequacy found in Confucian classics as well as eclectic Confucian-Daoist texts such as the *Commentary on Attached Phrases*.

How to connect recondite transcendent creative activity with concrete composition has always been the greatest problem, one that Chinese critics since the Western Jin have worked tirelessly to resolve. Their efforts have been buttressed by a firm belief in the inherent bond between language and reality, explicitly articulated or subtly endorsed by many thinkers. Generally speaking, Chinese philosophy has moved along two different but mutually complementary routes in trying to connect different phases of the creative process. The first consists of the *yi→xiang→yan* paradigm established in the *Commentary on Attached Phrases*: "The sages created the Symbols (*xiang*) to fully convey intended meaning [*yi*]; set forth the trigrams and hexagrams to fully present truth and falsehood; and attached phrases to give full expression in words" (§17). This statement connects *yi*, *xiang*, and *yan* within the same continuum. Here writing, when read together with the hexagrams, can adequately convey the latter's hidden meaning. Later, Wang Bi, using the logic of causation and inference, proposed that as *xiang* begets *yan*, *yan* also contains *xiang*; by the same token, as *yi* begets *xiang*, *xiang* also contains *yi*. This chain of causation grants *yan* a measure, however small, of ontological quality. And even though pre-Qin Daoist philosophers like Laozi and Zhuangzi insist that language cannot represent the highest cosmic principle, Dao, they concede the necessity of using it to describe Dao. This amounts to a tacit admission of language's capacity to reveal a metaphysical meaning beyond itself, so that "forgetting language after grasping conception" can be construed to imply language's capacity to reveal even Dao.

The second route involves the mind-body continuum established by Warring States philosophers and the Huang-Lao school in the early Han. Unlike the mind-body discrepancy common to Western thinkers, most Chinese thinkers affirm a mind-body unity. Mencius and Zhuangzi often use *qi* (lifebreath), a term related to the physical body, in discussing transcendent spiritual communion (§§24 27). But if *qi* or lifebreath is simultaneously connected to the physical body and transcendent communion, language can likewise play a similar mediatory role, conveying *qi* (as in "voice" or "intonation" [*ciqi* 辭氣]). The "Ji Gate Daoists" 稷下道家

text *Guanzi*, in discussing the relationship between transcendent mind and Dao, introduces notions of *qi* and bodily form, declaring sages are necessarily "perfect in mind and form" (§32). Sima Tan, the pioneer among early Han Huang-Lao thinkers, applied the principle of spirit-form unity to state governance in his "Treatise on the Essentials of the Six Schools" (§32), while Wang Chong of Eastern Han further broadened the scope of the spirit-form link, laying the foundation for later literary criticism to recognize the importance of the body (especially the uttering and transmission of sounds enabled by *qi*) for literary creation (§34).

Chinese literary exploration of the two routes (visual vs. acoustic) connecting conception to composition proved a lengthy process. From Western Jin to the High Tang, they focused mainly on the *yi→xiang→yan* paradigm. Lu Ji and Liu Xie both discussed the creative process within this paradigm but were able to elucidate only the mental activities involved in going from *yi* to *xiang*. Despite their awareness of artistic conception (*yi* or *shensi*) as a determining factor in compositional success, they could not explain how *yi* drives composition. The first person to successfully connect conception and execution was not in fact a literary critic but the Eastern Jin calligrapher Wang Xizhi. Wang used the term *yi* to refer exclusively to the calligrapher's envisagement of the shape and movement of characters before setting brush to paper. He believed that only by letting envisagement drive the brush can fine calligraphy be produced. Subsequently, Tang calligraphers such as Zhang Huaiguan and Sun Guoting connected this dynamic "envisagement" with spirit, thereby endowing it with transcendent import (§83). Wang Changling borrowed the term *yi* from Wang Xizhi and the Tang calligraphers' discussions to reveal all the mental activities involved in the entire compositional process, from creating overall structure to constructing lines and couplets, and finally to the fusion of emotion and scenery (§§82–85). Wang Changling's innovative approach of introducing dynamic *yi* from calligraphic discourse into poetics enabled him to successfully resolve the problem left by Lu Ji and Liu Xie, thereby revealing the operations performed by poetic imagination in enacting the compositional process. Within the evolution of literary creation discourse, Wang Changling's notion of dynamic *yi* undoubtedly marks a momentous breakthrough, one laying a solid groundwork for *yi*-centered creation discourse in the Ming-Qing period.

It took even longer for traditional literary criticism to explore the creative process via the second axis: the interactive relationship between mind/spirit and the physical body. Admittedly, Cao Pi, in his essay "A Discourse on Literature," noted how local atmosphere and the writer's temperament constitute crucial factors in determining writing style (§36). But "atmosphere" and "temperament" are intangible, elusive phenomena, while writing is material and tangible; how, then, could the former imbue the latter with a "style" both coinciding and differing from writing as a material act? Cao Pi failed to address this issue directly but offered an important hint: "Compare it to music: though melodies be equal and though the rhythms follow the rules, when it comes to an inequality in drawing on a reserve of *qi*, we have grounds to distinguish skill and clumsiness. Although it may reside in a father, he cannot transfer it to his son; nor can an elder brother transfer it to the younger."[6] Here, "drawing on a reserve of *qi*" refers to voicing (including singing, chanting, and reading out loud). Whether consciously or unconsciously, Cao had discovered the significance of voice as a crucial link. On the one hand, it inextricably linked the writer's mind and body, issuing from a bodily organ but obviously connected (as a kind of "breath") to local customs (such as Cao Pi's "atmosphere of *qi*"), as well as metaphysical cosmic energy (including Mencius's notion of "flood-like lifebreath" possessing transcendent moral significance). At the same time, voice manifests in words while abiding in writing and the classics. *Qi* connects metaphysical "energy" and material writing in the same way *xiang* connected metaphysical conception (*yi*) and concrete words. In both instances, we get a crucial link between the physical and metaphysical.

In discussing *qi* in writing, however, Cao Pi focused on assessing literary style and remained reticent about the creative process. Not until Han Yu put forth the notion of *yangqi* in the Middle Tang does *qi* fully enter into critical thinking about literary creation and play its special role as link between the author's transcendent creative and compositional activity. If Mencius manages to integrate moral cultivation and cosmic energy into a "flood-like lifebreath," Han Yu advocated nourishing that lifebreath by careful study of the sages so as to achieve spiritual communion with them, in the belief that this would ultimately make one capable of reproducing their achievements in "conveying meaning" and "establishing authorship." Han believed such splendid, proactive metaphysical lifebreath, accumulated to the full and flowing out naturally as the writer sets brush to paper, would produce perfect writing where "words and sounds would all be appropriate regardless of length or pitch" (§113).

If *xiang*—or *visual* perception (both inward and outward) for Lu Ji, Liu Xie, and Wang Changling—acts as the crucial intermediary between *yi* at the most recondite level and *yan* at the most concrete, then *qi*, a close associate of *acoustic* perception, links the mental activity in creative conception to actual composition. So while sound possesses the capacity for entering the spiritual dimension by connecting to *qi* and the mind, it also assumes linguistic expression via writing. One may regard Han Yu's theory of *yangqi* as a kind of physiological metaphysics because it connects spirit and form, internal and external. It opens a universally accessible passageway (distinct from Lu and Liu's *yi→xiang→yan* paradigm and Wang Changling's *yi→jing→xiang→yan* framework) nourishing *qi* to produce great writing. Han has reworked the sage tradition of "establishing oneself through writing" into a method of literary creation that common individuals would find accessible, reinforcing the underlying connection between an author's various resources. This *qi*-centered theory, originating with Mencius and matured by Han Yu, would gain further depth and sophistication at the hands of Song masters of ancient-style prose such as Su Shi and Su Che, while ever deepening Chinese literary thinking about the interaction between transcendent creative activity and the language by which it achieves expression (§§108–10).

In the roughly hundred-year period from High Tang to Mid-Tang, theorizing about literary creation witnessed two successive breakthroughs by Wang Changling and Han Yu, both of whom discovered new ways to resolve the stubborn problem posed by the apparent gap between transcendent creative activity and material execution. Wang Changling innovatively reappropriated *yi* from calligraphic discourse, applying it to a writer's mental activities during the compositional process, even though he neglected to provide a direct discussion of *yi*. Similarly, Han Yu noted the causative link between "nourishing vital lifebreath" and "forming words," without going into detail about it. But in the Ming-Qing period, *yi*, in association with *qi*, rose to prominence in discussions of the compositional process. Numerous literary critics, mostly from the Archaist camp, explored the compositional process from the perspective of *yi*. Especially prominent were discussions of *yi*'s relationship with overall structure, with emotive sublimation, with choices of tone, image, and diction. By meticulously following these discussions, a spectacular *yi*-centered theory of literary creation gradually emerges (see chapter 7).

This flourishing of *yi*-centered theorizing about literary creation in the Ming-Qing period presents a stark contrast to the relative neglect of material aspects of composition in Western critical discourse, throwing underlying cultural differences between Chinese and Western literary theory into sharp relief—in other words, the application of a holistic versus dualistic scheme to the creative process. Here the Western mind-body dichotomy comes into play, as does, in a different way, the notion of *logos* with its underlying meaning not only of speech but also of reason, making it more remote from living speech or the speech act. The fact that the Greek term *logos* covers such a wide spread of possible meanings was no doubt at least partly responsible for the lack of emphasis in the West on language in the literal sense of the spoken or written word. But equally significant was the notion—going all the way back to pre-Socratic philosophy and continued by Philo of Alexandria and Alexandrian Christianity (Clement of Alexandria, Origen Adamantius) all the way up to Coleridge (with his Logosophia project)—of Logos as a kind of conceptual or rational ordering built into the very structure of the world, rendering it apprehensible or graspable by the mind. Admittedly, in the Chinese scene some branches of Buddhist and Daoist thinking also sought to downplay language at the expense of mind or spirit. Nonetheless, within the mainstream tradition, a hidden passageway always remained open between language and ultimate reality—witness Zhuangzi's metaphors of the weir and trap (§13), Chan literary meditation practices (*wenzi Chan*), the Confucian belief in language's representational adequacy found in the *Commentary on Appended Phrases* in the pre-Qin era, the "Ji Gate Daoist" Guanzi's notion of mind and breath, Mencius on the "flood-like lifebreath," and the equalist view of spirt and form of the Huang-Lao school in the early Han (see §§1–2, 17–18, 31–32, 38). This exploring, reinterpreting, and applying of philosophical terms was a long and gradual process spanning all the way from Western Jin to the Ming-Qing period, but ultimately it accomplished the impressive feat of linking the spoken or written word to spirit.

In using the word *magnificent* to describe the Ming Archaists' development of a *yi*-centered theory of literary creation, I do so advisedly: although it may come as a surprise to some of my colleagues in the Chinese academy for whom Ming literary discourse is often derogatively associated with "rules of poetry," I believe this negative assessment of Ming theory can be traced to the powerful influence of Western literary thought on early twentieth-century China, and specifically on the leaders of the New Culture movement and May Fourth movement who adhered closely to Western values. Thus, Lu Xun, for example, in "On the Demonic Poetic Power" lamented China's lack of an imaginative power like that of Lord Byron to sweep away the old world and create it anew (§§179–84) and hence, likewise, the attack on "monsters of *Wenxuan* studies" (*Xuanxue yaonie* 選學妖孽) and "spawns of the Tongcheng school" (*Tongcheng miuzhong* 桐城謬種). Today, a century later, it's now time for a reassessment—neglect of the final stage of the compositional process is a regrettable flaw in any study of literary creation.

In the evolution of Chinese thinking about literary creation, the establishment of a *yi*-centered theory in the Ming-Qing period had momentous and far-reaching consequences because it successfully infused the pulse of transcendent mental activity and emotion-scene interaction into every step of the compositional process. In fact, when Zhang Huiyan and Zhu Tingzhen declared that *yi* turns "dead rules" into "live principles" (§§159–60), they meant to transform material syntax and diction into a kind of linguistic pulse not only beating in synchrony with the writer's spiritual and cosmic consciousness but also one capable of invoking an empathic response in the reader's mind. And all this is very much like the transformation of calligraphy into vital beats of life by calligraphic theorists since Wang Xizhi. In addition, just as *yi*-centered calligraphic discourse could and did elevate calligraphy into a great art, the *yi*-centered creative paradigm prevalent in the Ming-Qing period could lead writers to a new, more flexible application of rules in prose and poetry, thus revivifying composition as an artistic activity and infusing new life into traditional composition studies (*wenzhang xue* 文章學), which could now take on more theoretical depth and aesthetic sensibility.

From a broad cross-cultural perspective, it's not hard to see how aspects of the compositional process came to be excluded from Western creation theory for the same reason that Western calligraphy came to be excluded from the fine arts. Different forms of Western formalism (British and American New Criticism, Russian formalism) and phenomenological criticism all opposed traditional rhetoric for its treatment of writing as a polished, finished object and thus as not capable of radical formal innovation. At the same time, perhaps because of reaction against nineteenth-century Romanticism, all these forms of criticism were equally set against any attempt to connect writing to the author's transcendent activity of mind or, more broadly, subjectivity. For this reason, one of my main goals in writing this book is to try to encourage Western critical discourse to reconnect writing to subjectivity in a fashion similar to what we find in Ming theory. And just as Ernest Fenollosa and Ezra Pound, by their translations of classical Chinese poetry, helped foster modernism in Western poetry, I see no reason why Chinese literary theory might not help foster the invention of a new literary creation discourse in the West. And if this historical/critical introduction can help toward that end, it would represent the fulfillment of a lifetime dream.

////////////////////////////////////

Notes

1. Coleridge, *Biographia Literaria*, 304.
2. See Shelley, *Shelley's Poetry and Prose*, 513, 515, 535.
3. Owen, *Readings in Chinese Literary Thought*, 96.
4. Please note that this Hao Jing 郝經 (1223–1275) is not the same person as the late Ming critic Hao Jing 郝敬 (1557–1639).
5. Shelley, *Shelley's Poetry and Prose*, 531.
6. Owen, *Readings in Chinese Literary Thought*, 65.

References

Frequently Cited Primary Texts

CLSHJJ   Zhang Jian 張健, ed. *Canglang shihua jiaojian* 滄浪詩話校箋 (Canglang's Remarks on Poetry, with Collations and Annotations). Shanghai: Shanghai guji chubanshe, 2012.

CQFLYZ   Su Yu 蘇輿, annot. *Chun Qiu fanlu yizheng* 春秋繁露義證 (Luxuriant Gems of the Spring and Autumn Annals, with an Investigation of Its Meanings). Beijing: Zhonghua shuju, 1992.

GZJZ   Li Xiangfeng 黎翔鳳, annot. *Guangzi jiaozhu* 管子校注 (Guangzi, with Collations and Annotations). Beijing: Zhonghua shuju, 2004.

GZZQJ   Gong Zizhen 龔自珍. *Gong Zizhen Quanji* 龔自珍全集 (Complete Works of Gong Zizhen). Shanghai: Shanghai renmin chubanshe, 1975.

LXQJ   Lu Xun 魯迅. *Lu Xun quanji* 魯迅全集 (Complete Works of Lu Xun). Vol. 1. Beijing: Renmin wenxue chubanshe, 1973.

LYYD   *Lunyu yinde* 論語引得 (Concordance to the Analects). Harvard-Yenching Institute Sinological Index Series, supp. 16. Reprint, Shanghai: Shanghai guji chubanshe, 1986.

QMSH   Zhou Weide 周維德, ed. *Quan Ming shihua* 全明詩話 (Complete Poetry Talks of the Ming Dynasty). 6 vols. Jinan: Qilu shushe, 2005.

QSH   Wang Fuzhi 王夫之 et al., comp. *Qing shihua* 清詩話 (Collected Poetry Talks of the Qing Dynasty). Shanghai: Shanghai guji chubanshe, 1978.

QSHXB   Guo Shaoyu 郭紹虞, comp. *Qing shihua xubian* 清詩話續編 (A Sequel to the Poetry Talks of the Qing Dynasty). Shanghai: Shanghai guji chubanshe, 1983.

QTWDSG   Zhang Bowei 張伯偉, comp. *Quan Tang Wudai shige huikao* 全唐五代詩格彙考 (Complete Poetry Manuals of the Tang and Five Dynasties, with Collated Investigations). Nanjing: Jiangsu chubanshe, 2002.

SCJ   Su Che 蘇轍. *Su Che ji* 蘇轍集 (Collected Works of Su Che). Beijing: Zhonghua shuju, 1990.

SSJZ   Ruan Yuan 阮元 (1764–1849), comp. *Shisan jing zhu shu* 十三經注疏 (Commentaries and Subcommentaries on the Thirteen Classics). 2 vols. Beijing: Zhonghua shuju, 1980.

T   *Taishō Edition of Tripiṭaka* 大正新脩大藏經. Popular Edition in 1988. 大正新修大藏經刊行會 編 / 東京：大藏出版株式會社.

WFJS   Zhang Shaokang 張少康. *Wen fu jishi* 文賦集釋 (A *Fu* Exposition on Literature, with Collected Annotations). Beijing: Renmin wenxue chubanshe, 2002.

PRISM: THEORY AND MODERN CHINESE LITERATURE • 20 (ANNUAL SUPPL.) • DECEMBER 2023
DOI 10.1215/25783491-11325756 • © 2023 LINGNAN UNIVERSITY

WJMFL   Kūkai 空海. *Wenjing mifu lun huijiao huikao* 文鏡秘府論彙校彙考 (Bunkyō Hifuron, with Collected Collations and Examinations). Compiled by Shengjiang Lu 盧盛江. 4 vols. Beijing: Zhonghua shuju, 2006.

WXDL   Zhu Yingping 朱迎平, ed. *Wenxin diaolong suoyin* 文心雕龍索引 (Indexes to *Wenxin diaolong*). Shanghai: Shanghai guji chubanshe, 1987. [This index is based on the standard edition of *Wenxin diaolong*: Fan, Wenlan 范文瀾, annot. *Wenxin diaolong zhu* 文心雕龍注 (The Literary Mind and the Carving of Dragons, with Commentaries). Beijing: Renmin wenxue chubanshe, 1958.]

XZJJ   Wang Xianqian 王先謙, annot. *Xunzi jijie* 荀子集解 (Works of Xunzi, with Collected Commentaries). 2 vols. Beijing: Zhonghua shuju, 1988.

ZGLDWLX   Guo Shaoyu 郭紹虞 and Wensheng Wang 王文生. *Zhongguo lidai wenlun xuan* 中國歷代文論選 (An Anthology of Chinese Literary Criticism through the Ages). 4 vols. Shanghai: Shanghai guji chubanshe, 2001.

ZZJS   Guo Qingfan 郭慶藩 and Xiaoyu Wang 王孝魚, eds. *Zhuangzi jishi* 莊子集釋 (Zhuangzi, with Collected Annotations). 4 vols. Beijing: Zhonghua shuju, 2012.

Works Cited

Aśvaghoṣa (attributed to). *Awakening of Faith*, translated with commentary by Yoshito S. Hakeda. New York: Columbia University Press, 1967.

Ban, Gu 班固, comp. *Han shu* 漢書 (History of Han). Beijing: Zhonghua shuju, 1962.

Beijing daxue guwenxuan yanjiusuo 北大大學古文獻研究所, comp. *Quan Song shi* 全宋詩 (Complete Shi Poetry of the Song Dynasty). 72 vols. Beijing: Beijing University Press, 1998.

Bi, Shikui 畢士奎. *Wang Changling shige yu shixue yanjiu* 王昌齡詩歌與詩學研究 (Studies on Wang Changling's Poetry and Poetics). Nanchang: Jiangxi renmin chubanshe, 2008.

Birch, Cyril, trans. *The Peony Pavilion*. Bloomington: Indiana University Press, 2002.

Bush, Susan. "Tsung Ping's Essay on Painting Landscape and the 'Landscape Buddhism' of Mt. Lu." In *Theories of the Arts in China*, edited by Susan Bush and Christian Murck, 132–64. Princeton, NJ: Princeton University Press, 1983.

Cai, Zong-qi, ed. *A Chinese Literary Mind: Culture, Creativity, and Rhetoric in Wenxin diaolong*. Stanford, CA: Stanford University Press, 2001.

Cai, Zong-qi. *Configurations of Comparative Poetics: Three Perspectives on Western and Chinese Literary Criticism*. Honolulu: University of Hawai'i Press, 2002.

Cai, Zong-qi. "The Early Philosophical Discourse on Language and Reality and Lu Ji's and Liu Xie's Theories of Literary Creation." *Frontiers of Literary Studies in China* 5, no. 4 (2011): 477–510.

Cai, Zong-qi. "Six Dynasties Parallel Prose: Descriptive and Expository." In *How to Read Chinese Prose: A Guided Anthology*, edited by Zong-qi Cai, 210–26. New York: Columbia University Press, 2022.

Cai, Zong-qi. "Sound over Ideograph: The Basis of Chinese Poetic Art." In "Sound and Sense of Chinese Poetry," special issue, edited by Zong-qi Cai. *Journal of Chinese Literature and Culture* 2, no. 2 (2015): 251–57.

Cai, Zong-qi, "A Synthesis Rhythm, Syntax, and Vision of Chinese Poetry." In *How to Read Chinese Poetry: A Guided Anthology* edited by Zong-qi Cai, 379–99. New York: Columbia University Press, 2008.

Cai, Zong-qi. "Weishi sanleijing yu Wang Changling shixue sanjing shuo" 唯識三類境與王昌齡詩學三境說 (Three Types of Inscape in Consciousness-Only Buddhism and the

Three Types of Inscape in Wang Changling's Writings on Poetry). *Wenxue yichan* 文學遺產 (Literary Heritage), no. 1 (2018): 49–59.

Chan, Wing-tsit. *A Source Book in Chinese Philosophy*. Princeton, NJ: Princeton University Press, 1963.

Chen, Chuanxi 陳傳席. *Hua shanshui xu dianjiao zhuyi* 〈畫山水序〉點校注譯 (Annotated Edition of "A Preface to the Painting of Landscape"). In *Chen Chuanxi wenji* 陳傳席文集 (Collected Works of Chen Chuanxi). Hefei: Anhui meishu chubanshe, 2007.

Chen, Guying 陳鼓應. *Yi zhuan yu Daojia sixiang* 易傳與道家思想 (Commentaries on the *Changes* and Daoist Thought). Beijing: Sanlian shudian, 1996.

Ch'ien, Mu 錢穆. *Zhonguao jin sanbai nian xueshu shi* 中國近三百年學術史 (Chinese Intellectual History of the Last Three Hundred Years). 2 vols. Changsha: Shangwu yinshuguan, 1938.

Coleridge, Samuel Taylor. *Biographia Literaria*, vol. 1, edited by James Engell and W. Jackson Bate. Princeton, NJ: Princeton University Press, 1983.

Dai, Fugu 戴復古. *Dai Fugu shiji* 戴復古詩集 (Poetry Collection of Dai Fugu). Edited by Jin Zhishan 金芝山. Hangzhou: Zhejiang guji chubanshe, 2012.

Daoxuan 道宣. *Guang Hongmingji* 廣弘明集 (Expanded Collected Writings for the Propagation and Clarification of Buddhism). In *Taishōzō* 大正藏, vol. 52. Taipei: Taiwan New Wenfeng, 1983.

Dong, Gao 董誥 et al., comp. *Quan Tang wen* 全唐文 (Complete Prose Works of the Tang Dynasty). Shanghai: Shanghai guji chubanshe, 1990.

Egan, Ronald. "Poet, Mind, and World: A Reconsideration of the 'Shensi' Chapter of 'Wenxin diaolong.'" In Cai, *Chinese Literary Mind*, 101–26.

Eliot, T. S. *The Sacred Wood*. London: Methuen, 1920.

Engell, James. *The Creative Imagination: Enlightenment to Romanticism*. Cambridge, MA: Harvard University Press, 1981.

Fan, Xiangyong 范祥雍, annot. *Luoyang qielan ji jiaozhu* 洛陽伽藍記校注 (Annotated and Collated Record of the Buddhist Temples of Luoyang). Shanghai: Shanghai guji chubanshe, 1978.

Fan, Ye 范曄, comp. *Hou Han shu* 後漢書 (History of the Later Han). Beijing: Zhonghua shuju, 1959.

Foguang dacidian bianxiu weiyuanhui 佛光大辭典編修委員會, ed. *Foguang dacidian* 佛光大辭典 (Great Dictionary of Foguang [Buddha's Light]). Kaohsiung: Taiwan foguang chubanshe, 1988.

Gao, Heng 高亨, comp. *Gu zi tong jia hui dian* 古字通假字典 (A Dictionary of Interchangeable Ancient Characters). Jinan: Qi-Lu chubanshe, 1987.

Guan, Lin 管林 et al. *Gong Zizhen yanjiu* 龔自珍研究 (Studies on Gong Zizhen). Beijing: Renmin wenxue chubanshe, 1984.

Han, Fei 韓非. *Hanfeizi jijie* 韓非子集解 (Works of Master Han Fei, with Collected Commentaries). Beijing: Zhonghua shuju, 1998.

Hao, Jing 郝經. *Lingchuan ji* 陵川集 (Collected Works from Lingchuan). In *Siku Quanshu* 四庫全書 (Complete Library in the Four Branches of Learning), 1192:215.

Hao, Jing 郝敬. *Maoshi yuanjie* 毛詩原解 (Originative Interpretation of the Mao Text of the Book of Poetry). In *QMSH*, 4:2859–63.

Hsia, Tsi-an. "Aspects of the Power of Darkness in Lu Hsün." In *The Gate of Darkness*, edited by Tsi-an Hsia, 146–62. Seattle: University of Washington Press, 1968.

Hsü, Immanuel C. Y., trans. *Intellectual Trends in the Ch'ing Period*. Cambridge, MA: Harvard University Press, 1959.

Huang, Hui 黃暉, ed. *Lunheng jiaoshi* 論衡校釋 (Collations and Explanations of Lunheng). 4 vols. Beijing: Zhonghua shuju, 1990.

Huang, Jingjin 黃景進. "Chongdu *Jingtuzong sanjing* yu "Hua shanshui xu"—shi lun Jingtu, Changuan yu shanshui hua, shanshui shi" 重讀《淨土宗三經》與〈畫山水序〉—試論淨土、禪觀與山水畫、山水詩〉 (Rereading *Jingtuzong sanjing* and "A Preface to the Painting of Landscape": A Discussion of Pure Land, Chan, and Landscape Painting and Poetry). *Zhongguo wenzhe yanjiu tongxun* 中國文哲研究通訊 (Newsletter for Research on Chinese Letters and Philosophy) 16, no. 4 (2006): 217–43.

Huang, Jingjin 黃景進. *Yijing lun de xingcheng: Tangdai yijinglun yanjiu* 意境論的形成：唐代意境論研究 (The Making of the Theories of Inscape: Studies on the Tang Theories of Inscape). Taipei: Taiwan xuesheng shuju, 2004.

Huang, Kan 黃侃. *Wenxin diaolong zaji* 文心雕龍札記 (Notes on *Wenxin diaolong*). Shanghai: Shanghai guji chubanshe, 2000.

Huiyuan 慧遠. *Lushan donglin zashi* 廬山東林雜詩 (Poems from the Eastern Forest of Mt. Lu). In *Xian-Qin Han Wei Jin Nanbei chao shi: Jin shi* 先秦漢魏晉南北朝詩·晉詩 (Poetry of the Pre-Qin, Han, Wei, Jin, and Northern and Southern Dynasties [Jin Poetry]), edited by Lu Qinli 逯欽立, 1085. Beijing: Zhonghua shuju, 1983.

Hurvitz, Leon. "Tsung Ping's Comments on Landscape Painting." *Artibus Asiae* 32, no. 2/3 (1970): 146–56.

Jiang, Yin 蔣寅. *Qing shihua kao* 清詩話考 (Textual Studies on the Qing Poetry Talks). Beijing: Zhonghua shuju, 2005.

Jin, Shengtan 金聖嘆. *Jin Shengtan pingdian caizi quanji* 金聖嘆評點才子全集 (Complete Collection of Jin Shengtan's Commentaries on the Talented Writers). Beijing: Guangming ribao chubanshe, 1997.

Jindai mishu 津逮秘書 (Secret Texts for Crossing the Ford). Facsimile ed. Shanghai: Shangwu yinshuguan, 1936.

Kuang, Zhouyi 況周頤. *Huifeng cihua jizhu* 蕙風詞話輯注 (Ci Poetry Talks from Huifeng). Annotated by Qu Yuguo 屈興國. Nanchang: Jiangxi renmin chubanshe, 2000.

Kūkai 空海. *Kōbō Daishi Kūkai zenshū* 弘法大師空海全集 (Complete Works of Kūkai, the Great Master in Disseminating the Buddhist Law). 8 vols. Tokyo: Chikuma Shobō, 1984.

Langer, Susan. *Form and Feeling: A Theory of Art*. New York: Scribner's, 1953.

Lau, D. C., trans. *Lao Tsu: Tao Te Ching*. London: Penguin, 1963.

Lau, D. C., trans. *Mencius*. 2 vols. Hong Kong: Chinese University Press, 1979.

Lawal, Sarah. *Critics of Consciousness: The Existential Structures of Literature*. Cambridge, MA: Harvard University Press, 1968.

Lee, Leo Ou-fan. "Genesis of a Writer: Notes on Lu Xun's Educational Experience, 1881–1909." In *Modern Chinese Literature in the May Fourth Era*, edited by Merle Goldman, 161–88. Cambridge, MA: Harvard University Press, 1977.

Lee, Leo Ou-fan. "Tradition and Modernity in the Writings of Lu Xun." In *Lu Xun and His Legacy*, edited by Leo Ou-fan Lee, 3–31. Berkeley: University of California Press, 1985.

Lee, Leo Ou-fan. *Voices from the Iron House*. Bloomington: Indiana University Press, 1987.

Li, Limin 李利民. "Wang Changling *Shige: Tangdai shige de zhuangzhedia*" 王昌齡《詩格》— 唐代詩格的轉折點 (Wang Changling's *Shige*: A Turning Point in the Tang *Shige* Writing). *Hubei shehui kexue* 湖北社會科學 (Hubei Social Sciences) 7 (2006): 94–96.

Li, Shan 李善 et al., eds. *Liuchenzhu wenxuan* 六臣註文選 (Selection of Refined Writing, Annotated by Six Officials). Beijing: Zhonghua shuju, 1987.

Li, Yanshou 李延壽. *Nanshi* 南史 (History of the Southern [Dynasties]). Beijing: Zhonghua shuju, 1975.

Li, Zhenhua 李珍華 and Fu Xuanzong 傳璇琮. "Tan Wang Changling de *Shi ge*: Yibu you zhengyi d shu" 談王昌齡的《詩格》— 一部有爭議的書 (On Wang Changling's *The Norm of Poetry*: A Controversial Book). *Wenxue yichan* 文學遺產 (Literary Heritage) 6 (1988): 85–97.

Li, Zhi 李贄. *Fenshu, Xu Fenshu* 焚書、續焚書 (Burning Books, A Sequel to Burning Books). Beijing: Zhonghua shuju, 1975.

Li, Zhi 李贄, and Liu Dongxing 劉東星. *Daogu lu erjuan* 道古錄二卷 (Records of Accounts of Antiquity, Two Volumes). Reprint of the Wanli reign woodblock edition. Collected in *Xuxiu siku quanshu* 續修四庫全書 (Sequel to the Complete Library in the Four Branches of Learning), vol. 1127.

Liang, Qichao 梁啓超. *Yinbing shi heji* 飲冰室合集 (Collected Works from the Yinbing Studio). 40 vols. Shanghai: Zhonghua shuju, 1936.

Lin, Shuen-fu. "Liu Xie on Imagination." In Cai, *Chinese Literary Mind*, 127–60.

Lin, Yü-sheng. *The Crisis of Chinese Consciousness: Radical Antitraditionalism in the May Fourth Era*. Madison: University of Wisconsin Press, 1979.

Liu, Yingqing 劉義慶. *Shishuo xinyu [jiaojian]* 世說新語校箋 (A New Account of the Tales of the World). Beijing: Zhonghua shuju, 1984.

Lu, Ji 陸機. *Wenfu jishi* 文賦集釋 (Rhyme-Prose on Literature, Collected Annotations). Edited by Zhang Shaokang 張少康. Beijing: Renmin wenxue chubanshe, 2002.

Lu, Qinli 逯欽立, ed. *Xian-Qin Han Wei Jin Nanbei chao shi: Jin shi* 先秦漢魏晉南北朝詩·晉詩 (Poetry of the Pre-Qin, Han, Wei, Jin, and Northern and Southern Dynasties [Jin Poetry]). Beijing: Zhonghua shuju, 1983.

Luo, Zongqiang 羅宗強. *Sui Tang wudai wenxue sixiang shi* 隋唐五代文學思想史 (A History of Literary Thought of the Sui-Tang Period). Shanghai: Shanghai guji chubanshe, 1986.

Lyell, William A. *Lu Hsün's Vision of Reality*. Berkeley: University of California Press, 1976.

Lynn, Richard John, trans. *The Classics of Changes: A New Translation of the I Ching as Interpreted by Wang Bi*. New York: Columbia University Press, 1994.

Mather, Richard B. "The Controversy over Conformity and Naturalness during the Six Dynasties." *History of Religion* 9, nos. 2–3 (1969–70): 160–80.

Mou, Shijin 牟世金, and Kanru Lu 陸侃如. *Liu Xie lun chuangzuo* 劉勰論創作 (Liu Xie on Literary Creation). Hefei: Anhui renmin chubanshe, 1982.

Ouyang, Xun 歐陽詢, comp. *Yi wen lei ju* 藝文類聚 (Classified Compilation of Belles Lettres). Collated by Wang Shaoying 汪紹楹. 4 vols. Shanghai: Shanghai guji chubanshe, 1982.

Owen, Stephen. *Readings in Chinese Literary Thought*. Cambridge, MA: Council on East Asian Studies, Harvard University, 1992.

Peterson, Willard J. "Making Connections: 'Commentary on the Attached Verbalizations' of the *Book of Changes*." *Harvard Journal of Asiatic Studies* 42, no. 1 (1982): 77–79.

Pollard, David. "'Ch'I in Chinese Literary Theory." In Rickett, *Chinese Approaches to Literature from Confucius to Liang Ch'i-ch'ao*, 43–66.

Sengyou 僧祐. *Hongmingji* 弘明集 (Collected Writings for the Propagation and Clarification of Buddhism). In *Taishōzō*, vol. 52.

Sengyou 僧祐. *Hongmingji* 弘明集 (Collected Writings for the Propagation and Clarification of Buddhism). Vol. 2. Reprint of the [Song] Sixi edition. Beijing: Guojia tushuguan chubanshe, 2018.

Sengyou 僧祐. *Hanging* 弘明集 (Collected Writings for the Propagation and Clarification of Buddhism). Reprint of a Ming edition. Taipei: Xinxing shuju, 1960.

Shaw, Miranda. "Buddhist and Taoist Influences on Chinese Landscape Painting." *Journal of the History of Ideas* 49, no. 2 (1988): 183–206.

Shelley, Percy Bysshe. *Shelley's Poetry and Prose*. Edited by Donald Reiman and Neil Fraistat. New York: Norton, 2002.

Shen, Yue 沈約. *Songshu* 宋書 (History of the Song [Dynasty]). Beijing: Zhonghua shuju, 1974.

Shih, Vincent Yu-chung, *The Literary Mind and the Carving of Dragons*. Hong Kong: Chinese University Press, 2015.

Su, Shi 蘇軾. *Su Shi shiji* 蘇軾詩集 (Collected Poetical Works of Su Shi). Beijing: Zhonghua shuju, 1982.

Su, Shi 蘇軾. *Su Shi wenji* 蘇軾文集 (Collected Prose Works of Su Shi). Collated and punctuated by Kong Fanli 孔凡禮. Beijing: Zhonghua shuju, 1986.

Sun, Guangde 孫廣德. "Gong Zizhen di jingshi sixiang" 龔自珍的經世思想 (The Statecraft Thought of Gong Zizhen). In *Jinshi Zhongguo jingshi sixiang yantaohui lunwen ji* 近世中國經世思想研討會論文集 (Collected Essays on Chinese Statecraft Thought of Late Imperial China), edited by the Institute of Modern History, 275–89. Taipei: Academia Sinica, 1984.

Sun, Guoting 孫過庭. *Sun Guoting shupu jianzheng* 孫過庭書譜箋證 (Genealogy of Calligraphy by Sun Guoting, with Annotations). Annotated by Jianxin Zhu 朱建新. Shanghai: Shanghai guji chubanshe, 1982.

Sun, Yueban 孫岳頒 et al. *Peiwenzhai shuhuapu: Lunhua wu* 佩文齋書畫譜·論畫五 (Peiwenzhai Collection of Calligraphy and Painting. Discussions of Painting, 5). Woodblock edition, 1708.

Tan, Yuanchun 譚元春. *Tan Yuanchun ji* 譚元春集 (Collected Works of Tan Yuanchun). Shanghai: Shanghai guji chubanshe, 1998.

Varsano, Paula. "Whose Voice Is It Anyway? A Rereading of Wang Changling's 'Autumn in the Palace of Everlasting Faith: Five Poems.'" *Journal of Chinese Literature and Culture* 3, no. 1 (2016): 1–25.

Varsano, Paula. "Worlds of Meaning and the Meaning of Worlds in Sikong Tu's Twenty-Four Modes of Poetry." In *The Rhetoric of Hiddenness in Traditional Chinese Culture*, edited by Paula Varsano, 153–75. Albany, NY: SUNY Press, 2016.

Waley, Arthur, trans. *The Analects of Confucius*. New York: Random House, 1938.

Wang, Bi 王弼. *Wang Bi ji jiaoshi* 王弼集校釋 (Collected Works of Wang Bi, Collated and Annotated). Annotated by Lou Yulie 樓宇烈. Beijing: Zhonghua shuju, 1980.

Wang, Bi 王弼. *Zhouyi zhengyi* 周易正義 (Correct Meanings of the Classic of Changes). Annotated by Kangbo Wei 魏康伯 and Yingda Kong 孔穎達 et al. Shanghai: Shanghai guji chubanshe, 1990.

Wang, Changling 王昌齡. "Lun Wen Yi" 論文意 (On the Roles of *Yi* in Refined Writing). In *WJMFL*, 3:1282–1449.

Wang, Deming 王德明. "Wang Changling yu zhongguo gudai houqi shige qingjing lun de zhouxiang" 王昌齡與中國古代後期詩歌情景理論的走向 (Wang Changling and the Orientation in the Development of Theories of Feeling and Scene in Late Imperial China). *Hebei shifan daxue xuebao: Zhexue shehui kexue ban* 河北師範大學學報 (哲學社會科學版) (Journal of the Hebei Normal University: Philosophy and Social Sciences Edition) 7 (2004): 99–104.

Wang, Eugene Y. *Shaping the Lotus Sutra: Buddhist Visual Culture in Medieval China*. Seattle: University of Washington Press, 2005.

Wang, Fuzhi 王夫之. *Jiangzhai shihua [jianzhu]* 薑齋詩話箋注 (Jiangzhuai's [Wang Fuzhi] Remarks on Poetry, with Annotations). Annotated by Hongsen Dai 戴鴻森. Beijing: Renmin wenxue chubanshe, 1981.

Wang, Fuzhi 王夫之. *Ming shi pingxuan* 明詩評選 (Commented Anthology of Ming Poetry). Changsha: Yuelu chubanshe, 2011.

Wang, John C. Y. "Lu Xun as a Scholar of Traditional Chinese Literature." In *Lu Xun and His Legacy*, edited by Leo Ou-fan Lee, 90–103. Berkeley: University of California Press, 1985.

Wang, Shihan 汪師韓. *Su Shi xuanping jianshi* 蘇詩選評箋釋 (Commented Collection of Su Shi's Poems, with Annotations and Explanations). In *Jingyin Wenyuange Sikuquanshu* 景印文淵閣四庫全書 (Reprint of the Wenyuange Library in Four Branches of Learning), vol. 1448, *juan* 36, 698. Taipei: Taiwan Shangwu yinshuguan, 2008.

Wang, Shizhen 王世貞. *Wangshi huayuan* 王氏畫苑 (Garden of Painting of the Wang Family). 1590 woodblock edition. Shanghai: Shanghai guji chubanshe, 1991.

Wang, Shuang 文爽. "Jintishi de chengshu yu xin meixue yuanze de jueqi" 近體詩的成熟與新美學原則的崛起 —— 王昌齡詩學理論與創作實踐 (The Maturation of Recent-Style Poetry and the Rise of New Aesthetic Principles). *Anqing shifan xueyuan xuebao: Shehui kexue ban* 安慶師範學院學報(社會科學版) (Journal of Anqing Normal Institute: Social Sciences Edition) 11 (2011): 27–33.

Wang, Xianshen 王先慎. *Hanfeizi jijie* 韓非子集解 (Hanfeizi Collected Explanations). Beijing: Zhonghua shuju, 1998.

Wang, Y. C. *Chinese Intellectuals and the West*. Chapel Hill: University of North Carolina Press, 1966.

Wang, Yao 王瑤. *Lu Xun yu Zhongguo wenxue* 魯迅與中國文學 (Lu Xun and Chinese Literature). Shanghai: Pingming chubanshe, 1952.

Wang, Yuanhua 王元化. *Wenxin diaolong chuangzuo lun* 文心雕龍創作論 (The Theory of Literary Creation in *Wenxin diaolong*). Shanghai: Shanghai guji chubanshe, 1979.

Wang, Yunxi 王運熙. "Wang Changling de shige lilun" 王昌齡的詩歌理論 (Wang Changling's Poetic Theory). *Fudan xuebao: Sheshui kexue ban* 復旦學報(社會科學版) (Fudan University Journal: Social Sciences Edition) 5 (1989): 22–29.

Watson, Burton, trans. *The Complete Works of Chuang Tzu*. New York: Columbia University Press, 1968.

Weimojiesuoshuojing: Busiyiping diliu 維摩詰所說經：不思議品第六 (Vimalakīrti-Nirdeśa: Acintya, no. 6). In *Taishōzō*, vol. 14. Taipei: Taiwan New Wenfeng, 1983.

Wong, Shirleen S. *Kung Tzu-chen*. Boston: Twayne, 1975.

Wordsworth, William. *The Prose Works of William Wordsworth*. Edited by W. J. B. Owen and Jane Worthington Smyser. 3 vols. Oxford: Clarendon, 1974.

Xiao, Chi 蕭馳. "Dacheng fojiao de shourong yu Jin Song shanshui shixue" 大乘佛教的受容與晉宋山水詩學 (The Reception of Mahayana Buddhism and Landscape Poetry of the Jin and Song Dynasties). In *Fofa yu shijing* 佛法與詩境 (Buddhist Dharma and the Realm of Poetry), 11–76. Beijing: Zhonghua shuju, 2005.

Xu, Shen 許慎. *Shuowen jiezi [zhu]* 說文解字[注] (Explanations of Simple and Compound Characters, with Commentaries). Annotated by Duan Yucai 段玉裁. Reprint, Yangzhou: Jiangsu Guangling chubanshe, 1997.

Yan, Kejun 嚴可均. *Quan Jin wen* 全晉文 (Complete Writings of the Jin [Dynasty]). Beijing: Commercial Press, 1999.

Yang, Bojun 楊伯峻, trans. and annot. *Mengzi yizhu* 孟子譯注 (Mencius, with Translation and Annotations). Beijing: Zhonghua shuju, 1960.

Ye, Lang 葉朗. *Zhongguo meixue shi dagang* 中國美學史大綱 (History of Chinese Aesthetics: An Outline). Shanghai: Shanghai renmin chubanshe, 1985.

Yu Jianhua 俞劍華, ed. *Zhongguo lidai hualun leibian* 中國歷代畫論類編 (Compendium of Chinese Writings on Painting through the Ages). Beijing: Renmin meishu chubanshe, 1998.

Yu Jiaxi 余嘉錫, Zumo Zhou 周祖謨, and Shuyi Yu 余淑宜, eds. *Shishuo xinyu jianshu* 世說新語箋疏 (Annotated Commentary on *A New Account of Tales of the World*). Beijing: Zhonghua shuju, 1983.

Yu, Yuan 郁沅 and Zhang Minggao 張明高, eds. *Wei Jin Nanbei chao wenlun xuan* 魏晋南北朝文論選 (Selected Works of Literary Criticism of Wei-Jin and the Northern and Southern Dynasties). Beijing: Renmin wenxue chubanshe, 1996.

Yuan, Hongdao 袁宏道. *Yuan Zhonglang quanji* 袁中郎全集 (Complete Works of Yuan Zhonglang). In *Siku quanshu cunmu congshu* 四庫全書存目叢書 (Collectanea of Extant Titles from the Complete Works of the Four Treasures). Jinan: Qilu chubanshe, 2001.

Yuan, Mei 袁枚. *Xiachang fang shiwen ji* 小倉山房詩文集 (Collected Poems and Prose Works from the Xiaochangshan Studio). Shanghai: Shanghai guji chubanshe, 1988.

Yuan, Xingpei 袁行霈. *Zhongguo shige yishu yanjiu* 中國詩歌藝術研究 (Studies on the Art of Chinese Poetry). Beijing: Peking University Press, 1987.

Zhang, Bowei 張伯偉, ed. *Quan Tang wudai shige jiaokao* 全唐五代詩格校考 (Comprehensive Collated Edition of Instructions on Poetry from the Tang and Five Dynasties). Xi'an: Shaanxi renmin jiaoyu chubanshe, 1996.

Zhang Chao 張超. *Shulun jiyao* 書論輯要 (Essentials of Calligraphy Criticism: A Collection). Beijing: Jiaoyu chubanshe, 1988.

Zhang, Huiyan 張惠言. *Ci xuan* 詞選 (An Anthology of Ci Poetry). Reprint of the Sibu beiyao 四庫備要 edition. Beijing: Zhonghua shuju, 1957.

Zhang, Huiyan 張惠言. *Mingke wenbian* 茗柯文編 (Refined Tea: A Collection of Prose and Poetry). Shanghai: Shanghai guji chubanshe, 1984.

Zhang, Jian 張健. "*Shijia yizhi* de chansheng niandai yu zuozhe——jianlun *Ershisi shipin zuozhe wenti*" 《詩家一指》的產生時代與作者——兼論《二十四詩品》作者問題 (*The One-Finger Chan for Poets*: Dating and Authorship, with an Additional Discussion of the Authorship of *Twenty-Four Modes of Poetry*). *Beijing daxue xuebao: Zhexue shehui kexueban* 北京大學學報(哲學社會科學版) (Journal of Peking University) 5 (1995): 34–44.

Zhang Jing 張晶. "Yijing yu shenti: Zhongguo shixue de shenmei ganwu zhi si" 意境與身體——中國詩學的審美感悟之四 (Conception-Inscape and the Body: Inspired Aesthetic Reflections about Chinese Poetics). *Beijing daxue xuebao: Zhexue shehui kexueban* 北京大學學報(哲學社會科學版) (Journal of Peking University) 1 (2016): 69–77.

Zhang, Shaokang 張少康. *Zhongguo gudai wenxue chuangzuo lun* 中國古代文學創作論 (Traditional Chinese Theories of Literary Creation). Taipei: Wen shi zhe chubanshe, 1991.

Zhang, Yanyuan 張彦遠. *Fashu yaolu* 法書要錄 (A Collection of Essential Writings on Calligraphy). Shanghai: Shanghai shuhua chubanshe, 1986.

Zhang, Yanyuan 張彦遠, ed. *Lidai minghua ji* 歷代名畫記 (Records of Famous Paintings Through the Ages). In *Wangshi huayuan* 王氏畫苑 (Garden of Painting of the Wang Family), by Wang Shizhen 王世貞, *juan* 3. 1590 woodblock ed.

Zhang, Yuzhao 張裕釗. *Zhang Yuzhao shiwen ji* 張裕釗詩文集 (Collected Poetical and Prose Works of Zhang Yuzhao). Punctuated and collated by Wang Damin 王達敏. Shanghai: Shanghai guji chubanshe, 2007.

Zhongguo meixueshi ziliao xuanbian 中國美學史資料選編 (A Collection of Material in the History of Chinese Aesthetics). Edited by Peking University Philosophy Department, 2 vols. Beijing: Zhonghua shuju, 1980.

Zhou, Ji 周濟, comp. *Song sijia cixuan* 宋四家詞選 (An Anthology of Four Song Poets). Shanghai: Gudian wenxue chubanshe, 1958.

Zhu, Jieqin 朱傑勤. *Gong Ding'an yanjiu* 龔定盦研究 (Studies on Gong Ding'an). Reprint, Taipei: Taiwan shangwu yinshuguan, 1966.

Zhu, Qianzhi 朱謙之. *Laozi jiaoshi* 老子校釋 (Laozi, with Annotations and Explanations). Beijing: Zhonghua shuju, 1984.

Zhu, Xi 朱熹. *Zhuzi quanshu* 朱子全書 (Complete Works of Master Zhu [Xi]). Shanghai: Shanghai guji chubanshe, 2002.

Zong, Baihua 宗白華. *Meixue yu yijing* 美學與意境 (Aesthetics and Ideational Realms). Beijing: Renmin chubanshe, 1987.

Zou, Jinxian 鄒進先. *Gong Zizhen lungao* 龔自珍論稿 (Papers on Gong Zizhen). Haikou: Nanhai chubanshe, 1992.

Glossary-Index

ālaya-vijñāna (storehouse consciousness), 114

Amitābha Sutra 阿彌陀經, 71, 78

anāsrava-jñāna 以有漏智修善根者 (untainted wisdom), 67

Anti-Archaists (*Fan fugu pai* 反復古派), 9, 138–39, 156, 184, 188–89, 191, 196–97

Archaists (*Fugu pai* 復古派) 9, 138–39, 152, 156–57, 173–74, 184–85, 188–89, 191, 196, 233

Aśvaghoṣa 馬鳴 (ca. 80–ca. 150) 115–17, 121

Bai Juyi 白居易 (772–846), 7

"Baihua shishuo" 白華山人詩說 (Discussions on Poetry from the Man of the Baihua Mount) 161

bi 比 (metaphor), 199

bianshuo 辨說 (argumentative discourse), 17

biliang 比量 (inference), 148

"Bing mei guan ji" 病梅館記 (An Account of the Hall of Sick Plum Trees), 205

bixing 比興 (metaphor and affective image), 200–203

Bodhiruci 菩提流支 (?–527), 114

bu jin 不盡 (does not fully [do something]), 24

Buddha, 10, 61, 63, 68–72, 74, 78–79, 85, 88, 146, 223, 225, 227

Buddhism, 6–7, 10–11, 60–66, 68–70, 72–75, 79, 82, 87, 93, 96, 114, 117, 119, 123, 131–32, 135–36, 141, 145–46, 158, 173, 223–25, 227, 236

Buddhist dharma, 75

Bunkyō Hifuron 文鏡秘府論 (The Literary Mirror and the Secret Repository of Literature), 6, 97

Byron, George Gordon (1788–1824), 212, 216–18, 233

cakṣur-vijñāna (eye consciousness), 114

can 參 (deliberation), 7, 147

Canglang shihua 滄浪詩話 (Canglang's Remarks on Poetry), 123, 135, 137, 139

canwu 參悟 (meditation-enlightenment), 7, 9

Cao Pi 曹丕 (187–226), 40, 42, 186, 230–31

Chan 禪 (term for *samadhi*, "enlightenment"), 122–23, 129–30, 132–38

Chen Tingzhuo 陳廷焯 (1853–1892), 201

Chen Zi'ang 陳子昂 (ca. 659–ca. 700), 7, 136

chengming 成名 (establishment of names), 17

chi ren xingqing 持人性情 (controls one's disposition and emotion), 215

chigou 喫詬 (Wrangling Debate, a fictional character in the *Zhuangzi*), 25

Chunqiu fan lu 春秋繁露 (Luxuriant Gems of the *Spring and Autumn Annals*), 18

ci 辭 (phrases, the finest literary phrasing), 15–17, 171

Coleridge, Samuel Taylor, 181, 203, 222, 228, 232, 234

Commentary on the Attached Phrases (Xici zhuan 繫辭傳), 10, 13, 15, 23, 26–29, 41, 44–45, 54, 73

conception-image (*yixiang* 意象), 4–5, 10, 43, 45, 50, 53–54, 104–8, 140, 163–64, 179, 195, 225–26

Confucius 孔子 (551–478 BCE), 14–17, 23, 26, 35, 62–63, 77, 120, 143, 170–71, 197–98

couli 湊理 (the perfect running of lifebreath), 48

da 達 (get across/convey), 16

da gong wu shi 大公無私 (great public spirit and unselfishness), 208

"Da Li Yi shu" 答李翊書 (Letter in Reply to Li Yi), 125, 130

Dai Fugu 戴復古 (1167–1248), 134, 136

Dao 道 (the Way, eternal principle), 17, 20–31, 61–79, 89, 209–10, 225, 229

PRISM: THEORY AND MODERN CHINESE LITERATURE • 20 (ANNUAL SUPPL.) • DECEMBER 2023
DOI 10.1215/25783491-11080946 • © 2023 LINGNAN UNIVERSITY

Printed and bound by CPI Group (UK) Ltd, Croydon, CR0 4YY

08/10/2024

14570400-0001